T0316820

Tobacco Control in Africa

Tobacco Control in Africa

People, Politics and Policies

Edited by
Jeffrey Drope

ANTHEM PRESS
LONDON · NEW YORK · DELHI

International Development Research Centre
Ottawa • Cairo • Dakar • Montevideo • Nairobi • New Delhi • Singapore

Anthem Press
An imprint of Wimbledon Publishing Company
www.anthempress.com

This edition first published in UK and USA 2011
by ANTHEM PRESS
75-76 Blackfriars Road, London SE1 8HA, UK
or PO Box 9779, London SW19 7ZG, UK
and
244 Madison Ave. #116, New York, NY 10016, USA

A copublication with the
International Development Research Centre
PO Box 8500, Ottawa, ON K1G 3H9, Canada
www.idrc.ca / info@idrc.ca
ISBN: 978 1 55250 510 6 (eBook)

British Library Cataloguing-in-Publication Data
A catalogue record for this book is available from the British Library.

Library of Congress Cataloging-in-Publication Data
Tobacco control in Africa : people, politics, and policies /
edited by Jeffrey M. Drope.
p. ; cm.
Includes bibliographical references and index.
ISBN-13: 978-0-85728-783-0 (hardback : alk. paper)
ISBN-10: 0-85728-783-4 (hardback : alk. paper)
I. Drope, Jeffrey M.
[DNLM: 1. Smoking–prevention & control–Africa South of the Sahara.
2. Health Policy–Africa South of the Sahara.
3. Smoking–legislation & jurisprudence–Africa South of the Sahara.
4. Tobacco Industry–legislation & jurisprudence–Africa South of the Sahara. HV 5740]
LC classification not assigned
362.29'6096–dc23
2011032528

ISBN-13: 978 0 85728 783 0 (Hbk)
ISBN-10: 0 85728 783 4 (Hbk)

This title is also available as an eBook.

CONTENTS

LIST OF FIGURES AND TABLES

Figures

Tables

Foreword

TOBACCO CONTROL IN AFRICA – PEOPLE, POLITICS AND POLICIES

This magnum opus on tobacco control in Africa could not be timelier as we begin to confront the next global epidemic of noncommunicable diseases. Its 19 chapters and 12 country situational analyses carry the message effectively for all those who care to listen – governments, industry, health professionals and most poignantly of all, consumers, particularly today's youth. As this is a book on the African odyssey relating to a dreaded risk factor to health in world history, two timeless African proverbs seem apposite:

- *"The choreographer has given birth to her child; it not remains for the child to know how to dance."* That is, there is no longer any excuse for not knowing how to proceed.
- *"To prevent the branch of the tree sticking out dangerously from hurting your eyes, you must begin to contemplate that possibility from afar."* The epidemic is already upon us, not looming, so we must act now.

Anti-smoking policies have been developed and strategies mounted at global, regional and country levels, but the tepid response and lackluster attention paid to implementation have continued to thwart our efforts. The political will has not yet been consummated, and the shifting of the theater of "war" and skillful manipulation of unsuspecting nations by the tobacco industry continue to exact hardship on the expected impact on tobacco control.

Yet populations are acutely aware of the pervasive and devastating complications of the short- and long-term use of tobacco. A few may be ignorant, but many are simply indifferent or even defiant. The politics of tobacco control is a complex one: the lobby is often strong and determined, but at one point or other it meets with an equally powerful pro-tobacco counterlobby. In a corrupt political system it is easy to guess which side eventually triumphs.

Twelve countries in Africa have been appraised out of a total of over fifty, but the findings apply to the rest *mutatis mutandis*. But as the concluding chapter emphasizes, the approach varies with the social, political and economic environment and the solution cannot be "one size fits all." At the end of the day, political leadership is the most powerful activator for change and its impact on social, lifestyle, habit, environmental and economic integrity will determine whether a country is winning or losing this battle.

Africa has a responsibility to resist the carrot of industrial temptation. History will judge leaders harshly, including the health professions themselves, if we continue – like the proverbial ostrich – to bury our heads in the sand. The solution demands a doggedness that must permit us to shun quick returns and instead to focus on long-term gains, the types of dividends in human health that we cannot begin to compare with material resources.

The developed world has devised its own approach and the wily industrialists in the tobacco camp have relocated to the less-developed world, knowing that the index of compromise in this new environment is high. They increasingly dazzle the economically weak with ephemeral incentives. Impoverished populations must hold their destinies in their hands and hearken to the remonstrating cries of those in their indigenous communities who never tire of explaining the ruinous effects of tobacco on health. Advice, like water constantly dripping, will eventually wear away stone.

I warmly recommend this monumental work – a true *vade mecum* – to all stakeholders, policymakers and real and potential consumers in the African setting. Dr Jeffrey Drope and his team must be congratulated for putting together a compendium that clearly addresses the various facets of this problem. It is a compelling read and a clarion wakeup call, and I hope that the "Doubting Thomases" on the continent will no longer be content to sit on the fence.

O. O. Akinkugbe, MD, PhD
Emeritus Professor of Medicine
University of Ibadan, Nigeria
October 2010

PREFACE

In recent years the tobacco control community has shifted its focus to low- and middle-income countries (LMICs), which are becoming a major market for tobacco companies seeking to expand their profits and compensate for dwindling markets in higher-income countries. While some LMICs already have alarming smoking prevalence levels, many currently hover on the cusp of the epidemic. Such is the case in much of Sub-Saharan Africa (SSA). Already burdened by infectious diseases, the region now faces the extra burden of noncommunicable diseases related to tobacco use. The goal is to prevent another epidemic. This objective raises unique challenges in an area where the negative health effects of tobacco use are not yet widespread and where governments do not yet consider tobacco control as a health or development priority.

Attracted to the notion of staving off another epidemic in SSA, the Bill and Melinda Gates Foundation and the International Development Research Centre (IDRC) partnered in the fall of 2007 to analyze the status of the tobacco problem in a number of SSA countries, and to identify those countries in which an intervention might be most effective. The original plan was to conduct situational analyses in these countries; that is, to gather all existing data on current tobacco use, tobacco farming, tobacco control policies and the key players involved in the field. African researchers would gather, synthesize and analyze data at the country level so that local governments, civil society, universities and potential funders could use this information to understand opportunities for and obstacles to tobacco control, as well as the capacity for action in each country. Furthermore, this information would be used to inform broader health and development strategies and guide immediate and long-term actions for tobacco control in Africa.

After a competitive process, 12 countries were selected to conduct an in-country stakeholder consultation and a baseline assessment of readily available data and to submit a full proposal for an in-depth situational analysis. Before submission of the final proposals, the IDRC conducted a meeting in Nairobi for team leaders to present a summary of their country baseline assessments and the outcomes of the stakeholder meetings. Reports on stakeholder meetings were particularly positive, with most country team leaders emphasizing what a unique and valuable opportunity it was to bring together a large number of old and new stakeholders from a variety of disciplines and sectors to share information on tobacco control. A common finding in many baseline assessments was that the data were very uneven in availability and quality. A final revelation was the overwhelming emphasis of stakeholders on the need for policy change.

With the policy focus in mind, the second part of the Nairobi meeting was a political mapping training intended to guide teams toward writing a proposal to collect information focused on policy change in their specific country context. The session began with some skepticism and concern as participants expressed general confusion over the definition of a "situational analysis," the need to map their context and how the mapping fit into their situational analyses. By the end of the training, however, the majority of participants embraced the exercise, and, most importantly, understood the utility of it.

But the first round of final proposals continued to emphasize general and/or epidemiological goals such as "policy change" or prevalence studies. In response, the IDRC and the Gates Foundation agreed to set clearer parameters for the teams by diminishing the focus on epidemiology and data gathering and instead emphasizing the development of an improved understanding of the "politics" and policy. The foundation underscored that it was seeking the "stories" of tobacco control in each country and an understanding of what interventions might be most successful in each country. This emphasis echoed IDRC's perspective that what was most lacking in understanding the determinants of success for tobacco control and developing effective interventions was a systematic, rigorous understanding of sociopolitical contexts and how they evolve over time. The consensus was a reorientation toward developing a fundamental understanding of the key stakeholders and their abilities/contributions, tobacco company activities, the role of political institutions, and legislation and its level of development, implementation and enforcement.

The foundation also promoted immediate action focusing on narrow and sustainable policy interventions with the most potential for impact in the near future, as outlined in the international Framework Convention on Tobacco Control (FCTC). The principal interventions included increased tobacco taxes, smoke-free places, bans on tobacco advertising and promotion and graphic health warnings on packages. It was explicitly agreed that prevalence studies, national plans and assistance with writing wide omnibus national legislation did not fit within the parameters of the initiative.

The revised strategy resulted in the decision to anchor the analyses in a political mapping format and use policy interventions as case studies to achieve change while simultaneously deepening an understanding of tobacco control in each country. Though large-scale data collection was discouraged, in the interest of presenting data to policymakers it was agreed that existing prevalence and related data needed to be collected, organized and evaluated. A new round of in-country meetings saw IDRC staff and consultants assisting country teams through a process of identifying one or two policy priorities, mapping the political context and developing a work plan to implement those priorities.

For most, the in-country meetings were a major achievement. Some meetings started with a reluctant team, but most ended with satisfaction because the process enabled them to articulate the larger political, social and economic context within which their priorities fit and to develop a plan for action for both the immediate and longer term. Commonly, teams started with a very broad, ambitious goal, but then quickly narrowed their scope as the mapping evolved and the layers of complexity were revealed. Though the mapping process generated some initial uncertainty, as teams began working their way through identifying all of the actors and institutions – including their relative level of importance and interactions – team members quickly started to identify the main objectives and activities that needed to be fulfilled. The "story" behind tobacco control in their countries began to emerge, including an increasing understanding of country priorities, readiness and capacity. Many participants noted that they had never dissected an issue in such depth and found the process enlightening. Many of the teams ultimately employed the process several times as they mapped subsequent priorities and expressed plans to continue utilizing the tool in areas beyond tobacco control.

This book clearly demonstrates that tobacco control was on the radar of key people and organizations on the continent many years before this analysis was conducted. Despite a lack of both financial and human resources, tobacco control was growing in the region. But outside of the FCTC process, the level of interaction and exchange between these actors was limited. In recent years, however, regional organizations such as the Africa Tobacco Control Regional Initiative (ATCRI) and the African Tobacco Control Alliance (ATCA) have formed in order to provide the network building and technical assistance needed to support the growth of tobacco control capacity and resources for countries in SSA. These organizations have supported and promoted the ATSA syntheses and have embraced the importance of political mapping in all of their planning and implementation of programs and policies. In the past year ATCRI has continued the work of ATSA by conducting "mini-ATSAs" in six more countries. With new funding, they have also planned for more analyses in ten more countries by 2012.

In countries where precious few are tackling a looming epidemic, this rigorous documentation and analysis is an amazing feat. I extend much admiration to my colleagues in Africa who not only compiled and analyzed their country data looking at the broader political, social and economic context in which tobacco control exists but also continued to push forward their policy priorities at the same time. I also commend Jeffrey Drope for guiding staff, consultants and team members through the political mapping process and tireless consultation with all of the team leaders in an effort to capture each country team's stories in their own voice.

Jacqui Drope

ACKNOWLEDGMENTS

There are many people who helped to develop, execute and bring this important piece of the Africa Tobacco Situational Analyses (ATSA) initiative to publication. At risk of exclusion, I will attempt to acknowledge individually the people who were most central to this endeavor.

First and foremost, however, this narrative project would never have been realized without the many participants in the ATSA initiative. They are too numerous to name and their contributions cannot be accurately measured. While the actual writers get direct credit through authorship, it is important to note that the narratives were generated in most circumstances by sizeable groups of stakeholders and other participants who all contributed to the project.

The Research in International Tobacco Control (RITC) team at the International Development Research Centre (IDRC) has been very helpful in the production of this volume through both financial and human resources. First, by far the largest debt is to Jacqui Drope, who was the senior program officer for the ATSA initiative. She spent months conceptualizing the initiative and making certain that it was executed effectively. She also believed in, helped to develop and then championed the narrative component. Eugène Gbedji was the ATSA program officer and provided a great deal of general input, particularly concerning the Francophone countries. The initial (acting) RITC program leader, Christina Zarowsky, first embraced the narrative component of the project, but it was her successor Greg Hallen who was most supportive and active in making certain that this print publication came to fruition. Bill Carman was instrumental throughout the publication process. Jean-Michel Labatut provided input to the volume's production. Luis Caceres was a near constant supply of important background materials, and Rosemary Kennedy and Wardie Leppan commented on the process at several junctures. Edita Lindsey provided valuable administrative support.

By far the largest debt in terms of support for writing and editing the volume is owed to Linda Waverley. Linda read every single chapter multiple times with an incredibly keen eye for logic, writing and accuracy. She always demonstrated good humor through a long and sometimes challenging process. It is a richer collection for the comments and suggestions that come from her wisdom, strong writing skills and vast experience in public health. She bears no responsibility for any remaining shortcomings.

Many other experts in the field provided information or valuable feedback on the project. Colleagues from or associated with the Bill and Melinda Gates Foundation – which supplied the principal funds for the entire ATSA initiative – were very helpful with input and insight throughout the ATSA process. In particular, Michael Eriksen and Mike Stark were great sources of wisdom at the beginning of the program. Kate Teela offered helpful input at the meeting when the initial syntheses were discussed. In an impressive demonstration of interorganizational cooperation, Pam Sumner Coffey and especially Dave Elseroad from the Campaign for Tobacco-Free Kids offered valuable input and resources, as did their former colleague, Ross Hammond, who commented on preliminary versions of the country chapters. Evan Blecher from the American Cancer Society provided vast and helpful comments on the taxation chapter. Similarly, both Veronique LeClezio and Massamba Diouf generously gave valuable input on their home country chapters.

The overall project benefitted from superb research assistance. As editor, I sincerely thank the team of researchers involved in the general research for the volume for their hard work: Jason Ardanowski, Melanie Baier, Grace Cochon, John Madigan, Arie Molema, Tony Ocepek, Lauren Reeves, Dave Ruigh, Anne-Marie Schryer-Roy, Craig Shockley, Joe Struble and Ashley Tikkanen. Several of the researchers became coauthors in the volume – a testament to their beyond-the-call hard work – and one, Anne-Marie, even traveled extensively throughout the region to make certain that the information that we were collecting was accurate.

From the actual production perspective, there were still more instrumental people. The principal cover graphic was provided to the volume as a courtesy by Yussuf Saloojee and Peter Ucko of the National Council Against Smoking in South Africa. The powerful Smoke-Free Africa symbol is the organization's logo and thanks to their generous permission to use it, the cover's boldness properly represents the efforts of public health advocates throughout the continent. I am also thankful to Tej Sood, Janka Romero and the Anthem Press staff for all of their hard work and skillful assistance.

On a deeply sad note and on behalf of her many colleagues in tobacco control in Africa, I would like to pay very special tribute to one of our authors, Sophia Twum-Barima, who passed away in December 2010. Sophia not only played a significant role in the Ghana chapter and discussions about the development of the volume but more generally was enormously important to tobacco control and public health in her role as public relations officer at the

Accra office of the World Health Organization. Her dedication to the cause of public health greatly reflected the personal side of Sophia: kind, generous of time and spirit, and very sharp.

On a much happier final note, acknowledging gratefully that many families have sacrificed for the cause of tobacco control in Africa, I wish to thank my wife Victoria and our two children for their support and putting up with my absences, both literal and figurative, during the writing and editing of the volume with kindness and understanding.

Jeffrey Drope
Milwaukee, WI
May 2011

LIST OF ABBREVIATIONS
AND ACRONYMS

ABSP	Association Burkinabe de Santé Publique (Burkina Faso Public Health Association)
AD	Alliance for Democracy (Nigeria)
AFCO	Armed Forces Canteen Organization (Kenya)
AFRO	Africa Regional Office (World Health Organization)
AG	attorney general
AGM	annual general meeting
AIDS	acquired immune deficiency syndrome
AJD-PASTEEF	Association des Jeunes pour le Developpement (Senegal – Association of Youth for Development)
AMMP	Adult Morbidity and Mortality Project (Tanzania)
ANC	African National Congress (South Africa)
ANCOMU	All Nigeria Consumers Movement Union
ANPP	All Nigerian People's Party
APCON	Advertising Practitioners Promotion Control (Nigeria)
AORTIC	African Organization for Research and Training in Cancer
APS	advertising, promotion and sponsorship
ASPAT	Association Sénégalaise pour la Paix, la Lutte contre l'Alcool et la Toxicomanie (Senegalese Association for Peace and the Fight Against Alcohol and Addiction)
ATCA	Africa Tobacco Control Alliance
ATCC	Africa Tobacco Control Consortium
ATCRI	Africa Tobacco Control Regional Initiative
ATSA	African Tobacco Situational Analysis
ATTT	Association of Tanzania Tobacco Traders
BAT	British American Tobacco
BATK	British American Tobacco–Kenya
BATN	British American Tobacco–Nigeria

BMGF   Bill and Melinda Gates Foundation
BMA   British Military Administration
CAMBoD   Cameroon Burden of Diabetes Project
CAMH   Centre for Addiction and Mental Health
                (Canada)
CANSA   Cancer Association of South Africa
CAT   Coalition Against Tobacco (Nigeria)
CCAP   Church of Central Africa Presbyterian
CCM   Chama Cha Mapinduzi Party (Tanzania)
CEMAC   Communauté Economique et Monétaire de l'Afrique
                Centrale (Economic and Monetary Community of
                Central Africa)
CEPS   Customs, Excise and Prevention Service (Ghana)
CES   Conseil Économique et Social (Burkina Faso – Social
                and Economic Council)
CETAC   Compagnie d'Exploitation des Tabacs Camerounais
                (Cameroon Tobacco Development Company)
CFAF   Central African CFA (Colonies françaises d'Afrique)
                Franc (currency)
CfDC   Communication for Development Centre (Ghana)
CFSC   Centre for Social Concern (Malawi)
CIF   cost, insurance, and freight
CNTC   Coalition of Non-government Organizations in
                Tobacco Control (Ghana)
CONGOMA   Council of NGOs in Malawi
COP   Conference of the Parties
COTU   Central Organization for Trade Unions (Kenya)
CPC   Consumer Protection Council (Nigeria)
CPHA   Canadian Public Health Association
CRES   Consortium pour la Recherche Economique et Social
                (Senegal – Consortium for Economic and Social
                Research)
CRTV   Cameroon Radio and Television
CSO   civil society organizations
CSR   corporate social responsibility
CTFK   Campaign for Tobacco-Free Kids (also TFK)
CUF   Civil United Front (Tanzania)
DA   district assembly (Malawi)
DAT   Doctors Against Tobacco
DDG   deputy director general
DEC   Drug Enforcement Commission (Zambia)

DED	Direction de enquêtes douanières (Burkina Faso – Office of Customs Investigation)
DFID	Department for International Development (United Kingdom)
DG	director general
DGD	Direction général des douanes (Burkina Faso – General Customs Office)
DGI	Direction général des impôts (Burkina Faso – General Tax Office)
DGSS	director general for social service (Eritrea)
DHPES	Direction de l'hygiène et de l'éducation sanitaire (Burkina Faso – Directorate of Hygiene and Health Education)
DHS	Demographic Health Survey
DLM	Direction de la lutte contre les maladies (Burkina Faso – Directorate of Disease Control)
DMTP	Dimon Morogoro Tobacco Processors (Tanzania)
DPP	Democratic Progressive Party (Malawi)
DSF	Direction de la santé de la famille (Burkina Faso – Directorate of Family Health)
DSRP	*Document de stratégies de réduction de la pauvreté* (Cameroon – *Strategies for Poverty Reduction Document*)
DTI	Department of Trade and Industry (South Africa)
ECOWAS	Economic Community of West African States
EDIF	Export Development and Investment Fund
EEG	Export Expansion Grant
EHO	environmental health officers (Zambia)
EPA	Environmental Protection Agency
ERA	Environmental Rights Action (Nigeria)
EU	European Union
FAO	Food and Agriculture Organization of the United Nations
FAOSTAT	Food and Agriculture Organization of the United Nations – Statistics
FCA	Framework Convention Alliance
FCT	Federal Capital Territory (Nigeria)
FCTC	Framework Convention on Tobacco Control
FDB	Food and Drugs Board (Ghana)
FIFA	Fédération Internationale de Football Association (International Federation of Association Football)
FLAZ	Female Lawyers Association of Zambia

FOB	free on board
FoEN	Friends of the Earth Nigeria
FPTC	Fédération des Planteurs de Tabac et autres Cultures Vivrières du Cameroun (Cameroon Federation of Growers of Tobacco and other Agricultural Crops)
GATS	General Adult Tobacco Survey
GATUA	Ghana Anti-Tobacco Use Alliance
GCF	Gash Cigarette Factory (Eritrea)
GDHS	Ghana Demographic Health Survey
GDP	gross domestic product
GES	Ghana Education Service
GG	*Government Gazette* (various countries)
GHPSS	Global Health Professions Students Survey
GHS	Ghana Health Service
GPRTU	Ghana Private Road Transport Union
GSHS	Global School-based Student Health Survey
GSPS	Global School Personnel Survey
GTB	Ghana Tourist Board
GTSS	Global Tobacco Surveillance System
GYTS	Global Youth Tobacco Survey
HCC	Health Centre Committees
HIV	human immunodeficiency virus
HoPiT	Health of Population in Transition (Cameroon)
ICRIS	International Crops Research Institute for the Semi-arid Tropics
ICRAF	World Agroforestry Centre
IDRC	International Development Research Centre (Canada)
IEC	Electoral Commission (Tanzania)
IEC	information, education, and communication
IGAE	Inspection générale des affaires économiques (Burkina Faso – General Inspection of Economic Affairs)
IHE	Institutes of Higher Education (Eritrea)
ILA	Institute for Legislative Affairs (Kenya)
INB	Intergovernmental Negotiating Body
INESOR	Institute for Economic and Social Research (Zambia)
INGO	international nongovernmental organization
INSD	Institut national de la statistique et la démographie (Burkina Faso – National Institute for Statistics and Demographics)
IPAR	Institute for Policy Analysis and Research (Kenya)

IPPA	Institute of Public Policy Analysis (Nigeria)
ISODEC	Integrated Social Development Centre (Ghana)
ITC	international tobacco control
JTI	Japan Tobacco International
KABP	knowledge, attitudes, beliefs and practices
KANU	Kenyan African National Union
KDHS	Kenya Demographic and Health Survey
KETCA	Kenya Tobacco Control Alliance
KIPPRA	Kenya Institute for Public Policy Research and Analysis
KRA	Kenya Revenue Authority
LEAT	Lawyers Environmental Action Team (Tanzania)
LEG	Linking Education and Governance (Malawi)
LGAZ	Local Government Association of Zambia
LMIC	low- and middle-income countries
MABUCIG	Manufacture Burkinabé de Cigarettes (Burkinabé Cigarette Manufacturers)
MATOSA	Movement Against Tobacco and Substances of Abuse (Ghana)
MCP	Malawi Congress Party
MCPEA	Ministère du commerce, de la promotion de l'entreprise et de l'artisanat (Burkina Faso – Ministry of Commerce and the Promotion of Enterprises and Handicrafts)
MCT	Mount Cameroon Tobacco
MD	medical doctor
MEF	Ministère de l'économie et des finances (Burkina Faso – Ministry of the Economy and Finances)
MEJN	Malawi Economic Justice Network
MGDS	Malawi Growth and Development Strategy
MHAZ	Mental Health Association of Zambia
MIH	Mauritius Institute of Health
MIJ	Malawi Institute of Journalism
MINEPAT	Ministère de l'Economie, de la Planification, et du Amenagement du Territoire (Cameroon – Ministry of the Economy, Planning and Land Use)
MMD	Movement for Multi-party Democracy (Zambia)
MMSM	Mauritian Militant Socialist Movement
MoE	Ministry of Education
MoH	Ministry of Health
MOH&QL	Ministry of Health and Quality of Life (Mauritius)
MoPH	Ministry of Public Health (Cameroon)

MoU   memorandum of understanding
MP   member of parliament
MTOA   Manufacture de Tabacs de l'Ouest Africain
                 (Senegal – Tobacco Manufacturers of West Africa)
MUR   Mauritian rupee (national currency)
N   naira (Nigerian currency)
NACADA   National Agency for the Campaign against Drug
                 Abuse (Kenya)
NACADAA   National Campaign Against Drug Abuse Authority
                 (Kenya)
NAFDAC   National Agency for Food Drug Administration and
                 Control (Nigeria)
NARC   National Rainbow Coalition (Kenya)
NATOCC   National Tobacco Control Committee (Nigeria)
NBHE   National Board of Higher Education (Eritrea)
NCAS   National Council Against Smoking (South Africa)
NCD   noncommunicable disease
NCS   Nigerian Cancer Society
NECPAD   Network for Community Planning and Development
                 (Ghana)
NGO   nongovernmental organization
NHF   Nigerian Heart Foundation
NHIL   National Health Insurance Levy (Ghana)
NIPC   Nigerian Investment Promotion Commission
NMA   Nigeria Medical Association
NMC   Nyasa Manufacturing Company (Malawi)
NONM   National Organisation of Nurses and Midwives
                 (Malawi)
NORAD   Norwegian Agency for Development Cooperation
NSSF   National Social Security Fund (Kenya)
NTCA   Nigeria Tobacco Control Alliance
NTSA   Nigeria Tobacco Situational Analysis
NUEW   National Union of Eritrean Women
NUEYS   National Union of Eritrean Youth and Students
ODA   official development assistance
ODM   Orange Democratic Movement (Kenya)
PADDI   People Against Drug Dependence and Ignorance
                 (Nigeria)
PARTEC   Projet d'Appui à la Relance de la Tabaculture à
                 l'Est Cameroun (Project Supporting the Revival of
                 Tobacco Farming in Eastern Cameroon)

PDP	People's Democratic Party (Nigeria)
PDS	Parti démocratie du Sénégal (Democratic Party of Senegal)
PF	Patriotic Front (Zambia)
PFDJ	People's Front for Democracy and Justice (Eritrea)
PH(T)R	Public Health (Tobacco) Regulation (Zambia)
PM	prime minister
PMI	Philip Morris International
PMXD	Parti Mauricien Xavier Duval (Xavier Duval Party of Mauritius)
PNU	Party of National Unity (Kenya)
PPP	purchasing power parity
PPTE	(fonds de) Pays Pauvres Très Endettés (Heavily Indebted Poor Countries (initiative) or HIPC)
RDA	Resident Doctors Association (Zambia)
RDCP	Rassemblement Démocratique du Peuple Camerounais (Cameroon People's Democratic Movement)
RDD	Research and Development Division (Ghana)
REPOA	Research on Poverty Alleviation (Tanzania)
RITC	Research for International Tobacco Control (Canada)
SACU	Southern African Customs Union
SAFA	South African Football Association
SARS	South African Revenue Services
SCT	Société Camerounaise des Tabacs (Cameroon Tobacco Company)
SEITA	Société Nationale d'Exploitation Industrielle des Tabacs et Allumettes (Cameroon – National Tobacco and Match Company)
SFCT	Société Franco-Camourounese des Tabacs (French-Cameroonian Tobacco Company)
SHEP	School Health Promotion
SHS	second-hand smoke
SITABAC	Societé Industrielle des Tabacs du Cameroon (Cameroon Tobacco Manufacturing Company)
SoM	School of Medicine
SON	Standards Organization of Nigeria
SRH	Services de ressources humaines (Burkina Faso – Human Resources Service)
SSA	Sub-Saharan Africa
STC	State Transit Corporation (Ghana)

SUA	Sokoine University of Agriculture (Tanzania)
TAG	Tobacco Action Group (South Africa)
TAMA	Tobacco Association of Malawi
TAZ	Tobacco Association of Zambia
TCA	Tobacco Control Act (Kenya)
TCC	Tanzania Cigarette Company
TCT	Tobacco Council of Tanzania
TEACH	Training Enhancement in Applied Counseling and Health
TFK	Tobacco-Free Kids (also CTFK)
TFSEI	Tobacco-Free Schools Initiative (Eritrea)
TOFAZA	Tobacco Free Association of Zambia
TOPSERV/TLTC	Tanzania Leaf Tobacco Company
TOTAWUM	Tobacco Tenants and Allied Workers Union of Malawi
TPHA	Tanzania Public Health Association
TPRA	Tobacco (Products Regulation) Act of 2003 (Tanzania)
TTB	Tanzania Tobacco Board
TTCF	Tanzania Tobacco Control Forum
UACT	Union des associations contre le tabac (Burkina Faso – Union of Associations Against Tobacco)
UDA	United Democratic Alliance (Zambia)
UEMOA	Union économique et monétaire ouest-africaine (West African Economic and Monetary Union or WAEMU)
UICC	Union Internationale Contre le Cancer (International Union Against Cancer)
UK	United Kingdom
UN	United Nations
UNDP	United Nations Development Programme
UNESCO	United Nations Educational, Scientific and Cultural Organisation
UNFPA	United Nations Population Fund
UNICEF	United Nations Children's Fund
UNZA	University of Zambia
USA	United States of America
USD	United States dollar
VALD	Vision for Alternative Development (Ghana)
VAT	value added tax
WHO	World Health Organization

WHOSIS	World Health Organization Statistical Information System
WHS	World Health Survey
WNTD	World No Tobacco Day
YASED	Youth Alliance in Social and Economic Development (Malawi)
YMCA	Young Men's Christian Association
YWCA	Young Women's Christian Association
ZACA	Zambia Consumer Association
ZAHVAC	Zambia Association of High Value Crops
ZAMNAT	Zambia Media Network Against Tobacco
ZASS	Zambia Anti-Smoking Society
ZEGA	Zambia Export Growers Association
ZMA	Zambia Medical Association
ZNA	Zambia Nurses Association
ZNFU	Zambia National Farmers' Union
ZTCC	Zambia Tobacco Control Campaign
ZWIA	Zambia Women in Agriculture

Chapter 1

INTRODUCTION

Jeffrey Drope

The harmful effects of tobacco use pose an imminent threat to the health of African people. As the tobacco epidemic shows signs of waning in some northern countries, a combination of factors such as low prevalence rates, young and burgeoning populations, growing disposable incomes and aggressive and unscrupulous advertising by multinational tobacco companies threatens to create a massive tobacco-related burden of disease in Africa, which will unfortunately add to existing public health challenges. The World Health Organization (WHO) reports that tobacco kills approximately 5.4 million people annually, which is more than HIV/AIDS, malaria or tuberculosis. More than half of these tobacco-related deaths are now in developing countries. Fortunately, in recent years, proponents of tobacco control have increased their efforts in Africa and there is now some notable progress in policy reform. However, a great deal of work remains. Moreover, more country-specific or locally relevant research in Africa and across developing countries is necessary to complement these nascent efforts. While the research must be theoretical and empirical, it must also be highly relevant, accessible and useable by advocates of policy change.

Accordingly, the principal focus of this research is to examine the political, economic and social determinants of policy change in the area of public health generally and tobacco control more specifically. The research in the book is based on the 2008–10 African Tobacco Situational Analyses (ATSA) initiative, which was spearheaded by the International Development Research Centre's (IDRC) Research for International Tobacco Control (RITC) with funds from the Bill and Melinda Gates Foundation. The initiative sought to collect and analyze comprehensive tobacco-related data in 12 countries across the African continent: Burkina Faso, Cameroon, Eritrea, Ghana, Kenya, Malawi, Mauritius, Nigeria, Senegal, South Africa, Tanzania and Zambia. Participants from across sectors in these countries gathered a panoply of data about policies, prevalence, actors and institutions. Uniquely, the ATSA initiative sought to analyze these data using political mapping, which is a tool (explained in Chapter 2) that helps to examine the relationships between the actors and institutions in the particular political context of each country in order to consider tractable policy changes for the political situation.

One of the most important and exciting findings of this research is that the politics of public health remain decidedly local in fundamental ways. While no one would question the importance of international forces in public health – including, of course, in the case of tobacco control, the WHO's highly influential Framework Convention on Tobacco Control (FCTC)[1] – each of the contributions in this volume points to the fact that much of the daily work of making policy change is happening in significant part at the country level. Indeed, while international organizations and donors still shape much of the agenda and are helpful by providing resources and expertise, most of the significant agents of policy reform within countries – a major component of success in tobacco control – are endogenous to countries, not exogenous to them.

The structure of this volume greatly reflects the broad and inclusive nature of the ATSA initiative. When the program began, there was a strong focus on data gathering and analysis. However, after a few months of proposal writing and vigorous discussions, there was a significant move toward actual planning and executing of policy interventions, and resources were shifted firmly toward these new goals. Participants noted that the shift facilitated and necessitated a whole new set of analyses of policy in motion and every team regrouped to be reflective on their own efforts and actions as they were occurring. This self-reflexive dynamic is evident in many of the narratives as authors, all of whom participated actively in the ATSA initiative, discuss and analyze the complexities of policy interventions almost in real time.

From a theoretical perspective, this research borrows heavily from policy and political science approaches. In recent years, the two approaches have become increasingly exclusive of the other. The policy-specific literature has become more pragmatic and often idiographic, while the political science literature has become overwhelmingly theoretical, often to the point of forsaking application. In this volume, there is a concerted effort to link the two approaches and to be mindful of making the research relevant to advocates and policymakers. Political science and the subfield of political economy more specifically offer very useful lenses through which we can discuss and analyze the determinants of policy change in major areas of global public health. While the inherent complexities of public health policy in the developing world preclude the development of a unified theory in which to place the discussion of tobacco control, this integrative approach seeks to provide clear and complementary frameworks in which proponents of policy reform can consider change both broadly and specifically.

Throughout the volume, the authors emphasize both the "agents" of change – the individuals and organizations that are seeking policy change – and the institutions that mediate these demands. Thus, the research draws from both interest group and institutions literatures. In addition, in large part due to the breadth of expertise and interest of the authors – including medical doctors, public health professionals, social scientists, government officials (elected and unelected) and development specialists – there is a keen eye to move beyond just a narrow politics-only approach by situating the actors and institutions within the larger sociocultural context of each country.

Knowing and Articulating Your Context

Undoubtedly, policy has been a principal focus of the ATSA teams – after all, much of what needs to be accomplished in tobacco control in Africa has a direct policy component. Even activities that might not appear to be immediately policy-relevant, such as education campaigns or cessation programs, can be inherently political if they involve any government institution. More than once in the course of the ATSA program, country teams undertook a rigorous process of identifying, examining and then explicating the relative policy positions of relevant actors and the roles that institutions were playing in mediating the demands for different policies. In general, all of the teams acknowledged that knowing the policy process and having the requisite skills to navigate it effectively were paramount to the success of their various initiatives and to developing a comprehensive and meaningful synthesis of tobacco control in their countries.

In presenting the pertinent information on policy context, the country authors seek to balance two important goals. On one hand, the authors wish to illustrate abstractly which types of actors and institutions play a role in influencing and shaping tobacco control policy, so that at any future point, readers can identify who are likely to be the central policy players. On the other hand, many of the contributors want to place actual individuals into the context so that the reader can gain from the narrative a genuine sense of what happened or is happening on the ground in terms of the politics of tobacco control in the 12 countries.

Some reviewers of earlier versions of this research raised the legitimate issue that this information could become "dated" quickly if it became overly descriptive. The authors were mindful of this potential pitfall, but also offer three important responses. First, as many of the participants in the several ATSA workshops brought to light, the political elite in most (if not all) countries is pretty small, and perhaps particularly small in most African countries. So while individuals' specific positions might change, the people at the highest levels of leadership tend to be remarkably static. The relatively fixed nature of politics in some countries is evident in the syntheses where teams note that a particular individual now runs a given ministry, but had been the minister of a different one just a short time before. In some cases, people have not changed their positions in decades. Secondly, in terms of turning an abstract exercise into something tangible, the process of actually identifying the actors is a useful one. Because the teams elucidate both the overall context and the specific roles of the relevant institutions and organizations, it is not a conceptual stretch to contemplate what might happen – or not happen – when the position is taken over by someone new. Finally, this exercise provides a neat snapshot in time – arguably a critical juncture as countries accede to the FCTC and seek to implement the agreement's specific articles – and begins to generate a contemporary history of tobacco control across the 12 countries.

The ATSA Narratives

The narratives that the country authors develop (Chapters 7–18) are both snapshots in time – generally, late 2009/early 2010 with some updating into early 2011 – and contemporary histories from approximately the previous 20 years, though sometimes longer or shorter depending on a country's experiences. Furthermore, in every case there is much more than just a casual glance toward the future. The authors developed the narratives not only to provide valuable description, explanation and discussion of the recent and current state of affairs in tobacco control in Africa, but also the foundation for more data gathering and analysis. As of writing, the Africa Tobacco Control Consortium (ATCC) has already expanded the in-depth analysis to six more countries with plans and resources for 11 more.[2] Moreover, through this synthesis and discussion, the authors are demonstrating the trajectory of tobacco control efforts on the continent more broadly and are directly emphasizing the work that will need to be done and how it might be realistically undertaken.

   The country syntheses intensively utilize the qualitative research technique of developing narratives. In work across the social sciences and humanities, scholars use narratives to furnish significant context of a particular topic – in this case, to chronicle the development of (or attempts to develop) new and/ or the reform of existing tobacco control policies and then the subsequent implementation and enforcement of them.[3] The rigor of these narratives derives from several key sources. First, the theoretical foundation of institutions and interest groups that guides the volume helps to maintain a consistent set of themes and data-gathering efforts that frame the narratives. Every team focuses on interest groups and institutions in a systematic manner.[1] Second, for the sake of meaningful cross-country comparison, the overall structure of the narratives is consistent across the countries. Third, the structure was determined through vigorous discussion among dozens of participants both within each country and subsequently among the 12 country teams in a series of face-to-face meetings. In other words, they are not the narratives of the specific authors, but rather of the various stakeholders that took part in the process of producing them. In the cases of Kenya, Nigeria and Tanzania, the organizational authorship actually speaks directly to this collective effort. More importantly, none of these efforts attempts to reach a consensus, but rather encourages different interpretations of how policymaking happened or is transpiring and then attempts to articulate these complexities. Lastly, the syntheses, where possible, are anchored by empirical data. For example, the tobacco "problem" discussion in each country chapter highlights and discusses most of the relevant survey research on prevalence and related issues that has been executed in each country. These data help to furnish as accurate a portrayal of the challenges as is possible within the constraints in each country. Similarly, the discussions of policy are based on actual pieces of legislation and regulation, and the public hearings, media accounts, discussions and other discourse that often occurred around them.

On a related issue, it is important to discuss briefly how traditional scholarly citation expectations fit into the form and style of the country narratives. In the volume, when the authors are citing direct fact and other people's research and/or opinion, they seek to provide the proper citation. Because much of the information was generated in stakeholder and similar types of meetings, however, some of the information is less directly attributed to a specific source. In some instances, authors are giving their impressions or those of other actors deeply involved in tobacco control and/or public health more generally in Africa. In these cases, the authors make a concerted effort to attribute the observations to either the ATSA team or the stakeholders who attended the formal meetings in each country. It is important to note, too, that in some less democratic countries there was genuine concern about retribution from governments or other actors, so not every stakeholder was comfortable going on the record about sensitive issues. That said, in the interest of rigor and validity, if readers wish to follow up on the more ambiguous sources, they are encouraged to contact the authors directly. In all cases, there is contact information in the contributors section and the authors are pleased to engage about these issues.

In some cases, it is clear that the narratives are very much ongoing. In some countries, it is possible to observe nearly completed actions; in two short years, a number of advocacy teams participating in the ATSA program identified a policy or related goal, mapped out its possible progression and then followed through with action. For example, in the cases of the Nigerian smoke-free Abuja enforcement and the new Osun State smoke-free legislation, the narrative tracks nearly the entire process from what the team members initially thought would be central to their objective to what turned out to be more instrumental in achieving their policy goals. Similarly, the Zambian team mapped out an initial understanding of and a strategy to enforce a smoke-free Lusaka. In less than a year, the team had fully initiated the program and could report back in their narrative on the effort's accomplishments and to where the program was headed.

Overview of the Book

The structure of the book is explicitly designed to be utilized in at least two ways: as a complete set of analyses and discussion of tobacco control in a major collection of developing countries, or as the individual pieces of the set, each of which stand on their own independently or as logical subsets. For example, some readers will wish to learn about the politics of public health policy and/or the status of tobacco control in a specific country or set of countries (e.g. East African or Francophone African countries, etc.). Other readers will be interested in discussions across a specific policy area (e.g. taxation) or a set of policies (e.g. major policies related to FCTC articles). Still other readers will be interested in the process that the ATSA teams employed to develop their analyses. Finally, some readers will want to fast-forward to the conclusions. The collection is designed explicitly to accommodate all of these users. While the total collection seeks to offer unique and helpful insights, each of the constituent parts has its own intrinsic value.

Chapter 2 presents the flexible process or template that the 12 country teams used to analyze their political contexts, develop their narratives and execute their interventions, with the expectation that the template can be used for any such endeavor by proponents of policy reform in any country or political context. The template guides users through a systematic assessment of the major institutions in any country, particularly by emphasizing the major branches of government including the executive, the legislature and the judiciary. It also underscores the role of the bureaucracy, which consistently plays a significant role in public health policy. It provides additional focus on the institutions that often have particular public health relevance such as ministries of health and legislative health committees. It also strongly implores users to consider relevant interest groups such as nongovernmental organizations and research institutions, particularly their organizational characteristics and the roles they play (or seek to play) in the policy process. Above all, it presses users to contemplate systematically the complex interactions between the actors and institutions that shape or are attempting to influence policymaking.

Examinations of major tobacco control policies

Chapters 3 through 6 examine four of the most significant tobacco control policies across Africa: smoke-free policies; tobacco taxation; advertising, promotion and sponsorship bans; and health warning labels on tobacco packaging. These synthetic analyses utilize the central principles of the mapping process to permit systematic comparisons of what is working in some countries (so-called "best practices") in terms of tobacco policy reform and what is not working, as well as how to address more effectively these ongoing challenges. The policy-specific analyses also provide an opportunity to reflect comparatively on how political structures, the relative strengths of civil society organizations and the effectiveness of research support are affecting policy reform.

Chapter 3 explores the complexities of smoke-free policies – protection from second-hand smoke in public spaces and private workplaces. This policy area has probably received the most attention from policymakers and tobacco control researchers alike across the globe. Because it is estimated that less than 10 percent of Africans are protected by smoke-free regulations,[5] it demonstrates enormous potential for positive public health impact in the short term. While a number of countries have been able to pass such legislation – either as narrow regulation or as part of broader health legislation – the real stumbling block consistently proves to be implementation and enforcement. Proponents of smoke-free policies need to be thinking about what mechanisms can ensure effective enforcement. In particular, convincing municipal-level officials to make enforcement part of their responsibilities and finding ways to train these actors and earmark budgetary resources for them are the pivotal challenges in this policy area.

Chapter 4 examines tobacco taxation, a strategy that presents enormous potential to effect positive public health change. The chapter particularly examines the central role played by finance ministries and argues specifically that accessing these ministries – sometimes relatively neutral agencies – in order to present strong evidence-based research demonstrating the long-term fiscal and health benefits of increased tobacco taxation is one of the key components to successful taxation reform.

Chapter 5 focuses on advertising, promotion and sponsorship bans and makes the argument that this is the policy area that the tobacco industry most creatively and insidiously seeks to circumvent. Again, vigilance in terms of monitoring and enforcement is a key factor for successful policy. Across the continent, the industry continues to host "smoking" parties, flout advertising rules and, ironically, sponsor children's health programs and other so-called corporate social responsibility (CSR) activities. Countries are clearly challenged to keep up with the industry's relentless pursuit of breaking the rules. The results of this research suggest that civil society monitoring coupled with a willing and effective official enforcement mechanism (e.g. police or courts) help to promote success.

Chapter 6 tracks the recent push in many countries to introduce graphic health warning labels on packages. Unlike many other policy areas, most countries permit agency-level regulation of packaging, which means that the pursuit of legislation, while perhaps desired, is not totally necessary for the actual policy objective, at least in the shorter term. Particularly for countries where more comprehensive legislation is stalled in the legislative process, pursuing this alternative moves countries to a goal of graphic warning labels quickly and effectively. Again, similar to taxation, successful advocates are using evidence-based research to convince the relevant agency – often, but not always, the health ministry – to pass and implement the regulations, and then to help them do it effectively.

Examinations of tobacco control in 12 African countries

Chapters 7 to 18 analyze the public health challenges of tobacco control policy reform in 12 African countries.[6] In order to provide broad and even competing viewpoints from an African perspective, each country's analytical narrative is authored by leading development and public health professionals from the specific country, all of whom participated in some manner in the ATSA initiative. The authors were drawn from across major sectors including government, civil society, the academic community and international organizations. Moreover, as outlined briefly above, the narrative is the fruit of multiple intra- and intercountry meetings and workshops that involved a wide variety of participants from across each country.

For the sake of clarity and easy comparison, each individual country chapter follows a standard outline. First, each chapter begins with a brief overall summary that also effectively serves as an introduction to the broader narrative. After a short presentation of country-level vital statistics, there is a discussion of the scope and magnitude of the tobacco problem using the available empirical data, with particular emphasis on adult prevalence, youth smoking, exposure to second-hand smoke and the extent of industry advertising and promotion. Next, the authors analyze the politics of public health generally and tobacco control specifically. They then develop the themes that most help to explain public health and tobacco policy reform in their countries. Often, the authors use one or more of the specific policy interventions pursued with ATSA resources as the centerpiece of discussion. As one might expect, most chapters also examine the activities and behavior of the tobacco industry specific to the country. Finally, most chapters end with a recap of the achievements of the ATSA-related activities, and in some cases, further discussion of the challenges encountered by the teams along the way and suggestions for best practices. Each final review hews closely to the presentation made by each ATSA team leader at a reunion meeting hosted by the American Cancer Society and the WHO (with funds from the Gates Foundation) in Johannesburg in February 2011.

From a social scientific perspective, it is critical to note the wide variation in the countries in this research in terms of the "values" of both the dependent variables (the extent of tobacco control policy and/or tobacco policy change) and the independent variables (the characteristics shaping these policies). In terms of magnitude and scope of tobacco control policies, there is enormous variation: on one end of the scale, Mauritius and South Africa are in multiple ways world leaders in tobacco control policy, while on the other end of the scale, Malawi has almost no tobacco control legislation or regulation and has yet to sign the FCTC. Across significant independent variables, the countries vary considerably in terms of geographical size, population, ethnicity, language, country-level and personal incomes, and types of political systems (including levels of democracy), just to name a handful of characteristics. In fact, the ATSA program officers and their outside reviewers considered these variables – along with the quality of the initial proposals – when selecting the countries for the program.

In Chapter 7, the authors argue that Burkina Faso's quickly decentralizing government offers an excellent opportunity for reform in the area of policy implementation. While the government has moved recently toward new tobacco control legislation, the authors point out that implementation and enforcement of most policies will take place mainly at the local level. Thus, they argue that these local political actors – including mayors and councilors – must be engaged successfully in public health programs in order for the policies to do well.

In Chapter 8, the authors make an argument that in highly centralized Cameroon the government must be the key initiator of policy change. With only a small civil society organized around public health issues, the existing catalysts for reform are limited. However, the authors do make the additional compelling case that academic researchers are playing an integral role in terms of helping to inform better health policy, have access to key decision makers in the government and can help to shape public health policy.

Chapter 9 examines the case of Eritrea. Similar to Cameroon, Eritrea is another highly centralized regime and the authors demonstrate how working within the governmental system is currently the most viable strategy for policy change. Furthermore, with only a limited civil society, the academic sector is ideally and uniquely situated to offer well-researched public policy options to the government.

Chapter 10 examines recent tobacco policy challenges in Ghana. The authors weigh the relative merits of pursuing targeted policies through less legally binding instruments such as ministerial directives versus comprehensive national legislation. They find that the former is eminently feasible though possibly less effective in the longer term, while the latter requires enormous investment from civil society and internal governmental pressure to move the policy. Though Ghana has a strong civil society that is highly active in the public health sector, the burden of changing a huge part of the public health code continues to be challenging.

Chapter 11 acknowledges the importance of Kenya's 2007 comprehensive tobacco control legislation, but makes a plea that the focus must now shift in large part from the national to the more local politics of implementation and enforcement. The authors argue that it is only through the coordinated partnership of civil society, several levels of government (national and subnational), and at least for the time being the help of external donors that successful enforcement of public health policies will happen. Because no one actor can execute these actions alone, genuine reform will not happen without this team effort.

Chapter 12 examines the case of Malawi, one of the world's leading producers of tobacco leaf. The authors argue that because tobacco comprises such a key part of the economy (greater than 60 percent of foreign exchange), the emphasis must be strictly focused on health in order to gain any – and much-needed – political traction. Since it is unlikely that the government will initiate policy reform, the burden falls on civil society organizations and research institutions to spur the effort. Finally, alternative livelihoods for tobacco farmers must be part of the discussion in order to convince both policymakers and ordinary citizens of the benefits of tobacco control policies.

Chapter 13 explores the recent enormous public health legislative successes in Mauritius. Like Kenya, with the passing of broad public health legislation and subsequent regulation, much of the focus in Mauritius is shifting to implementation and enforcement. The emphasis in this small, vibrant democracy is on the central role that government should play in these efforts and the watchdog role that its small but highly effective civil society plays.

Chapter 14 offers a lively and comprehensive discussion about the possible routes to policy change in Nigeria. In particular, the authors demonstrate the creative possibilities in a federal system. While the National Senate finally approved new comprehensive national legislation in early 2011, proponents of health reform have been successfully pursuing major public health policy changes at the subnational level for a number of years. For countries where national legislative reform seems unrealistic or very slow, the two-pronged Nigerian model is very attractive, particularly considering the diffusion effect that has been occurring as new jurisdictions see the positive changes in other parts of the country and begin to seek policy reform. The two-pronged model will also likely prove useful for implementation and enforcement because it is often subnational actors that are charged with putting much of the legislation into action.

Chapter 15 follows recent challenges in Senegal to improve public health policy with a government that demonstrates little interest in policy reform. In particular, the chapter argues that creativity is the key when neither the government nor most of civil society is engaged with an issue. In Senegal, tobacco control policy advocates have elected to pursue relationships with religious authorities in key locales that are potentially more sympathetic to their public health cause with the hope that there will be a "trickle-up" effect to the national government.

Chapter 16 on South Africa tracks one of the continent's great public health success stories. In many ways, South Africa is a leading worldwide model of tobacco policy reform. The authors argue that the formula for success is the powerful combination of government engagement, civil society activism and valuable evidence-based research support from the academic sector.

Chapter 17 tracks the recent frustrations of public health advocates in Tanzania. This narrative in many ways is a cautionary tale wherein ineffective comprehensive legislation has led to widely ignored regulation, and the authors argue that changing existing bad rules is turning out to be more difficult than generating new legislation.

Chapter 18 introduces the dynamics of public health policy in Zambia. In particular, the authors neatly demonstrate how academic institutions can team up successfully with civil society in order to convince government to generate more active public health policy, even in a country with increasing tobacco leaf cultivation. In this case, government appears energized by the external prompting, and the three entities are well on their way to enforcing smoke-free laws.

In the conclusion, the editor draws together the many common themes that are raised in the policy and country chapters. While each country narrative is unique, together they provide a myriad of lessons. At one level, these lessons may guide tobacco control activists in countries throughout the world in the development of new tobacco-related policies. But the lessons extend beyond tobacco control. They are, first and foremost, stories of policymaking. While an age-old adage suggests that two processes that should never be closely examined because of their gory components are the making of either sausages or policy, the narratives in this text scrutinize the latter in significant detail. In doing so, they provide observations on policymaking in general – a sometimes orderly, incremental process, but not infrequently a serendipitous and somewhat chaotic procedure that leads to the institutionalization and/or promotion of social norms on a multitude of issues. The narratives underscore the importance of people, individually and collectively; of institutions of all types including governmental, nongovernmental, academic, health and charitable; and perhaps most importantly, of the broader political context in which those individuals and institutions function. For those who are fascinated by policymaking, the narratives are captivating. For all readers, whatever their discipline, the narratives offer a thoughtful, in-depth look at the determinants, the process and the overwhelming complexity of policymaking.

Notes

1 For example, see K. Warner, "The Framework Convention on Tobacco Control: Opportunities and issues," *Salud Pública México* 50.3 (2008).
2 See atsa.atcri.org for more information (last accessed 19 July 2011).
3 For example, B. Czarniawska-Joerges in the organization literature (*A Narrative Approach to Organization Studies* (Thousand Oaks, CA: Sage Publications, 1998)) and A. MacIntyre (*After Virtue* (University of Notre Dame Press, 1984)) in philosophy have championed the use of the narrative technique to help explain human interactions.
4 R. Bates, A. Grief, M. Levi, J. Rosenthal and B. Weingast make a compelling case in *Analytic Narratives* (Princeton University Press, 1998) for the use of narratives as a tool to generate testable hypotheses, but they vigorously endorse the use of a rational choice framework. This research does not employ rational choice, but like D. North does with economic outcomes in *Institutions, Institutional Change and Economic Performance* (New York: Cambridge University Press, 1990), we heavily emphasize the role that institutions play in conditioning public policy outcomes.
5 Global Smokefree Partnership, "Global Voices: Rebutting the Tobacco Industry, Winning Smokefree Air – Status Report 2009." Online at: http://www.globalsmokefreepartnership. org/index.php?section=artigo&id=109 (accessed 19 July 2011).
6 For expanded treatment of each country, see the African Tobacco Control Regional Initiative's (ATCRI) website at atsa.atcri.org or the International Development Research Centre's electronic library at http://www.idrc.ca/en/ev-152233-201-1-DO_TOPIC. html (last accessed 11 July 2011).

Chapter 2

THE POLITICAL MAPPING PROCESS

Jeffrey Drope

This chapter explains the political mapping process that teams from the African Tobacco Situational Analyses (ATSA) initiative utilized to examine the political, economic and social contexts in which they were seeking to reform tobacco control policy. In brief, the process asks proponents of policy change to identify relevant domestic and international institutions and interests, and to consider how their roles and interactions help to shape policy in a particular country. The process is broadly framed by two theoretical constructs borrowed from the political science literature: both political *institutions* and *interest groups* influence policymaking and policy outcomes – independently and interactively. More specifically, it is the principal structural and organizational characteristics of the two entities, in addition to how they interact, that significantly shape policy. In other words, the individuals may change, but the types of actors and the institutional structures tend to be relatively static and deeply influence the making of policies and the outcomes generated by them. Understanding the fundamental nature of these central components can contribute markedly to successful navigation of the policy process.

Proponents of the so-called "new institutionalism" maintain that the actual structure of the political system will significantly condition outcomes.[1] These structures include major features such as presidential versus parliamentary systems, unitary versus federal designs and the relative development and influence of the judicial branch, but also less obvious ones such as the autonomy and power of government ministries and the cabinet.

This mapping process also underscores the role of nonstate actors, particularly civil society organizations, and seeks to conceptualize how formal institutions mediate the demands of the nongovernmental actors.[2] In many developing countries, where the tobacco industry has for many years strongly influenced existing policy, an effective and appropriate way to characterize the coalitions that develop to reform public health policy is what Eisner et al. term *competitive*.[3]

In short, the coalition forms to challenge the entrenched interest, in this case the tobacco industry. The new coalition must fight to establish "presence" in the policy area.[4] The approach also draws conceptually from what Sabatier calls an advocacy coalition framework. This framework is particularly relevant because it suggests that groups organize around a shared set of policy beliefs or goals, and emphasizes not just the importance of national government and interest groups, but also multiple levels of government and the influence of researchers.[5] The narratives in this volume illustrate unequivocally the importance of these nonstate actors in public health policy development and enforcement.

While there is no universal template for achieving tobacco control legislation and/or regulation, it is essential to develop an understanding of the policy processes in an effort to determine potential options. Moreover, once the basic system is understood, it is critical to identify the principal variables that are contributing to significant progress and discover which variables are typically obstacles.

Over a series of country-level stakeholder meetings to which individuals and organizations interested in tobacco control policy reform were invited, every country team analyzed the actors and institutions – and the interactions among them – that are shaping public health policy in their countries. While it is impossible to identify a single, consistent process across countries, it became readily evident that the same types of actors and institutions are influencing the policymaking process in all 12 countries. Moreover, every team noted that a systematic and sophisticated understanding of the domestic political structure and context was paramount to any policy reform. While many international forces were identified as key partners and allies, particularly for agenda-setting, legitimacy and resources – discussed in some length later in the chapter – participants overwhelmingly focused on understanding better how to navigate their own complex domestic political situations.

Domestic Institutions

Across all 12 countries in this volume, participants noted the essential role of domestic political institutions. Whether it was new legislation, better regulation or an executive decree used to reform policy, the nature of national-level political institutions and their interactions with other actors, in large part, dictated the outcome. The lengthy process of passing legislation is a prime example: the more complex the legislation, the more substantial the institutional obstacles become as more actors fear the consequences of a potential policy change and seek to find an opportunity to stop or modify it. In the case of tobacco control policies, which face many entrenched opponents within the political structure – such as ministries protecting their tobacco-growing and/or manufacturing constituents, members of the government in some way indebted or otherwise closely connected to the industry or officials who promote a laissez-faire economic management style – there were a number of consistent and identifiable places that policies stalled.

While not identical, there are many similarities in the general public health policy processes across African countries. In order to better understand these processes, it is helpful to work systematically through the roles of the pertinent institutions. To begin, new legislation is typically drafted in the relevant national ministry, which in the case of tobacco control legislation is most often the health ministry or its equivalent. Next, the proposed law is usually presented to the national cabinet for consideration.[6] If the cabinet chooses to place the proposal on its agenda and discuss it, the ministers can decide to vote on it. If the proposal meets some threshold of majority approval in cabinet, it is passed on to the legislature for further consideration. Once in the legislature, the proposed law will first be considered by a relevant committee (again, usually health-related) and even subjected to public and/or private hearings in which interested parties can present their views and preferences. If the proposed legislation receives sufficient approval from the committee, it will go to the full legislature for a vote. In most countries, legislation requires simple majority approval. Upon legislative endorsement, in most cases, at least in presidential systems, the executive must sign the proposed bill for it to become law. At that point, a new law is still vulnerable to legal challenges that can be taken up by the judicial branch. This basic outline of the process, of course, does not address the additional hurdles that must be surmounted for implementation and enforcement.[7]

Clearly, there are many stages in the process at which policy can be stopped or changed, most of which involve a wide variety of actors. These critical stages in the policy process are often termed "veto points" by scholars. The key actors at these stages are generally called "veto players."[8] But, more proactively, reformers can also conceptualize these veto points and players as opportunities precisely because this is where policy is shaped institutionally. Reformers need to be able to identify these key points and actors and develop strategies to access them effectively. This chapter will develop the roles of these veto points and actors in more depth.

The (mostly) indirect role of executives

Though the role of executives is not a central part of the policy process outlined above, in Africa's often highly centralized political systems possibilities for major policy change can sometimes begin or end at the highest levels of the overall governmental structure. Therefore, it is critical to identify what policy preferences executives – e.g. presidents and prime ministers – have and what actual powers they wield in a particular country. For example, can and does the executive propose legislation? Can the executive veto legislation passed by the legislature (and is there a working mechanism for the legislature to override an executive veto)? How much decree power (if any) or other extraordinary authority does the executive have? If the system is not democratic or is only partly democratic (e.g. Burkina Faso, Cameroon or Eritrea), does the president have power over most or all policy areas? And equally as importantly, does the president choose to exercise this power in every circumstance or does he or she defer authority in specific areas to other actors?

From both basic institutional and de facto perspectives, many executives in Africa wield enormous amounts of power. While having presidential support is very helpful in any country, in some countries it is paramount to effecting policy change. In Eritrea, the public preferences of most major official actors – e.g. ministers, regional administration officials, etc. – essentially represent the views of the president. This is probably true in Cameroon, and mostly true in Senegal as well. While less true in vigorously democratic countries such as Mauritius and South Africa, there is little doubt that presidential or prime ministerial support is extremely helpful.

However, in the case of these 12 African countries, the evidence in this volume suggests that executives have only played a limited role in tobacco control policy. It is not entirely clear why executives generally choose not to engage this policy area, though public health in general does not usually frame presidential agendas. Despite executives' typical hands-off approach to tobacco control, there are occasional opportunities to garner support – or perhaps just attention – from the president or the prime minister. For example, in Mauritius, Prime Minister Ramgoolam explicitly and vigorously promoted tobacco control in his March 2009 official speech to the entire national constituency on Mauritius Independence Day, which gave newly passed regulation a considerable public endorsement. In contrast, in Senegal President Wade appeared to play a nontrivial role in helping to attract Philip Morris International to the country to build a large cigarette manufacturing plant that opened in 2007. This event served to stymie the efforts of tobacco control advocates to reform the country's weak tobacco control policies. Most notably, though the president's role in affecting tobacco policy may have been somewhat indirect, it has nevertheless had a monumental effect, which reinforces that executives can potentially wield enormous power when they choose.

Cabinets – The mostly silent power

Cabinets may be one of the more overlooked institutions in terms of policymaking in Africa and perhaps other developing regions of the world.

Cabinets appear to have a stronger institutional role in many African countries compared particularly to their North American and even their Western European counterparts. Institutionally, in many countries, as a general policymaking process, proposed legislation must pass first through the cabinet before it is considered by the wider legislature. In essence, it becomes a major veto point and a gatekeeper of potential policy reform. Less formally, cabinets throughout the continent continue to be dominated by the highest levels of each country's political elite, which in many cases is exceptionally small and demonstrates little turnover. In other words, the cabinet is often the semicollective voice of a country's entrenched political – and often economic – elite. While technocrats tend to dominate cabinets in more established democracies such as South Africa and Mauritius, the qualifications of cabinet members in many other countries sometimes better reflect family connections and political loyalties. As interest groups trying to change policy, public health advocates have to find creative ways to access these small, powerful groups of influential actors.

Within cabinets, there appears to be a general pattern as to how the actors line up for or against tobacco control. The minister of health typically leads proponents in cabinet, which is consistent with the minister's responsibility for addressing the health of the nation. Of course, not all health ministers are supportive of tobacco control, but this is usually a foundation of support for policy change. Other overt support often comes from ministers who have potentially more vulnerable constituencies, including those ministers with portfolios that cover issues related to children, youths and women.

The ministers of agriculture, trade and industry are frequently the most challenging to convince to support tobacco control initiatives. In countries with substantial tobacco leaf cultivation, the agriculture minister is often reluctant to support tobacco control initiatives lest they be seen as harming constituents. Ministers of trade, too, can have a vested interest in maintaining the status quo because changes in tobacco policy can affect export flows in either tobacco leaf or manufactured tobacco products. Similarly, industry ministers have direct concerns about effects on manufacturing and jobs.

The position of the typically powerful finance minister toward tobacco control issues can be complex. In most cases, evidence-based research is necessary to gain the support of this minister. If persuaded by the compelling case that the direct and indirect costs of tobacco use exceed tobacco tax revenues, they may be swayed by the opportunity to increase revenue through higher taxes on tobacco products. However, the finance ministry is likely to face vigorous countervailing pressure from the tobacco industry, which consistently presents doomsayer scenarios of job and revenue losses as a result of tobacco tax increases.

Ghana provides a highly relevant recent illustration of the political power of cabinets. From at least 2004 to 2010, tobacco control reform stagnated in cabinet. It was not even a case of ministers voting down the proposed legislation, but of the legislation not even making it onto the agenda. In contrast, in a much shorter time in Burkina Faso, tobacco control proponents in and out of government fought to have tobacco control legislation on the cabinet agenda and in 2010 it was passed on to the legislature for approval.[9]

Government ministries – The independent strength of bureaucracies

Beyond the important deliberations in cabinet, the ATSA country teams consistently note the enormous role that national ministries usually play in tobacco control and other areas of public health, whether in actual policymaking or in implementation and enforcement. It is therefore important to identify the basic institutional parameters of ministries and their leadership. For example, how much codified autonomy do ministers have to make policy and/or regulation (i.e. new rules that are not passed by the legislature)? Do the ministers make their own major policy decisions – i.e. without executive or legislative meddling? How actively do ministers and/or their staffs participate in the development of legislation?

In Africa, ministries and other national-level agencies are usually important because they tend to be highly active in helping to develop legislation, and then in helping to promulgate the policies eventually passed by the legislature and/or the executive. But many teams also identified the importance of the independent policymaking role of ministries. Making laws is a complex process and legislatures are not equipped or expected to make every law, rule and regulation, so much of that responsibility falls on the relevant ministries. While some legislation spells out its parameters in significant detail, most laws simply enable the further development of corresponding regulation. For example, in South Africa, legislation from 2007 calls for graphic warning labels on packages, but the actual implementation – particularly developing corresponding regulations – is left explicitly to the Department of Health. In a more dramatic example in Ghana beginning in 2010, the Food and Drugs Board (FDB), under the control and supervision of the health ministry, is using its codified institutional authority to implement new stricter packaging and labeling requirements for tobacco products without any highly specific corresponding legislation.

Similar to Ghana's FDB, much of the real authority in terms of taxation is often left to ministries – usually that of finance, or its equivalent. In such instances, the case for increased tobacco taxation is taken – at least initially – directly to the finance ministry, not the legislature. While executives would no doubt have input – after all, ministers report to them – the ministries often have considerable policy autonomy in these instances and the executive and legislature often defer to the expertise of the finance professionals in the ministry.

Beyond the ministry's inherent power, it is clear that the interactions between bureaucratic agencies and the executive and/or the legislature also condition the policy that is being generated and/or implemented.[10] Social scientists often employ a principal-agent model to represent this dynamic wherein either the executive or the legislature is the principal and the agency is the agent.[11] In theory, the agent simply does what the principal wants or requires, while in practice, the relationship between principal and agent is much more complex. In making public health policy, executives and legislators will press ministries to make, implement and/or enforce specific rules and regulations, and understanding how these interactions transpire is important to navigating the process and predicting outcomes. In countries such as Eritrea or Malawi, where ministries have limited autonomy, the will of the executive will largely dictate policy. In contrast, in a more established system such as South Africa's, the executive and legislature will be more bound by institutional – even constitutional – constraints as they seek to affect the activities of the bureaucracies charged with executing policy and regulation. In fact, an agency's insulation from elected officials is often deliberate – by actual institutional design – in order to protect it from nefarious political influence and allow it to make decisions that promote the general welfare of society, not the overly particularistic political goals of elected officials that promote the well-being of some groups at the expense of others. In Africa, agencies typically do not yet demonstrate high levels of autonomy, though this is improving in some democratizing countries.

In reaction to the limitations of the basic principal-agent model, scholars have argued that bureaucracies consistently generate their own preferences. In other words, the bureaucracy is not the simple register of demands from the executive and legislative branches. For example, bureaucrats can seek to maximize their agency's budget[12] or their own influence.[13] It is reasonable to expect independent agendas within ministries – sometimes completely at odds with other powerful actors and institutions – as they seek to make and/or execute policy.

Legislatures – A rapidly emerging lawmaking authority

In a number of African countries, the power of the legislative branch to make real policy has been growing.[14] In the arena of public health, some legislatures are playing pivotal roles in shaping tobacco control policy. For example, in the countries that have passed comprehensive national legislation (e.g. Kenya, Mauritius, South Africa and most recently, Nigeria) and also in many countries that have passed more targeted tobacco control laws and/or regulations (e.g. Zambia), legislatures have been playing integral roles in the development and eventual approval of new policies. The implementation and enforcement phase will now largely fall to other national and subnational government agencies.

Though legislatures and the legislative process are maturing in many African countries, the politics of legislators can still be largely influenced by the narrow interests of the most powerful groups at the direct expense of other constituencies. In countries with geographically designated representation, this phenomenon appears most pronounced. In the tobacco leaf–growing (particularly Malawi and Tanzania, and to some extent, Kenya and Zambia) or manufacturing countries (most of the ATSA countries), for example, legislators representing districts with these interests are usually vehemently opposed to reforming existing tobacco-related laws and regulations.

There are also distinct structural hurdles that require consideration by agents of policy change. In many countries, proposed legislation must pass through relevant legislative committees; before the full legislature will consider a legislative proposal, it must meet the approval of a majority in the relevant committee. Most commonly, though not always, it is a health-specific committee that considers the proposal. The relative power and varying sets of responsibilities of the committees is an important feature in the policy reform process. In many of the ATSA countries, the relevant committee becomes the veritable gatekeeper – and a potential veto point – of policy on its way (or not) to the full legislature. Furthermore, it is often in committee that public hearings take place on the proposed new law or changes to existing laws. Hearings are an opportunity not only for public health advocates to make their cases to elected officials and the public for tobacco control policy reform, but also for the tobacco industry to mobilize its forces to oppose changes. In Nigeria, the 2009 National Senate hearings on the comprehensive tobacco control legislation pitted vigorous civil society organizations against a well-organized and vociferous industry machine led by British American Tobacco–Nigeria (BATN). The dogged pursuit of policy change and the evidence-based presentations by the well-organized civil society organizations clearly contributed markedly to the bill's eventual passage in both the committee and the full Senate.

The coming role of the judiciary

Though it has only played a limited role in tobacco control to date in Africa, the role of the judiciary is almost guaranteed to increase over the coming years in two overarching ways: in arbitrating over questions of constitutionality, and in the prosecution of the violators of the new laws and regulations. Tobacco control policy reformers need to be prepared for both scenarios.

In terms of constitutionality, as countries begin to press for better legislation – either targeted or comprehensive – the tobacco industry and/or its allies are going to question the legality of the new statutes and the corresponding regulations as they have done in the majority of developed countries. Already, in South Africa, proponents of the most recent legislative amendments in 2007 and 2008 have contended – successfully thus far – with legal challenges, particularly to new person-to-person marketing restrictions. The industry maintains that its fundamental right to communicate with its adult customers is being impinged upon by the new laws. South Africa's Gauteng High Court denied the claim in May 2011. Similarly, in 2008 in Kenya, Mastermind Tobacco challenged the constitutionality of the Tobacco Control Act 2007, though perhaps in a sign of its concern over the legitimacy of its case, the firm has sought several long delays in filing its case. As of 2011, the case was still pending.

In both South Africa and Kenya, there have been prosecutions of violators of tobacco control legislation. In South Africa, the National Council Against Smoking (NCAS) has pursued a number of cases – particularly pertaining to smoke-free regulations – through the legal process, though the organization has reported that the threat of prosecution is often sufficient to get violators to reverse their behavior. In 2009, authorities in three Kenyan municipalities (Nairobi, Kakamega and Eldoret) arrested and fined violators of the new smoke-free laws, though the fines were small. In some contrast, violations by the tobacco industry of the ban on advertising, promotion and sponsorship have yet to be prosecuted, which according to Kenya's independent Institute for Legislative Affairs (ILA) is principally a result of a lack of cooperation from agencies that are supposed to enforce the ban.

Subnational-level politics – The frequent lynchpin for enforcement

Across countries in this collection of narratives, the authors consistently identify the significant role that subnational governments play in tobacco control, sometimes in terms of policymaking (depending on the country in terms of overall structure and/or devolution of lawmaking power), but almost always in terms of implementation and enforcement. The task of executing many tobacco-related laws frequently falls to subnational authorities and/or agencies.

In some countries, new tobacco control policies have occurred first at the state or municipal level, which should prove to be very valuable even after national policy is realized. In Nigeria, the promulgation of a smoke-free Federal Capital Territory was specific to the city of Abuja. Similarly, the smoke-free Osun State law passed in the state's legislature and was signed into law by its governor in 2009. Particularly in countries where the process of passing national comprehensive legislation is very slow or is not even currently on the legislative agenda, the pursuit of alternative or simultaneous options at different levels of government is increasingly a viable choice. In the case of Nigeria, the situation is even more complex. The National Senate finally passed comprehensive legislation that includes a set of strict smoke-free provisions in 2011, but in all likelihood much of the implementation and enforcement burden of these provisions will fall on the states and/or municipalities. However, in addition to the obvious state-level progress in Abuja and Osun, several other states have indicated a strong and explicit public interest in pursuing smoke-free policies, which is encouraging for Nigerian advocates. In Senegal, the options to pursue tobacco control reform appear limited, and advocates hope that the influential city leadership in Touba – a major Islamic religious center that bans smoking in public – can affect national-level policy. In such a case, advocates hope that these efforts have a "trickle-up" effect to the national level.

In many countries, the implementation and enforcement of national-level public health policy is already occurring mainly at lower levels of government. For example, though there is a national smoke-free law in Zambia, it is at the city level in the capital of Lusaka that policymakers and advocates have been seeking to implement and enforce the law since 2009. Similarly, in Kenya, the 2007 comprehensive legislation banned smoking in public places throughout the country. However, it is specifically in some of the major urban centers, including the capital, Nairobi, that local-level officials with their civil society partners are seeking to implement and enforce the regulations.

Domestic Interests

Civil society – A significant driver of public health policy change

All of the country narratives clearly identify a central and important role for civil society in tobacco control in Africa. By civil society, this research employs a broad definition similar to the one articulated by the London School of Economics' Centre of Civil Society: "the arena of uncoerced collective action around shared interests, purposes and values."[15] Across these 12 country narratives, without exception, stakeholders identified nongovernmental organizations as pivotal actors in successful tobacco control initiatives. Many of the organizations have a specific tobacco control focus, including the NCAS in South Africa, Kenya's ILA and ViSa in Mauritius, while broader organizations have played key roles in seeking policy reform in other countries, including the Tanzania Public Health Association and the Zambia Consumer Association.

Though not at the level of a social movement in any African country, at least yet, other types of organizations can play and are playing key supporting roles. For example, medical-related professional associations (e.g. doctors, nurses, midwives, etc.) have a vested interest in promoting policies that have positive effects for overall public health. Similarly, organizations dedicated to advocating for or assisting potentially more vulnerable populations such as children or those affected by diseases with a direct tobacco link (e.g. cancer or heart disease) or with comorbidity issues (e.g. HIV/AIDS and tuberculosis) are often active in tobacco control advocacy or some related supporting role.

Labor organizations frequently take a direct, though often mixed, interest in tobacco control activities. From a healthy workplace perspective, tobacco control proponents have often found allies in labor organizations seeking to improve working conditions or overall quality of life for their members. On the other hand, some proposed tobacco-related policies can have effects on employment and labor organizations can therefore demonstrate fundamental concerns about proposed policy change. For example, in a number of countries, organizations that represent hawkers (street vendors) have often opposed new tobacco control policies for fear of jeopardizing a major component of their members' sales.

Research institutions

The country narratives highlight an important emerging trend in Africa wherein academic and/or research institutions and independent researchers are increasingly playing large and important roles in tobacco control policy reform on the continent. Obviously, as they have in many other countries, researchers can help to provide evidence-based research to assist policymakers and actors advocating for policy change in making new and better tobacco control policy. This research component is perhaps especially critical because policymakers in Africa often demand country-specific research to support proposals, rather than general research from other countries.

Researchers are also increasingly playing stronger direct advocacy roles. For example, in Zambia, faculty from the University of Zambia have been active far beyond their research and training roles in the ATSA program, and in particular, have taken prominent advocacy roles in the Zambia Tobacco Control Campaign (ZTCC) by helping to spearhead the 2009 smoke-free Lusaka campaign.

The media

The media's role in tobacco control is a complex one in Africa. On one hand, many media rely on revenues from the tobacco industry's efforts to market its products. On the other hand, particularly in established democracies and also in some emerging democracies, the media take considerable pride in delivering the news in a relatively unbiased manner. Advocates can even use the media to expand the focus from just health-related issues specifically to the more pivotal policy discussions.[16] In the ATSA countries, there is ample evidence of these different scenarios.

In the early 1980s, Senegal passed very progressive tobacco control legislation that would have even been mostly compliant with the World Health Organization's (WHO) Framework Convention of Tobacco Control (FCTC) by today's standards. However, within five years, most of the legislation had been repealed or dramatically diluted. By most accounts, the tobacco industry and owners of media put considerable pressure on the government to reverse the legislation because of the negative impacts on their revenue as a result of the bans on advertising and sponsorship. They argued specifically – and apparently, effectively – that cross-border tobacco advertising they could not control gave competitors an unfair economic advantage.[17] Senegal has yet to recover from this major policy regression.

In contrast, in countries with free or increasingly freer media, there has been more evenhanded coverage of tobacco issues. In some countries, media outlets even donate time to tobacco issues as a public service. In Nigeria, there is a radio show in the three largest markets that discusses the perils of tobacco use. In Zambia, during the smoke-free Lusaka campaign, the ZTCC took advantage of multiple opportunities to publicize the effort in multiple media including radio, television and print, an effort that has reportedly raised awareness among the general public.[18]

The International – Institutions and Interests

In recent decades, public health has become increasingly globalized and a number of key international forces continue to play notable roles in this development area, including intergovernmental organizations, individual governments and international nongovernmental organizations (INGOs). There is no doubt that in public health generally and tobacco control specifically, international governmental organizations wield genuine influence. Clearly, the WHO's FCTC is the principal agenda setter in tobacco control, and it has continued to shape the structure of the discussions and many of the major efforts in tobacco control in recent years. For example, the interactions generated as a result of the convention's first three Conferences of Parties have alone pushed the agenda for tobacco control in specific directions, including stronger emphases on smoke-free policies, advertising bans and taxation strategies. More scholarly inquiry into international institutions' effects on the behavior of central actors is an important next step in the broader public health research agenda.[19]

In some specific important cases, other supranational governmental institutions can also play a direct role in shaping tobacco control policy and therefore add another layer of international complexity to the policy context. The European Union, for example, has compelled its members to reach certain public health benchmarks, including in tobacco control. In Africa, too, there have been recent significant efforts to integrate economically, and arguably, politically to some extent. Two important agreements have included the Southern African Customs Union and the Economic Community of West African States (ECOWAS). The specific example of taxation in both African agreements provides an excellent illustration of how such institutions can affect tobacco control. As signatories of the agreements, the member states are obligated to coordinate tax policy, including import duties and excise taxes. As the chapter on taxation discusses, the most effective taxation strategies focus on using excise taxes to affect affordability of tobacco products. But these international agreements obligate countries to keep taxes for discrete categories of products below a specified ceiling (for example, as of 2009 in ECOWAS, it was 40 percent), thereby complicating tobacco taxation strategies. In other words, countries would be violating their commitments to the international economic agreement if they go above the tax ceiling. Ultimately, to resolve such issues, it is necessary not only to access each country's political system, but also to access the political structures of the larger multilateral organization.

Major individual government-sponsored donor organizations from specific countries are also continuing to play major roles in international tobacco control. For example, the United Kingdom's Department for International Development (DFID), Canada's International Development Research Centre (IDRC) and the Norwegian Agency for Development Cooperation (NORAD) have been involved for many years in sponsoring tobacco-related public health research to help promote tobacco control across developing nations, including countries in Africa.

A number of other major international organizations are also playing critical roles in international tobacco control in Africa. In some cases, organizations are private foundations, while in others, they are not-for-profit INGOs. For example, the Bill and Melinda Gates Foundation funded ATSA and is currently funding the Africa Tobacco Control Consortium (ATCC) through a major INGO, the American Cancer Society. Similarly, the Bloomberg Initiative to Reduce Tobacco Use (using funds from a private foundation), through the Campaign for Tobacco-Free Kids (CTFK) and the International Union Against Tuberculosis and Lung Disease (an INGO) among other organizations, continues to fund major programs in Africa and elsewhere in the developing world.[20] The literature is just beginning to examine the implications for transparency and agenda-setting as global public health is increasingly funded by enormous private donors who do not have the same levels of accountability as governments or international governmental – or even nongovernmental – organizations that rely on external support.[21]

Perhaps more dramatically – and with considerable potential for additional effectiveness – these different international forces interact with each other and with domestic organizations and governments to form a dense public health information and advocacy network. For example, many of the international organizations are strongly linked with partner organizations in specific countries as proponents seek policy reform. This increasing international-national collaboration effectively comprises what Keck and Sikkink have termed a transnational advocacy network.[22] The network of organizations, which communicates partly through electronic platforms such as GlobaLink,[23] is deeply shaping tobacco control across the globe and also merits additional scholarly attention.[24]

Finally, of course, it is an understatement to suggest that the tobacco industry is entirely global. Companies such as British American Tobacco (BAT), Philip Morris International (PMI) and Japan Tobacco International (JTI) have a major economic and marketing presence in dozens of countries around the world. In fact, BAT boasts in its promotional materials that it operates in over 180 countries and the *Wall Street Journal* reported that in 2008 profits had increased 17 percent from the previous year to £2.7 billion, on revenues of £12.1 billion.[25] To put these numbers into economic size perspective, BAT's revenues are frequently larger than Malawi's total GDP, and of course, are singularly derived from selling tobacco products and dedicated to the promotion and sale of them. The industry and particularly its strengths and strategies have proven to be particularly opaque in many African countries, and future examination of this crucial topic must be at the top of the near-term research agenda.

Conclusion – A Dynamic Interaction

The country narratives, individually and collectively, remind us that it is imperative to think not only about the parts of the system, but also about the whole. In all countries (and internationally), there is a clear policy system that is comprised of a variety of institutions and actors. In different countries, certain actors will take on larger roles – for example, in an autocracy the president may become a major champion of or an impediment to tobacco control, or, in a newly democratizing country where the media is suddenly free, these actors may come to play a vital role – but the overall types of interactions are remarkably consistent. While international actors can make a valuable contribution, nothing gets done on the ground in terms of national-level policy change without the hard work of the various domestic-level players. These actors must access their own political systems, and the only way to navigate them effectively is to understand them. The individual country chapters document how individuals in each country sought to understand the unique context of their particular country and to work effectively with political institutions and interest groups both independently and in a dynamic interaction to achieve policy reform and broader public health goals.

Notes

1 R. K. Weaver and B. A. Rockman, *Do Institutions Matter: Government Capabilities in the United States and Abroad*. (Washington DC: The Brookings Institution, 1993).

2 In *Tobacco Control: Comparative Politics in the United States and Canada* (Peterborough ON: Broadview Press, 2002), D. Studlar employs an integrative theoretical approach that includes institutions and interest groups, though they are two components among a handful of other major approaches.

3 M. A. Eisner, J. Worsham and E. Ringquist, *Regulatory Policy* (Boulder, CO: Lynne Rienner Publishers, 2000).

4 C. Bosso, *Pesticides and Politics* (Pittsburgh, PA: University of Pittsburgh Press, 1987).

5 P. A. Sabatier, *Theories of the Policy Process* (Boulder, CO: Westview, 1999).

6 In some countries, a law is scrutinized for constitutionality by the attorney general/ justice ministry or its equivalent before being sent to the cabinet (or legislature). If a proposed law fails this test, it is returned to the ministry that wrote it for revision and resubmission.

7 Some of the text in the preceding two paragraphs is borrowed from J. M. Drope, "The politics of smoke-free policies in developing countries: Lessons from Africa," *CVD Prevention and Control* 5.3 (2010): 65–73.

8 For further development of the idea of veto points and players, see M. D. McCubbins, R. G. Noll and B. R. Weingast, "Structure and Process, Politics and Policy: Administrative Arrangements and the Political Control of Agencies," *Virginia Law Review* 75 (1989): 431–82, and G. Tsebelis, "Decision-Making in Political Systems: Veto Players in Presidentialism, Parliamentarism, Multicameralism and Multipartyism," *British Journal of Political Science* 25.3 (1995): 289–325.

9 In a related development, the tobacco industry vigorously supported the introduction of a competing private member's bill in the legislature that circumvented the cabinet, the Council of Ministers. Ultimately, in late 2010, the legislature approved the private member's bill, which was weaker than the proposal that the cabinet approved.

10 For a comprehensive general discussion of the politics of bureaucracy, see G. Peters, *The Politics of Bureaucracy* (London: Routledge, 2010), chapter 5. For an overview of the specific literature on bureaucracy, see K. J. Meier and G. A. Krause's introduction "The Scientific Study of Bureaucracy: An Overview" in *Politics, Policy, and Organizations: Frontiers in the Scientific Study of Bureaucracy* (Ann Arbor, MI: University of Michigan Press, 2003), 1–22.

11 T. M. Moe, "The New Economics of Organization," *American Journal of Political Science* 28 (1984): 739–77.

12 W. Niskanen, *Bureaucracy and Public Economics* (Cheltenham: Edward Elgar, 1994).

13 J. Q. Wilson, *Bureaucracy* (New York: Basic Books, 1989).

14 J. Barkan, "Legislatures on the Rise," *Journal of Democracy* 19.2 (2008): 124–37.

15 London School of Economics Centre for Civil Society, "What is civil society?" (2010).

16 L. Wallack and L. Dorfman, "Media Advocacy: A Strategy for Advancing Policy and Promoting Health," *Health Education and Behavior* 23.3 (1996): 293–317.

17 San Francisco Department of Public Health (Tobacco Free Project), "Country Case Study: Senegal" (Washington DC: Campaign for Tobacco-Free Kids, 1998–9).

18 E. Stokes, "Postcards from Lusaka: No smoking. *Really* no smoking," *This Magazine*, 17 August 2009.

19 More broadly, this is the central argument in L. Martin and B. Simmons, "Theories and Empirical Studies of International Institutions," *International Organization* 52.4 (1998): 729–57. This research also offers a comprehensive literature review of the subfield.

20 Campaign for Tobacco-Free Kids, "What we fund" (2010). Online at: http://tobaccocontrolgrants.org/Pages/40/What-we-fund (accessed 20 August 2010).

21 D. McCoy, G. Kembhavi, J. Patel and A. Luintel, "The Bill & Melinda Gates Foundation's grant-making programme for global health," *Lancet* 373.967 (2009): 1645–53. In the interest of full disclosure, it is important to reiterate that a considerable part of the research that comprises this book was funded indirectly by funds from the Bill and Melinda Gates Foundation as the principal sponsors of the ATSA program.

22 K. Sikkink and M. Keck, *Activists Beyond Borders* (Ithaca, NY: Cornell University Press, 1998).

23 See www.globalink.org (last accessed 20 July 2011).

24 H. L. Wipfli, K. Fujimoto and T. W. Valente, "Global Tobacco Diffusion: The Case of the Framework Convention on Tobacco Control," *American Journal of Public Health* (published ahead of print, 13 May 2010).

25 S. Turner, "British American Tobacco fiscal-year net profit up 17%," *Wall Street Journal*, 26 February 2009.

Chapter 3

PROGRESS ON SMOKE-FREE POLICIES[1]

Jeffrey Drope

The public health rewards of smoke-free policies have been well established and substantiated empirically, and include a decrease in tobacco consumption and youth smoking initiation[2] as well as an overall reduction in heart attacks among other benefits.[3] But this chapter demonstrates that what might seem like an obvious prescription to improve the overall health of a community can get easily mired in the daily political struggles of a country, state or city. Moreover, both advocates and policymakers frequently underestimate the sustained and vigorous effort – often coordinated between multiple, not always agreeable, parties – required to pass such policies and then to implement and enforce them effectively. Scholars are only beginning to examine the importance of the role of politics in the shaping of successful smoke-free policies, particularly in developing nations. This chapter seeks to help fill this significant lacuna in the literature.

The word "politics" is multifaceted and in this chapter it refers both to the process of decision making within and by governments, and the contestation for new policies that can involve nonstate actors such as civil society organizations and individuals in addition to the government. The two definitions are used more or less interchangeably, but should be evident in the context of the specific discussion.

The African Tobacco Situation Analyses (ATSA) countries demonstrate considerable variation in terms of tobacco control legislation generally and smoke-free policies specifically. As Table 3.1 illustrates, the extent of tobacco control legislation varies markedly. A number of these countries have already passed comprehensive national tobacco control legislation (all of which include smoke-free policies); some are actively working on passing new or improved general tobacco control laws or ones specific to smoke-free places; while others have just begun seeking new policies. Furthermore, some countries have passed subnational (e.g. state or city) and/or more targeted

Table 3.1. Status of smoke-free policies in the 12 ATSA countries

Country	National comprehensive policy	Active enforcement of smoke-free policies	Subnational smoke-free policies	Passed other smoke-free policies
Burkina Faso	1988 – "Raabo" (some smoke-free provisions)*	No (except several targeted initiatives beginning in 2006)		
Cameroon	No		Ban in government buildings in Yaoundé	Bans in buildings of the Ministry of Health, Ministry of Economy and Ministry of Finance
Eritrea	2004 – Proclamation 143	No (except 2009 educational institutions initiative)		
Ghana	No*			Ministry directives for education, health and transportation facilities; government offices and restaurants and cinemas
Kenya	2007 – Kenya Tobacco Control Act (almost 100% FCTC-compliant)	Yes		
Malawi	No			Bans at airports, on domestic flights and in fueling areas
Mauritius	1999 and 2008 – Public Health Act (almost 100% FCTC-compliant)	Yes		

Nigeria	1990 – Tobacco Smoking (Control) Act and Decree 20 (some smoke-free provisions)*	No (until 2009 efforts in Abuja)	Yes (Abuja and Osun State)
Senegal	No		Yes (Touba)
South Africa	1993, 1999, 2007 and 2008 – Tobacco Products Control Act, and amendments (almost 100% FCTC-compliant)	Yes	
Tanzania	2003 – Tobacco (Products Regulation) Act*	No	
Zambia	1992 – Public Health (Tobacco) Regulation and subsequent instruments*	No (until 2009 Lusaka initiative)	

*Indicates that there is pending FCTC-influenced or FCTC-compliant legislation that is either entirely new (Ghana and Nigeria) or seeks to improve on older, weaker, non-FCTC-compliant legislation (Burkina Faso, Tanzania and Zambia). In the case of Nigeria, the legislation was passed by the National Senate in early 2011, but implementation has not yet taken place.

laws or regulations such as prohibiting tobacco use in healthcare facilities, workplaces and public transportation. Finally, many of the countries continue to address significant challenges related to implementation and enforcement of smoke-free policies.

This chapter demonstrates that the broad patterns for success in smoke-free policies are pretty clear. Success in the context of these countries translates into the passage of laws and/or regulations that prohibit smoking in public (and sometimes private) places, and evidence that appropriate authorities have begun to implement the laws and are making sincere efforts to enforce them. In the countries that have achieved success in this area or appear to be progressing toward success, there is always an active network of civil society organizations pushing for change, evidence of at least some will for such policies on the part of key relevant government institutions, and in some cases, active involvement from research and/or academic institutions.

In many of the most successful cases, there is a pattern of civil society organizations and relevant government entities working together to pursue smoke-free policies, often with the academic community playing a supporting role by providing evidence-based research that both substantiates the advocates' arguments and education efforts and informs policymakers' shaping of policy. In most cases, the advocacy organizations not only had to work initially to press actors in the political system for the policy, but also then continued to work within the system with their government colleagues to implement and enforce the new policies and to monitor subsequent progress. This combination is the clearest route to successful smoke-free policies.

The Path of National Comprehensive Tobacco Control Policy

Several ATSA countries have passed national comprehensive tobacco control legislation framed by compliance with the World Health Organization's (WHO) Framework Convention on Tobacco Control (FCTC), while most others are actively seeking to do so. In all cases, smoke-free policies comprise an important component of the broader legislation. Among the countries that have passed major legislation, there is considerable variation in terms of effectiveness. The countries with the most effective current national legislation are Mauritius[4] and South Africa.[5] Beyond just passing the legislation, both countries have made considerable progress in terms of implementation and enforcement.[6] Kenya passed national comprehensive legislation in 2007, but in terms of smoke-free policies (and other areas), enforcement continues to present challenges. In fact, enforcement is a challenge that these governments and each country's tobacco control community in general have been addressing directly. In all three countries, civil society organizations with tobacco control focus and expertise are working actively with government institutions to meet these challenges.

Because there are myriad places where proposed legislation can get stalled or squelched, it is essential that at every step in the legislative and/or regulatory process the proposed legislation has the strong support of vocal and active proponents outside of the elected and nonelected government officials who support it. In South Africa, for example, the Tobacco Action Group (TAG) is the umbrella group of organizations that has been actively involved in pursuing and promoting improved tobacco control policies. A strong network of academics provides evidence-based research to help TAG in its efforts to educate government on the dangers of tobacco and how better policy can mitigate and even eliminate these problems.[7] The tobacco control community has made considerable efforts over many years to meet with legislators and other government officials, provide information and training and raise these issues prominently in the media and with the general public.

Countries with less complex governmental structures arguably have fewer barriers to overcome in seeking new legislation. In Mauritius, for example, because the country is a parliamentary system, the legislative process is more streamlined. There are fewer steps toward making policy change, and therefore fewer actors and/or opportunities to affect the proposed legislation. Furthermore, the national Ministry of Health and Quality of Life (MOH&QL) has played a very active role guiding tobacco control legislation through the cabinet and legislature. There have also been other major proponents in the legislature, including the prime minister,[8] who have promoted the new policies. However, there is also an advocacy and watchdog organization, ViSa, partly funded by the government that continues to play a major role in educating officials and the general public on tobacco control issues and influences the agenda.

Working with Existing Policies

Recognizing the considerable obstacles to achieving comprehensive legislation, tobacco control proponents in a number of ATSA countries, both in government and in civil society, have elected to pursue implementation and enforcement of existing smoke-free policies, often while simultaneously pursuing new, improved comprehensive policies. Furthermore, recognizing the enormous resources that effective enforcement inevitably requires, advocates in some ATSA countries have elected to pursue enforcement either in a narrow area (e.g. educational institutions) or in specific regions or municipalities. In all cases, there is a hope that the preliminary efforts will diffuse to other areas and/or regions.

In 2004, Eritrea's president declared Proclamation 143/2004, which was comprised of a wide variety of tobacco control measures including smoke-free policies.[9] In its first five years, however, efforts to implement the components of the proclamation, let alone enforce them, were limited. In 2009, with funding from the ATSA initiative, a team of tobacco control proponents spearheaded the Tobacco Free Schools Environment Initiative (TFSEI) in an effort to begin with enforcement of smoke-free policies in educational institutions. Though tobacco-free schools are considered a very small step by most tobacco control activists and scholars, particularly in developed countries, the program had important symbolic status because the government had not yet followed up meaningfully on the proclamation. Since the schools initiative's launch, the ministers of health and education have publicly embraced it and have vowed to put tobacco control higher on the agenda of the executive branch of government. Being highly centralized politically, executive level support is a necessary component for tobacco control in Eritrea. Furthermore, tobacco control proponents have been using evidence-based research to buttress their case. Part of the ATSA project was the execution of a new and improved set of prevalence studies so that advocates could make their case for these policies substantively and clearly to policymakers. Furthermore, in addition to reaching out to high-level ministry officials, advocates have identified that actual enforcement of the TFSEI will be mostly decentralized. Therefore, they have reached out to the leaders of the regional (*zoba*) administrations who tend to be pivotal in actual policy implementation, and work closely with schools and their staffs.

Burkina Faso,[10] Tanzania[11] and Zambia[12] all have existing national tobacco control legislation that incorporates smoke-free policies. In all three countries, the legislation is not FCTC-compliant, and even more importantly, tobacco control proponents have found that legislation has been largely ineffectual and enforcement has been mostly nonexistent. But while advocates in all three countries pursue new legislation, recognizing the time and resource constraints and the complexity of seeking a new comprehensive set of laws, they are also simultaneously seeking to enforce the legislation and/or regulation that they already have.

In Burkina Faso, a broad coalition of tobacco control advocates from both government and civil society has been actively pursuing smoke-free initiatives that are more focused to specific substantive or geographical areas. In 2006–7, the country's principal public health association, the Association Burkinabe de Santé Publique (ABSP), worked with the Canadian Public Health Association on the development of advocacy activities around creating smoke-free hospitals and school curricula on smoking.[13] Since 2008, the main tobacco control coalition, the Union des associations contre le tabac (UACT), which is facilitated by the ABSP, has been working with the Bloomberg Initiative focusing on advocacy to strengthen enforcement of existing smoke-free policies from the broader legislation, the Raabo, in four major cities.[14] In this context, a public tobacco control campaign was also launched in the media.

Tobacco control proponents in Burkina Faso are also seeking to take advantage of a recent shift in the overall organization of government as the previously highly centralized government is devolving considerable policymaking authority to the 359 municipalities. Since early 2009, under the ATSA initiative, a team of tobacco control proponents from both government and civil society has been seeking to raise awareness among 45 mayors about the dangers of tobacco use and about existing laws – including smoke-free policies – that are not currently applied. To encourage these elected officials to implement the existing laws, the program has been educating high-level municipal administrators and helping them to identify and implement relevant activities in their action and development plans. Like all countries, this team of advocates is working within significant resource constraints, and hopes that the 45 mayors will become the team's intermediaries and will become catalysts to expand their work to other mayoralties in order to reach many more people without expending excessive efforts and resources.[15]

In Zambia, the situation is similar to Burkina Faso with vigorous recent efforts to enforce existing legislation while major new FCTC-compliant comprehensive legislation is pursued. In this case, a coalition of civil society and academic organizations is actively soliciting the support of national and subnational elected and nonelected government officials for smoke-free enforcement. In May of 2009, the Zambia Tobacco Control Campaign (ZTCC) successfully launched a program to enforce the existing smoke-free laws in the capital, Lusaka.[16] The team included the city council's town clerk, mayoral and environmental health officers, civil society organizations including the Zambian Consumer Association (ZACA), and academic institutions such as the University of Zambia. In a show of broad official support at the inaugural event in Lusaka, participants included the deputy minister of health (officially representing the vice president), the mayor, the deputy mayor, the town clerk, an official from the district commissioner's office, the permanent secretary for Lusaka Province, the commissioner of the Drug Enforcement Commission as well as members and leaders of the ZTCC. The city council has since expressed interest in following up on the enforcement of the law – an interest that the ZTCC is actively seeking to cultivate.

Though it does not yet have national tobacco control legislation, official institutions in Cameroon have recently begun to seek more actively to implement existing smoke-free regulations and directives. For example, the

Department of Mfoundi (Yaoundé),[17] and the ministries of Economy and Finance,[18] Education, and Public Health all officially banned smoking in government buildings. There is also reportedly an informal ban on smoking on public transportation. In late 2009, the Cameroon ATSA team began a program to implement smoke-free policies in Mfoundi beyond just government buildings to include other public (e.g. hospitals, educational institutions, healthcare facilities and tourist establishments) and private environments (e.g. workplaces).[19] In this effort, the team engaged civil society organizations, enforcement officials and the local authorities as key partners.

Creative Alternative – Or Complementary – Solutions

Sometimes, or even often, optimal outcomes such as a fully implemented and enforced comprehensive set of national tobacco control laws are simply unrealistic, and both advocates and governments must be more creative in seeking to pass new policies that restrict public and workplace smoking. As a result, proponents in many countries have hedged their options and have either stopped or slowed in their pursuit of national policy and instead are pursuing other policy options, or are pursuing national and subnational policies simultaneously. The main options include pursuing smoke-free policies at the subnational level (e.g. state or municipal) or in specific public realms (e.g. educational institutions).

In Nigeria, the comprehensive tobacco control legislation was only passed by the National Senate in early 2011,[20] and while seeking this goal, advocates were concomitantly pursuing other policy options. In Nigeria, a federal system, states and even municipalities have considerable policy autonomy. As long as state governments in Nigeria do not violate federal law, they have considerable vested powers in generating and enforcing their own laws. For example, in 2006, with active support and encouragement from civil society organizations, the minister of the Federal Capital Territory (FCT) Administration passed a smoke-free law for all public places, including workplaces, in Abuja, the nation's capital.[21] Unfortunately, there was little immediate subsequent effort to implement or enforce the law. However, in 2008–9, civil society organizations worked actively to sensitize elected – including the new chief minister – and nonelected officials in the FCT to the existing law and what it would require to implement and enforce it. In late 2009, the minister in charge of the FCT Administration directly earmarked resources in the FCT budget for tobacco control awareness and enforcement, which should greatly help the law to become self-sustaining.

Similarly, in October 2009, Nigerian advocates achieved a major policy victory with the passing of a statewide smoke-free policy in southwestern Osun

State.[22] The institutional barriers to passing this legislation were significant. First, the proposed legislation had to pass through the state legislature. One of the principal strategies that advocates used to achieve this goal was education: they developed and facilitated workshops on the benefits of smoke-free policies for legislators in early 2009. They also actively sought the public support of influential members of the legislature, particularly the speaker. After the legislative hurdle was cleared, the legislation still needed to be signed by the state governor. Again, advocates used education: in face-to-face meetings with the governor and his staff, they successfully articulated why it was in the best health and economic interests of the state to pass the legislation. In this circumstance, both a majority of legislators and the governor recognized the huge public health benefits and embraced the initiative.

In Senegal, where national tobacco control legislation does not appear to be on the main policy agenda, advocates are continuing to put considerable energy into the pursuit of smoke-free policies in carefully chosen municipalities. For example, the city of Touba, an important Muslim religious centre, is smoke free.[23] As a city that demonstrates moral authority (Senegal is more than 95 percent Muslim),[24] tobacco control advocates hope that it will encourage other municipalities to pass similar laws and the national government to put the issue much higher on the policy agenda.

In Ghana, where national comprehensive legislation has been stalled at least since 2004–5, there are already a number of smoke-free policies in place, principally as a result of national ministry directives. There are existing bans in all health-related institutions, educational institutions and in vehicles and buildings related to public transportation. Though not nearly as legally binding as actual legislation, Ghana has demonstrated that these directives are actually quite effective in ensuring smoke-free places. In countries where there is limited political will for broader legislation, Ghana's experiences suggest that it is worthwhile considering other options, at least until larger initiatives gain traction. It may also be possible that these directives that are smaller in scope can serve to catalyze more comprehensive efforts.

Even in Malawi, one of the world's largest producers of tobacco leaf and a country with almost no tobacco control law, governments have been able to pass limited tobacco control directives such as those prohibiting smoking on airplanes, in airports and near fuel stations. While not ideal, it is evidence that well-supported proposals to introduce tobacco control regulations can be successful even in environments more sympathetic to tobacco than tobacco control. In recent years, a new, energized tobacco control movement in Malawian civil society has actively been pressing the government for new health-based tobacco control laws including smoke-free policies.[25]

Post-legislative Challenges: Implementation and Enforcement

After the general excitement of passing comprehensive legislation, or even a more targeted smoke-free policy, proponents then face the often difficult reality of implementation and enforcement. Burkina Faso, for example, has had official smoke-free policies for more than 20 years with almost no implementation or enforcement. Similarly, Tanzania passed major tobacco control legislation in 2003, but enforcement continues to be an enormous challenge. In terms of smoke-free policies specifically, the Tanzania Public Health Association reports that the legislation calls explicitly for health supervisors to enforce the law, but these officials have never been selected nor empowered by subsequent regulation. Across Africa (and elsewhere), the availability and/or willingness of officials to enforce the smoke-free policies remains a central challenge. Furthermore, for many countries that have codified an enforcement mechanism, a lack of appropriate training and sufficient resources for the designated agency remain related central issues.

Kenya passed national comprehensive legislation in 2007 with one of the strongest smoke-free policies in the world – smoking is even banned in outdoor public places such as streets. While this policy may sound ideal, it has actually generated a set of challenges not totally anticipated. By all accounts, implementation and enforcement have been major challenges. In 2009, there was a substantial joint effort by the Ministry of Public Health and Sanitation and civil society organizations, including the Institute for Legislative Affairs (ILA), to train public health officers (approximately 1,000), particularly in major urban areas including Nairobi.[26] In an attempt to address potential corruption issues with enforcement officers – particularly to encourage the actual prosecution of offenders rather than the extortion of bribes – public health officers now have performance contracts and must provide monthly reports on their efforts. As of 2010, the training project has demonstrated mixed success. With completed trainings in ten towns or cities, only a handful of communities have subsequently agreed to enforce the smoke-free provisions with actual arrests of violators of the ban. Officers report insufficient resources for the execution of their duties and a lack of coordination between public health officers and the police in enforcement, particularly for facilitating arrests. There are ongoing efforts to convene discussions among all of the relevant departments to resolve these issues.[27]

In Mauritius, the MOH&QL has its own smoke-free enforcement unit, the Flying Squad. The unit has some proscribed powers to inspect venues that come under the jurisdiction of the legislation, and then to fine violators. Importantly, the ministry dedicates funds and some limited personnel to this effort. One of the main challenges is that the very small squad cannot possibly keep up with the demand for their services, as there are thousands of public environments and workplaces that fall under the tobacco control regulations. Nonetheless, dedicated government resources and staff for tobacco control remain the exception, not the norm, in Africa, so Mauritius is in fact a leader in this respect.

Closely tied to the issue of enforcement training is the codified existence of actual penalties for violators. In other words, trained government enforcement officials must be able to enact a penalty, such as a fine, to serve as a genuine deterrent to violators or would-be offenders. More importantly, this component of enforcement must have the firm backing of government, including particularly the public safety and judicial arms. Public safety officials must be willing to make certain that fines are levied and collected, and then, as a final authority, the justice system must be willing to prosecute offenders. Across many African countries, both comprehensive legislation and the more targeted or subnational policies have a codified penalty component, but the real issue continues to be enforcement: no one will enforce the legislated penalty. As more countries enact new and better tobacco control legislation, enforcement is rapidly becoming the new battle front for advocates, perhaps most conspicuously in the area of smoke-free policies. Particularly in light of the sizeable number of smoke-free policies passed in the 1980s and 1990s in Africa that were never implemented or enforced, sustained commitment to the enforcement component of new tobacco control policies by government and civil society organizations will largely dictate the ultimate success of these policies.

A Final Key Component: Public Awareness

A final cornerstone in successful smoke-free policy implementation and enforcement has to be vigorous efforts to increase public awareness of the laws and corresponding regulations. Again, the evidence in Africa suggests that the laws are most effective when civil society and government partner together in this awareness effort. In many cases, it is civil society organizations that lead the initial effort, but buy-in by government and media appears to have tremendous positive impacts.

In 2009, in their effort to implement and enforce existing smoke-free policies in Lusaka, Zambia, advocates made awareness central to their activities. After the 2009 Lusaka inaugural event, the ZTCC followed up with considerable public awareness efforts including leaflets, brochures and a major distribution of "no smoking" signs. Furthermore, members of the ZTCC have sought and obtained appearances on high-profile radio and TV programs. Zambian media outlets have been increasingly receptive to giving air time to smoke-free messages.

In Mauritius, civil society and the government have been working toward raising awareness of the smoke-free component of the 2008 regulations. For a number of years, the most active awareness-raising entity has been the civil society organization, ViSa. Though it receives a small annual amount of government money (approximately Rs 250,000), it is fully autonomous and also acts as a vigorous watchdog of both industry and government tobacco-related activities.[28] It actively sponsors and engages in myriad education and awareness programs in the country.

In Kenya, in a follow-up to the enforcement initiative discussed above, the ILA prepared a series of awareness-raising and sensitization activities, which included the distribution of information, education and communication materials. These materials were posted in hospitals, schools, bars and other public places. Also, the ILA and its partners facilitated a series of awareness workshops and personal visits to secure support from key local and national-level officials.

In Nigeria, there have been efforts by many civil society organizations to increase awareness of smoke-free policies. Civil society organizations such as the Nigerian Heart Foundation and Environmental Right Action/Friends of the Earth Nigeria regularly provide press releases and seek coverage of tobacco control issues in the national media on television, radio and in print. Additionally, there is a popular weekly radio program *Tobacco and You* that airs on stations in the three largest cities, Lagos, Abuja and Kano.

A final central issue related to all components of enforcement is resources. In an ideal world, the resources will be self-sustaining, or at least internally generated, wherein governments recognize the substantial public health benefits of smoke-free and other tobacco control policies and earmark specific resources for programs such as those related to tobacco awareness. In Mauritius, the MOH&QL has noted that it plans to organize more advocacy and awareness sessions related to the 2008 legislation, and followed up in 2009 with assessments of air quality in relevant smoke-free environments including workplaces.[29] In Nigeria, there has been official support for World No Tobacco Day activities, and in Abuja, Nigeria, as discussed above, the minister in charge of the FCT for the first time included a line item in the budget for awareness and enforcement of smoke-free policies for 2009–10.[30]

Conclusion

The potential for smoke-free policies to influence attitudes and behavior is significant. Official smoke-free policies institutionalize the governments' acknowledgement of the dangers associated with exposure to second-hand smoke and respond to increasing public desire for clean air. The 12 ATSA countries have taken different paths to achieve these policies, but all have acknowledged the need to achieve this policy by whatever means possible.

In a final appraisal of African smoke-free policies, several major components for increased likelihood of policy success emerge. First, a strong partnership between active tobacco control civil society organizations and government institutions – often, but not always, health ministries – is a key element of most success stories. Second, the support of researchers who provide relevant materials to advocates and policymakers is proving to be enormously helpful in shaping policy. Finally, the last piece of the puzzle continues to be the availability of resources not only to change policy, but also to implement and enforce new programs. While internally funded programs are the ultimate goal, it is incumbent upon external donors to continue to nurture the considerable progress that is being made in Africa toward smoke-free environments.

Notes

1 An expanded version of this chapter appears in J. M. Drope, "The politics of smoke-free policies in developing countries: Lessons from Africa," *CVD Prevention and Control* 5.3 (2010): 65–73.

2 C. M. Fichtenberg and S. A. Glantz, "Effect of smoke-free workplaces on smoking behaviour: Systematic review," *British Medical Journal* 325 (2002): 7357.

3 J. M. Lightwood and S. A. Glantz, "Declines in Acute Myocardial Infarction After Smoke-Free Laws and Individual Risk Attributable to Secondhand Smoke," *Circulation* 120.14 (2009): 1373–9; D. G. Meyers, J. S. Neuberger and J. He, "Cardiovascular Effect of Bans on Smoking in Public Places: A Systematic Review and Meta-Analysis," *Journal of the American College of Cardiology* 54.14 (2009): 1249–55.

4 Government of the Republic of Mauritius, Public Health Act (1999); Public Health Act (2008).

5 Government of the Republic of South Africa, Tobacco Products Control Act, No. 83 (1993); Tobacco Products Control Amendment Act, No. 12 (1999); Tobacco Products Control Amendment Act, No. 23 (2007); Bill B24-2008 (2008).

6 Global Smokefree Partnership, "Global Voices: Rebutting the Tobacco Industry, Winning Smokefree Air – Status Report 2009." Online at: http://www.globalsmokefreepartnership. org/index.php?section=artigo&id=109 (accessed 20 July 2011).

7 B. E. Asare, "Tobacco regulation in South Africa: Interest groups and public policy," *African Journal of Political Science and International Relations* 3.3 (2009): 99–106; M. Malan and R. Weaver. "Political Change in South Africa: New Tobacco Control and Public Health Policies," in J. de Beyer and Bridgen L.Waverley (eds), *Tobacco Control Policy: Strategies, Successes and Setbacks* (Washington DC: The World Bank, 2003), 121–51; C. P. Van Walbeek, "Tobacco control in South Africa in the 1990s: A mix of advocacy, academic research and policy," *South African Journal of Economic History* 19 (2004): 100–31.

8 N. Ramgoolam, Prime Minister of Mauritius, national address on Mauritius Independence Day, 12 March 2009.

9 Government of the State of Eritrea, Proclamation 143/2004 – A Proclamation to Provide for Tobacco Control (2004).

10 Government of Burkina Faso, Raabo N°AN IV-0081/FP/SAN/CAPRO/DP of 1988; Law N°25-2001 (2001).

11 Government of the United Republic of Tanzania, Tobacco (Products Regulation) Act (2003).
12 Government of the Republic of Zambia, Public Health (Tobacco) Regulation (1992); Health regulation-Statutory Instrument No. 163 (1992); Government Statutory Instrument No. 39 (2008).
13 Canadian Public Health Association website. Online at: www.cpha.ca/en/programs/substance-use/gtc/gtc-a/gtc-a-bf.aspx (website discontinued – last accessed 25 March 2010).
14 Bloomberg Initiative to Reduce Tobacco Use, "Promotion and creation of smoke free spaces in Burkina Faso." Online at: www.tobaccocontrolgrants.org/Pages/40/What-we-fund (accessed 20 July 2011).
15 ATSA, Project #105895. Information online at: http://idris.idrc.ca/app/Search?request=directAccess&projectNumber=105895&language=en (accessed 20 July 2011).
16 ATSA, Project #105676. Information online at: http://web.idrc.ca/en/ev-83072-201_105676-1-IDRC_ADM_INFO.html (accessed 20 July 2011). See also E. Stokes, "Postcards from Lusaka: No smoking. *Really* no smoking," *This Magazine*, 17 August 2009.
17 Mfoundi Department, Cameroon, Memorandum N°1913, 12 June 2007.
18 Ministry of Economy and Finance, Cameroon, Memorandum N° 07/788, 15 June 2007.
19 ATSA, Project #105799. Information online at: http://web.idrc.ca/en/ev-83035-201_105799-1-IDRC_ADM_INFO.html (accessed 20 July 2011).
20 National Senate of Nigeria. "A Bill for an Act to Repeal the Tobacco (Control) Act 1990 Cap T16 Laws of the Federation and to Enact the National Tobacco Control Bill 2009 to provide for the Regulation or Control of Production, Manufacture, Sale, Advertising, Promotion and Sponsorship of Tobacco or Tobacco Products in Nigerian and for other Relates Matters" (National Tobacco Control Bill, 2009).
21 *This Day*, "Nigeria: The Abuja Smoking Ban" (editorial), 24 June 2008.
22 Government of Osun State (Nigeria), Prohibition of Smoking in Public Places Bill (2009).
23 G. Griffith, *Global map of smokefree policies* (2008), prepared for the Global Smokefree Partnership, online at: http://www.tobaccofreecenter.org/files/pdfs/en/GSP-GlobalMap-SmokeFreePolicies.pdf (accessed 20 July 2011).
24 E. Ross, "Touba: A spiritual metropolis in a modern world," *Canadian Journal of African Studies* 29.2 (2006): 222–59.
25 Smoke Free Malawi, "Malawi Should Not Be an Exception: Sign FCTC and Ban Public Smoking," press release, 26 June 2009.
26 Bloomberg Initiative to Reduce Tobacco Use, "Building capacity for the enforcement of the Tobacco Control Act of 2007 in Kenya." Online at: www.tobaccocontrolgrants.org/Pages/40/What-we-fund (accessed 25 March 2010).
27 A. Schryer-Roy, "Kenya: Bridging the Gap Between Policy and Practice," Africa Tobacco Control Regional Initiative news update (2010).
28 World Health Organization, "World No Tobacco Day awardees 2004." Online at: www.who.int/tobacco/communications/events/wntd/2004/awards/en/index1.html (accessed 20 July 2011).
29 P. Burhoo, "African Tobacco Situational Analysis: Tobacco Control in Sub-Saharan Africa, Mauritius," presentation at the 14th World Conference on Tobacco or Health, Mumbai, India, March 2009.
30 K. K. Akinroye, "Promoting smoke-free worksites and public places in Abuja and Osun State, Nigeria," presentation at the 14th World Conference on Tobacco or Health, Mumbai, India, March 2009.

Chapter 4

TAXATION AS A TOBACCO CONTROL STRATEGY

Jeffrey Drope and John Madigan

Despite the demonstrated efficacy of increased tobacco taxation as a primary deterrent to tobacco use, the vast majority of the countries participating in the Africa Tobacco Situational Analyses (ATSA) initiative do not yet employ taxation as a tobacco control strategy. Though all 12 ATSA countries levy taxes on tobacco products, only South Africa has been able to create, implement and enforce significant tobacco taxation aimed purposefully at reducing consumption.[1] This chapter seeks to furnish a regional context of tobacco taxation in Africa and to analyze the challenges that countries face in attempting to utilize such policy instruments.

Tobacco taxation generates a distinct set of important policy dynamics that merit serious consideration, particularly for advocates seeking policy change. Proponents of tobacco tax policy reform – i.e. targeted tax increases – must take their well-researched, ironclad case for change to government in order to convince them of the tangible revenue and public health benefits. They also have to be prepared for vigorous opposition from the tobacco industry and/or their allies, which will inevitably present a doomsayer scenario of decreased tax revenue and job loss. On the side of actual policy provision, proponents within government must develop policies that will be effective over the long term, particularly instituting a codified system of substantial specific excise tax increases that will account effectively for changes in personal income and inflation. Proponents within the government must also be prepared for opposition from colleagues towards these reforms, based on concerns over their constituency support and/or ideological preferences (e.g. lower taxes).

Broadly speaking, the current state of tobacco taxation policies in the ATSA countries can be grouped into four categories. First, there are countries that currently have essentially no meaningful tobacco taxation, such as Burkina Faso and Tanzania.[2] Second, there are countries that have low rates of tobacco taxation, which include Cameroon, Kenya, Mauritius, Nigeria, Senegal and Zambia. Third, two countries, Eritrea and Ghana, have significant rates of tobacco taxation though not as a public health measure. Malawi also employs significant taxes, but it is a special case as the government is using taxation as a strategy to encourage the domestic manufacturing of cigarettes. Finally, the only country that has used significant tobacco taxation as a deterrent to consumption is South Africa, though in the late 2000s it began to encounter some challenges with taxation strategies that will be discussed in depth below.

In terms of strategies to address tobacco consumption, it is not taxation per se that is the most effective way to reduce consumption, but rather, regular increases in the rate of tobacco taxation relative to inflation and gains in personal income that are most effective.[3] Other important taxation strategies include applying tax increases to all tobacco products to discourage substitution; earmarking government revenues from tobacco taxation to fund tobacco control activities; and encouraging regional cooperation to prevent illicit trade.

The 12 ATSA countries vary considerably in current tobacco taxation measures, but the challenges they each face are similar. Looking ahead, these countries and developing countries like them will need much more complete data on existing tax policies and trends (e.g. increasing or decreasing rates relative to inflation, the effects of changes in national and individual income, the likely effectiveness of specific versus ad valorem excise taxes, tariffs, other consumption-based taxes, etc.). Advocacy teams lobbying government officials for tax policy change will also need to be equipped with better evidence-based research supporting the relationship between increased taxation and reduced consumption and the near certainty of increased tax revenues in the long term.

Review of Key Tax-Related Terms

In general, taxation is very specialized and typically the domain of professionals (e.g. lawyers, accountants, economists, etc.) who practice in the area. Accordingly, for the lay reader, it is important to develop at least a rudimentary understanding of taxes, taxation and tax policy. For example, it is important to distinguish between different types of taxes including excise tax (specific and ad valorem), sales tax, value added tax (VAT) and tariffs (also referred to as import taxes or duties), among others.

An excise tax is a tax on selected goods produced for sale within a country or imported and sold in that country. Typically, an excise tax is levied on an item that produces a negative externality such as the pollution generated by gas, oil and other energy products. Tobacco products not only generate pollution but also produce or exacerbate negative health outcomes that the state must then address. Specific excise taxes are based directly on quantity or weight, independent of price (e.g. $x per 1,000 cigarettes, or per pack, or per carton, etc.). Ad valorem excise taxes are based on value (e.g. a percentage of manufacturer or retail prices). The World Health Organization (WHO) has identified specific excise taxes on tobacco products, assessed on manufacturers and *increased regularly* (specific taxes do not index automatically for inflation), as the most effective type of tax for curbing tobacco consumption. The specific excise tax's main advantages are that it treats all products (e.g. all cigarettes regardless of price, brand, etc.) equally and is generally easier to administer because quantity can be measured more accurately than value.[1] Ad valorem taxes by nature do automatically index for inflation, but tax amounts can be affected directly by the industry's overall pricing and/or the production of lower-priced cigarettes, which effectively gives significant power to the industry. For a variety of reasons, many countries use a combination of both excise taxes, though research demonstrates that countries at lower levels of economic development tend to generate better public health and revenue-generating results relying more on specific taxes.[5]

Taxes that apply generally to all goods or services include a general sales tax – usually charged as a percentage of price at the point of purchase – and a VAT, which is levied on the value added to goods at each stage of transaction from production to purchase. Because sales taxes and VATs generally apply to all goods at the same rate and do not target tobacco products specifically, they are widely considered to be much less effective than specific excise taxes in reducing tobacco consumption. Also, manufacturers have no incentive as a result of a VAT or a similar tax to shift production to other nontobacco goods because the tax would be applied equally to any type of good.

Import taxes are levied against goods that have been imported into a country. An import tax is commonly called a tariff or a duty, and such taxes tend to vary from one product class to another. But unlike excise tax rates, import tax rates often stay the same for many years, as tariff rate schedules are only occasionally altered in most countries because the process of changing these rates is usually complex. Import taxes are considered to be less effective than excise taxes as a tobacco tax strategy because: a) they can be only applied to imported goods and multinational tobacco firms can establish domestic manufacturing to circumvent them; b) firms can take advantage of duty-free zones and similar arrangements; and c) producers can utilize regional free trade agreements to mitigate or avoid tariffs altogether.

Cigarette Affordability

Affordability is a cornerstone of all tobacco taxation strategies because it takes into account the simultaneous effect of income and price on people's decisions to make purchases.[6] Furthermore, for the purposes of this discussion, we employ Blecher and Van Walbeek's (2009) definition of affordability: the resources (time or money) required to buy a pack of cigarettes. Table 4.1 presents World Health Organization (WHO) data on the affordability of cigarettes in the 12 ATSA countries. The data represent the price of the most popular brand, so it is important to note that prices can vary considerably below and above this price. For example, in 2006, retail prices for a pack of 20 cigarettes in Zambia ranged from 5,600 kwacha (US$1.96 at purchasing power parity or PPP) on the low end to 7,800 kwacha ($2.74) for the premium foreign brand, Dunhill.

Several important patterns emerge in terms of comparative affordability. In countries such as Eritrea and Ghana, the price (by purchasing power

Table 4.1. Affordability of a 20-cigarette pack of the most widely consumed brand

Country	Price (in local currency)	Price in international dollars (USD at PPP), 2006	GDP per capita in international dollars (USD at PPP), 2006	Price as % of GDP per capita*	Adult prevalence (%)
Burkina Faso	500 (XOF)	2.77	1,084	0.25	13–15
Cameroon	500 (XAF)	2.09	2,042	0.10	18
Eritrea	20 (ERN)	5.96	621	0.96	7–8
Ghana	13,500 (GHC)	6.83	1,281	0.53	5
Kenya	120 (KES)	3.63	1,442	0.25	15–20
Malawi	65 (MWK)	2.06	705	0.29	15
Mauritius	60 (MRU)	5.15	10,577	0.05	18
Nigeria	200 (NGN)	2.31	1,852	0.10	15–20
Senegal	400 (XOF)	1.89	1,660	0.10	32
South Africa	15.70 (ZAR)	5.15	9,141	0.05	23
Tanzania	1,000 (TZS)	–	1,108	–	–
Zambia	6,000 (ZMK)	2.11	1,206	0.17	15

* The figures in this column have been multiplied by 100 for ease of cross-country comparison.
– Data not reported/not available.
Sources: World Health Organization, *WHO Report on the Global Tobacco Epidemic, 2008: The MPOWER Package* (2008); World Bank Group, *World Development Indicators* (2009).

parity or PPP) as a proportion of GDP per capita – a crude proxy for income – is high, particularly compared to other African countries.[7] Notably, as described below, both countries have high excise tax rates, which likely explain part of the higher price. Though a causal relationship cannot be accurately inferred from such limited data, it is worthwhile to note that Ghana and Eritrea also have among the lowest cigarette-smoking prevalence rates on the continent.[8] In contrast, cigarettes are relatively affordable in Cameroon, Senegal and Zambia. Zambia and Cameroon have above-average prevalence rates while Senegal has one of the highest prevalence rates compared to the rest of the continent (and even across all developing nations).

Strategies for Tobacco Taxation

Raising the rate of taxation on tobacco products is widely shown to be the most effective way to reduce tobacco consumption.[9] On average, increases of 10 percent on the real (inflation-adjusted) price of cigarettes reduces cigarette consumption by 4 percent in high-income countries and up to 8 percent in middle- and low-income countries.[10] The young and the poor, in particular, tend to be the most responsive to price changes resulting from increased taxation. This responsiveness is largely due to the fact that spending on tobacco products constitutes a relatively greater share of disposable income for these demographic groups.[11] In order to be effective in reducing tobacco consumption, increases in specific excise taxes on tobacco must outpace both inflation and increases in per capita income, and lead to an increase in real price.[12] In brief, the less affordable tobacco products are, the less consumption there will be. Less tobacco consumption means lower mortality and morbidity rates.

To appeal to skeptical and/or reluctant governments, it is critical to emphasize that increased tobacco taxation will increase government revenue. For example, in South Africa between 1993 and 2007, real excise taxes increased by 357 percent and price increased by 146 percent, while consumption decreased by 48 percent. In this time period, revenue increased by 215 percent, bearing in mind that revenue increases, *ceteris paribus*, occur up to a certain tax maximizing point, after which the revenues begin to decrease.[13]

A component of taxation strategy that further supports tobacco control is for the government to earmark revenues from tobacco to fund certain tobacco control activities. Technically, Ghana's government sets aside a small percentage of its tobacco tax revenue for health promotion and education, though by all accounts, this earmark has never been institutionalized fully. Tobacco control advocates in Mauritius and South Africa are actively seeking such an earmark. Other countries outside of Africa that earmark tobacco tax revenues for similar health-related purposes include the United Kingdom, Ireland, Qatar, Australia, Egypt, Iran and Thailand.[14]

Finally, while the industry continues to argue that tax increases generate more illicit trade, scholars have recently demonstrated that the link between the two is speculative at best. Joosens et al. (2010) demonstrate empirically that countries with higher tobacco taxes do not have higher levels of illicit trade in tobacco products.[15] Nevertheless, this tax-illicit trade connection persists and is strongly promoted by the industry. Perhaps not surprisingly, policymakers continue to voice specific concern in this area. For example, policymakers in Senegal expressed concern to ATSA team members that the country's 2009 ad valorem excise tax increase on cigarettes would result in higher rates of cigarette smuggling from neighboring countries. Scholars and tax experts have suggested that countries can confront this supposed issue by achieving regional cooperation on tobacco taxation.[16] If Senegal works with its neighbors to harmonize tobacco taxes, it will create a disincentive for regional illicit trade. To help to address these challenges, many countries – including South Africa – are employing tax stamps to help identify the origin of products and which taxes have been paid. Cameroon officially has a tax stamp program, though by all accounts, it has never been officially implemented. Even in Malawi, a country with almost no tobacco control provisions, Finance Minister Gondwe raised the issue of tobacco smuggling and proposed addressing the problem with the introduction of a tax stamp system in his budget for 2008–9.

State of Tobacco Taxation in the ATSA Countries

Substantial tobacco taxation as a deterrent

Of the 12 ATSA countries, South Africa stands out because of its use of tobacco taxation specifically as a way to curb consumption. As described above, between 1993 and 2007, real (inflation-adjusted) excise tax rates on tobacco increased substantially, as did real prices. These increases – in part – led both to a major decline in consumption and a large increase in real government tobacco-based revenues. Importantly, the increases in taxes only accounted for half of the real price increase in tobacco products. Industry-imposed price increases aimed at increasing profit margins at the cost of sales volumes accounted for the other half of the change. In essence, increased tobacco taxation had a positive corollary effect on the industry's pricing structure.

There is still room for stronger tobacco taxation policy in South Africa that will decrease consumption and bolster government revenue. According to the National Council Against Smoking (NCAS) in South Africa, the national government has recently been reluctant to increase tobacco taxation further. Substantial increases in both personal income and inflation have steadily eroded the effects of the tax on prices, and cigarettes have become more affordable since 2005. In 2010, the NCAS was preparing material to present to the government to support a renewed policy initiative to increase excise taxes systematically above the rate of inflation and to account for economic growth.

Significant tobacco taxation, though not as a deterrent

As Table 4.2 demonstrates, both Eritrea and Ghana tax tobacco more aggressively than most of their African neighbors. However, these rates – at least until recently in Ghana – have not been designed explicitly as a deterrent to tobacco use; rather, these higher rates have been meant to increase state tax revenues.

Eritrea imposes a 100 percent ad valorem excise tax on all tobacco products. It also levies a 25 percent import customs tax, though this is not too relevant since imports are rare (BAT–Eritrea reportedly has a government-sanctioned monopoly on production). Finally, there is a 12 percent sales tax that applies to all goods at the point of retail sale. There is no evidence that any of these rates are set to increase. All taxes considered, cigarettes, as demonstrated in Table 4.1, are less affordable in Eritrea compared to other African countries.

In the 2011 national budget, Ghana increased its ad valorem excise tax on cigarettes from 140 to 150 percent of factory price (snuff and other products are reportedly levied at 170.65 percent of factory price). In his budget speech to parliament, the minister of finance cited health reasons and alignment with international agreements as the reasons for the increase.[17] Advocates, however, continue to lobby for a sustained tobacco taxation strategy because there is still no regular, codified schedule of tobacco taxation increases. Also, notably, Ghana previously employed a mix of specific and ad valorem excise taxes on tobacco, but has now elected to utilize only ad valorem taxes. This change could potentially permit tobacco firms to affect tax revenues through price manipulation, which might generate a new set of challenges. It will be important to identify the effects of this decision. All of these recent changes considered, as in Eritrea, cigarettes remain comparatively more expensive in Ghana than other countries – though still affordable to many – and prevalence rates are lower.

While both of these countries have significant tobacco taxation in place that appears to have some effect on consumption, these taxes cannot be effective in reducing consumption in the longer term without regular increases

Table 4.2. National tobacco taxes – 2009–10

Country	Specific excise*	Ad valorem excise	Sales tax	Value added tax (VAT)	Import duties
Burkina Faso	12%**	10–14% *** (possibly 17–22%)	12.5%	18%	–
Cameroon	–	25–42.5%***	–	19.5%	30%**
Eritrea	–	100%	12%		25%**
Ghana	–	150% (cigarettes) 170.65% (other)	–	12.5%	–
Kenya	30% (cigarettes)	–	–	16%	–
Malawi	–	39%**	–	16.5%	11%*
Mauritius	44 MRU/pack (cigarettes) 7,500 MRU/ kilogram (cigars)	–	–	15%	–
Nigeria	40% (cigarettes)				5%
Senegal	–	20–40%***	20%	18%	20%
South Africa	R6.82/pack (cigarettes) R8.67/50g (cigarette tobacco) R2.30/20g (pipe tobacco) R39.72/23g (cigars)	–	–	14%	–
Tanzania	20%**	–	20%	–	–
Zambia	14.5%***	34%**	–	20%	–

– Data not reported/not available.
* The specific excise taxes presented as percentages represent the tax as a percent of price at the time of reporting to the WHO.
** The tax applies to a pack of 20 cigarettes (World Health Organization, *WHO Report on the Global Tobacco Epidemic, 2008: The MPOWER Package* (2008)).
*** It is not clear as to which specific tobacco products the tax applies.

relative to changes in inflation and per capita income. Inflation and economic growth will likely catch up to these higher prices, perhaps even quickly. As Blecher and Van Walbeek demonstrate (2009), affordability is driven more by income than by price, and it is the affordability that matters most for affecting consumption.[18] But with a history of higher tobacco taxes, this type of taxation is at least not new and may even be viable in the short term. Clearly, Ghana has recently been contemplating more seriously the possibility of taxation as a tobacco control strategy.

Weak or ineffective tobacco taxation

The most common status of tobacco taxation across ATSA countries (and many developing nations more generally) is the existence of excise taxes that have limited demonstrable effect on the pricing of tobacco products. This characterization includes Cameroon, Kenya, Mauritius, Nigeria, Senegal and Zambia. Existing tobacco taxation is weak or ineffective in these countries for a combination of reasons. First, the excise taxes are limited to only certain tobacco products, as in Nigeria and Kenya, where it is not clear if these taxes apply to tobacco products other than cigarettes. Therefore, product substitution by consumers may pose a problem. Second, the excise taxes are generally low, averaging less than 30 percent of the total price. Third, none of the countries have regular tax increases institutionalized in the tax code.

In Cameroon, there is an excise tax that applies to all luxury goods generally, which includes tobacco products. The ad valorem excise tax is 25 percent, which applies to domestically manufactured and imported products. There is also a 30 percent import duty regulated by the Economic and Monetary Community of Central Africa (CEMAC). Finally, there is a VAT of 19.2 percent that applies to the value of goods at different stages of production (including retail), though by all accounts implementation of this tax remains problematic as businesses seek exemptions and officials remain uncertain about how to apply it.

In the late 2000s, there were some encouraging signs for advocates of tobacco taxation in Kenya. First, the new Tobacco Control Act of 2007 includes a broad provision for tobacco taxation. Second, from 2006 to 2008, there was an annual increase of 10 percent in the excise tax on tobacco products. The excise rate as of early 2010 was the equivalent of 30 percent of the price of cigarettes. However, in the 2009 and 2010 tax code changes, the minister of finance elected not to increase tobacco tax rates again even though the ministry had the power to make such changes. Tobacco control advocates continue to pursue this opportunity in Kenya.[19]

Like Kenya, Mauritius is also moving in the direction of higher tobacco taxes. Until late 2010, there were specific excise taxes of Rs 2,200 per thousand sticks on cigarettes and Rs 7,500 per kilogram on cigars. This tax was increased by 25 percent in November 2010 for the 2011 budget (there was no change in 2010). As of May 2008, there is also an import tax of 15 percent that has been imposed on all tobacco. This change in import taxes is particularly important because there is no longer any domestic manufacturing of tobacco products, so all products are imported. This import-only scenario thus offers two different taxation options – excise and import duty – for proponents of tobacco tax reform in Mauritius, though again, excise taxes are arguably more manipulable than tariffs. There is also reportedly a final tax of 15 percent of the total of both aforementioned taxes plus the base cost of cigarettes prior to sale. Changes in tax rates on tobacco products are imposed regularly (almost annually) by the minister of finance, which has fairly consistently led to price increases; however, there is no institutionalized mechanism for tax increases, particularly ones that stay ahead of growing incomes.

In Nigeria, there is a quantity-specific excise tax on cigarettes equivalent to 40 percent of the price and a 5 percent import duty. Nigerian tobacco control activists are advocating for changes in the excise tax rate, particularly with consistent increases over time. Import taxes will not be a particularly effective strategy since most tobacco products are now domestically manufactured.

Senegal applies tobacco-specific taxes at a moderate level. Three tax laws passed between 1992 and 2004 built a tax structure that included ad valorem excise taxes of 16 percent on low-end cigarettes, 31 percent on standard cigarettes and 40 percent on premium brands. Most recently, tax legislation passed in 2009 actually increased the ad valorem tax to 40 percent for all brands, though it is not yet clear to which tobacco products this change applies, thus generating concern that substitution of noncigarette tobacco products could pose a problem. Furthermore, the tax on premium brands did not increase, which raises the concern that premium brands will not see a reduction in consumption. Furthermore, some government departments have expressed explicit concern that this tax increase will lead to an increase in smuggling. A VAT of 18 percent applies to all goods and services. A 20 percent tariff applies to imported tobacco products, but this is almost irrelevant because most tobacco products are manufactured locally, particularly since the opening of a large Philip Morris International plant in 2007. Finally, several other minor tax measures apply to imported tobacco products only, including a West African Economic and Monetary Union (UEMOA) customs fee, a statistical tax, a community solidarity deduction, an Economic Community of West African States (ECOWAS) deduction, an interior tax and a surcharge.

In the case of Zambia, there is little else in the way of tobacco taxation beyond a 14.5 percent specific excise tax on tobacco products (as a percentage of price at the time of data collection by the WHO in 2006). The excise rate has not changed in recent years and it does not have any effect on price changes that occur. There is also a 20 percent VAT on all goods and services.

Most notably, across all of these countries, there are no regular increases in excise tax rates relative to inflation or systemic gains in personal income.

To repeat the nearly unequivocal findings of the scholarly and empirical literature: tobacco taxation rates outstripped by inflation and gains in per capita income are not effective as a tobacco control strategy because the relative affordability of tobacco eliminates its potency as a price deterrent.[20]

No meaningful tobacco taxation

As Table 4.2 demonstrates, Tanzania and Burkina Faso currently lack tobacco-specific taxation. There are either very low or no national excise taxes on tobacco products, though details of the tax structures in both countries are unclear. Tanzania has recently undertaken a program to assess taxation broadly and the viability of tobacco taxation strategies more specifically.[21]

Similarly, Burkina Faso has very limited tobacco-specific taxation. Government sources suggest that there are ad valorem excise taxes of 10–14 percent, though it is not clear how effectively the taxes are implemented.[22] In fact, actual tax collection remains a struggle in many developing countries.[23] In 2008–9, there were unsubstantiated reports that the government actually decreased tax rates on tobacco products (to 4 percent). However, in a more optimistic development, the National Assembly passed a comprehensive tobacco control bill in November 2010 that includes a taxation clause, though as of writing, no actual tax reforms had yet occurred. Reports from tobacco control advocates in Burkina Faso suggest that the new proposed ad valorem tax rate is 60 percent. This is a very positive step for tobacco taxation. There are no details, however, as to the possibility of regular increases to help to address future changes in inflation and/or income levels.

The complex case of Malawi

The case of Malawi is arguably more complex than many of the other countries because of the motivation behind recent tax code changes. Specifically, the excise tax provisions from 2008–9 on tobacco are designed to stimulate domestic cigarette production by favoring cigarettes that use Malawian-grown tobacco. Since 2008–9, there is a duty system that is based on the quantity of cigarettes being imported or produced rather than based on value, but has differential rates depending on the place of manufacture and the origin of the inputs (particularly tobacco leaf). The basic duties on cigarettes are flat rates as follows: (a) the equivalent of US$18 per 1,000 sticks for a hinge-lid packet and (b) the equivalent of US$12 per 1,000 sticks for a soft packet.[24] As is reportedly done in neighboring tobacco-producing countries including Uganda, there is a much-reduced rate of excise tax on cigarettes that contain at least 70 percent Malawian tobacco. The excise taxes on these cigarettes are reportedly half of what they are for tobacco products using foreign inputs.

While the combined effect of the new excise rates and the introduction of tax stamps to encourage compliance is expected to generate a tax revenue gain of K600 million annually, there could actually be a loss of revenue if the new Nyasa Manufacturing Company cigarette factory successfully takes advantage of the lower excise rate and gains significant market share. This new policy could ironically have significant negative economic implications for the government, not to mention poor consequences for public health.

The Political Challenges of Tobacco Taxation

Tobacco taxation strategies taken at face value would appear to be a ready and effective fix for tobacco consumption challenges in almost any country. However, the political challenges associated with executing such strategies are real and often substantial. Several important political trends emerge across these countries, and it is particularly important to identify the key actors and what their particular stake in tax policy change might be.

In a process of mapping out the key political actors in their countries in regard to tobacco taxation, ATSA team members identified key players in taxation and tobacco control more broadly. Not surprisingly, across all 12 countries, ministries of finance are consistently identified as the most critical actors in terms of support for – or opposition to – tobacco-specific excise tax increases. Finance ministries often have considerable discretion in setting tax rates and can change them to a certain point without seeking wider approval from either the higher executive (the president or prime minister, and/or the greater cabinet) or the legislature. In many countries, ministries employ tax experts to help inform policy. Notably, actors in these ministries vary across and within countries as both allies and opponents of increased tobacco taxation.

Within these ministries, particular departments consistently play important roles in shaping and implementing tax policy. First, in each country, the revenue service (or its equivalent) is responsible for collecting taxes. In most countries, the revenue service helps the ministry develop an annual estimate of future national revenue. When there is a proposed change in the tax code, the revenue service has to consider potential implications for overall revenue. Since the collection of taxes in general in most developing countries is challenging, revenue services are generally suspicious of any changes that will alter the streams of money coming to the government. It is crucial to be able to demonstrate unequivocally to the revenue service that tobacco taxation changes will actually increase revenues over the medium and long term, if not immediately. Contrary to conventional wisdom and tobacco industry lobbying, the empirical evidence demonstrates that in most circumstances, increases in tobacco taxation actually bolster government revenue while simultaneously driving down consumption.[25] Explaining and demonstrating this revenue-rich dynamic to revenue authorities were key parts of the strategy that advocates in South Africa successfully employed to help garner tax changes.

In the last couple of decades, a handful of revenue authorities in Africa have gained greater autonomy. Although in most places the tax agency technically remains a part of the ministry of finance or its equivalent, it often has extraordinary powers, including to hire, fire and remunerate on its own professional and pay scale (typically to compete for talent with the private sector).[26] The impetus behind such institutional reforms has been ostensibly to professionalize the authority and to insulate it better from politics. While international finance experts and scholars have noted some success, anecdotally it has created in some cases a more direct relationship between the chief executive (e.g. the president) and the revenue chief. This additional link may affect taxation in certain circumstances.

The department(s) in the finance ministry that handles customs and excise issues is also a central actor in most discussions of tobacco tax, both in regard to tax collection and problems associated with illicit trade. First, customs and excise divisions are usually charged with collecting taxes from producers and importers (the agents who import goods produced in other countries). In many cases, this agency collects the tax that is then passed on to the revenue service. Similar to the broad concerns of the revenue authorities, when the revenue streams are potentially going to shift, the customs and excise departments are likely going to question how and why these shifts are occurring. So while these actors do not typically have a "pro" or "anti" taxation stance, they do have concerns about their accountability on a different but still important level. In several countries including Ghana and South Africa, customs and excise authorities can be quite supportive of tobacco taxation reforms, particularly when presented with evidence-based research demonstrating that revenues generally grow in the long term after such reforms.

Furthermore, shifts in taxation can create incentives for those involved in the illicit trade of tobacco products to increase their efforts, and it is usually the customs and excise authorities that have immediate jurisdiction over such issues, particularly in developing countries.[27] Not surprisingly, in countries such as Nigeria and Ghana, there is concrete evidence of the tobacco industry openly supporting customs and excise departments with resources (often in the form of gifts such as jeeps for pursuing smugglers). Of course, this relationship is fraught with conflict of interest as the agency receiving the gifts is also responsible, in part, for collecting taxes from the donor of these gifts. Clearly, keeping these relationships as transparent as possible is central to mitigating any conflicts of interest or blatant corruption.

Beyond the bureaucratic level, some tax policy changes require broader consideration and approval by authorities other than the finance ministries. In most African countries, the national-level executive in the form of the cabinet (or its equivalent) has considerable input into the policy process. In some countries such as Burkina Faso, Ghana and Zambia, almost all bills are approved first by the cabinet before being passed on to the legislature for approval. It is therefore critical to ascertain the support for prospective policies across the cabinet. Thus, if there is a more comprehensive tax bill that requires the broader approval of the government, obtaining sufficient support from the cabinet becomes necessary.

The ATSA teams identified the ministries of trade, industry and agriculture as the most likely potential opponents to tobacco tax increases at the cabinet level. For trade ministries, increased taxation runs the risk of adversely affecting trade, particularly exports. In the countries with significant exports of manufactured tobacco products (e.g. Kenya, Nigeria, Senegal and South Africa) or tobacco leaf (e.g. Kenya, Malawi, Tanzania and Zambia), trade ministers may oppose major tax changes that they believe might affect these important economic sectors. It is vital to note that exports are not subject to excise taxes, which is a very persuasive argument when making a case for excise tax increases to the trade ministry.

Industry ministries are typically charged with helping businesses and if a tax policy proposal could potentially affect a particular industry negatively, it could be a genuine problem for the minister to endorse. Moreover, as African countries aggressively seek growth to provide jobs for growing populations, it is not just the countries with established industries, but also the ones that aspire to create more industry (e.g. Malawi and Tanzania) where these ministers might demonstrate vehement opposition to increased tobacco taxation.

In tobacco leaf–growing countries, the ministries of agriculture tend to have a strong vested interest in their farming constituents. There is a perception that tobacco taxation will affect farmers adversely. Increases in taxation, however, are unlikely to affect the overall demand for tobacco leaf in the short term, partly due to worldwide population growth, which creates natural increases in demand. The best possible solution to this challenge is the simultaneous introduction of programs to support crop alternatives (and truly viable alternatives that will produce equal or more income). Changes stemming from increased tobacco taxation should leave sufficient time for agricultural ministries to help farmers transition to profitable crops that also have far fewer health and environmental implications.

Fortunately, there are also natural allies among cabinet-level actors. Among the most obvious supporters of tobacco control efforts are health ministries. In Kenya, Ghana, Mauritius, Nigeria, Zambia, Cameroon and Burkina Faso, each of the ATSA teams had principal team members who are working within national ministries of health, which indicates at least some support for tobacco control. Tobacco control advocates consistently identify ministries that have responsibilities for the welfare of potentially more vulnerable societal groups such as children, youths and women as possible cabinet-level allies for tobacco-related policy reforms. Selling the potential health and revenue benefits of tobacco tax reform across cabinet members becomes a very important task for advocates.

Though rarely central to the tobacco taxation policy process, presidents and prime ministers can be important advocates or adversaries of policy change. For example, in Nigeria, the former president Umaru Yar'Adua sought aggressively and publicly to stimulate tax revenues and was openly sympathetic to increased tobacco taxation. Though it was not his policy decision to make ultimately, the finance ministry reports directly to the president's office, which is likely to have considerable influence. Similarly, the prime minister of Mauritius publicly declared a fight against tobacco and his support is no doubt helpful as advocates seek tax reform. In contrast, in Senegal, a country with a highly centralized political system, most anecdotal accounts suggest that President Wade opposes most measures that hurt economically the important and politically powerful tobacco manufacturing industry. In fact, Senegal steadily diluted most of its tobacco control laws from the early 1980s, and sought aggressively – and successfully – to attract Philip Morris International to invest in a large manufacturing plant in the country.

The role of national legislatures in tobacco taxation varies across the region. In some countries with strong executives, the legislature is mostly a formality (the proverbial "rubberstamp"). Increasingly, however, national legislatures play a larger role. In some countries, a majority in the legislature must approve the annual budget, and if a tobacco tax change is part of that budget it is then vulnerable to legislative scrutiny. Although a tobacco tax change will be part of a number of other reforms in such a circumstance, it will be necessary to determine the level of support for the change. Similarly, if the broader tax code is being partly or entirely rewritten, the legislature may turn out to be a major obstacle. Not surprisingly, it is legislators in districts that grow tobacco and/or manufacture tobacco products or have direct or indirect economic interests in the tobacco industry who are consistently the strongest opponents to increased tobacco taxation. While challenging, it is necessary to map the policy preferences of legislators. In particular, tax reformers have found previously that accessing the legislature's finance committee, including particularly the committee chair, in order to demonstrate the sound logic and benefits of the proposed tobacco tax change, is an important step toward achieving wider legislative support. Encouragingly, tobacco control advocates have successfully pursued and obtained major tobacco control legislative victories in Kenya, Mauritius and South Africa in the last decade and very recently in early 2011 in Nigeria. Many legislators in Africa appear to be aware of the public health crisis posed by tobacco and some are clearly open to making significant policy changes to mitigate the problems.

It is also crucial for proponents of tobacco taxation strategies to know their opponents outside of government. Across nearly all of the ATSA countries, the tobacco industry was identified as a formidable political adversary to increased tobacco taxation.[28] Tobacco leaf cultivation and/or tobacco product manufacturing are among the largest sectors in the national economies of each of the 12 ATSA countries. Most notably, British American Tobacco (BAT) is the largest tobacco producer or manufacturer in South Africa, Eritrea, Kenya and Nigeria. In several other ATSA countries, other multinationals have a strong presence (e.g. Philip Morris International in Senegal; Japan Tobacco International in Tanzania) or there is an emerging domestic manufacturer (e.g. Nyasa Manufacturing Company in Malawi and MABUCIG in Burkina Faso). Even in the countries without major manufacturing (Cameroon, Ghana, Mauritius and Zambia), the marketing and sales divisions of large multinational tobacco firms maintain a very strong presence both through marketing and seeking to influence politics.

Specific to tobacco taxation, the most common argument made by BAT, Philip Morris and other tobacco firms to government officials in all ATSA countries is that increases in tobacco taxation would hurt sales volumes, thereby decreasing government revenues from taxation, threatening employment and crippling the national economy. In South Africa, for example, the industry strategy has been to exaggerate price increases on tobacco products in response to government tax increases as a way of driving down consumption and government revenue in the short term.[29] The industry has held out hopes that this strategy would pressure government concerned with generating revenues to abandon tobacco taxation increases. Fortunately, the strategy has mostly failed as the tobacco firms could not maintain the artificial price increases for a sustained period of time.

A New International Dimension

Taxation has another potential set of international political constraints and implications because it is sometimes a significant part of regional economic and political agreements. For example, there are direct tax implications for countries that belong to ECOWAS, UEMOA, the Economic and Monetary Community of Central Africa (CEMAC) and the Southern African Customs Union (SACU). The case of Senegal provides a useful illustration. In 2009, the government increased tobacco excise taxes on most products to 40 percent, which is the excise tax ceiling in the UEMOA, in which Senegal is a member. However, the ECOWAS agreement, in which Senegal is also a member, has a higher excise tax ceiling. Proponents of tobacco tax reform are pressing for policymakers to reform tobacco tax levels using the ECOWAS guidelines. It is not clear how the government will resolve its international commitments.

Realistically, there are several options to resolve this tension between agreements that reduce trade barriers and a tobacco tax strategy that in principle can generate barriers to the free flow of goods. In the best case scenario, the agreement would incorporate an excise tax minimum ("floor") for tobacco products rather than the maximum ("ceiling") that many agreements are currently employing – and then permit countries to increase the rate as they so choose, particularly on public health grounds. The EU has taken this policy path by imposing a minimum total excise duty of €64 per 1,000 cigarettes (€1.28 per pack of 20) in 2006. Additionally, the minimum total level of excise tax on the most popular price category (MPPC) must be 57 percent of the tax-inclusive (excise tax and VAT) retail price. Notably, actual tobacco taxation rates differ markedly between EU members by up to 300 percent, which generates potential problems with illicit trade between members.[30] A less desirable option in Africa would be to petition for higher excise rate ceilings for tobacco products. The central stumbling block with this strategy is that the ceiling would have to be sufficiently high to be able to accommodate future increases in excise taxes. Recalling that excise taxes only work when they are affecting affordability, it would be difficult to predict what this ceiling should be since in some countries, aggressive sustained taxation increases would be the only way to affect affordability effectively.

In either scenario, a complex political dimension evolves because it is now necessary to affect the policymaking of the supranational entity (e.g. ECOWAS, CEMAC, etc.). This effort will entail identifying the exact tax policy–making structures within these organizations. The appropriate tax officials will have to be introduced to the possibility in ways that will be congruent with the broader goals of the economic integration that the agreement is seeking, which is a potentially challenging task. Beyond lobbying these organizations directly, which will be necessary in every circumstance, it will likely be necessary to lobby some or all of the governments and particularly the finance ministries of the member countries. There are also potential power asymmetries within these agreements. For example, until recently in SACU, South Africa generally dictated excise tax rates for the union.[31] Today, while the new SACU agreement shares decision making more equitably among members, South Africa remains an essential power broker in tax policy decisions. Similarly, in ECOWAS, the minister of finance of the larger and more powerful countries, such as Nigeria, will have marked influence within the broader ECOWAS organization and the ongoing negotiations that define its institutional development. These national-level actors will have some ability to affect the rules that are ultimately adopted by the supranational body.

Conclusion

At the annual meeting of the African Organization for Research and Training in Cancer (AORTIC) in Tanzania in November 2009, Dr Yussuf Saloojee of the NCAS in South Africa summed up tobacco taxation eloquently: "Taxation is the most powerful weapon governments have at their disposal to control tobacco consumption and ultimately decrease deaths."[32] This statement is powerful and persuasive, and as we observe from the 12 ATSA countries, it is a strategy that has been scarcely utilized in Africa thus far. The reason that tobacco control advocates have not been employing taxation strategies is twofold: taxation is both highly technical and very political. These two challenges frame the efforts of successful tobacco taxation.

Tobacco control advocates are not usually tax policy experts and in order to proceed with a taxation strategy, there must be much more technical assistance provided to African advocates. The first task will be to assess rigorously the state of taxation in each country. The next task will be to offer likely – though concrete – scenarios in terms of the consequences of any tax policy change. It is this evidence-based research that advocates will need to present convincingly to their finance ministries – and possibly to other governmental institutions – to demonstrate that this is a favorable policy for the long-term fiscal and health needs of the country.

Beyond the technical nature of taxation, there is a lingering problem in most developing countries, including many in the ATSA program, of the basic execution of efficient tax collection. High levels of corruption and limited capacity to administer tax programs are just two of a number of major obstacles for many developing countries in reaching their taxation goals.[33] In short, many governments are simply not adept at implementing their own taxation programs. Until governments figure out how to tax effectively, the prospects for tobacco taxation as a tobacco control strategy remain bleak. Moreover, the process of reforming any country's entire taxation structure is bound to be complex and resource-intensive. While a noble and desirable goal, the tobacco control community – both internationally and in the specific domestic scenario – needs to be prepared for this challenge.

Finally, the tobacco control community cannot underestimate the political complexity of successfully changing taxation policy in a country. As with technical tax assistance, some countries will need technical policy assistance in terms of helping to identify, reach out to and then successfully influence the appropriate political actors. In many countries, public health advocates are public health professionals and do not have a policy background, let alone in the areas of national finance and taxation. It is therefore reasonable to expect that it is just as important to provide appropriate policy support to domestic tobacco control civil society organizations.

In spite of the challenges to implementing tobacco tax reforms, it is a strategy that cannot and should not be ignored. Empirical evidence demonstrates unequivocally that tobacco taxation is a pivotal component of successful comprehensive tobacco control strategies.

Notes

1 Enforcement, however, continues to be a challenge, particularly in the area of the illicit trade of tobacco products. See E. Blecher, "A mountain or a molehill: Is the illicit trade in cigarettes undermining tobacco control policy in South Africa?" *Trends in Organized Crime* 13.4 (2010): 299–315. For a broader treatment of industry involvement in illicit trade, see E. LeGresley, K. Lee, M. Muggli, P. Patel, J. Collin and R. Hurt, "British American Tobacco and the 'insidious impact of illicit trade' in cigarettes across Africa," *Tobacco Control* 17 (2008): 339–46.

2 In November 2010, the National Assembly in Burkina Faso passed comprehensive legislation reportedly with provisions for tobacco tax increases. At the time of publication, the government had not yet implemented any changes.

3 E. H. Blecher and C. P. van Walbeek, "Cigarette Affordability Trends: An Update and Some Methodological Comments," *Tobacco Control* 19 (2009): 463–8.

4 As a way to seek to undermine specific excise taxes, tobacco firms sometimes elect to manufacture longer cigarettes.

5 For a comprehensive discussion, see World Health Organization, *WHO Technical Manual on Tobacco Tax Administration* (Geneva: World Health Organization, 2010). Table 3 (27) has an illustration of the different effects of specific and ad valorem excise taxes.

6 Blecher and Van Walbeek, "Cigarette Affordability Trends."

7 The PPP measure is the most appropriate because it takes into account relative costs of living and countries' inflation rates.

8 WHO, *Technical Manual on Tobacco Tax Administration*.

9 See F. J. Chaloupka and K. E. Warner, "The economics of smoking," *National Bureau of Economic Research* (1999): 7047 and World Health Organization, *WHO Report on the Global Tobacco Epidemic, 2008: The MPOWER Package.* (Geneva: World Health Organization, 2008). See also WHO, *Technical Manual on Tobacco Tax Administration*.

10 The World Bank, *Curbing the Epidemic: Governments and the Economics of Tobacco Control* (Series: Development in Practice) (Washington DC: The World Bank, 1999).

11 G. E. Guindon, S. Tobin and D. Yach, "Trends and affordability of cigarette prices: Ample room for tax increases and related health gains," *Tobacco Control* 11 (2002): 35–43.

12 E. H. Blecher and C. P. van Walbeek, "An international analysis of cigarette affordability," *Tobacco Control* 13 (2004): 339–46; Blecher and Van Walbeek, "Cigarette Affordability Trends."

13 E. H. Blecher, "Targeting the affordability of cigarettes: A new benchmark for taxation policy in low-income and middle-income countries," *Tobacco Control* (Online First), 7 June 2010.

14 See Guindon, Tobin and Yach, "Trends and affordability of cigarette prices," 41–2.

15 L. Joossens, D. Merriman, H. Ross and M. Raw, "The impact of eliminating the global illicit cigarette trade on health and revenue," *Addiction* 105 (2010): 1640–9.

16 Guindon, Tobin and Yach, "Trends and affordability of cigarette prices."

17 Hon. Dr Kwabena Duffuor, Minister of Finance and Economic Planning (MOFEP), "Government of Ghana Budget Statement and Economic Policy for 2011 Financial Year," 37 (item no. 119).

18 See Blecher and Van Walbeek, "Cigarette Affordability Trends."

19 M. Wahome, "Health agencies seek more cash from smokers in Budget," *Business Daily Africa (The Nation)*, 26 April 2011.

20 See Blecher and Van Walbeek, "An international analysis of cigarette affordability" and "Cigarette Affordability Trends."

21 International Development Research Centre, "Cigarette Taxation in Tanzania," Project #103440. Information online at: accessed August 3, 2010. http://www.idrc.ca/en/ev-83069-201_103440-1-IDRC_ADM_INFO.html (accessed 20 July 2011).

22 Some government sources cite a slightly higher range of 17–22 percent, where higher taxes apply to premium brands, but these rates are not clearly codified in the national tax guidelines.

23 M. Keen and A. Simone, "Tax Policy in Developing Countries: Some Lessons from the 1990s and Some Challenges Ahead," in S. Gupta, B. Clements and G. Inchauste (eds), *Helping Countries Develop: The Role of Fiscal Policy* (Washington DC: International Monetary Fund, 2004), 302–52.

24 The government presents these rates in US dollars, which is the reason we do not present the rates in the local currency here.

25 C. P. van Walbeek, "The Economics of Tobacco Control in South Africa," Economics of Tobacco Control Project (Cape Town: University of Cape Town, 2000).

26 See M. Kidd and W. Crandall, "Revenue authorities: An evaluation of their impact on revenue administration reform," IMF Working Paper WP06/240. (Washington DC: IMF, 2006). Also, see O. Fjeldstad and M. Moore, "Revenue Authorities and State Capacity in Anglophone Africa," CMI Working Paper 2008:1 (Bergen: Chr. Michelsen Institute, 2008).

27 LeGresley et al. demonstrate that the industry has played a direct role in promoting illicit trade often after a tax increase.

28 For a general discussion of industry tactics, see LeGresley et al. For an in-depth discussion of South Africa, see E. Blecher, "A mountain or a molehill."

29 See Van Walbeek, "The Economics of Tobacco Control in South Africa."

30 S. Cnossen, "Tobacco Taxation in the European Union," CESIFO Working Paper No. 1718, Category 1: Public Finance, 2006.

31 R. Kirk and M. Stern, "The New Southern African Customs Union Agreement," *The World Economy* 28.2 (2005): 169–90.

32 A. Thom, "More tax=less smoking," Health-e, 13 November 2009. Online at: http://www.health-e.org.za/news/article.php?uid=20032568 (accessed on 8 July 2011).

33 M. Keen and A. Simone, "Tax Policy in Developing Countries."

Chapter 5

THE CHALLENGES OF IMPLEMENTING BANS ON ADVERTISING, PROMOTION AND SPONSORSHIP

Jeffrey Drope and Joseph Struble

Research indicates that comprehensive bans on tobacco advertising, promotion and sponsorship (APS) are effective in reducing tobacco consumption.[1] Across the 12 African Tobacco Situational Analysis (ATSA) countries, there is considerable variation in terms of the countries' progress in instituting such restrictions. Several countries, including South Africa and Mauritius, have strong provisions in place, while some countries, such as Senegal and Ghana, have much weaker provisions. In most countries, there is a need for stronger legislation and/or regulation to create bans or to improve existing ones. In all countries, there is a significant need to improve efforts at enforcement, particularly considering the tobacco industry's ongoing efforts to subvert the bans.

This chapter has several broad goals. First, it lays out the Framework Convention on Tobacco Control (FCTC) interpretation of these bans so that the reader can understand the legal basis for the strategy. Second, it discusses the status of and variation in the bans in the 12 ATSA countries by meaningfully grouping countries together by performance and/or common challenges. Finally, it raises some of the most pressing issues facing this tobacco control strategy that require further research, discussion and/or resolution.

FCTC Definitions and Article 13

Building on research findings that advertising, promotion and sponsorship bans are effective tobacco control strategies, a comprehensive strategy has been enshrined in Article 13 of the World Health Organization's (WHO) FCTC to provide broad guidelines for country-level implementation and enforcement.

In the FCTC's Article 1, the "Use of Terms," tobacco advertising and promotion are defined as "any form of commercial communication, recommendation or action with the aim, effect or likely effect of promoting a tobacco product or tobacco use either directly or indirectly." This definition encompasses the traditional forms of television, radio and print advertising as well as product giveaways and promotions. Article 1(g) defines tobacco sponsorship as "any form of contribution to any event, activity or individual with the aim, effect or likely effect of promoting a tobacco product or tobacco use either directly or indirectly."[2] The tobacco sponsorship definition covers contributions that help fund cultural or sporting events, and more broadly, any academic scholarships and other types of so-called corporate social responsibility (CSR) activities.

In Article 13, the FCTC identifies measures that may be undertaken to restrict or ban advertising, while recognizing that the ability of some governments to undertake comprehensive bans may be limited by constitutional and/or other legal restrictions. More specifically, Section 4 of the article contains a list of clauses that detail the minimum APS controls that a party to the treaty should implement within five years of ratification, while Section 3 allows a country to implement less restrictive controls for legal, technical or constitutional reasons.

All of the political challenges of making, implementing and enforcing FCTC-compliant laws, and the broad language of the article itself, likely contribute to the variation in laws banning advertising promotion and sponsorship in the ATSA countries. In an effort to develop more consistency and clarity in the application of FCTC Article 13, and to offer advice on best practices, the Conference of the Parties (COP), the governing body of the FCTC, adopted guidelines for the implementation of Article 13 in November 2008.[3]

ATSA Country Overview and Model Laws

Across the ATSA countries, there is a range of the depth and breadth of laws related to advertising, promotion and sponsorship and the standards of enforcement. Table 5.1 presents a rough outline of the components in each country. Some countries, including Mauritius and South Africa, have extensive laws and regulations, and even report some enforcement or are actively seeking to improve it.[4] In many of the ATSA countries – including Burkina Faso, Eritrea, Nigeria, Tanzania and Zambia – there are national laws or proclamations banning particularly tobacco advertising, but with limited or no reported enforcement. In a few of the countries – including Ghana and Malawi – there are only very limited pieces of relevant legislation and/or regulation.

Achieving success

In South Africa and Mauritius, comprehensive tobacco control legislation is in place, and both countries have strong provisions for advertising, promotion and sponsorship bans. Both countries continue to face the challenges of enforcement, but are showing evidence of success. In Kenya, as of 2007–8, there is new comprehensive legislation that includes FCTC-compliant bans on advertising, promotion and sponsorship, and both government and civil society are actively pursuing enforcement. In Cameroon, a targeted national law (i.e. not part of national comprehensive tobacco control legislation) has proven to be effective against advertising and some forms of promotion and sponsorship.

Since its first round of major tobacco control legislation in 1993, South Africa has created and implemented very progressive advertising, promotion and sponsorship policies – there is a near complete ban in place. Importantly, civil society and government have monitored the laws since implementation, and successive amendments to the initial laws have sought to close common loopholes exploited by the industry, including such strategies as coupons for promotions and the use of misleading advertising claims such as "mild." Tobacco control advocates continue to pursue certain other aspects that are especially exploited by the industry, such as flagrant abuse of point-of-sale displays (discussed below). Promotion and sponsorship are also almost completely banned with only a few remaining issues, including only limited restrictions on charitable contributions (in contrast to a total ban on these contributions) and other CSR strategies on the part of the industry.

In Mauritius, a combination of government leadership and initiative, NGO activism and media attention keep the 1999 ban on advertising, promotion and sponsorship effective. Civil society organizations and the media put pressure on the government to uphold the rules, particularly by encouraging increased enforcement measures. These efforts appear to be leading toward renewed action by enforcement officials within the Ministry of Health and Quality of Life (MOH&QL) to increase compliance. While the 1999 legislation created a total ban on tobacco advertising, promotion and sponsorship, some issues persisted and the government followed up in 2008 with new regulations. These new regulations help to close some of the loopholes that had been exploited by the industry, for example extending the advertising ban to anything closely associated with a tobacco product and prohibiting the supply of free products, discounted tobacco and tobacco as prizes. In perhaps the most exciting development, the 2008 regulations ban all CSR activities in Mauritius, and British American Tobacco (BAT) reports that it has been forced to curtail its charitable giving almost completely.[5]

Table 5.1. Status of advertising, promotion and sponsorship requirements and prohibitions in the 12 ATSA countries

Country	Name of legislation	13:4(a) False and misleading APS prohibited	13:4 (b) Health warning on APS	13:4 (c) Incentives to consumers prohibited	13:4 (d) Company reports on APS expenditures	13:4 (e) Ban on radio (R), TV and print (P) advertising	13:4 (f) Ban on event sponsorship	Corporate social responsibility	Penalty
Burkina Faso	Raabo (1988), amended 2001	No	No	No	No	R, TV, billboard (U)	No	No	Unknown
Cameroon	Law #2006/018 (2006)	Yes	No	No	No	R, TV, billboard, P, films (U)	Sports	Scholarships	Unknown
Eritrea	Proclamation #143 (2004)	Yes	Yes	Yes	No	R, TV, P (some enforcement)	Yes	No	Up to 5,000 NkF
Ghana	1981 ministerial directive	No	No	No	No	R, TV, P	No	No	N/A
Kenya	Tobacco Control Act (2007)	Yes	Yes	Yes	Yes (by request of the MoH)	All media (nascent enforcement)	Yes	No	Up to Ks 1,000,000/ prison (6 months– 3 years)
Malawi	—	No	No	No	No	R, TV	No	Scholarships	Unknown

Country	Legislation								Penalties
Mauritius	Public Health Act (1999); Public Health Regs (2008)	Yes	N/A (total advertising ban)	Yes	N/A	Yes	All media, including the internet (some enforcement)	Yes	Rs 5,000–10,000/prison (≤ 12 months)
Nigeria	Tobacco Smoking Act (Decree #20) (1990); APCON*	Yes (U)	Yes (U)	No	No	No	No	No	N5000/prison (3 years)
Senegal	Law n°81–58 (1981)	No	No	No	No	No	Limited (U)	No	N/A
South Africa	Tobacco Products Control Act (1993); amended in 1999, 2007 and 2008	Yes	Yes	Yes (except point of sale)	Yes	Some	Yes (some enforcement)	No	< R50,000
Tanzania	Tobacco (Products Regulation) Act (2003)	No	No	Yes (U)	No	No	Not clear	No	5–20 million TSh, and/or prison (3 years)
Zambia	1992, reiterated in 2008 (I#39)	No	No	No	No	No	No	No	Unknown

(U) = Unenforced; * Nigeria's National Senate passed comprehensive tobacco control legislation in March 2011 that has FCTC-compliant provisions for a total ban, but the ban is not yet in effect.

While it might be premature to identify Kenya as a success story, its recent efforts to enforce the advertising, promotion and sponsorship ban from the new comprehensive legislation – the Tobacco Control Act of 2007 (TCA) – are very encouraging. The act is FCTC-compliant, for example prohibiting tobacco advertising of any kind (Article 25.2: "on any medium of electronic, print or any other form of communication); the use of "lifestyle advertising"; sponsorship of all public and private events including sporting, cultural and artistic performances; and personal promotions such as free gifts or rewards.[6] While advocates have expressed serious concern about enforcement, recent efforts to police violators of the advertising ban pair civil society organizations and government together in the effort. The TCA (Part VII) authorizes existing public health and law enforcement officials to enforce the act, but a great deal remains unclear in terms of how this will happen effectively. Fortunately, recent efforts have concentrated on training public health inspectors to enforce both advertising and public smoking bans. The nongovernmental Institute for Legislative Affairs (ILA) and the Ministry of Health (MoH) have been training inspectors on the use of a checklist for inspections, and these officials are now compelled to give monthly reports on actions they have taken. Nevertheless, significantly more still needs to be done for effective monitoring of the ban's implementation. To date, it continues to be civil society organizations that are executing and funding much of the monitoring of enforcement. The ministry is convening official meetings between the key stakeholders including civil society and the enforcement agencies to discuss progress and future strategy.

In Cameroon, the government has thus far taken the path of targeted legislation. Though Cameroon does not yet have comprehensive tobacco control legislation, Act N° 2006/018 (29 December, 2006) directly addresses tobacco advertising by banning any advertising advocating tobacco use in print media; on television, radio, billboards and posters; or in movies (see Article 39). There is also a ban on outgoing cross-border advertising and several types of sponsorship. In terms of CSR, the act prohibits the offering of tobacco industry-sponsored scholarships to students at all grade levels. Though there is no empirical research yet, anecdotally the ban is thought to be well observed and enforced. Furthermore, the ATSA team from Cameroon reports that corresponding fines are substantial. More research on the efficacy of Cameroon's ban would be useful to understanding the option of a targeted law.

"Medium" cases

Among ATSA countries with more limited laws or regulations pertaining to advertising, promotion and sponsorship, there are two common scenarios: a law exists restricting or banning advertising and sponsorship but it is vague and easy to circumvent, and/or a law exists – even a good one – but it has not been enforced effectively. Generating political and institutional enthusiasm to enforce vague laws and/or unfunded mandates is proving to be challenging in any context.

In Nigeria, tobacco control advocates have struggled for over two decades first with poorly developed rules and then with subsequent rules that had particularly strong influence from the industry. First, in 1990, the Tobacco Smoking Act had not much more than provisions for warnings on advertising and sponsorship – strategies that have never been proven to be effective from a public health perspective.

In 2002, the government's Advertising Practitioners Promotion Control (APCON) directives created partial bans on tobacco advertising. The directives ban tobacco advertisement on television, radio and in the print media. Anecdotally, these bans have been well observed. But the bans allow for nonproduct advertising such as CSR activities and sponsorships of events (with no product advertising), which have allowed the industry to keep a high profile in the country. Many advocates argue that these bans are only a limited improvement on the initial rules because the industry had considerable influence in making them, and they sought to make the rules in anticipation of foiling any future legislation that would be much harsher for them. The tobacco advocacy community in Nigeria explicitly cites the enormous weaknesses in the existing rules. In part in reaction to the experience with these substandard rules, the new comprehensive tobacco control legislation passed by the National Senate in early 2011 has strong provisions for complete FCTC-compliant bans on advertising, promotion and sponsorship. The new challenges will be to implement and enforce the new and improved rules.

Tanzania also has limited legislated bans on advertising, promotion and sponsorship through the Tobacco (Products Regulation) Act of 2003 (TPRA), but the law has proven to be both weak and full of loopholes and enforcement has been problematic. The most successful part of the act is a near-total ban on radio and television tobacco advertising. There is, however, no clear ban on print advertising for tobacco products. In fact, by statute, tobacco advertising in print is not prohibited and instead must only carry health warnings. Similarly, promotional activities are legislated only in a limited way with most provisions targeted only at the protection of minors. For example, product giveaways remain legal involving consenting adults, and the Tanzania Tobacco Company continues to sponsor major public events such as music concerts.

Even provisions that Tanzanian tobacco control advocates thought were in effect seem to lack any force of law. For example, tobacco control advocates thought that the TPRA prohibited billboard advertising, but the tobacco lobby requested an interpretation from the attorney general, who suggested that such advertising did not fall under the law. Billboard advertising remains widespread. Similarly, the act is supposed to prohibit advertising that suggests sporting, professional or sexual prowess, but such lifestyle advertising persists widely. In general, the government continues to allow sexually charged advertising aimed at young people with only minimal health warnings.

Finally, in Tanzania, there are no limitations of any kind on CSR activities. The law does not prohibit tobacco manufacturers or marketers from giving to anything that might be considered a good cause. Remarkably, donations are even permitted to health, social service, educational or religious institutions. All decisions to accept such gifts are at the total discretion of the donor and beneficiary.

In Burkina Faso, both an insufficient law and a lack of implementation and enforcement contribute to a troubled ban on advertising, promotion and sponsorship. The Raabo of 1988 has basic provisions for regulating tobacco advertising. In 2001, Law N° 25-2001 increased controls on advertising, including banning tobacco publicity from radio and television, but it is reportedly frequently subject to various interpretations and manipulation.[7] Empirically, it is clear that advertising activities continue. The 2006 Global Youth Tobacco Survey (GYTS) reports from interviews with 13–15-year-olds that 69 percent had seen pro-cigarette advertisements on billboards in the previous 30 days; 64 percent saw pro-cigarette advertisements in newspapers or magazines in the previous 30 days; nearly a quarter of respondents had an object with a cigarette brand logo; and 11.6 percent were offered free cigarettes by a tobacco company representative. It is not clear what the new comprehensive legislation passed by the legislature in 2010 will accomplish toward a complete ban on advertising, promotion and sponsorship.

In Zambia, the Public Health Regulations of 1992 restricted tobacco advertising, promotion and sponsorship, but the provisions were broad, somewhat ambiguous and poorly enforced. For example, the 1992 regulation bans or restrains tobacco advertising in the "mass media," free products or samples, the giving of money and/or cigarettes to winners of contests and tobacco companies sponsoring sporting activities. By all anecdotal accounts from Zambian ATSA team members, it is clear that none of these measures have been well enforced. The ATSA team from Zambia does note that the government has expended some resources to sensitize the public to the issue of the dangers of tobacco use, and ongoing research is examining this issue more systematically. The 1992 ban was reiterated in 1999, and again after FCTC accession in 2008 (Instrument #39), but tobacco control advocates believe that even the new instrument is not specific and comprehensive enough in its wording. There is ongoing research to determine the extent of ban violations, and the ways in which the tobacco industry is circumventing or could circumvent the ban.

In Eritrea, Proclamation 143/2004 of 2004 calls for total bans on advertising, promotion and sponsorship, but the principal issue remains a lack of enforcement. In fact, most importantly, the proclamation identifies no body that is responsible for enforcing the law. Most advocates believe that until such a body is identified and empowered, there will be little to no enforcement. By FCTC standards the statute is actually pretty strict, and even extends to offers of free gifts, indirect sponsorships and other manners in which the industry commonly seeks to circumvent weaker legislation. Nevertheless, ATSA team members from Eritrea report significant exposure to advertisements and promotional messages, particularly from non-Eritrean television channels. The team's 2009 survey of students and school staff revealed that 37 percent of students and 33 percent of school personnel reported seeing tobacco advertisements in magazines or on the internet in the previous 30 days; 41 percent of the students and 46 percent of school personnel said they saw tobacco advertisements on billboards; and 52 percent of the students and 47 percent of school personnel said they saw tobacco advertisements when they watched live sports or cultural events.

Minimal provisions

Several ATSA countries demonstrate very low standards in terms of advertising, promotion and sponsorship bans. Senegal is a particularly troubling case because extremely progressive legislation from 1981 was mostly reversed in 1985, and advocates have only been able to regain small pieces of it. However, in at least two other country cases – Ghana and Malawi – there are some encouraging signs of strong societal norms of support for such bans.

In 1981, Senegal introduced Law n°81-58, which was rather progressive for the time and place. The law banned radio, television and print tobacco advertising, particularly emphasizing tobacco-free media for youths; banned posters, billboards, leaflets and neon signs; had point-of-sale provisions (permitting brand and contents only); banned product giveaways and person-to-person selling; and prohibited sponsorship of arts, sports and other public events. In another show of its progressive nature, the law included action against cross-border advertising, a feature still lacking in many countries' provisions across the globe. But Law n°85-23 (25 February 1985) overturned most or all of the sponsorship bans in the earlier tobacco legislation. According to anecdotal accounts, the media industry was vehemently in opposition to the law and lobbied the government vigorously to change it. While there is no empirical record that any part of the 1981 provision was ever effectively enforced, the spirit was impressive. Since 2005, there have been pieces of legislation that have started to reintroduce some of the original tobacco control bans – including those on advertising, sponsorship and promotion – but by all anecdotal accounts by stakeholders at ATSA country-level meetings, enforcement of these new laws has been limited.

While there is some ambiguity about the exact nature of bans related to advertising, promotion and sponsorship in Malawi, it is clear that these laws are limited, and there is ample evidence of ongoing advertising and promotion. There is reportedly a directive issued by the Ministry of Health in the 1990s that bans radio advertising. The ban apparently may also apply to television, though no written directive has been produced by the government or tobacco control advocates. In an encouraging sign, however, both bans are well observed according to the 2009 survey conducted by the ATSA team from Malawi.[8] There is no ban in the print media, and such advertisements are prevalent in Malawi. The ATSA team reports that BAT and the new domestic manufacturer, Nyasa, are actively promoting tobacco, particularly through smoking parties (often with paid celebrities and tobacco-inspired games and prizes); branded umbrellas, sunshields and ashtrays; and visually attractive, digitally produced posters and flyers distributed and posted in many public places.

In Ghana, there is no national legislation banning tobacco advertising, promotion and sponsorship, but there is a directive from 1981 by the Provisional National Defense Council banning advertising on television and radio and in print that appears to have significant positive effect. In this case, it appears to be as much a strong societal norm as anything clearly legal that is perpetuating the ban. Advocates report plenty of violations of the directive, but there is also plenty of circumstantial evidence of societal pressure against a strong public presence of tobacco. In one instance in 2002, for example, BAT attempted to paint one large wall of Kaneshie Market with a giant logo of a popular brand. But people demanded emphatically that the advertisement be removed, and BAT acquiesced and painted over the advertisement.[9]

The Central Challenge of Enforcement

Enforcement of existing restrictions on advertising promotion and sponsorship is arguably the largest challenge facing every ATSA country. Not only must penalties and types of banned media be clearly stated and well understood, but the power of the state must be vested in an authority capable of enforcing the advertising ban. The designated enforcement authority must also have appropriate training for its workers and an incentive to enforce the ban. It is helpful if the enforcement authority is a government agency, and has the strong and explicit backing of the state, but it also may be possible for civil society and some level(s) of government to collaborate to raise awareness of advertising bans and identify flagrant violations, as has been occurring in Kenya since 2009. Developing enforcement capacity will continue to be a major challenge for years to come in all ATSA countries.

An enforceable ban must also have clearly defined penalties that fit the crime effectively. An example of a case where the crime and possible penalties do not align effectively is in Nigeria, where the penalty for an infraction of the advertising ban is 5,000 naira (approximately US$30) or three years imprisonment. There is an obvious major difference between the severities of these two possible penalties and no clear provision for when one or the other of the punishments would be invoked – what firm would not just pay the small fine? Furthermore, without proper codification of the penalties, any application of these disparate punishments would appear arbitrary to even a casual observer. In contrast, in Mauritius and South Africa, the penalties for violating advertising bans are incremental and better match the severity of the infraction. Thus, there is a rather low penalty for a violation of an advertising ban by a street merchant or shopkeeper and a much higher penalty for a violation of a television or radio ban by a media company. If a penalty appears to be arbitrary or is applied inconsistently, there is less of a possibility that a ban will be enforced or accepted by society.

Youths and Advertising: Empirical Findings

The ongoing struggle to implement and enforce advertising, promotion and sponsorship bans is particularly relevant to the broader goal of reducing youth smoking. In short, it is evident that advertising and promotion efforts are aimed particularly at young people. The empirical evidence, particularly from the GYTS, is troubling. The GYTS findings from each country provide comprehensive quantitative data addressing the penetration of tobacco advertising in ATSA (and many other) countries. First, as Table 5.2 presents, the GYTS surveys find that advertising for cigarettes in the print media and on billboards is widespread in nearly every ATSA country. Across the ATSA countries, the most recent GYTS surveys indicate that an average of 62 percent of youths (defined as 13–15-year-olds) had seen pro-cigarette advertisements on billboards within the previous 30 days, and that 57 percent saw pro-cigarette advertisements in newspapers or magazines.[10] In a more encouraging sign, however, on average, 75 percent of youths in ATSA countries had seen an anti-smoking message in the previous 30 days. In the eight ATSA countries where comparative GYTS data exist from two different time periods, six countries reported decreases in the amount of

Table 5.2. Youths and tobacco in the 12 ATSA countries

Country (survey year)	Anti-smoking message	Tobacco ad – billboard	Tobacco ad – print	Have object with brand logo	Offered free tobacco by rep.
Burkina Faso (2006)	76.80	69.00	64.00	24.40	11.60
Cameroon (2008)	79.00	65.90	54.40	13.50	6.40
Eritrea (2006)	67.50	44.60	49.10	20.00	12.40
Ghana (2006)	65.90	48.80	44.50	15.70	14.50
Kenya (2007)	81.70	81.10	68.40	19.50	13.20
Malawi (2005)	84.90	53.20	50.30	22.30	13.20
Mauritius (2008)	84.90	N/A	51.40	N/A	8.40
Nigeria (2008)	66.00	50.15	53.15	21.10	11.85
Senegal (2007)	76.40	75.50	64.70	20.60	11.40
South Africa (2002)	75.40	68.10	69.50	18.80	15.00
Tanzania (2003)	71.90	70.47	57.07	19.43	7.70
Zambia (2007)	73.75	53.35	54.60	18.10	16.00
Average:	75.35	61.83	56.76	19.40	11.80

Source: Global Youth Tobacco Survey (various countries, various years).

pro-cigarette advertising to which youths reported being exposed, while two actually reported increases. However, both the increases and decreases were generally small. Another troubling finding from the GYTS advertising data is that two of the relatively successful countries, South Africa and Mauritius, have a higher than average percentage of youths reporting exposure to cigarette advertising. It is readily apparent from these data that cigarette advertising is widespread and not enough is being done to eliminate, or even mitigate, its presence among the youth.

The Continued Cunning Ways of the Tobacco Industry

Even in countries like South Africa or Mauritius that have complete bans on advertising and promotion, the industry continues to find new and creative ways to circumvent the law. One of the more common recent efforts has been the use of point-of-sale advertising to promote products. It is not unusual, for example, to enter a supermarket in either country and see a veritable wall of tobacco branding (sometimes many packages stacked together) that the industry claims is only "point of sale." Clearly, such efforts – often called "power walls" – are thinly veiled marketing ploys.[11]

Another technique that tobacco companies have been employing aggressively is what they describe as one-to-one communication between the tobacco firm and the customer. As Jimmi Rembiszewski, marketing director at BAT describes it: "We see this as marketing for a new era, where product brand communication is primarily based on one-to-one permission marketing to adult smokers, in much more focused, narrower channels, with tight standards for age verification."[12] In fact, tobacco companies have recently touted their commitment to marketing and advertising principles that seek to target individual adults through strict market segmentation. These principles are endowed in a document created in 2001 and frequently referenced by tobacco companies, the International Tobacco Marketing Standards.[13] In this document, the tobacco companies outline their commitment to engage in advertising, promotion and sponsorship only in media and events that are primarily targeted at adult audiences. Unfortunately, it is often impossible to differentiate an audience profile, particularly in developing countries where there is little quantitative audience analysis. In addition, verification of this enforcement commitment by company subsidiaries is not accounted for in any of the available documentation. One might surmise from these statements that tobacco companies have interest only in marketing to adults, but the on-the-ground reality is different. In South Africa and Malawi for example, stakeholders at ATSA meetings report that tobacco companies are throwing "smoking parties" for their customers. Not only are these parties often for people of all ages – many patrons are below the legal age for smoking – but the industry defends its actions by claiming that such activities are communication between its firms and consenting adult consumers of tobacco products. Perhaps most troubling in the South African case is that the industry is aggressively defending this behavior as a legal right and is seeking to protect it constitutionally in the judicial system.[14] In early 2011, the North Gauteng High Court rejected the industry's claim.

Importantly, countries must be prepared to follow up with revisions to initial regulations when necessary, particularly as the industry tests the boundaries of the existing laws. Both Mauritius and South Africa continue with these efforts to keep up with the industry. In Mauritius, since the 2008 regulations, tobacco advocates continue to monitor closely all aspects of tobacco control, particularly the activities of the tobacco industry. Civil society organizations such as ViSa regularly inform the MOH&QL about the industry's latest tactics and the noncompliance of tobacco regulation by other businesses. Another key aspect in Mauritius continues to be the positive role of the media, which regularly reports on noncompliance by businesses.

Unfortunately, one of the principal problems is that the industry has the resources to keep finding new ways to test the laws, and both civil society and government have to expend their own resources just to keep up. While this might be feasible in wealthier African countries, there is genuine concern that the industry can simply outspend its opponents as necessary. In Malawi, for example, the Youth Alliance in Social and Economic Development (YASED) reported in 2009 that the industry has been manipulating language in the warnings attached to its advertisements. Instead of stating that smoking "is" hazardous to your health, the domestic Nyasa Manufacturing Company has been running advertisements in national newspapers that state in Chichewa, one of the country's principal languages, that smoking "may" be hazardous to your health. In most countries, this type of warning is unacceptable, but other than speaking out publicly, the tobacco control community in Malawi has little alternative recourse.

The scourge of corporate social responsibility

As advertising and promotion are banned in an increasing number of countries, tobacco companies have increasingly turned to CSR activities as an alternative marketing strategy. Documented corporate responsibility projects in the ATSA countries include school supply giveaways, reforestation projects (Eritrea), HIV/AIDS awareness education (South Africa and Zambia), black economic empowerment (South Africa), crime prevention, anti-malarial spraying (Zambia), water well projects, athletics sponsorships and academic scholarships. A number of ATSA countries have included restrictions or bans on various forms of CSR projects in their tobacco control legislation, most notably Mauritius, which bans all such activities. The most common recent bans relating to CSR are on academic scholarships (e.g. Cameroon and Malawi) and sponsorship of national cultural events (e.g. Ghana and Tanzania).

The shift of tobacco companies from direct advertising in mainstream media to CSR and other forms of marketing is nothing more than a sharp-edged business decision in response to social pressure.[15] The return from CSR activities for tobacco companies is increased respectability, legitimacy and the right to continue marketing a product that kills people when used as intended.

Tobacco company CSR should be seen for what it is – an attempt to subvert the intention of the FCTC Article 13 and to restrict the development and/or implementation of effective global health policy.

Conclusion

Developing comprehensive tobacco control legislation that effectively bans advertising, promotion and sponsorship is a worthy goal for every country. However, a law itself is not a panacea that will solve the public health problem of widespread tobacco consumption. The obstacle of enforcing comprehensive bans is particularly daunting in developing nations that lack a strong central government and the capacity – including resources – to enforce tobacco laws. When the myriad of law enforcement challenges confronting most developing countries are considered, it is unlikely that enforcing a ban on tobacco advertising tops the list of any law enforcement agency. However, by combining the talents of civil society and the authority of public health officials, it is possible to develop awareness and more effective enforcement initiatives.

Moreover, a reasonable case can be made for promoting new or amended legislation – as opposed to attempting to enforce existing laws that are poorly conceived – as the best way forward. In recent years, the countries that have begun to enforce comprehensive advertising, promotion and sponsorship bans have done so with laws specifying the precise types of advertising, promotion and sponsorship that are outlawed and providing details on how enforcement would be carried out. These statutes provide a body of laws that can serve as a model for other countries. Having a codified plan to make such bans a reality is an important first step.

Finally, it is particularly important to reemphasize that tobacco companies form a powerful lobby in many ATSA countries, and it will require the coordinated efforts of civil society, academic scholars and government to develop and enforce advertising, promotion and sponsorship bans. The challenge of controlling advertising is particularly important when one considers that youths are often the primary targets of tobacco company marketing efforts. Consistently, surveys across the developing world indicate just how pernicious and widespread cigarette advertising is in both the mainstream and alternative media. Also, tobacco companies are beginning to market nonsmoking tobacco products more aggressively, such as snuff and snus, which will present a whole new set of challenges. Ensuring that comprehensive advertising bans cover nonsmoking tobacco products is important. Civil society organizations and governments must monitor the implementation and enforcement vigilantly, and be sufficiently flexible to amend the regulations where necessary.

Notes

1　H. Saffer and F. Chaloupka, "The Effect of Tobacco Advertising Bans on Tobacco Consumption," *Journal of Health Economics* 19.6 (2000): 1117–37. This research also demonstrates that limited restrictions on tobacco advertising and promotion have little or no effect on consumption.

2　World Health Organization, *Framework Convention on Tobacco Control* (2005). Online at: http://whqlibdoc.who.int/publications/2003/9241591013.pdf (accessed 20 July 2011).

3　For the COP FCTC Article 13 guidelines (November 2008), see the World Health Organization official website: http://www.who.int/fctc/guidelines/article_13.pdf (accessed 20 July 2011).

4　Kenya, which passed comprehensive tobacco control legislation in 2007, is working on initial enforcement measures.

5　British American Tobacco, "*British American Tobacco Annual Report 2009*" (2009). Online at: http://www.bat.com/annualreport2009 (accessed 20 July 2011).

6　Goverment of the Republic of Kenya, Tobacco Control Act (2007).

7　Ministry of Health, Burkina Faso, "National Strategic Plan on Tobacco Control 2009–13," 29 April 2009, 17.

8　Malawi ATSA Team, "Tobacco advertising, promotion and sponsorship: A Malawi research agenda towards MPOWER No.5," working paper, December 2009.

9　*Accra Daily Mail*, "British American Tobacco Sensitive to Public Opinion," 6 February 2002.

10　Unfortunately, the GYTS survey does not ask about cigarette advertising on the radio or on television.

11　Physicians for a Smoke-Free Canada, "Filter Tips: Taking the Power out of Power Walls" (2006). Online at: http://www.smoke-free.ca/filtertips-5/retail.htm (accessed 27 August 2010).

12　Public statement from the marketing director of BAT, J. Rembiszewski (2009). Online at: http://www.bat.com/group/sites/uk__3mnfen.nsf/vwPagesWebLive/DO78BDW6?op endocument&SKN=1&TMP=1 (accessed 4 November 2009).

13　Companies that claim to adhere to the International Tobacco Marketing Standards include British American Tobacco, Imperial Tobacco and Philip Morris. The standards are available online at: http://www.bat.com/group/sites/uk__3mnfen. nsf/vwPagesWebLive/DO52ADRK/$FILE/medMD74MLPM.pdf?openelement (accessed 10 July 2011).

14　See BAT–SA's website for their explanation of the legal challenge: http:// www.batsa.co.za/group/sites/BAT_7N3ML8.nsf/vwPagesWebLive/ DO7YELCZ?opendocument&SKN=1 (accessed 10 July 2011).

15　G. Hastings and J. Liberman, "Tobacco corporate social responsibility and fairy godmothers: The Framework Convention on Tobacco Control slays a modern myth," *Tobacco Control* 18 (2009): 73–4. Also, for background on BAT's corporate social responsibility program, see J. Collin and A. Gilmore, "Corporate (Anti)Social (Ir) Responsibility: Transnational Tobacco Companies and the Attempted Subversion of Global Health Policy," *Global Social Policy* 2.3 (2004): 354–60.

Chapter 6

THE PURSUIT OF PACKAGING AND LABELING REQUIREMENTS

Jeffrey Drope and Melanie Baier

According to the FCTC "Guidelines for the Implementation of Article 11," well-designed health warnings and messages are an important part of a range of effective measures to communicate health risks and to reduce tobacco use.[1] Research evidence demonstrates that the effectiveness of health warnings and messages increases with their prominence.[2] In comparison with small, text-only health warnings, larger warnings with pictures are more likely to be noticed, better communicate health risks, provoke a greater emotional response and increase the motivation of tobacco users to quit or to decrease their tobacco consumption.[3] Larger picture warnings are also more likely to retain their effectiveness over time and are particularly effective in communicating health effects to low-literacy populations, children and young people. Other elements that enhance effectiveness include locating health warnings and messages at the top of the principal display areas; the use of color rather than just black and white; requiring that multiple health warnings rotate and appear concurrently; and periodic revision of health warnings and messages.

One of the particularly compelling possibilities with packaging and labeling restrictions is that it is not always necessary to address this issue using national legislation, though it certainly can be – and has been – done this way. In countries that are struggling with the passing of new legislation, this less burdensome option offers many possibilities. In fact, as this chapter demonstrates, many countries allow regulatory agencies, often but not always in health ministries, to handle many and even most issues regarding packaging and labeling. Health warnings can often be made obligatory through bureaucratic instruments. Furthermore, in the cases where there is national legislation mandating new packaging and labeling requirements, these specific health- and/or standards-related agencies remain central actors

Table 6.1. Packaging and labeling provisions in the 12 ATSA countries

Country	Pictorial	Size and placement	Font and color	Language	Content and rotation	Constituents and emissions
Burkina Faso	No	None	None	French	No rotation	Yes
Cameroon	No	50% (two principal sides)	Black text on white background; 16 pt and uppercase	French and English	No rotation	Yes
Eritrea	No	30–50%	Black text on white background	Tigrigna, Arabic and English	Rotating collection (6 warnings)*	Yes
Ghana	No	50%	Black text on white background	English	Rotating collection (3 warnings)*	No
Kenya	Yes (not implemented)	50% of total 30% of front	Black text on white background; 17 pt	English and Kiswahili	Rotating collection (13 warnings)*	Yes (but no actual amounts)
Malawi	*No packaging and labeling provisions*					
Mauritius	Yes	65% (total) 40% front (French) 90% back (English)	White and black; minimum of 10 pt Helvetica font	French and English (both official languages)	Rotating collection (10 picture and 8 text warnings)*	Prohibited

Nigeria**	No	No size requirement; placed on base of front	White text on black background; minimum of 6 pt font	English or Nigerian language (only in English)	No rotation required (but 5 different messages)	Yes
Senegal	No	None	None	French	No rotation	Yes
South Africa	Yes (not implemented)	15% front 25% back 20% of one side	Multiple and rotating colors; text 60–70% of warning		Rotating collection; quitline*	Yes (but under review as of 2010)
Tanzania	No	None	None	English and Kiswahili	Rotating collection (10 warnings)	No
Zambia	No	None	Black on white, or white on black	No regulation	No rotation	No

* Prohibit false and misleading warnings labels such as "mild." ** Nigeria's National Senate passed a new law in 2011, but regulations mandating new packaging regulations have not been developed yet. The legislation, however, gives the MoH the legal mandate to promulgate FCTC-compliant labeling rules.

because they ultimately generate the relevant regulation and undertake the task of implementing and enforcing the law and regulation.

Another theme that emerges in this chapter is that advocates and policymakers alike have to be flexible and anticipate revising the regulations or even changing the laws as time passes and new challenges develop. Both Mauritius and South Africa have amended their regulations as the countries sought to improve their regulation and as they needed to close loopholes that the tobacco industry had discovered. Countries have to be prepared for a lengthy process that will be ongoing and require competent and vigilant monitoring.

It is also evident that enforcement may be more tractable for packaging and labeling than many other potential tobacco control interventions. Efforts to inspect packages can be a small part of relevant agencies' existing mandates. For example, the agencies that maintain standards look at all aspects of consumer products, and customs officials randomly inspect any imports. With some well-targeted training and without too much additional resource expense, enforcing these laws and regulations can be done quickly and effectively.

As Table 6.1 illustrates, as in most areas of the Framework Convention on Tobacco Control (FCTC), the levels of packaging and labeling regulations and requirements demonstrate considerable variation across the African Tobacco Situational Analysis (ATSA) countries, and are progressing at varying paces. Mauritius represents the most advanced country in the region, with not only pictorial warnings but also with warnings that comprise among the largest proportion of the package in the world (as of 2011). In contrast, Malawi lags significantly behind every other country, having yet to enact any substantial tobacco control legislation or even narrow regulations.

This chapter follows a slightly different structure than the other policy-specific chapters. Instead of grouping the countries in terms of their overall performance in the policy area, the chapter is organized by the different components of packaging and labeling including pictorial warnings, size and placement, font size and color, language, content and rotation, and the disclosure of constituents and emissions. Within each subsection, however, there is a discussion and comparison of the performance of each country in that area. What is interesting is that certain countries perform well in a particular area. For example, Mauritius is a world leader in the size and graphic nature of the warning, while South Africa is still seeking pictorial warnings, but uses color in its text warnings better than most countries in the world.

The Ultimate Goal – Graphic Pictorial Warnings

Article 11.1(b)(v) of the FCTC specifies that health warnings and messages on tobacco product packaging and labeling may be in the form of or include pictures or pictograms.[1] Evidence shows that health warnings and messages that contain both pictures and text are far more effective than those that use text only. Moreover, graphic pictures tend to communicate risk more effectively. They also have the added benefit of potentially reaching people with low levels of literacy and those who cannot read the language(s) in which the text of the health warning or message is written.[5] For these reasons, the FCTC suggests that each party consider the placement of pictorial warnings on each of the principal sides of the package. These images should be in full color and be of appropriate size (as per the size requirements).

Currently, among the 12 ATSA countries, only Mauritius has graphic warning labels. In fact, Mauritius has extremely comprehensive and explicit legislation regarding pictorial warnings. The country's Public Health Act of 2008 (Fourth Schedule, Point 4-D) requires that pictograms should be on the front and the back and must be "displayed in such a manner and in such a template as approved by the Minister [of Health]." As of 2009, there are ten different pictorial messages that rotate along with a collection of text-driven messages.

Several other ATSA countries are in process or perhaps soon-to-be in process in regard to graphic health warnings. South Africa's legislation also includes the requirement of pictorial warnings, and proposed new graphic warnings are currently in the regulatory process in the Department of Health (the South Africa ATSA program provided resources to a major civil society organization seeking to support the department with relevant research). Similarly, Kenya's comprehensive legislation in 2007 permits the health ministry to regulate pictorial warnings, but as of early 2011, nothing has yet been done in this regard.

Size and Placement are Essential

Research demonstrates unequivocally that the size and placement of the warning labels affect their effectiveness: larger and more prominent labels are more effective. Accordingly, Article 11.1(b)(iii) of the FCTC specifies that each party shall adopt and implement effective measures to ensure that health warnings and messages are large, clear, visible and legible. Article 11.1(b)(v) mandates that health warnings and messages on tobacco product packaging and labeling should be 50 percent or more – but no less than 30 percent – of the principal display areas. The FCTC guidelines also emphasize that the location and layout of health warnings and messages on a package should ensure maximum visibility, meaning that warnings should be placed on both the front and the back principal areas. Research indicates that health warnings and messages are more visible at the top rather than the bottom of the front and back of packages.[6] Also, the labels are required to be positioned in such a way that the opening of the package does not damage or conceal the warning message. Finally, the FCTC suggests that parties consider requiring additional labels to be placed on the remaining sides of the package.

The variation in size and placement is considerable across the ATSA countries, but at least a handful of countries have FCTC-compliant or better rules. Mauritius currently has the most rigorous legislation in terms of size. Mauritius' new 2008 legislation codifies the obligation to cover 65 percent of the total tobacco packaging with the warning. A warning in French covers 40 percent of the front panel, while the back panel is to be occupied with a warning label in English that covers at least 90 percent of the surface area. The Public Health Act requires that one of the remaining sides have a message reading "smoking kills" in English while the opposite side should read "*la cigarette tue*" in French. Both of these labels should occupy 65 percent of the side panels. None of these labels should be placed in such a location that they are severed upon the opening of the package.

Cameroon, Eritrea and Kenya's laws closely follow the recommendations of the FCTC, requiring between 30 percent and 50 percent of tobacco products' principal areas to be covered by warnings. Cameroon's Decree 967 from the Ministry of Health (MoH) and the Ministry of Commerce (25 June 2007) details new regulations that state that health warnings must cover at least 50 percent of the two principal covers. Proclamation 143/2004 of Eritrea requires that warnings should cover 50 percent or more of the two principal display areas (front and back), but must be no less than 30 percent of the principal display areas. Kenya's legislation, the Tobacco Control Act of 2007, stipulates that packaging is to display two warning labels covering at least 50 percent of the total surface area, which includes a regulation that 30 percent of the front of the package be covered by a warning.

South Africa's warning size regulations from 1994–5 fall slightly short of FCTC-compliance, but are in the process of revision. The regulations require that the health warnings cover 15 percent of the front principal panel (at the top, but unbroken by the package opening), 25 percent of the back principal panel (at the top) and 20 percent of the top of one of the long sides of the package. However, as compelled by Bill B24-2008, the MoH is in the process of developing new regulations that will require not only pictorial warnings but also FCTC-compliant sizing.

From 1989 until 2009, Ghana had only minimal regulation obligating warning labels of 5 percent of the front of tobacco product packaging, but new administrative policies passed in 2009 – and intended as a stopgap until new comprehensive legislation is passed – now obligate that warnings cover

50 percent of both the front and back of the package. The pending legislation has strict labeling requirements that surpass FCTC minimum standards.

Until 2011, Nigeria had very poor packaging and labeling rules, but with new legislation, positive changes should come quickly. The Advertising Practitioners Promotion Control (APCON) directive for warning labels had no size requirement, but stipulated that the warning must be printed at the base of the front of the pack or at the side with the added ambiguous provision, "without detracting from its prominence."[7] In 2011, Nigeria passed new comprehensive legislation that will make new packaging and warning policies FCTC-compliant. As of May 2011, the law was awaiting reconciliation between the two houses in the legislature and then presidential assent. After assent, the government will need to draft new packaging regulations to implement new labels.

The remaining ATSA countries lag considerably behind their peers in terms of warning size and placement requirements. While Zambia's Instrument #39 from 2008 improves upon the 1992 Public Health regulation by specifying that warnings must appear on the two largest sides of the pack, it still does not specify the size or placement of these labels. Currently, Burkina Faso, Tanzania and Senegal have vague warning requirements but prescribe no regulations regarding the size or placement of warning labels on tobacco products. Malawi has no formal warning regulations for packages.

Font and Color Requirements of Warnings

FCTC Article 11 specifies that the text of health warnings and messages should be in bold print in an easily legible font size and in a specified style and color(s) that enhance overall visibility and legibility. In most cases, ATSA countries use the direct wording of the FCTC in their legislation or regulation, requiring that the font of warning labels be "large, clear, visible, and legible."[8] In some cases, the countries are very precise about the meaning of "large, clear, visible, and legible," while in some cases there is no further explanation of its meaning, which generates considerable ambiguity. Following FCTC standards, it is also common for countries to require that labels be designed using contrasting colors. The popular method is to contrast black and white, although some research has argued that the use of color in warning labels is more effective.[9]

South Africa has some of the most progressive stipulations in terms of the color and font size of the required health warnings. The regulations require the following for each brand: black, red or blue print on a white background on one half of the packages, and white print on a black, red or blue background for the remaining packages. These color variations are required to be rotated.

The actual text must comprise a minimum of 60 percent of the warning but no more than 70 percent.[10] When South Africa's Department of Health publishes its regulations to implement pictorial warnings – perhaps in 2011 – color of text and background will likely be less important.

Consistent with the strict restrictions placed on the size and placement of warning labels, Mauritius also sets forth stringent guidelines on the font to be used for the warnings. Packaging of cigarettes, cigars (including cigarillos) and pipe tobacco must include labels that are white with black letters. For all other products, the labels must be in such a template that is approved by the health minister. Furthermore, the text of the labels for cigarettes, cigars and pipe tobacco must be displayed in Helvetica font that is no smaller than 10 point.

While relevant pieces of tobacco control legislation in both Cameroon and Kenya include the basic requirements of the FCTC, they also include more stringent regulations for font size and type. Article 4 of Decree 967 of the MoH and the Ministry of Commerce in Cameroon explicitly states that the text of the warning labels should be black on top of a white background. The decree also specifies that the warnings are required to be in at least a 16-point font and written in all uppercase letters. Kenya's 2007 legislation states that the warnings must be color-contrasting, which generally means that they should ideally be designed as white on black or black on white – however, if the company's box is principally black or white then the warning should have a different contrasting color scheme. The word "warning" must appear in all capital letters and the rest of the message in 17-point font unless this would take up more than 70 percent of the panel.

Nigeria, Zambia and Ghana all have some stipulations regarding color, and font as well in the case of Nigeria (though very weak). In Nigeria, the APCON directive's Section IV (iii) prescribes that the color of the warning on the pack is white type over a black background, with the type size to be no less than 6 points on packs of 10 or 20 cigarettes. When new regulations from the 2011 comprehensive bill are promulgated, Nigeria's font and color regulations will be FCTC-compliant. Zambia compels a contrasting color scheme (black on white, or white on black), but has no provision for font size. Ghana's recent directive from the Food and Drugs Board requires that the warnings be in black on a white background, with no font stipulation. Eritrea employs the FCTC wording of "large, clear, visible, and legible" in its legislation, and requires a black text on a white background.

The remaining ATSA countries – Burkina Faso, Senegal and Tanzania – do not have any font or color requirements for their warning labels and do not employ the FCTC language of "large, clear, visible, and legible." Malawi does not have warning label requirements.

Language of the Warning

Article 11 of the FCTC requires that all warnings be in the native language(s) of the principal party. Most ATSA countries currently require that the warning be in the official language(s). One of the principal language issues in many countries, however, is the sometimes large disconnect between "official" languages and the languages that many people actually speak and read. In other words, the warnings are ultimately in a language that a large proportion of the literate population cannot read. This dynamic – particularly coupled with low literacy rates – strongly reinforces the case for pictorial warnings.

Mauritius is perhaps fortunate in that it has both a high rate of literacy and that the vast majority of citizens read in one or both of the two official languages, French and English. By statute, warnings must be in both languages. As described above, Mauritius is also the only country that explicitly regulates the placement of the messages in each language.

Several other ATSA countries have language policies on packaging that effectively reach a significant majority of citizens. In Kenya and Tanzania, warnings must be in English and Kiswahili. While there are other languages in both countries, the addition of Kiswahili ensures that a much larger proportion of both countries' literate populations can read the warning. In Eritrea, warnings must be in Tigrigna, Arabic and English.

In most other ATSA countries, the laws only require warnings in the official language or languages. Cameroon's labeling regulations require that the warnings be in French and English, the two official languages. Similarly, the laws only require warnings in the official language in Ghana (English), Burkina Faso (French) and Senegal (French). In all four cases, the proportion of people speaking and reading the official language(s) is relatively small, which renders the text warnings much less effective.

In Nigeria, the 2002 APCON rules require that warnings be in "English or a Nigerian language." Not surprisingly, the industry has not developed any warnings in a Nigerian language. While any stipulation would be challenging in a country with at least nine major languages, it is clear that English warnings alone are ineffectual. The new law passed by the National Senate in 2011 permits the minister of health to obligate pictorial warnings, which once implemented should help to mitigate the enormous language challenge that Nigeria will face.

Zambia currently lacks language regulations for the warnings on their tobacco packaging. Malawi has no regulations for warnings, though the two principal manufacturers, British American Tobacco (BAT) and Nayasa Manufacturing Company (NMC) reportedly voluntarily use small letter warnings in English.

Content and Rotation of Warnings

In regards to message content, the FCTC states that using a range of health warnings and messages increases the likelihood of impact, as different health warnings and messages resonate with different people. The FCTC suggests that health warnings relate to different areas of tobacco use, including: advice on cessation, the addictive nature of tobacco, adverse economic and social outcomes, and the impact of tobacco use on significant others. Article 11 advises that regardless of the exact content of the warning, the message should be presented in a way that is authoritative and informative, but nonjudgmental. The FCTC also believes that health warnings and messages are likely to be more effective if they elicit unfavorable emotional associations with tobacco use and personalize the information to make the health warnings and messages more believable and personally relevant. The inclusion of a "quitline" number is also recommended in the 2008 FCTC guidelines to Article 11.[11]

Research has shown that the impact of health warnings and messages that are repeated tends to decrease over time, whereas changes in health warnings and messages are associated with increased effectiveness. Therefore, the FCTC's Article 11 requires that parties establish a period of rotation for both their text and pictorial warnings. Along with this, when warning labels are rotated, it is suggested that the size and/or layout of the message be altered so that the change is more effectively noticed. A number of ATSA countries have begun to incorporate rotation and a variety of messages in their labeling.

In Mauritius, in accordance with the Public Health Act 2008, there are eight rotating specified warnings on all cigarette packages, which are in both English and French.[12] As of 2010, there were ten rotating pictorial warnings. These warnings are in addition to the standard "smoking kills/*la cigarette tue*" stipulation on the smaller sides of every package described above.[13]

Kenya's Tobacco Control Act of 2007 requires that each package display two different warnings. In total, there are 13 different labels that are displayed on a rotational basis randomly through a 12-month period.[14]

South Africa has one of the longer histories of health warnings on packages in Africa, having started large rotating (eight in total) messages in 1995. The message on the front of the package is always short (and in emphatic uppercase letters), while the message on the back of the back has much greater detail including a quitline telephone number. Refer to Appendix A for a listing of South Africa's extensive warnings.

In Eritrea, statute requires that there are six messages in rotation at any given time. In 2010, the messages included "smoking kills" and "smoking causes cancer."

The Tobacco (Products Regulation) Act passed in Tanzania in 2003 is generally dismissed as weak and mostly ineffective, and not surprisingly it does not provide clear regulations regarding the packaging and labeling of tobacco products. Beyond the ten warnings stipulated in a schedule in the legislation, there is no further precision to the labeling requirements.[15]

Ghana's recent (2009) directive from its Food and Drugs Board (FDB) requires a rotation of three different sets of warnings.[16] Tobacco control advocates in Ghana hope that this stipulation is improved in pending legislation, including rotating graphic pictorial warnings (which is permitted in the directive, but not compelled). Nigeria's APCON directives do not require rotation, but compel manufacturers to display one of five possible messages.[17] The 2011 legislation passed by the National Senate gives power to the MoH to regulate messages and rotation.

Burkina Faso, Senegal and Cameroon still lack regulation for message rotation. Burkina Faso's "Raabo" (1988) gives the national health authority the power to regulate the message of the warnings on the packaging of tobacco products, but there is only one current approved message, which reads: "Careful, dangerous for your health." Senegal's main tobacco control legislation from 1981, Law n°81-58, Ch. 1 Art. 8, requires only one warning: "Excessive smoking is dangerous for your health (*"Abus dangereux pour votre santé"*). Ministry bylaw n°8236 MSP-DPH (30 July 1982) reiterates the gist of Law 81-58. In Cameroon, Decree 967 from the MoH and the Ministry of Commerce (25 June 2007) obligates tobacco producers to include statements about the harm of nicotine and tar as well as the exact phrase, *"le tabac nuit gravement à la santé du fumeur et de celle de son entourage"* ("tobacco severely harms the health of the smoker and those surrounding him/her"). The decree does not obligate the inclusion of additional messages.

Finally, scholarly research demonstrates that labels such as "mild" and "low-tar" are misleading and inaccurate because such products are not actually lower health risks.[18] Accordingly, some countries prohibit such labeling on packages (and in advertisements). Eritrea, Ghana (through the 2009 FDB directive), Kenya, Mauritius and South Africa prohibit false and misleading warnings. However, Burkina Faso, Cameroon, Malawi, Nigeria, Senegal, Tanzania and Zambia do not yet have prohibitions on the use of false or misleading language on tobacco product labeling.

Inclusion of Constituents and Emissions

Article 11.2 of the FCTC specifies that each unit packet and package of tobacco products and any outside packaging and labeling of such products shall, in addition to the warnings specified in Article 11.1(b), contain information on relevant constituents and emissions of tobacco products as defined by national authorities.[19] However, the qualitative and quantitative statements on the products should not imply that one brand is less harmful than another. Recent research demonstrates that emissions information is widely misrepresented by manufacturers and misunderstood by consumers. Research also suggests that descriptive information (e.g. the types of harmful ingredients in a cigarette) is much more meaningful, and several countries have begun to employ these new standards.[20] There is considerable variation across the ATSA countries in terms of compliance to this subarticle.

Mauritius, perhaps not surprisingly because of its comprehensive tobacco legislation, is thus far the only ATSA (and African country) *prohibiting* the display of tar and nicotine contents on the package. According to PHA08, regulation 4(a)(vi), cigarette packages must not display the tar content, nicotine content or carbon monoxide yield. The new regulations, however, do not compel a more descriptive explanation of the constituents.

Kenya and South Africa are grappling with the issue of what information to include on packages. In Kenya, the Tobacco Control Act of 2007 specifies that only a statement of tar, nicotine and other constituents must appear on the right side of the package in a clear and prominent format and that there be no disclosure of the actual quantities of these chemicals. This part of the statute is designed so that consumers are not fooled into trying to compare the amounts of certain ingredients. While the packaging and labeling regulations in South Africa that have been in effect since 1995 compel the disclosure of tar and nicotine on the package, the MoH is currently developing new regulations that will remove these disclosures. The ministry has not yet determined (as of early 2011) what will replace them.

Burkina Faso, Cameroon, Eritrea, Kenya, Nigeria and Senegal all have a simple requirement that the tobacco's contents and emissions be listed on the packaging. Ghana, Malawi, Tanzania and Zambia currently do not require (or prohibit) that constituents and emissions be displayed on the package.

Opportunities for Enforcement

As with many areas of the tobacco control policy, some countries continue to struggle with enforcement challenges in the area of packaging and labeling restrictions. However, some countries report strong compliance and/or evidence of governments taking their enforcement responsibilities seriously. In some ways, enforcement of this article may be somewhat easier because it is manufacturers that need to be policed, and they tend to be few in most countries (especially compare this task to attempting to police every public and workplace establishment in order to enforce smoke-free policies). Similarly, all imports must pass through a customs authority so if inspecting for proper tobacco labels – as such an agency must do for other products (e.g. alcohol, firearms, etc.) – is incorporated into officials' duties, it is tractable. Finally, because it can be one small additional part of an existing government agency's mandate, it arguably can be less resource-intensive than other tobacco control efforts.

Mauritius and South Africa report strong compliance with their labeling regulations. But even in Mauritius, a country with strong rule-of-law, advocates faced a cunning effort by the industry to delay using the new graphic warning labels in 2009. Exploiting a loophole in the wording of the legislation, BAT stockpiled packages in-country using the older text warnings. Fortunately, the delay was only a few months. In Cameroon, Law (Decree) No. 0016 in 1990 actually makes a violation of the packaging and labeling restrictions part of the penal code. Reportedly, after the decree, the Ministry of Finance gave the order to conduct inspection visits and burned several large loads of noncompliant packages.

In contrast, in Burkina Faso, even though legislation stipulates fines and six months of imprisonment for failure to include warnings on cigarette packages, a bylaw that was supposed to make the law enforceable was never passed.[21] Though bylaws are not technically necessary to make laws enforceable, they generally codify the enforcement process and identify the officials who will implement them. Despite these difficulties, manufacturers have mostly complied, but having the force of law would give the regulations considerably more vigor. Similarly, in Ghana, a recent needs assessment expressed concern about the ability to implement and enforce measures related to FCTC Article 11. In particular, the responsibility to inspect packages currently lies with the FDB, and since this is a fairly new duty to the agency, they will need more resources to be able to fulfill this responsibility effectively.[22]

Conclusions

The status of warning labels in the ATSA countries is generally not up to international – and specifically FCTC – standards or norms, but there is considerable cause for optimism that progress will be considerable and quick in this area. Clearly, certain countries including Mauritius and South Africa are performing well and have either surpassed FCTC standards or likely soon will. In both of these cases, there has been a positive contemporary history of advocates and policymakers implementing better standards and then improving them. Any aspiring country seeking better warning labels could use these countries as an example of doggedly pursuing and then reaching high goals in this area.

It is very important to note the possibilities in many countries for pursuing new and improved packaging and labeling requirements outside of the more demanding legislative process are considerable and real. Going through the process of developing, passing and then implementing new legislation is daunting. Though it is a worthwhile goal, the opportunity to pursue packaging and labeling within the regulatory framework rather than the legislative one is a very attractive one. Moreover, these two strategies can be pursued simultaneously. In Kenya, it took over a decade to pass the 2007 comprehensive tobacco control legislation, and it could take that long or longer in many other countries. While pursuing this end goal, advocates in and out of government in many countries could be seeking warning labels within existing health and/or standards regulations and could therefore score a quick and big "win."

Language continues to be an issue with packaging and labeling initiatives. In most ATSA countries, as in many developing countries in general, there are multiple major languages. In short, developing an effective strategy for text warnings in multiple languages is very challenging in many countries. The short but effective resolution to this issue is pictorial warnings. While pictorial warnings must be sensitive to the multiple cultural contexts in countries, this is arguably easier than providing text warnings with multiple languages or expecting the industry to distribute the correct language warnings regionally. Moreover, when the language complexity is coupled with low literacy in many countries, the only viable strategy is to pursue graphic pictorial warnings much more aggressively.

Finally, there are some encouraging signs that enforcement is more tractable with warning labels. With a limited number of manufacturers in many countries (or only imported products) and an existing infrastructure in many countries for inspecting consumer goods, the burden for enforcement and monitoring is arguably lower than many other areas of tobacco control.

For many years, the tobacco industry has used attractive packaging to great effect in promoting their product and advancing an image of smoking as sophisticated, sexy and even a part of a healthy lifestyle. Packaging and labeling requirements offer countries an opportunity to retaliate and, furthermore, to require that the tobacco industry pay for the messaging. Tobacco packages are read immediately by those who use the products and discarded packages disseminate the health warning messages even further. The use of graphic warnings makes messaging accessible to almost all sectors of the population. With no real need for national legislation and enforcement strategies that are often within mandate of existing organizations, packaging and labeling regulations are one of the most effective and affordable strategies in preventing the uptake of tobacco use and encouraging cessation.

Notes

1 World Health Organization, "Guidelines for the Implementation of Article 11" (2008). Online at: http://whqlibdoc.who.int/publications/2009/9789241598224_eng.pdf (accessed 20 July 2011).

2 D. Hammond, G. Fong, G. McNeil, R. Borland and K. Cummings, "Effectiveness of cigarette warning labels in informing smokers about the risks of smoking: Findings from the International Tobacco Control (ITC) Four Country Survey," *Tobacco Control* 15 (2006): iii19–iii25, and Health Canada, "The health effects of tobacco and health warning messages on cigarette packages – Survey of adults and adult smokers: Wave 9 surveys," report prepared by the Environics Research Group, January 2005.

3 E. Strahan, K. White, G. Fong, L. Fabrigar, M. Zanna and R. Cameron, "Enhancing the effectiveness of tobacco package warning labels: A social psychological perspective." *Tobacco Control* 11.3 (2002): 183–90, and D. Hammond, G. Fong, R. Borland, K. Cummings, A. McNeill and P. Driezen, "Text and graphic warnings on cigarette packages: Findings from the ITC Four Country Survey," *American Journal of Preventive Medicine* 32.3 (2007): 202–9.

4 A pictogram may be an image that is not an actual photograph.

5 World Health Organization, "Guidelines for the Implementation of Article 11."

6 Strahan et al., "Enhancing the effectiveness of tobacco package warning labels."

7 Government of the Federal Republic of Nigeria, Act No. 55 (1998).

8 World Health Organization, *Framework Convention on Tobacco Control* (2005), Article 11.1 (b) (iii). Online at: http://whqlibdoc.who.int/publications/2003/9241591013.pdf (accessed 20 July 2011).

9 G. Bhalla and J. L. Lastovicka, "The impact of changing cigarette warning message content and format," *Adv Consumer Res* 11 (1984): 305–10.

10 Government of the Republic of South Africa, "Regulations relating to the labeling, advertising and sale of tobacco products," published in GN 2063 in *Government Gazette* 16111, 2 December1994, and amended by GN R1148 in *Government Gazette* 16588, 4 August 1995.

11 World Health Organization, "Guidelines for the Implementation of Article 11."

12 The eight warnings for the principal face of cigarette packaging in Mauritius are: (a) "A cigarette is a highly addictive drug"; (b) "Tobacco smoke harms the health of children"; (c) "Smoking causes heart diseases"; (d) "Smoking causes strokes"; (e) "Smoking causes lung cancer"; (f) "Smoking causes oral mouth cancer"; (g) "Tobacco use makes you impotent"; and (h) "Smoking causes a slow and painful death." In French, the warnings read: (a) "*La cigarette est une drogue qui crée une forte dependence*"; (b) "*La fumée de tabac nuit à la santé de l'enfant*"; (c) "*Fumer provoque les maladies du cœur*"; (d) "*Fumer provoque l'attaque cérébrale*"; (e) "*Fumer provoque le cancer du poumon*"; (f) "*Fumer cause le cancer de la bouche*"; (g) "*L'usage du tabac provoque l'impuissance sexuelle*"; or (h) "*Fumer cause une mort lente et douloureuse.*"

13 On cigar, cigarillo and pipe tobacco packages, the standard warning on the smaller sides reads in English on one side: "Smoking causes cancer, heart disease, bronchitis and early death." Its equivalent in French, "*Fumer provoque le cancer, les maladies du cœur, la bronchite et la mort prématuré*" appears on the opposite side.

14 The 13 warnings in Kenya are: (a) "Smoking harms people next to you"; (b) "Tobacco use kills"; (c) "Tobacco harms your unborn baby"; (d) "Tobacco use causes cancer"; (e) "Tobacco use causes heart disease"; (f) "Tobacco use causes lung disease"; (g) "This product can cause gum disease and tooth loss" (includes smokeless tobacco products);

(h) "This product can cause mouth cancer" (includes smokeless tobacco products); (i) "This product is not a safe alternative to cigarettes" (for smokeless tobacco products); (j) "Tobacco use causes impotence"; (k) "Tobacco use causes miscarriages"; (l) "Tobacco use causes infertility in women"; and (m) "Tobacco use causes mental retardation in children."

15 The ten warnings in Tanzania are: (a) "Smoking harms people next to you"; (b) "Cigarette smoking kills"; (c) "Tobacco use kills"; (d) "Cigarette smoking may cause cancer"; (c) "Tobacco use may cause cancer"; (f) "Cigarette smoking causes lung disease"; (g) "Tobacco use causes lung disease"; (h) "Cigarette smoking is dangerous to your health"; (i) "Tobacco seriously damages health"; and (j) "Smoking causes heart and fatal diseases."

16 The three sets of warnings in Ghana are – Set 1, front: "Smoking seriously harms you and others around you"; and back: "Stopping smoking reduces the risk of fatal heart and lung diseases." Set 2, front: "Smoking causes cancer"; and back: "Smoking damages the health of those around you" Set 3, front: "Smoking causes fatal diseases"; and back: "Smokers die younger."

17 The five nonrotating messages in Nigeria are: (a) "Smoking is addictive"; (b) "Smoking damages lungs"; (c) "Smoking can kill"; (d) "Smoking can cause cancer"; and (e) "Smoking can damage the fetus."

18 R. Pollay and T. Dewhirst, "The dark side of marketing seemingly 'Light' cigarettes: Successful images and failed fact," *Tobacco Control* 11.1 (2002): i18–31, and US Department of Health and Human Services, "Risks associated with smoking cigarettes with low machine measured yields of tar and nicotine," research paper created by the US Department of Health and Human Services, US Public Health Services, US National Institutes of Health, and the National Cancer Institute (2002). Online at: www.cancercontrol.cancer.gov/tcrb/monographs/13 (accessed 20 July 2011).

19 World Health Organization, "Guidelines for the Implementation of Article 11."

20 Health Canada, "Summary Report of Four Focus Groups in Toronto & Montreal on Awareness and Understanding on Toxic Emissions Information on Tobacco Packaging" (2007); Federal Trade Commission, "Federal Trade Commission Cigarette Report for 2004 and 2005" (2007), online at: http://www.ftc.gov/reports/tobacco/2007cigarette2004-2005.pdf (accessed 10 July 2010).

21 Ministry of Health, Burkina Faso, "National Strategic Plan on Tobacco Control 2009-2013," 29 April 2009, 17.

22 WHO FCTC Secretariat and Ministry of Health, Ghana, "Needs Assessment for implementation of the WHO Framework Convention on Tobacco Control in Ghana," June 2010, 2–3 and 15–17. Online at: http://www.ghanahealthservice.org/includes/upload/publications/Needs%20Assesment%20for%20Tobacco%20Control%20In%20Ghana.pdf (accessed 20 July 2011).

Appendix A – South Africa Health Warnings

Annexure 2. Warnings

Part A	Part B
Danger: smoking can kill you	Tobacco smoke contains many harmful chemicals such as carbon monoxide, cyanide, nicotine and tar, which can cause disease and death. Non-smokers and ex-smokers, on average, live longer and are healthier than smokers. For more information call (011) 720-3145. [Telephone number added by GN R1148 of 4 August 1995]
Danger: smoking causes cancer	Nine out of ten patients with lung cancer are smokers. Smoking also causes cancer of the lip, mouth, voice box, food pipe and bladder. Quitting smoking reduces your risk of cancer. For more information call (011) 720-3145.
Danger: smoking causes heart disease	Smoking is a major cause of heart attacks, strokes and blood vessel diseases. Quitting smoking reduces your risk of heart diseases. For more information call (011) 720-3145.
Smoking damages your lungs	A morning cough and shortness of breath are signs of lung disease. It is never too late to quit. Stop smoking now and you can prevent further harm. For more information call (011) 720-3145.
Pregnant? Breastfeeding? Your smoking can harm your baby	The babies of mothers who smoke during pregnancy are more likely to die before birth or to be born underweight. Stopping smoking before or during the first months of pregnancy reduces the risk to the baby. For more information call (011) 720-3145.
Warning don't smoke near children	Children who live with smokers suffer more from colds, coughs, ear infections, asthma and chest disease. Protect your children from the harmful chemicals in tobacco smoke. For more information call (011) 720-3145.
Tobacco is addictive	Nicotine in tobacco is a drug which acts on the brain and nerves. Most smokers are dependent on nicotine that is why they feel uncomfortable and get cravings when they go without smoking for a while. For more information call (011) 720-3145.
Your smoke can harm those around you	Every time you smoke, those around you smoke too. Your smoking increases their risk of lung cancer and heart disease. Stop smoking for the sake of your health and that of your family and friends. For more information call (011) 720-3145.
Causes cancer [special warning only on snuff and chewing tobacco]	

Source: GN 2063 in *Government Gazette* 16111 (2 December 1994), amended by GN R1148 in *Government Gazette* 16588 (4 August 1995).

Chapter 7

BURKINA FASO

Salimata Ki Ouedraogo, Laurent Ouedraogo and Kangoye Théodore

Executive Summary

Burkina Faso has several tobacco control measures in place as the result of a set of regulations – the "Raabo" – promulgated by the executive branch in 1988, which includes basic provisions for smoke-free policies, advertising bans and warning labels. However, like many countries in Sub-Saharan Africa, the regulation is weak in terms of its basic parameters, implementation and enforcement. As a result, the tobacco control in recent years has been pursuing comprehensive, FCTC-compliant tobacco control legislation (the country ratified the treaty in 2006). In 2010, the Council of Ministers approved a draft bill that had received significant input from the tobacco control community, which was then passed on to the National Assembly for legislative approval. At the same time, however, another bill was introduced into the National Assembly that had significant input from the tobacco industry. The latter of the two bills was approved by the legislature.

Concomitantly, tobacco control advocates continue to pursue the enforcement of existing smoke-free legislation. Although Burkina Faso has traditionally been a highly centralized government, in the last few years the government has taken sizeable steps to decentralize. As a result, significant powers, particularly in the area of health, have been devolved to the 359 mayors of the main municipalities. The ATSA team has been working with a sample of 45 of these elected officials and their staff to educate them about tobacco issues and to encourage and help them enforce smoke-free policies. They hope that success in some or all of the 45 municipalities will be a catalyst for change across the country.

Country Profile[1]

Population in 2009 (global and African ranking):	15,746,232 (62, 15)
Geographical size (global ranking):	274,200 sq. km (81)
GDP by purchasing power parity in 2008 (global ranking):	US$17.82 billion (128)
GDP real growth rate (2006–8):	4.5%
Main industries:	Cotton lint, brewing and bottling, agricultural processing, soap, cigarettes, textiles, mining gold, peanuts, shea nuts, sesame, sorghum, millet, corn, rice, livestock
Languages:	French (official), African languages belonging to the Sudanic family, Moore and Dioula (90%)
Official development assistance (ODA) – total commitments/disbursements (2007):	US$697.5/650.8 million
ODA as a percentage of GDP:	9.61728%
Largest donors (disbursements in millions of USD):	European Commission 204.4, France 129.9, Netherlands 65.7, Denmark 40.8, Germany 39.9, USA 21.8, Sweden 21.1, Japan 20.4, Switzerland 20.3
Tobacco production by volume in 2007 (global ranking):	525 tons (99)
Tobacco exports (2007):	Cigarettes: 136 tons at $8,897 per ton, #1 export
Tobacco imports (2007):	Tobacco products: 1,481 tons at $19,257 per ton, #13 import

Brief Description of Political System

Type: Burkina Faso is a semipresidential military republic based on France's Fifth Republic.

Executive: The president is Blaise Compaore, who has won every election since 1987. The prime minister is Tertius Zongo (2007), though he has only limited executive power.

Cabinet: The Council of Ministers is appointed by the president with the recommendation of the prime minister.

Legislature: The unicameral National Assembly – 111 seats are elected by popular vote every five years. As of late 2009: Congress for Democracy and Progress, 73 seats; African Democratic Rally Alliance for Democracy and Federation, 14 seats.

Judiciary: Supreme Court.

Scope of Tobacco Problem

The data on prevalence are limited in Burkina Faso, and firm statistics on adult prevalence rates are not available. Similarly, data broken down into meaningful categories, including age, gender, socioeconomic and high-risk groups, are also not widely available. The one exception is the availability of data relevant to youths. The most widely cited statistic, from the World Health Organization's MPOWER publication, reports a 14.7 percent adult smoking rate (age adjusted), but it is not based on well-substantiated data.

The most reliable data for youths come from the Global Youth Tobacco Survey (GYTS), which has been executed three times, in 2001 (Ouagadougou only), 2006 and 2009. The Association Burkinabe de Santé Publique (ABSP) helped to execute the GYTS 2001, and received Canadian Public Health Association capacity-building assistance for this activity. For the various youth-focused surveys, researchers have examined different age ranges from 11–30, and estimates of the prevalence of tobacco use have ranged from 13.6 percent to 36.7 percent. These studies are difficult to compare directly, however, because they were carried out by different individuals in different contexts, with different target populations and the use of different methodologies.[2]

The GYTS 2006, which covers 11–15-year-olds, reports that youth prevalence rates appear to be slightly lower than general adult rates (if we interpret the MPOWER statistic as current smokers). In terms of overall youth prevalence, the GYTS 2006 reports:

- 23.0 percent of students had smoked cigarettes (male 34.5 percent, female 9.7 percent)
- 17.3 percent currently use any tobacco product (male 25.0 percent, female 7.8 percent)
- 12.2 percent currently smoke cigarettes (male 19.8 percent, female 3.4 percent)
- 7.7 percent currently use other tobacco products (male 9.5 percent, female 4.9 percent)

The surveys demonstrate an alarming general acceptance of smoking by family and society. Of the youths from the GYTS 2006 survey who smoke, 56.4 percent reported usually smoking at home, 35.3 percent reported buying cigarettes in a store and 73.8 percent who bought cigarettes in a store were not refused purchase because of their age. While minors do not appear to face many difficulties purchasing cigarettes, organizations such as the ABSP have been executing awareness programs so that families become more sensitized and particularly children and youths develop negative perceptions of tobacco consumption, especially cigarettes.

Second-hand tobacco smoke is also a serious issue in Burkina Faso for young people. The GYTS 2006 reports that 35.7 percent of respondents live in homes where others smoke in their presence; 49.9 percent are around others who smoke in places outside their home; 16.4 percent have one or more parents who smoke; and 7.9 percent have most or all of their friends who smoke. Organizations are also working toward sensitizing older family members to these dangers.

Encouragingly, youth awareness of health issues related to smoking is fairly high in Burkina Faso. The GYTS 2006 reports the following:

- 88.3 percent think smoking should be banned from public places
- 71.3 percent think smoke from others is harmful to them
- 92.5 percent want to stop smoking
- 87.3 percent tried to stop smoking during the past year
- 100.0 percent have received help to stop smoking

The curricular record for tobacco control issues in schools is less impressive, with the GYTS 2006 reporting:

- 58.6 percent had been taught in class, during the past year, about the dangers of smoking
- 34.9 percent had discussed in class, during the past year, reasons why people their age smoke
- 49.7 percent had been taught in class, during the past year, the effects of tobacco use

Beyond prevalence statistics, tobacco control advocates express concern that the data on the economics of tobacco are particularly lacking. When making the public health argument for tobacco control to policymakers, advocates wish to have not only reliable prevalence statistics but also relevant economic data. These data are necessary to convince the ministries of Finance and Commerce that illnesses caused by tobacco consumption are harmful to

Burkina Faso's economy. Currently, there are insufficient economic tobacco-related data generally, and no basic data on the costs of tobacco to the public health system specifically. In a recent cursory examination, however, tobacco control advocates demonstrated that the cost of medical evacuations alone is higher than the earnings from tobacco taxation. The Ministry of Finance reports that taxes from local manufacturer, Burkinabé Cigarette Manufacturers (MABUCIG), generate approximately CFA 14 or 15 million per year, while the Ministry of Health estimates that evacuations for patients with respiratory illnesses for medical care outside of Burkina Faso, paid for by the government, cost significantly more.

Politics

Inventory of existing laws and regulations

Burkina Faso has had a multifaceted tobacco control regulatory framework for more than 20 years, but severe enforcement challenges have undermined these rules. The first piece of anti-tobacco national regulation, the "Raabo" N°AN IV–0081/FP/SAN/CAPRO/DP, was signed into action in 1988, prohibiting smoking in a variety of public spaces, workplaces, health and educational institutions; and providing for the regulation of advertising and warning labels.[3] However, the Raabo is very weakly enforced. In fact, even after Decree N°97–84/PRES/PM/MJ in 1997 established fines for infractions of the Raabo, its enforcement has remained minimal.

Burkina Faso has also been active internationally in tobacco control. It participated in the elaboration of the FCTC, signed it in 2003, and the National Assembly and executive branch authorized ratification in 2006.[1] The process toward FCTC-compliant legislation has been slow, however, and the newest legislation passed by the National Assembly in 2010 does not comply with the treaty.

Overall political context

The politics of tobacco in Burkina Faso are tied strongly to the highly centralized national government. The positions of the president and his key ministry officials will greatly shape the progress made in tobacco control in the short, medium and longer terms. While some preliminary mapping has begun and more has taken shape since the project began, the record of these exercises needs to be revisited in greater depth.

Recently, members of the tobacco control community – specifically, the partners in the ATSA initiative – overturned an initial decision to pursue a smoke-free schools program, citing the common argument that such tobacco control initiatives were popular but not cost-effective. Instead, the ATSA team and its partners decided that it was better to work for broader social impact as well as advocate for greater enforcement of existing anti-tobacco legislation. Accordingly, the Burkina ATSA team's priorities during the program were: 1) facilitating the adoption of a national anti-tobacco law and 2) capacity building for tobacco control with elected municipal officials. The former initiative built on an existing effort to develop FCTC-compliant legislation, which was sponsored by the Bloomberg Initiative. The idea with the latter initiative was to build on the work of a related project sponsored by HealthBridge, which focused on sensitization and development of municipal work plans with elected officials.

In early 2010, the proposed comprehensive legislation was approved by the Council of Ministers, and it was passed on to the National Assembly for discussion and approval. At the same time, however, a competing bill was introduced in the legislature. This proposal did not have provisions consistent with the FCTC. Unfortunately, the weaker legislation was passed by the assembly in late 2010.

The aim of the capacity-building projects has been to raise awareness among 45 municipal mayors with respect to the dangers of tobacco use and of existing tobacco-specific regulations that are not currently applied. These efforts have aimed to 1) discuss the mayors' role in implementing these regulations; 2) educate the permanent (i.e. nonelected) municipal administrations; 3) help mayors and administrators to identify and implement activities; 4) encourage them to include anti-tobacco activities in their action and development plans; and 5) ensure implementation of these activities for the benefit of citizens. Resource constraints precluded working with the 359 mayors in the country, but over time advocates hope to expand their work to other mayoralties. Furthermore, the team believes that if these mayors become the team's intermediaries, they will be able to help reach many more people in the future without expending additional effort and resources.

With the previous initiatives in mind, during the October 2008 ATSA meeting in Burkina Faso, the team and other stakeholders undertook a vigorous process to map out the preferences and positions on tobacco control of key actors and institutions. The participants came to the conclusion that within such a centralized political system, knowing and understanding the president's position on any major issue was critical. If the president supports tobacco control, advocates expect that his ministers will, too. The process of mapping tobacco control systematically also helped the participants realize how to use information – such as public health and economic statistics – to promote the project. They believe that such information is useful in helping to convince ministers and other key players that it is in their interest to support the proposed comprehensive tobacco control act. The team suggests that in order to know better where the president stands on tobacco control they would need to engage in an even more extensive mapping process, which would include personal interviews with relevant actors and other research techniques. There is some evidence of support from the government both because of the Raabo and FCTC ratification, but the lack of subsequent implementation and enforcement belies these efforts. Advocates need to examine and understand these contradictions better.

Beyond the president, the positions of ministers, deputy ministers and high-ranking bureaucrats in key ministries are certainly important. Key ministries include, but are not limited to, Health, Education, Economy and Youth. At ATSA stakeholder meetings, most tobacco control advocates voiced concern that tobacco control is not high on the government's current agenda. Unfortunately, there are no data available on the positions of these actors and more in-depth investigation is required in order to discuss these positions more meaningfully.

The relative position on tobacco control of the Ministry of Health is the most established and there are clear indications that it takes tobacco control seriously. The minister is supportive of tobacco control and in 2009 he met with officials from the ministry's Directorate of Family Health (DSF) and the Union of Associations Against Tobacco (UACT), a coalition of organizations with tobacco control goals, to discuss this topic in order to be well briefed and to request an action paper. Following this meeting, he signed a document banning smoking in all facilities run by the Ministry of Health, including administration and care services. There has also been a ministry focal point for over a decade. In the ministry, the DSF continues to play a pivotal role in tobacco control. The directorate's mandate includes a component on the health of young people, under which their strategic plan anticipates a certain number of initiatives, including tobacco control. It has initiated several significant tobacco control projects that have given it an advantage over the Directorate of Disease Control (DLM) and the Directorate of Hygiene and Health Education (DHPES) as the focal point for tobacco control. The DSF was also responsible for coordinating the preliminary comprehensive bill.

Beyond the public health issues related to tobacco, according to current statute and government organization, it is actually the Ministry of Commerce that is predominantly in charge of actually regulating the tobacco industry. The General Inspection of Economic Affairs/Ministry of Commerce (and the Promotion of Enterprises and Handicrafts – IGAE/MCPEA) has attended previous ATSA meetings, but the ministry's position on ongoing tobacco control efforts is not yet known.

Similarly, the Ministry of the Economy and Finances (MEF) has a significant stake in tobacco because it is responsible for taxation. Representatives from the ministry participated in the initial 2008 ATSA stakeholders' meeting – particularly officials from the Office of Customs Investigation/General Customs Office (DED/DGD). These officials explained taxation rules and demonstrated that taxation rates on tobacco products are generally low. Additionally, the Human Resources Service/General Tax Office (SRH/DGI) and the National Institute for Statistics (INSD) have also attended tobacco control meetings in recent years. These officials, however, are technocrats, and the actual positions of elected and higher-level appointed officials in the ministry toward tobacco control – and particularly taxation – have not yet been determined.

Some major tobacco control initiatives – for example, smoke-free policies – will likely need support from local officials for implementation and/or enforcement. In fact, there has been organizational decentralization in most ministries with local-level ministry representatives exercising specific powers to implement programs. When any specific initiatives requiring local participation are pursued, there will need to be a systematic examination of these actors.

Tobacco Industry

There is a substantial tobacco manufacturing industry in Burkina Faso. The national tobacco industry is controlled by Burkinabé Cigarette Manufacturers (MABUCIG). Available figures place national production at 62 tons in 2002 or 1.55 billion cigarettes (by contrast, only 6 tons were imported in 2000–2). Not surprisingly, as a large industry, it is well connected in the broader society of Burkina Faso. For example, the Chairman of the Administrative Board of MABUCIG is also currently the chair of the Chamber of Commerce, the first vice chair of the Social and Economic Council (CES), and the chair of the Poverty Fund of the CES, among other high-profile positions.

The tobacco industry in Burkina Faso is particularly aggressive in promoting its products. Direct marketing, the distribution of tobacco products and event sponsorships are its dominant strategies. Anecdotal evidence suggests that the industry regularly uses the technique of cigarette handouts, most often by attractive young women. Event sponsorship – including sports, culture and music events – is so prevalent that the majority of such events have some industry sponsorship.[5] There were multiple anecdotal reports from ATSA stakeholders' meetings of the omnipresent tobacco firm–branded vans that drive around the capital displaying and promoting tobacco products. In a country with few cars, particularly in the less urban areas, these displays are highly conspicuous.

In terms of nonindustrial production, small farmers frequently plant side plots of tobacco for sale, consumption and ceremonial purposes – these plots produce low quantities but are culturally valued in Burkina Faso.[6] There are reports that MABUCIG actually supervises some tobacco production, particularly in the western part of the country, though this is not well substantiated. There are no data on how much tobacco is produced for sale, though it is clear that Burkina Faso is not an exporter of tobacco leaf, or manufactured products. As reported previously, revenues from taxing tobacco do not generally exceed $15 million.

The industry was strongly opposed to the comprehensive legislation that was approved initially by the Council of Ministers, and lobbied the government not to follow through on the proposal. In particular, they argued that the 60 percent tax and the graphic warning labels would destroy the industry, and emphasized the loss to the economy for the tax revenue that it generates. They did, however, support the weaker legislation that was ultimately approved by the National Assembly.

ATSA Review

Despite the enormous challenges, the ATSA team has noted some recent breakthroughs in tobacco control, which were at least partly a result of their efforts. The most significant event, of course, was the initial adoption of the draft of comprehensive national legislation for tobacco control by the Council of Ministers, which was developed in considerable part by the team. Though the assembly ultimately passed the competing – and much weaker – proposal, advocates are heartened that tobacco control remains on the agenda. In other important developments, the team successfully pursued the decentralized strategy described above by working closely with the mayors that demonstrated interest in pursuing tobacco control policies, such as smoke-free initiatives. The team began training these officials and formed a coalition of mayors in support of tobacco control initiatives. This coalition will be instrumental in implementing many of the provisions in the new legislation. Finally, the ATSA program also helped to develop new anti-smoking materials such as posters that will support the impending changes in tobacco control policy.

Notes

1 Sources: CIA World Factbook https://www.cia.gov/library/publications/the-world-factbook/; except Organization of Economic Cooperation and Development (OECD) for development assistance statistics, and Food and Agriculture Organization of the United Nations – Statistics (FAOSTAT) for tobacco production. See http://stats.oecd.

org/index.aspx and http://faostat.fao.org/site/567/default.aspx#ancor respectively (accessed 20 July 2011).

2 Ministry of Health, Burkina Faso, "National Strategic Plan on Tobacco Control 2009-2013," 29 April 2009, 14.

3 The Raabo is not legislation, and is more like an executive decree in structure – it is promulgated directly by the executive branch, and has not been passed by the legislature.

4 Ministry of Health, "National Strategic Plan on Tobacco Control 2009–2013," 29 April 2009, 18.

5 Ibid., 17.

6 Ibid., 15.

Chapter 8

CAMEROON

Zakariaou Njoumemi, Daniel Sibetcheu, Tetanye Ekoe and Eugène Gbedji

Executive Summary

Though the prevalence of daily smokers is comparatively low in Cameroon at 4 percent, the prevalence of occasional smokers (~18 percent) and young smokers (~14 percent) is higher and increasing across most social groups. There are already a number of tobacco control measures in Cameroon, including some limited smoke-free provisions, an advertising ban and some labeling requirements, but improved implementation and enforcement and a comprehensive national tobacco control bill remain central goals of the tobacco control community. Though Cameroon has ratified the Framework Convention on Tobacco Control (FCTC), none of the existing measures are FCTC-compliant.

There is evidence of support for tobacco control at the level of the president and at the ministerial level. The establishment of a Group of Experts on Tobacco Use (2007) by the national government is evidence of government interest and support. This group is charged with developing new legislation. Civil society action on tobacco control is still nascent in Cameroon.

Through 2010, the African Tobacco Situation Analysis (ATSA) team has been working to promote smoke-free policies in the Mfoundi Department (which includes Yaoundé) in the hope that this pilot phase will serve as a model that can be replicated at the national level. Major priorities for the tobacco control community include fine tuning the existing regulations, generating new and improved tobacco control legislation (either comprehensive legislation or piecemeal by area) and developing strategies to implement and enforce these new rules.

Country Profile[1]

Population in 2009 (global and African ranking):	18,879,301 (59, 13)
Geographical size (global ranking):	475,440 sq. km (60)
GDP by purchasing power parity in 2008 (global ranking):	US$42.75 billion (94)
GDP real growth rate (2006–8):	2.5%
GDP per capita (global ranking):	US$2,300 (177)
Main industries:	Petroleum production and refining, aluminum production, food processing, light consumer goods, textiles, lumber, ship repair, coffee, cocoa, cotton, rubber, bananas, oilseed, grains, root starches, livestock timber
Languages:	270 African languages, 24 major African languages including Pidgin, Fulfulde, Ewondo, English (official), French (official)
Official development assistance (ODA) – total commitments/disbursements (2007):	US$2074.9/1964.8 million
ODA as a percentage of GDP:	9.5%
Largest donors (disbursements in millions of USD):	Germany 756.7, France 750.1, Belgium 87.8, EC 74.9, Sweden 73.6, UK 51.7, Switzerland 32.5, US 30.7, Global Fund 27.8
Tobacco production by volume (2007):	4,500 tons
Tobacco exports (2007):	Tobacco (unmanufactured): 274 tons at $2,905 per ton, #17 export
Tobacco imports (2007):	Tobacco products NES: 1,138 tons at $14,207 per ton #10 import; tobacco (unmanufactured): 751 tons at $12,614 per ton, #13 import; cigarettes: 908 tons at $7,700 per ton, #18 import

Brief Description of Political System

Type: Cameroon is a multiparty presidential regime, with a large state bureaucracy.

Executive: The president is Paul Biya. Prime Minister Philemon Yang was appointed by the president on 30 June 2009, though he has limited executive power.

Cabinet: Appointed by the president.

Legislature: The unicameral National Assembly is comprised of 180 seats, elected by popular vote every five years. The assembly is dominated by the RDCP (Rassemblement démocratique du Peuple Camerounais/Cameroon People's Democratic Movement) political party (140/180 seats in 2009). The constitution calls for an upper legislative chamber called the Senate, but it has yet to be established.

Judiciary: The Supreme Court is appointed by the president. The High Court is elected by the National Assembly.

Scope of Tobacco Problem

Though the rate of daily smokers is low by global standards, the rate of occasional smokers is much higher, and tobacco use of all kinds is clearly increasing. The Ministry of Public Health (MoPH) estimates that 17.5 percent of the population – 28.8 percent of all men and 8.1 percent of all women – smoke occasionally.[2] According to the same study, approximately 4 percent of adults (8 percent of men and 1 percent of women) describe themselves as regular or daily smokers.[3] Second-hand tobacco smoke (SHS) is also a significant public health challenge: in 1994, 35.7 percent of the population reported exposure to SHS,[4] while the MoPH reports a slightly higher percentage of 37 percent in a study executed in 2006.[5]

There are reliable surveillance data regarding young smokers that illustrate a genuine problem with tobacco use amongst school-aged children. The Global Youth Tobacco Survey (GYTS), conducted in 2008 among students 13 to 15 years of age, generated the following statistics: 13.4 percent of students (17.3 percent of boys and 9.7 percent of girls) currently consume a tobacco product; 5.7 percent of students (8.8 percent of boys and 3.0 percent of girls) currently smoke cigarettes; and 9.5 percent of respondents (11.6 percent of boys and 7.3 percent of girls) currently consume one or more other tobacco products. The reasons cited for consuming tobacco are numerous, including peer pressure, advertising and curiosity. Despite the widespread use of tobacco products, banning smoking in public places is popular with 87.6 percent reporting that they are in favor of such a policy.

There are also reliable data that demonstrate widespread tobacco use in the educational sector. The Global School Personnel Survey (GSPS 2008) reports that 25.3 percent of all school personnel (22.6 percent of teachers and 39.5 percent of administrative personnel) have tried smoking; 26.6 percent of all school personnel (24.0 percent of teachers and 39.0 percent of administrative personnel) currently consume a tobacco product;

19.3 percent of all school personnel (17.3 percent of teachers and 30.3 percent of administrative personnel) currently smoke cigarettes; and 14.0 percent of all school personnel (12.2 percent of teachers and 19.1 percent of administrative personnel) currently consume other tobacco products. This study shows that rates of tobacco use are systematically higher among administrative personnel (all personnel other than teachers) than among teachers, though the reasons for this discrepancy are not examined. It is also important to note that in contrast to the trend among students, cigarettes are a more popular product (19.3 percent) than other tobacco products (14 percent). This difference is likely due to the economic resources available to the tobacco user – cigarettes are more expensive and individuals with higher incomes are more likely to use them than other products.

Politics of Tobacco

Existing legislation and regulations

Cameroon has shown strong support for international tobacco control and the FCTC. The government signed the FCTC on 13 May 2004 and it was ratified by executive decree in 2006 (N° 2005/440, 31 October). In a demonstration of immediate official support for the agreement, Decision N° 0180 of 28 May 2004, issued by the MoPH, provided for the creation of the Tobacco Experts Group. The subsequent Decision N° 0615 of 29 November 2004, issued by the same ministry, appointed the group members.

Notably, Cameroon actually had a history of tobacco control policies before the ratification of the FCTC. In addition to the MoPH ban on smoking in health facilities in 1988, a piece of general legislation adopted in the late 1990s was a starting point for youth tobacco control. National Act N° 98/004 of 14 April 1998 regarding the Cameroon education system (specifically Article 35) addresses students' physical and moral well-being and prohibits the sale, distribution and consumption of alcoholic beverages, tobacco and drugs to young people. Anecdotally, some advocates at ATSA stakeholder meetings claimed that there is leniency when it comes to ensuring compliance, whereas others found that, in general, the legislation has been obeyed. Almost a decade later, Circular Letter N° 19/07 of 11 September 2007, issued by the Ministry of Secondary Education, reiterated the spirit of the act by stating that anti-tobacco groups would be created and that schools were smoke-free spaces.

Overall political context

There is an emerging political view that curbing tobacco consumption is important and that the government should aim to make certain that it is not a public health or a development issue in the future. The general political context of tobacco control is consistent with the implementation of the national health sector strategy and the poverty reduction strategy (*Document de stratégies de réduction de la pauvreté* or DSRP). Perhaps because of its consistency with the DSRP, ministers tend to be rhetorically supportive of tobacco control, though actual progress on these issues remains slow.

There is evidence of support for tobacco control in the executive branch. For example, the president of the republic, Paul Biya, demonstrated overt support for tobacco control when he signed and ratified the World Health Organization (WHO) FCTC in 2006. The French-style mixed regime also includes a prime minister whose policymaking role is important. Though the president must approve all legislation, before a bill is sent to him it must first go through the prime minister's office. Tobacco control advocates believe that the prime minister's office is supportive of tobacco control.

The MoPH is openly supportive of tobacco control and has been pivotal in recent efforts in reforming tobacco control policy. In 2002, a reorganization of the ministry created the Community Action and Prevention Sub-Directorate in the Health Promotion Directorate that includes, among other things, the tobacco control focal point, who was Mr Daniel Sibetcheu as of early 2010. This department is responsible for defining and implementing tobacco control strategies and action plans; developing tobacco legislation and regulations; promoting the creation of tobacco treatment and healing centers; and defining and implementing recovery strategies for tobacco users. On 7 October 2009, ATSA team leaders and International Development Research Centre (IDRC) staff met with the focal point, who demonstrated great support for tobacco control and is an active participant in the drafting of a proposed FCTC-compliant national bill. Similarly, Dr Virginie Owono Longang, a public health physician in the faculty of medicine at Université de Yaoundé 1, is head of tobacco and alcohol control at the subdirectorate. Though she has held this position only since 2009, she has informed herself about tobacco control issues, openly supports it and has made her office available if advocates require specific information.

In a major demonstration of official support for tobacco control in 2004, the Health Promotion Directorate created and implemented a 15-person, multisectoral Tobacco Experts Group (Decision No. 00615/D/MSP/DPS of 11 February). The group's mission was to lead brainstorming sessions and conduct studies on smoking and its impact on public health, and group members were chosen by their respective ministries or sectors. In 2008–9, in order to consolidate existing regulations and legislation, these experts helped to draft Cameroon's national bill on tobacco control. The proposed bill considers all aspects of tobacco control as prescribed by the FCTC and particularly focuses on public health protection. Adoption and promulgation of this legislation will constitute a strong foundation for starting the fight to reduce and regulate production, marketing and consumption of tobacco products, thereby also preventing exposure to second-hand smoke and saving more lives.

The MoPH has played other key roles in tobacco control as well. In 2006, the minister of public health openly encouraged the other ministers to support the FCTC, and his position against the tobacco industry is well known. Also, the National Committee for the Fight against Drugs and Tobacco (Comité national de lutte contre la drogue et le tabagisme) is another related initiative within the MoPH. Dr Flore Ndembiyembe is the committee's permanent secretary and is an active participant in the anti-tobacco campaign including the ATSA initiative and a member of the Tobacco Experts Group.

Beyond the MoPH, the tobacco control community believes – based on observed actions – that all relevant national ministries support tobacco control measures. For example, a number of ministries have passed regulations to prohibit smoking on their premises. The Ministry of Finance adopted a bylaw banning smoking in ministry offices to protect people from SHS. The Ministry of Secondary Education has also recently signed a bylaw banning smoking on school premises and establishing anti-tobacco groups. As of 2010, however, school programs do not include tobacco issues in the curriculum. The Ministry of Transport has a de facto smoking ban on all public transportation, which anecdotally is thought to be well observed, especially in taxis, on coaches, buses and trains and aboard air transport. These ministries are represented on the Tobacco Experts Group. Other ministries involved in the group include the Ministry of the Environment and the Ministry of Justice, which has appointed some judges to the group. These judges can preside over legal action in the event of infringement of regulatory measures. However, to date, no tobacco regulation cases have been reported to the judges or the minister of justice.

Other ministries, including the Ministry of Youth Affairs, Ministry of Women's Empowerment and the Family, Ministry of Social Affairs and the Ministry of Territorial Administration and Decentralization (which ensures community governance) are regarded as potential key partners. Also, because of ongoing tobacco leaf cultivation, tobacco control advocates consider the Ministry of Agriculture an important stakeholder. Before the signing of the FCTC, the ministry canceled funding to tobacco farming programs in the Eastern part of the country, but there is no evidence that this had a tobacco control-related motivation. Tobacco control advocates continue to explore the positions of and potential for partnerships and/or support with all of these ministries.

ATSA nonsmoking campaign

In 2009–10, the ATSA team pursued a smoke-free campaign in the Department of Mfoundi (the city of Yaoundé). The team's activities have affected a variety of sectors including workplaces and public spaces. The sectors include education (all levels), health (hospitals, dental and other clinics, etc.), transportation (taxis, buses, etc.), tourism (mainly hotels, restaurants and bars), businesses (supermarkets, hardware stores, bakeries, etc.) and administrative and community buildings (municipal halls, prefectures, national security, ministries, etc.). An official municipal-level memorandum (regulatory measure) on smoking in municipal buildings (the delegate offices and the seven town halls) is currently in effect. Part of the effort has been to pursue actual enforcement of this regulation. The team hopes that the pilot project will serve as a model for the rest of the country.

As in most countries, support from local authorities is essential to making public spaces smoke free. Their support is especially important in ensuring regulatory compliance; for example, support from each community's mayor can help with enforcement in town halls. The government delegate to the Yaoundé urban community recently adopted a regulatory measure banning smoking in community-owned buildings in the town. This delegate has authority over Yaoundé's seven urban communities. He is appointed by the president, and his post is similar to that of a minister. Mayors are elected by their fellow citizens. Currently, all mayors belong to the same political party (the governing party), which eases policy adoption and enforcement. Similarly, support from law enforcement agencies will be essential to ensuring compliance with tobacco legislation. Local and national police forces must be sensitized to any new legislation and given tools – training and resources – to enforce the provisions.

The ATSA team has argued that it takes much more than official support for successful tobacco control, including especially widespread and genuine interest and action from actors outside the government. Undoubtedly, civil society organizations are potential key partners in the efforts toward smoke-free policies. In particular, these organizations can be especially helpful in social mobilization, education, general public awareness, information dissemination and monitoring. Although there was no representative from civil society on the Tobacco Expert Group as of 2010, participation of civil society groups in tobacco control programs is beginning to take shape. In an encouraging sign, some women's groups have started integrating tobacco control into their general mandates. Based on their mandates and missions, the following nongovernmental organizations are some potential partners: the African Humanitarian and Economic Foundation, the Association de santé communautaire et de communication sociale sur le tabagisme (Association for Community Health and Social Communication on Tobacco), the Fédération des organisations non gouvernementales de la santé (Federation of Nongovernmental Health Organizations), the Coalition camerounaise de lutte contre le tabac (Cameroon Tobacco Control Coalition), the Association camerounaise de santé publique (Cameroon Public Health Association) and the Association camerounaise de défense des droits des consommateurs (Cameroon Association for the Defense of Consumer Rights).

There is enormous unrealized potential for help or support for tobacco control from professional associations and organizations. In the health sector, doctors, pharmacists, nurses and public health professionals all have a clear interest in public health policies that promote healthy living. It is also reasonable to seek support from other professionals that might be interested in the positive public health benefits, including journalists, lawyers, judges and teachers. These groups can also assist greatly in establishing initiatives that are not limited to promoting smoke-free spaces. However, as of early 2010, none of these groups had yet been successfully engaged.

In the labor sector, there is potential to tap the influence of associations that organize workers, including laborers, taxi drivers, urban and intercity bus drivers, hotel employees and restaurant and bar workers. Specifically, the team would like to be able to turn to these organizations to inform and raise worker awareness of smoke-free workspaces. Though these groups have yet to participate in tobacco control–related discussions and/or activities, the ATSA team does not anticipate their opposition. Similarly, the ATSA team identified a need to mobilize industry associations (i.e. owners' associations), especially in transport, the hotel business, restaurants and bars, health and education. If business owners could also be convinced of the benefit of healthier workers, such as lower costs and increased productivity, tobacco control advocates expect strong support of these often politically and economically powerful groups.

The influence of the public and private media is strong with the general population, and their participation is arguably critical in the successful promotion of smoke-free environments. Unfortunately, it is challenging to get coverage for tobacco control in the media. Though Cameroon has a national radio and television network and a public newspaper, in order to obtain print media coverage, it is necessary to reimburse journalists' travel expenses and even to remunerate them. Furthermore, health-related issues do not tend to receive a lot of media coverage. Despite these challenges, tobacco control advocates are making some progress with the media. For example, there is now a network of health journalists that is represented in most of the media. There has also been media representation on the ATSA team. Rodrigue Bertrand

Tueno, a journalist, has been an active member of the ATSA–Cameroon team, and the team believes that Mr Tueno's participation, contacts and interactions have been useful to the project and tobacco control more broadly. For example, the project received major coverage when the overall ATSA program leader and program officer made a site visit, and anecdotally it seems that many journalists are aware of tobacco control measures and demonstrate knowledge of the issues.

The team anticipates that the tobacco industry and its allies will be vehemently opposed to smoke-free policies. The tobacco industry will be opposed to any policy that will negatively affect the number of people that smoke and/or consumption. Similarly, some restaurant, bar and hotel owners will oppose such policies because they fear negative effects on their sales. It is possible that some media outlets will be against the policy because they receive money or support from the tobacco industry. The position of tobacco growers has not been determined, but tobacco control advocates stress the need to offer concrete ways of making a living through alternative crops.

Tobacco Industry

Though tobacco production in both manufactured products and leaf cultivation has been decreasing in recent years, the industry maintains a strong presence. The national tobacco industry consists mainly of raw tobacco leaf production, the industrial production of cigarettes and tobacco product imports. Historical data concerning tobacco production and importation may be inaccurate because of the shortcomings of the country's statistical system. Furthermore, official import statistics do not accurately reflect the illicit trade.

History

Tobacco has been part of the economy for more than a century. Historical data from the Ministry of Agriculture and Rural Development indicate that tobacco farming was introduced in Cameroon by the Germans in 1907 for cigar wrapping, particularly in the Mungo area. Dutch technicians pursued this farming after World War I, and it continued uninterrupted until World War II. In 1945, tobacco farming was resumed in Batschenga, in the Centre-South Region, by the French company, SEITA (Société Nationale d'Exploitation Industrielle des Tabacs et Allumettes). The Batschenga station long served as a research and tobacco seed production center for various training companies. In the early 1950s, tobacco farming expanded further and was popularized particularly in rural areas of the East Region.

The industrialization of tobacco farming developed steadily after World War II. Farming increased from 25 tons in 1945 to 950 tons in 1962. In 1963, a Franco-Cameroonian company, the Société Franco-Camourounese des Tabacs (SFCT), took over from SEITA. On 30 January 1974, the Société Camerounaise des Tabacs (SCT) resumed all of the former SFCT's operations with the government as a majority interest holder. Under the SCT's supervision, production reached 2,400 tons in 1973–4, including 1,740 tons of wrapper tobacco and 660 tons of cut tobacco, all auctioned on the Paris market. Eventually, 13 production centers were created to channel the tobacco produced by 10,000 producers in areas such as Batouri, Bertoua, Mindourou, Ngoura, Belita, Gribi, Bétaré-Oya, Bandagoué, Lolo, Bengué-Tiko, Boubara, Ngotto and Bounou. During this era, the population involved in tobacco farming, which employs growers and support personnel for six months of the year, was approximately 50,000 people. In addition, the SCT provided permanent employment for 800 people, including 35 executives. It also provided for 360 temporary workers hired during the conditioning period. The SCT always provided support for producers of wrapping tobacco.

Bastos–British American Tobacco (BAT) and the Societé Industrielle des Tabacs du Cameroon (SITABAC) set up tobacco factories in Cameroon in 1950 and 1980, respectively, and concentrated their businesses on cut tobacco production, conditioning and marketing infrastructure. These companies' cigarettes continue to be sold in Cameroon and/or exported (in the case of SITABAC).

Production

Though large-scale industrial tobacco production no longer exists in Cameroon, small-scale production, carried out mainly by smallholder farmers, still exists. Over the last couple of decades, the industry has put effort into engaging tobacco farmers and preparing them for tobacco production. After the SCT was liquidated in 1997–8, tobacco producers were left to their own efforts to maintain the industry. Some executives and producers took advantage of the government's disengagement to implement structures in an attempt to take over operations of the defunct SCT in the East Region again. It was with this purpose in mind that several joint initiative groups and support organizations were created. The four main ones founded in the region were: la Fédération des Planteurs de Tabac et autres Cultures Vivrières du Cameroun (Cameroon Federation of Tobacco Growers and Growers of other Agricultural Food Crops) (FPTC), created 13 January 1997; the Compagnie d'Exploitation des Tabacs Camerounais (Cameroon

Tobacco Development Company) (CETAC corporation) in Batouri, created 1 November 1997; Mount Cameroon Tobacco (MCT corporation) in Batouri, created in May 1998; and the Cameroon Wrapper First limited company, created in November 2003. Generally, these organizations focus on the following: pre-financing of production activities, input and phytosanitary product subsidies, training, follow-up, business advice, regular payment for crops, education or sickness funds (FPTC), development and maintenance of gathering routes (CETAC) and credit (CETAC). As a result of these efforts, there remain thousands of small tobacco leaf producers. The most recent official data from the agricultural ministry suggest that 6,000 smallholder farmers are currently involved in tobacco farming. In 2004, small-scale producers generated 510 tons of tobacco at a price per kilogram ranging from 300 to 2,000 CFAF for the five grades of tobacco, generating between 1,020,000 and 153,000,000 CFAF for farms.

In the early 2000s, the national government, aware that tobacco farming generated significant revenue for certain producers, approved the Projet d'Appui à la Relance de la Tabaculture à l'Est Cameroun (Project Supporting the Revival of Tobacco Farming in Eastern Cameroon) (PARTEC). The total amount of the project was roughly 2.1 billion CFAF, including 530 million CFAF as an FPTC contribution and 1.6 billion CFAF in anticipated grant money from the Fonds Pays Pauvres Très Endettés program (PPTE – Heavily Indebted Poor Countries initiative). However, this tobacco farming grant was suspended or withdrawn as a result of the combined efforts of various tobacco control stakeholders (including the health, agriculture, commerce and finance ministries) before Cameroon signed the FCTC in 2006. Some advocates believe that this policy change played a role in BAT's departure from the manufacturing sector, though this has not been confirmed.

Because of the number of small tobacco producers, tobacco control advocates recognize that future strategies must include provisions for helping farmers find alternative livelihoods. In fact, an agreement reached at the ATSA stakeholders' meeting in October 2009 emphasized the need to provide farmers with alternative crops or other means of earning a living, since tobacco is still a livelihood for many of them.

Unlike leaf cultivation, which has remained fairly steady in recent years, the production of manufactured tobacco products has decreased, as illustrated in Table 8.1. From 1983 to 2004, two firms, BAT and SITABAC, produced manufactured tobacco goods. But in 2004, SITABAC, citing counterfeiting and smuggling issues, closed its operations. In 2007, in its African operational regional consolidation effort, BAT closed its Cameroon manufacturing subsidiary. SITABAC subsequently reopened that same year.

Table 8.1. Manufactured tobacco production in Cameroon (tons)

Year	1999	2000	2001	2002	2003	2004
Production	3,249	2,984	2,814	2,785	1,905	1,485
Change		−8.20%	−6%	−1.10%	−32%	−22%

Perhaps as a result of the uncertainty in the tobacco manufacturing sector, tobacco imports and exports have fluctuated enormously in recent years. Although Cameroon produces tobacco products for the international market, it is also a tobacco product importer. Measures reported in Table 8.2 indicate that trade varied considerably from 1999 to 2003, the only recent period for which there are accurate data. Approximately 30 percent of the country's tobacco products are currently imported.

Taxation and illicit trade

The tobacco industry generates some tax revenues for the national government. Table 8.3 presents data on customs and excise duties for

Table 8.2. Tobacco imports and exports in Cameroon

Year	1999	2000	2001	2002	2003
Imports					
Quantities imported (thousands of tons)	1,772	750	1,753	1,694	529
Change		−58%	134%	−3.40%	−69%
Import value (CFAF, millions)	3,200	4,718.5	3,903.7	4,166	1,698
Change		47%	−17%	6.70%	−59%
Share of import spending for tobacco		0.50%	0.30%	0.36%	0.15%
Exports					
Quantities exported (thousands of tons)	171.3	229	327.9	262	248
Change		+34%	+43%	−20%	−5%
Tobacco export revenues (CFAF, millions)	305	424	1,078	1,355	1,163
Change		+39%	+154%	+25.7%	−14%
Share of export revenues from tobacco		0.03%	0.08%	0.10%	0.09%

Table 8.3. Customs and excise duties on imported tobacco in Cameroon (CFAF, millions)

	2000	2001	2002	2003	2004
Customs duties (CD)	2,341.7	1,176.0	1,540.0	1,534.7	1,234.3
Excise duties (ED)	423.1	305.5	497.1	529.1	474.3
Total (CD + ED)	2,764.8	1,481.5	2,037.1	2,063.8	1,708.6

Source: Direction de la statistique et de la comptabilité nationale, MINEPAT (Department of Statistics and National Accounts, MINEPAT).

imported products for the period of 2000–4. Table 8.4 presents tax revenues for domestic tobacco manufacturing for 2000–2. Countries in the CEMAC subregion, which includes Cameroon, are reportedly considering a specific excise tax on tobacco products as part of a concerted tobacco control effort. This initiative could potentially result in increased customs and excise duty rates on tobacco products.

Though (or because) there is a tax stamp program in place to address illicit trade, tobacco product smuggling is thought to be executed at a sophisticated level in Cameroon. The extent of cigarette smuggling is difficult to assess and there are no customs statistics that track these activities. It is believed widely that low taxes in Benin and Nigeria encourage tobacco product smuggling into Cameroon. According to BAT and CEMAC, there was an estimated decline in tobacco sales figures of 4.5 billion CFA francs in 2003. Cameroon's geographic location is a natural factor that facilitates smuggling. Its Southwest Province lies along the coast, and the country's border with Nigeria is nearly 1,500 km long and poorly controlled. The main brands of cigarettes smuggled are Delta menthol, Delta, Aspen, London, Benson, Fine, Business Club, Marlboro, Craven, Rothmans and Dunhill. In addition to the tax stamp program, to combat illicit trade (including fraud, smuggling and counterfeiting), the government created an ad hoc committee through Decree No. 2005/0528/PM of 15 February 2005. In particular, there is an effort to pursue businesspeople who are involved in the illicit tobacco trade.

Table 8.4. Taxes on domestic tobacco production in Cameroon (CFAF, millions)

Fiscal year	Excise taxes	Income taxes	Total
2000/2001	1,309.12	1,348.17	2,657.29
2001/2002	442.54	2,196.42	2,939.96

Source: Direction de la statistique et de la comptabilité nationale, MINEPAT (Department of Statistics and National Accounts, MINEPAT).

Market power and opportunities

The overwhelmingly young Cameroonian population – more than 50 percent of people are under 20 years old – continues to represent a potentially viable market for the tobacco industry, and tobacco control advocates anticipate enormous challenges from the industry in the coming years. Similarly, the low smoking rate (below 10 percent) among women constitutes another potentially profitable market for the industry in Cameroon. In addition, as in most African countries, improvement in Cameroon's socioeconomic conditions encourages an increase in smoking as people begin to have more disposable income. There is strong evidence that the industry is already using a wide range of marketing strategies and focused promotion to entice and recruit new consumers, especially young and female ones. The tobacco control community is positioning itself to counter these efforts.

ATSA Review

The principal achievements of ATSA-related activities include the development of significant information, education and communication (IEC) materials; steps toward better enforcement of smoke-free regulations in the capital, Yaoundé; and the active promotion of smoke-free policies in the mainstream media. In terms of new materials, there was the development and wide dissemination of a scientific paper on the economic, social and health impacts of tobacco (~1,000 copies distributed to government officials, public health professionals, etc.). Furthermore, the team developed and distributed 15,000 posters, leaflets and warning signs (bilingual in French and English) on the dangers of tobacco products. These materials are widely displayed in Yaoundé as part of the effort to implement the smoke-free effort. In terms of media promotion, the team helped to design and implement regular broadcast television magazine segments (i.e. news information rather than advertisement length) on the national broadcaster CRTV in both French and English about passive smoking and banning smoking in workplaces and public spaces in Yaoundé. As of mid-2011, these efforts were ongoing. In addition, the tobacco control community continues to pursue the passage of a national bill that is FCTC-compliant.

Notes

1 Sources: CIA World Factbook https://www.cia.gov/library/publications/the-world-factbook/; except Organization of Economic Cooperation and Development (OECD) for development assistance statistics, and Food and Agriculture Organization of the United Nations – Statistics (FAOSTAT) for tobacco production. See http://stats.oecd.

org/index.aspx and http://faostat.fao.org/site/567/default.aspx#ancor respectively (accessed 20 July 2011).

2 Ministry of Public Health, Cameroon "Aperçu du document de travail pour l'élaboration du plan national de lutte antitabac, Point Focal Tabagisme" (Yaoundé: Comité national de lutte contre la drogue, 2007).

3 Health of Population in Transition (HoPiT), Cameroon Burden of Diabetes Project (CAMBoD), "Final report on project implementation" (2008), paper prepared by the HoPiT research group.

4 O. Shafey, S. Dolwick and G. E. Guidon (eds), *Tobacco Control Country Profiles* (2nd ed.), prepared for the 12th World Conference on Tobacco and Health . Online at: http://www.who.int/tobacco/global_data/country_profiles/en/index.html (accessed 20 July 2011).

5 Ministry of Public Health, "Aperçu du document de travail pour l'élaboration du plan national de lutte antitabac, Point Focal Tabagisme."

Chapter 9

ERITREA

Zemenfes Tsighe, Stifanos Hailemariam,
Senai Woldeab, Goitom Mebrahtu,
Mussie Habte, Selamawi Sium,
Meseret Bokuretsion, Hagos Ahmed,
Ghidey Gberyohannes,
Andemariam Gebremicael
and Giorgio Solomon

Executive Summary

Eritrea presents some interesting and hopeful opportunities for tobacco control, even though it is not yet a signatory of the Framework Convention on Tobacco Control (FCTC). Prevalence rates in Eritrea are low at approximately 8 percent, but there is regional variation and anecdotal reports of higher rates amongst young men in the conscripted army.

In this highly centralized regime with a powerful executive body, approval of proclamations generally indicates the government's commitment to a policy. Though the Office of the President finally approves all proclamations, the national ministries play a major role in crafting them. Regional "*zoba*" administrations also play vital roles in making, implementing and enforcing policies. Notably, the president proclaimed a set of national tobacco control regulations in 2004 (Proclamation 143/2004). Many of the articles of this proclamation are compliant with the FCTC; however, the regulations are largely ignored due to a lack of both political will and public awareness.

Proclamation 143/2004 includes provisions for smoke-free schools, but there is evidence of noncompliance. As a result, the African Tobacco Situation Analysis (ATSA) team initiated aggressive implementation and enforcement of smoke-free educational institutions. There are encouraging signs that this activity is building a critical mass of broader support for tobacco control and raising public awareness. Recently, both the health and education ministers have publicly stated their strong support of tobacco control for the first time. The ATSA team, though small and not comprised of tobacco control experts, continues steadfastly to press the agenda with the political establishment. Since decision making in the government is highly centralized, if the president and his cabinet can be convinced of the benefits of tobacco control, there are very good prospects for the enforcement of existing regulations and perhaps even the development of better ones.

Country Profile[1]

Population in 2009 (global and African ranking):	3,800,000 (110, 30)
Geographical size (global ranking):	124,320 sq. km (107)
GDP by purchasing power parity in 2008 (global ranking):	US$3.945 billion (166)
GDP real growth rate (2006–8):	0.7%
GDP per capita (global ranking):	US$700 (220)
Main industries:	Food processing and dairy products, alcoholic beverages, clothing and textiles, light manufacturing, salt, cement and other construction materials
Languages:	Afar, Arabic, Tigre, Kunama, Tigrinya, Bilen, Bidawyet, Nara and Saho
Official development assistance (ODA) – total commitments/disbursements (2007):	US$165.7/102.9 million
ODA as a percentage of GDP:	7.5%
Largest donors (disbursements in millions of USD):	EC 36.6, Global Fund 11.1, Norway 10.2, Japan 8.4, UK 6.3, UNDP 6, Netherlands 4.4
Tobacco production/imports/exports:	N/A

Brief Description of Political System

Type:	Eritrea is officially a presidential system.
Executive:	Isaias Afworki has been president since 1993. He is the chief of state and head of government.

Legislature: As of 2010, the legislature is comprised of the transitional unicameral National Assembly made up of 150 members. Currently, the sole legal party is the People's Front for Democracy and Justice (PFDJ).

Judiciary: There is a Court of Final Appeal, as well as high courts, regional courts and community courts.

Scope of Tobacco Problem

A number of smoking prevalence surveys have been conducted in Eritrea and they generally demonstrate low prevalence rates by global standards, though rates are considerably higher in specific demographic groups. The National Non-Communicable Disease Risk Factors Baseline Survey conducted in 2004 by the Ministry of Health (MoH) in collaboration with the World Health Organization (WHO) reported that 8 percent of the sampled population smoked, with 7 percent reporting being daily smokers. Smoking prevalence, however, showed important variation by age and sex. It ranged from 6.2 percent of the 15–24 age group to 21.6 percent of the 35–44 age group, and declined thereafter. Prevalence rates for women are much lower (~1 percent) than for men. Regionally, overall prevalence ranged from 10.2 percent in Gash Barka to 7.7 percent in Zoba Maekel to 5.2 percent in Zoba Debub.[2]

Researchers have examined the prevalence of noncigarette tobacco products. The same survey found that 2.9 percent of the population (>15 years old) currently used smokeless tobacco. The highest smokeless prevalence rate was for males older than 45 years. Across regions, the prevalence of smokeless tobacco ranged from 6.6 percent in Zoba Semienawi Keih Bahri to 0.4 percent in Zoba Maekel. Most users used either chewing tobacco (53.5 percent) or snuff by mouth (35 percent).

There have been efforts to examine better the patterns of tobacco use amongst youths. The Global Youth Tobacco Survey (GYTS) 2005 data, conducted by the MoH and the WHO, found that 8.2 percent of school students used any tobacco products, with 2 percent (2.6 percent of boys and 0.7 percent of girls) currently smoking cigarettes and 7 percent currently using other forms of tobacco. Cigarette smoking ranged from 0.7 percent in Zoba Debub to 3.4 percent in Semienawi and Debubawi Keih Bahri. More research will need to be executed in order to identify the precise variables conditioning these different rates across *zobas*.

There has also been an effort to examine prevalence among adults who provide education to young people. The Global School Personnel Survey (GSPS), executed at the same time as the GYTS, provides notable evidence for higher tobacco use rates among certain Eritrean adults. For example,

14.6 percent of school personnel used some form of tobacco (17 percent of men; 6.4 percent of women). Daily smoking was reported by 10.3 percent (12.5 percent of men; 2.7 percent of women), while daily use of smokeless tobacco was reported by 6.4 percent (6.6 percent of men; 5.7 percent of women).

The most recent survey, conducted by the ATSA Eritrea team in March 2008, focused on middle, secondary and college students. It covered Zoba Maekel and Zoba Debub Grade 6–12 students and all college students in these regions. The survey determined that 6 percent of the sample currently use some form of tobacco product (7.6 percent of boys; 3.5 percent of girls). Prevalence rates varied among different age groups. Prevalence (any tobacco product) among middle school students was 5.6 percent (7 percent of boys; 4 percent of girls) and among secondary school students, it was 4.8 percent (5.4 percent of boys; 3.9 percent of girls). Rates were higher with older students: 8.8 percent among Grade 12 students (13.8 percent of boys; 0.8 percent of girls) and 7.1 percent among college students (9.9 percent of boys; 0.8 percent of girls). Nearly 5 percent of the students currently smoke cigarettes (6.2 percent of males and 2.5 percent of girls) compared to 2 percent reported in the national 2005 GYTS. The survey of school personnel working in Zoba Maekel and Zoba Gash Barka found that 25 percent of the school personnel have smoked (32.8 percent male; 1.7 percent female) and that 16.4 percent are current cigarette smokers (21.1 percent male; 1.7 percent female), while 4 percent of them have used other tobacco products and 2 percent of them are current users of other forms of tobacco (2.4 percent male; 0.6 percent female).

Politics of Tobacco

The ATSA team

The stakeholder meetings invited people from across Eritrean society, including from the highest levels of government (e.g. ministers), institutions of higher learning and businesses, as well as representatives from student, youth and women's groups. The eventual ATSA team also came from a wide variety of sectors including government (e.g. the Bureau of Higher Education Administration, the National Board for Higher Education, the ministries of Health and Education and the National Statistics Office), civil society (e.g. National Union of Eritrean Youth and Students and the National Union of Eritrean Women) and the academy, across a wide cross-section of disciplines (accounting, dentistry, finance, law, medicine and nursing).

Inventory of existing laws and regulations

The wide-ranging Proclamation 143/2004 governs many aspects of tobacco control in Eritrea. For example, it forbids smoking in all public places, sales of tobacco products to minors and all tobacco advertising. The law also mandates that all tobacco packages contain a health warning, preferably on 50 percent or more, but no less than 30 percent, of the principal display area. Yet, the ATSA team notes that the political will embodied in Proclamation 143/2004 has proven mostly toothless because neither institutional will nor broad public awareness for its effective implementation have existed.

The enforcement of specific provisions in Proclamation 143/2004 has been fraught with difficulties. For example, the proclamation forbids smoking or holding a lighted cigarette within the enclosed, indoor areas of "educational institutions of all levels,"[3] though anecdotally, tobacco control proponents have observed that this is regularly violated. As yet, there is no institutional body that takes the responsibility to enforce and monitor the proclamation. As discussed below, without such a body, violators go unpunished.

Overall context

The Eritrean government is comprised of executive, legislative and judicial branches, but the preponderance of political power lies with the executive. The executive branch is composed of the Cabinet of Ministers and the president. Approval of proclamations usually indicates the position on, and political commitment to, a policy by the government, including, in theory, public health measures such as tobacco. Moreover, national ministries, their corresponding bureaucracies and regional *zoba* administrations (there are a total of six *zobas* or regions) all play vital roles in making, implementing and enforcing policies.

Though the Office of the President provides the final approval for all proclamations with the help of its legal advisors, the national ministries play a major role in crafting them. For example, the MoH spearheaded the creation of Proclamation 143/2004. Furthermore, the budgets of all state agencies and the *zoba* administrations are negotiated through the Ministry of Finance and approved by the national Cabinet of Ministers (16 ministers in total). The *zoba* administrations, which have their own regional assemblies, can also make their own laws as long as they do not duplicate, violate and/or contradict national laws. In fact, most of the day-to-day responsibilities of governance fall to the ministry bureaucracies and the *zoba* administrations, so they are potentially critical to implementing and enforcing tobacco control laws.

There is concrete evidence of high-level support for tobacco control in the country among high-level government officials. The MoH is spearheading tobacco control policy efforts and oversees health studies and activities in Eritrea. As indicated above, it has conducted various surveys and prepared Proclamation 143/2004, the country's principal existing tobacco legislation. The Ministry of Education (MoE), which throughout 2009 has been under the direction of H. E. Mr Semere Russom, is also supporting anti-tobacco use activities and providing education on health hazards of tobacco through its Life-Skill Based Health Education and Health Science Technology Education curricula. The curricula on health education cover a variety of tobacco-related topics. Some schools have demonstration kits. Notably, after the conference in July 2009 to inaugurate the Tobacco Free School Environment Initiative, the minister of education spoke publicly about the importance of this initiative. Similarly, at the conference, Ato Berhane Ghebregziabiher, the director general of health services, representing H. E. Mrs Amna Nurhussein, the minister of health, highlighted the danger of the tobacco epidemic and expressed the ministry's support of the initiative. The Ministry of Information is also supportive of the anti-tobacco efforts, and it has recently started broadcasting anti-tobacco, pro-health programs.

During the ATSA-sponsored baseline assessment and the initial country consultancy meeting (9–10 June 2008), a representative from the Ministry of Defense expressed a concern that many of the young soldiers are smoking and showed an interest in any anti-tobacco use activities and programs. However, there is not any systematic study of the prevalence of tobacco use among members of the Eritrean Defense Forces, making this an area that merits attention in the future.

Additional nonministry key supporters of anti-tobacco use activities in Eritrea include the National Union of Eritrean Youth and Students (NUEYS) and the National Union of Eritrean Women (NUEW). These two organizations are actively engaged in promoting healthy lifestyles and their programs include anti-tobacco activities. In fact, the NUEYS has fully implemented Proclamation 143/2004 in all of its premises throughout the country.

Although Eritrea has issued a proclamation to provide for the control of tobacco use in the country, it has not yet acceded to the WHO FCTC. However, it is worth noting that many of the articles in Proclamation 143/2004 are based on and fully compatible with the FCTC. The necessary documents for accession to the FCTC have been forwarded to the appropriate authorities.[1]

Tobacco-free school environment

Proclamation 143/2004 seeks to address the problem of smoking amongst young people. It prohibits smoking or holding a lighted cigarette within "educational institutions of all levels."[5] Moreover, it prohibits sales of tobacco products to minors (under 18 years old), sales or offering of tobacco products in all educational institutions and distribution of free tobacco products or items bearing tobacco brand names or logos. Approval and promulgation of this proclamation by the Office of the President can be taken as a stated supportive position on tobacco control at the highest level. Moreover, the MoE issued the "Thirty Golden Rules" document, which establishes a code of behavior for students. One of these golden rules prohibits smoking and the use of any tobacco product by students inside school compounds.

However, due to lack of enforcement of the proclamation, this initial step forward in tobacco control is not yet as monumental as expected. For example, there is corroborated anecdotal evidence from every recent tobacco control stakeholder meeting of school personnel smoking in school compounds. More empirically, the 2008 survey effort indicates that more than one-third of current cigarette smokers and 69 percent of current smokeless tobacco users consumed tobacco products in school premises such as tea rooms and staff lounges. Moreover, ATSA team members have observed the selling of cigarettes in school compounds. Additionally, street vendors and shops sell cigarettes at or close to school gates, providing students easy access to tobacco.

Government institutions are expected to support the Tobacco-Free Schools Environment Initiative (TFSEI) because it is in line with the provisions of Proclamation 143/2004. However, there is concern from supporters of the proclamation that some bureaucrats who smoke may not be enthusiastic about abiding by or enforcing it. These actors will need to be monitored for compliance to existing laws.

The *zoba* administrations are powerful and work in very close connection with the schools. Every *zoba* administration has a director general for social service (DGSS), who is responsible for any activities in schools and to whom the schools report directly. They also have heads of *zoba* MoE and *zoba* MoH branch offices. All of these functionaries bear the responsibility of implementing any pertinent government proclamations. The ATSA team believes that if they are convinced of the importance of the TFSEI, they can take it as part of their mandate and oversee its effective implementation in their respective schools.

The government agencies that administer higher education are logical allies in the tobacco control effort. The National Board of Higher Education (NBHE) is an obvious potential ally because its key constituency is young people. All institutes of higher education (IHE) are under the NBHE. The executive director of the NBHE expressed his position against tobacco use in his opening speech at the initial country consultancy meeting and promised to support the research team in all its activities. The ATSA team has continued to receive excellent support from him. Some colleges such as the College of Health Sciences and Orotta School of Medicine have expressed their interest in the anti-tobacco drive in the country and are even working to include it in their curricula. Moreover, the IHE have a pool of expertise (sociologists, anthropologists, health professionals, biomedical researchers, demographers, etc.) that can easily be tapped to conduct research and generate the knowledge required to inform and influence policy and decision makers.

In Eritrea, all IHE are fully and completely funded by the government and to the best of the knowledge of the ATSA team members, there is no direct linkage between British American Tobacco–Eritrea (BAT) and any IHE in the form of funding or scholarships. Similarly, no schools to date have had any of their activities sponsored and/or supported by BAT.

Tobacco Industry Monitoring

Background

Tobacco has a lengthy and prominent history in Eritrea. It may have been introduced to Eritrea in the sixteenth century by Portuguese soldiers or travelers.[6] In the second half of the nineteenth century, the Senhit area (particularly around Keren) was producing and exporting tobacco to Egypt. One of the popular brands (Nargile and chew) in Egypt at that time, Senahit, may have derived its name from Senhit (now a province in modern Eritrea).

Production of tobacco increased markedly throughout the twentieth century. In the 1900s, the Italians were conducting tests on local varieties, but Keren tobacco was found to be poorly combustible and the project was abandoned. In 1918, interest in tobacco was revived, and cultivation increased around Keren and other localities, probably in Tokombia, Ghinda and Segheneiti. Anecdotal discussions with elders suggest that the Italians were distributing cigarettes to Eritrean soldiers (*ascaris*) as part of their salary.

In 1920, a Greek company, Mina Ananistilia, was established and started to produce hand-rolled cigarettes using hand tools. A cigarette without a filter, with the brand name of Ideal, was produced. In 1929, the company was taken over by the Italian government and renamed Monopolio Tobacco Del'Eritrea.[7] The Italians renovated it by bringing new machinery from Holland, and its capacity increased to 300 cigarettes per minute.

In 1941, the British Military Administration (BMA) took over the factory and brought second-hand machinery from Egypt that enabled 600–700 cigarettes to be produced per minute. In 1959, there were two tobacco farms in Tokombia owned by Italians, namely Azienda Agricola Camozzi Giovani and Azienda Agricola Gabba Pietro. The latter was experimenting with various exotic varieties, but production was for local consumption. In 1962, the Ethiopian government took over the cigarette factory and renamed

Table 9.1. Eritrean tobacco consumption
by product type, 2000

Imported cigarettes	14%
Local cigarettes	52%
Tobacco/raw	23%
Other	11%

it Tobacco Monopoly of Ethiopia. In 1976, it was again renamed Asmara Cigarette Factory. In 1988, new machinery was installed. This modernization raised the production capacity of the factory to 2,500 cigarettes per minute. A new Ideal cigarette brand with a filter was produced.

After the liberation of Eritrea in 1991, the factory's name was changed to Gash Cigarette Factory (GCF). The GCF was privatized and acquired by Rothmans of Pall Mall in 1998. A year later, BAT and Rothmans merged, and the new company took the BAT appellation. As Table 9.1 presents, the latest data (2000) demonstrate that local cigarettes continue to make up the largest proportion of tobacco products consumed in Eritrea, though there is also an import market and an informal market of less processed products.

Production

BAT–Eritrea is the only tobacco manufacturing company in Eritrea. As Figure 9.1 reports, the gross output of cigarettes of BAT in Eritrea increased steadily from 1995 and reached its peak value of 220 million Nakfa in 2005.

Figure 9.1. Eritrean tobacco production by value, 1995–2006

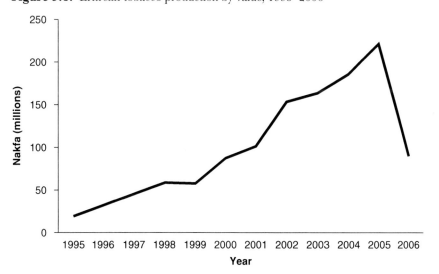

Privatization of the company and introduction of new advanced production technology by BAT increased the production capacity of the company fivefold. However, due to the lack of foreign currency, the production of cigarettes dwindled in 2006. Though no firm statistics are available, it is widely believed to have since increased once again.

Due to Eritrea's geographical isolation – it has long, sparsely populated borders with Sudan and Ethiopia, as well as a lengthy Red Sea coast – smuggling presents a concern. During 1995–2007, it is estimated by government agencies that approximately 20 million Nakfa's worth of cigarettes and chewing tobacco were smuggled into Eritrea (more cigarettes than chewing tobacco). Government officials believe that smuggling activities have increased since 2006, but more research on identifying the origins of the smuggled products needs to be done. Additionally, the reasons for smuggling (e.g. price differentials) need to be explored systematically by researchers.

Employment

According to Ministry of Industry and Trade official statistics, the number of employees in the tobacco industry declined from 139 in 1995, prior to privatization of the company, to 41 persons in 2006. The main reason for the decline is the modernization and automation of production facilities by BAT.

Employment in the Eritrean tobacco sector, however, is likely to be much higher in retail contexts (street vendors, agents for BAT, small shopkeepers) than in tobacco production or processing. There is ample anecdotal evidence of children hawking cigarettes on street corners to supplement meager family incomes.

Advertising and promotions

BAT, Eritrea's primary tobacco supplier, boasts of a strong public presence. It has a monopoly right to sell tobacco products in Eritrea. This means that without the permission of BAT–Eritrea, no one can sell cigarettes in Eritrea legally. It is technically legal, however, for those dealing in duty-free commerce to import non-BAT brands, or likewise when there is a supply shortage of BAT products. There are 19 wholesalers and 6,500 retailers duly licensed to sell BAT cigarettes in Eritrea. Although the government bans the advertising of cigarettes, anecdotal reports from stakeholders at the ATSA meetings report that BAT regularly gives out pens, pencils, bags, T-shirts, jackets, and other youth-centric items that carry tobacco company logos in direct violation of Proclamation 143/2004. Moreover, BAT continues to use point-of-purchase marketing techniques to promote its tobacco products. In terms of corporate social responsibility (CSR) activities, BAT employees in Eritrea take part in occasional community service events, such as a mass planting of several hundred trees to mitigate soil erosion.[8]

ATSA Review

Building on the framework of the 2004 proclamation, the ATSA team's achievements include: implementing a smoke-free policy in educational institutions; conducting one of the first major systematic examinations of smoking prevalence and other tobacco use; developing new anti-smoking materials specific for Eritrea; and offering direct assistance to organizations spreading a public anti-tobacco message. First, the team helped to formulate and submit a tobacco-free school policy to the Ministry of Education for final approval. As part of the effort, new, appropriate resource materials were developed and disseminated to pilot schools. Second, in terms of monitoring prevalence, the team conducted both a National Survey of Students and a National Survey of School Personnel. In a related effort, the team completed a Tobacco Marketing Study in order to determine better how the industry is reaching its customers and potential customers. Finally, in an effort to heighten awareness, the team hosted a widely attended seminar on the hazards of tobacco use for journalists, students and the general public. Media interviews and demonstrations were also organized to promote the anti-smoking message. The team has helped to establish anti-tobacco support group committees at the school level by empowering school health clubs. To help these organizations, the team developed and distributed new sensitization and awareness posters, cartoons and an anti-tobacco drama on CD-ROM. Finally, the team helped to develop anti-tobacco public announcements, which are being broadcast by the principal state media. Tobacco control proponents continue to pursue the implementation of more provisions from the tobacco control proclamation.

Notes

1 Sources: CIA World Factbook https://www.cia.gov/library/publications/the-world-factbook/; except National Statistical Office – Eritrea for population and land size; Organization of Economic Cooperation and Development (OECD) for development assistance statistics; and Food and Agriculture Organization of the United Nations – Statistics (FAOSTAT) for tobacco production. For the latter two, see http://stats.oecd.org/index.aspx and http://faostat.fao.org/site/567/default.aspx#ancor respectively (accessed 20 July 2011).

2 A *zoba* is a region in Eritrea.

3 Government of the State of Eritrea, Proclamation 143/2004, Article 7 (2004).

4 "Accession" is a one-step process equivalent to ratification.

5 Government of the State of Eritrea, Proclamation 143/2004, Article 7.

6 Amanuel Sahle, "Tobacco Comes to Eritrea," Shaebia, 19 March 2007. Online at: http://www.shaebia.org/cgi-bin/artman/exec/view.cgi?archive=16&num=4865 (accessed 21 July 2011).
7 D. Mulugeta, "Internship Report in British American Tobacco Eritrea Trade and Marketing Distribution Function," working paper, Department of Business Management, College of Business and Economics, University of Asmara, 30 December 2005.
8 Shabait, "Employees of BAT Company Plant Tree Seedlings at Martyrs Park," 21 July 2006.

Chapter 10

GHANA

Edith Wellington, John Gyapong, Sophia Twum-Barima, Moses Aikins and John Britton

Executive Summary

Despite considerable international activity in tobacco control, including shaping the Framework Convention on Tobacco Control (FCTC), comprehensive national legislation has been a struggle to achieve in Ghana. Accordingly, the most recent tobacco control efforts in Ghana, including the African Tobacco Situation Analysis (ATSA) initiative, have focused on advocating for national comprehensive legislation. Unfortunately, the legislation has been stalled for more than five years. It is not clear how much support there is for the legislation in either the new cabinet or the national legislature. High-level changes in the health ministry have complicated these efforts, so the advocacy community has been once again regrouping to assess the potential for high-level support.

In the interim, the tobacco control community has identified other goals that may be more feasible in the short term. With comparatively low prevalence rates (approximately 5 percent) and a public generally compliant with informal tobacco control norms – particularly smoke-free public places of various sorts (e.g. hospitals, educational institutions, public transport, etc.) – a formalization of existing rules and regulations with an emphasis on enforcement could be sought concurrent to the pursuit of the broader legislation.

The Research and Development Division (RDD, formerly the Health Research Unit of the Ghana Health Service (GHS)) has been the principal leader of the ATSA team. While this unit is well-poised to conduct health research (it has strong ties to the Universities of Ghana and Nottingham) and public education, it has limitations, as an official government entity, in advocating effectively for policy change. Civil society organizations, including Vision for Alternative Development (VALD) and Healthy Ghana, have become more outspoken publicly about tobacco control issues, and their participation will be central to the success of current initiatives. Furthermore, engaging other parts of the government in tobacco control will also put pressure on policymakers to effect change. Recently, in a very encouraging development for the tobacco control community, the Food and Drugs Board (FDB) has taken a more assertive role, particularly in the area of warning labels on packages. External donors have been supporting the push for broad national legislation.

Country Profile[1]

Population in 2009 (global and African ranking):	23,832,495 (46, 9)
Geographical size (global ranking):	238,533 sq. km (88)
GDP by purchasing power parity in 2008 (global ranking):	US$34.2 billion (100)
GDP real growth rate (2006–8):	6.4%
GDP per capita (global ranking):	US$1,500 (197)
Main industries:	Mining, lumbering, light manufacturing, aluminum smelting, food processing, cement, small commercial ship building, cocoa, rice, cassava (tapioca), peanuts, corn, shea nuts, bananas, timber
Languages:	Asante (15.8%), Ewe (12.7%), Boron or Brong (4.6%), Dagomba (4.3%), Dangme (4.3%), Dagarte or Dagaba (3.7%), Akyem (3.4%), Ga (3.4%), Akuapem (2.9%), other (including English (official), 36.1%)
Official development assistance (ODA) – total commitments/ disbursements (2007):	US$1675.4/825.8 million
ODA as a percentage of GDP:	5.5%
Largest donors (disbursements in millions of USD):	UK 152, Netherlands 142.2, EC 85.5, USA 70.7, Canada 54.5, Denmark 53.5, Germany 52.7, France 52.5, Global Fund 47, Japan 46.5
Tobacco production by volume in 2007 (global ranking):	2,700 tons (75)
Tobacco exports (2007):	Tobacco (unmanufactured): 2,455 tons at $2,637 per ton, #17 export
Tobacco imports (2007):	N/A

Brief Description of Political System

Type: Ghana is a constitutional democracy with a presidential system.
Executive: The president is John Atta Mills as of January 2009. He is the
               chief of state and head of government.
Cabinet: Members of the cabinet, the Council of Ministers, are appointed
               by the president and approved by the parliament.
Legislature: This is a unicameral parliament with 230 seats that are up for
               election every four years via direct popular vote. The 2008 election
               produced a legislature dominated by the National Democratic
               Congress (114 seats) and the National Patriotic Party (107 seats).
Judiciary: Supreme Court.

Scope of Tobacco Problem

Though data are scattered, it is apparent that the rates of tobacco use are lower
in Ghana compared to other countries in the region and globally. Nevertheless,
tobacco use is widespread and poses a genuine public health challenge. There
are several common forms of tobacco use, though cigarette smoking is the
most widespread. Other major forms of use include pipe smoking, chewing,
sniffing and oral or nasal use of smokeless tobacco. There were no national
prevalence data on tobacco use in Ghana until the early 2000s, and before that
time, prevalence data were not representative of the whole country. Earlier
prevalence data were in the form of small sample surveys and the Global
Youth Tobacco Survey (GYTS). These surveys conducted between 1970
and 2008 showed prevalence rates ranging from 3 percent to 33 percent due
to the variation in sample sizes, data collection tools and target population.
Apart from the 2008 study on "Smoking uptake and prevalence in Ghana"
undertaken in the Ashanti region, most of the earlier prevalence studies were
concentrated in Accra and its environs.

In one of the first major studies on cigarette smoking habits of secondary
school students in the Accra district of the Greater Accra Region in 1994,
it was found that 4.1 percent of students in a particular mixed school had
smoked before and 2 percent smoked cigarettes regularly (N=100). In
the survey, 88 percent of students reported that smoking was a problem
among secondary school students. According to the survey, those students
who smoked were aware that school rules stipulated a punishment for those
caught smoking in school.[2]

In a later and much larger national survey, Dennis-Antwi et al. (2003)[3]
sought to determine the prevalence and social consequences of substance
(i.e. drug) use among 2,500 second-cycle and out-of-school youths. They found

that 8.7 percent of respondents had smoked cigarettes. Users were influenced to smoke by friends (31.7 percent) and social pressure (31.2 percent), and a higher proportion (71.3 percent) smoked in groups while about 28.7 percent smoked individually. Of the reported smokers, 37.8 percent said that they were regular smokers who smoked daily in the six months prior to the study. About 27.1 percent of smokers had been smoking for about a year; 17.8 percent for two years; and 19.5 percent for three years. Apart from cigarette smoking, 27 percent of the users chewed or sniffed tobacco as a regular habit once or twice a day.

In 2000, Ghana joined the Global Tobacco Surveillance System (GTSS) and undertook the first GYTS. This study was repeated in 2005 and 2009, and data from these surveys are the most representative for youths in the country. The GYTS focuses on youths aged 13–15 and collects information in junior secondary schools. A total of 9,990 students participated in the Ghana GYTS in 2005. Table 10.1 presents some of the key findings, including current smoking rates of less than 5 percent for males and females.

For the current smokers, 18.5 percent mostly smoked at home. On the issue of second hand tobacco smoke, 39 percent reported being around others who smoke in places outside their home, while another 39.6 percent thought that smoke from others was harmful to them.[1]

The most recent national smoking prevalence data come from studies conducted as part of the GTSS and the Ghana Demographic Health Survey (GDHS). The first attempt at a national adult survey was in 2008 when the GDHS asked a few questions on the extent of smoking among Ghanaian

Figure 10.1. Ghana GYTS 2005 prevalence highlights

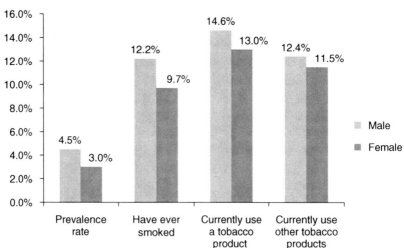

adults. Women and men were asked if they currently smoke cigarettes or use other forms of tobacco. Results from the GDHS demonstrate that smoking in Ghana is higher amongst men than women. Almost all women and 93 percent of men said they do not use tobacco at all and only 6 percent of men said they currently smoke cigarettes. Among men, the highest proportion of current smokers is in the Northern (11.9 percent), Upper East (11.6 percent) and Upper West (12.9 percent) regions.

Politics of Tobacco

Overall political context

Broadly speaking, Ghana has demonstrated commitment to tobacco control, particularly internationally. Notably, Ghana participated actively in the development of the World Health Organization's (WHO) FCTC and was one of the first five African countries to become a party to the convention in November 2004. Ghana has also played active roles by chairing committee meetings at the first and second Conferences of the Parties, in Geneva (2006) and Thailand (2007) respectively. It also played a leading role in tobacco control activities and programs worldwide that included the Framework Convention Alliance seminar for NGOs in the Africa Regional Office (AFRO) region in 2007; the first session of the Intergovernmental Negotiating Body on the Protocol on Illicit Trade in Tobacco Products in Geneva in February 2008; and hosting the WHO-sponsored Consultation on Regional Capacity Building for Tobacco Control in Africa.

Although the national government of Ghana has been rhetorically supportive of tobacco control, related policy development has been slow. Apart from ratifying the FCTC in 2004, governments have continued to show an unenthusiastic attitude toward passing the proposed Tobacco Control Bill. However, successive governments have adopted various narrower policies, including legislative and administrative measures concerning tobacco control. In fact, much of Ghana's tobacco control success has come from administrative rules, not national laws. Most directives have come out of pronouncements by government officials during commemorations of World No Tobacco Day. These pronouncements have held over time because of people's goodwill and not because they have any substantial legal basis.

There are clear examples of contemporary ministerial directives on tobacco control that have demonstrated some effectiveness. Firstly, the Ministry of Education (MoE) prohibits the smoking of cigarettes by both students and teachers at the pre-tertiary educational level during school and working hours, and there are prescribed stiff punishments for those caught smoking. Secondly, the Ministry of Transportation restricts smoking on public and private commercial transport, including the Ghana Private Road Transport Union (GPRTU), intercity State Transit Corporation (STC) buses and on both local and international flights. Thirdly, the Ministry of Health (MoH) has prohibited smoking in all of its healthcare facilities in the country, a measure that remains in force. Additional pronouncements by government officials in the 1980s placed restrictions on smoking in government facilities, offices and other public places, including restaurants and cinemas. The effectiveness of these measures has never been studied rigorously, so the actual levels of compliance are not well documented.

Beyond the ministerial support for tobacco control, there has been public pressure for new tobacco control measures. Based on the overwhelming support from the general public for tobacco control, the National Tobacco Control Steering Committee was set up by the government in January 2002 and mandated to draft a Tobacco Control Bill. The country's ratification of the FCTC gave the need for this legislation a further boost. The ratification led to the redrafting and editing of the draft bill in 2005 before submitting it to cabinet by the then minister of health. In 2008–9, the draft bill was reviewed by local and international experts and resubmitted to the attorney general's office for onward submission through the minister of health to the cabinet. For a variety of reasons, progress on the bill has stalled. As of mid-2011, it was not clear if the bill would be passed from the cabinet to the legislature, as is the legislative process in Ghana.

At the legislative level, there is some evidence of support for the bill. After several advocacy meetings with members of parliament (MPs), particularly the Select Committee on Health, several MPs have given assurances of their strong support for the passage of the bill. In demonstration of this support, members have made statements on the floor of the house and provided a signed statement of commitment to the advocacy team at a three-day exhibition in the parliament house.

Much of the support for and efforts to promote tobacco control are coming from the agency level in the national government. Encouragingly, this support is widespread and includes key institutions such as the ministries of Health; Education; Finance; Environment, Science and Technology; Tourism; and Justice. For example, the Ghana Education Service (GES) in the MoE is a major partner for the implementation of smoke-free policies in public places with specific reference to schools and all institutions of learning. The GES is a key partner in the provision of health services to the population. It is represented on the GHS council as a major policy decision-making body. Concerning implementation of relevant policy, the School Health Promotion (SHEP) coordinators at the

national, regional and district levels are already actively working with the focal
point for tobacco control.

The Environmental Protection Agency (EPA), under the Ministry
of Environment, Science and Technology, is also very active in tobacco
control. Generally speaking, the agency comanages, protects and enhances
the country's environment, as well as seeking common solutions to global
environmental problems. Though much energy is being exerted on outdoor
air pollution quality monitoring in Ghana, the EPA is also executing indoor air
pollution monitoring on a smaller scale. The agency has seven main divisions;
the two specifically involved in indoor air quality issues are the Information,
Education and Communication division and the Environmental Compliance
and Enforcement division.

One of key attributes of the EPA is that it already has a law on indoor-
air pollution that will support new smoke-free policies. This law, though not
specific to tobacco control, can be used by smoke-free advocates to illustrate
that indoor air pollutants should be eliminated. Through the National Steering
Committee meetings, the EPA has already expressed its willingness to use these
laws accordingly for tobacco smoke. The EPA is also important in that it has
offices across Ghana, and with its existing teams of inspectors, it can be one of
the agencies involved actively in enforcement.

The Ghana Tourist Board (GTB) is a major stakeholder in a smoke-free
policy intervention because it has jurisdiction over some of the largest public
places with broad visibility to the public. The GTB is the sole government
agency that implements the government's tourism policies. It is mainly a
research, marketing and regulatory body under the Ministry of Tourism
with a mandate to develop, promote and coordinate all tourism activities
in Ghana. The tourism sector in general, but especially the GTB, has been
an ally to the GHS in its tobacco control efforts. The GTB, working in
partnership with the hospitality industry (i.e. restaurants, bars, nightclubs
etc.), has gone ahead to create smoke-free places within their facilities and
even made public commitments to support a proposed broader ban on
smoking in public places.

Two departments of the GTB – quality assurance and public relations – will
be pivotal to tobacco control efforts. First, the Quality Assurance Department
inspects, classifies licenses, regulates and registers accommodation and
catering/eating enterprises, as specified under Legislative Instrument 1205.
This department and its teams of inspectors are particularly key to enforcement
of smoke-free policies. Second, the Public Relations Department ensures the
free flow of information between the board and the general public; evolves
strategies and machinery for explaining and promoting public understanding
of the activities of the board; prints publications on the activities of the board

and industry for the public and specified agencies; and monitors the print and electronic media on public opinion concerning activities of the board and industry. In terms of spreading messages related to tobacco control and the tourism sector, this department is pivotal.

The Food and Drugs Board (FDB) in the MoH is another pivotal agency in the tobacco control effort. In particular, the board has a Tobacco and Substance Abuse Department, which currently regulates imported tobacco products. It requires packages to state the place of origin and to bear the inscription "for sale in Ghana" in order to better identify licit from illicit cigarettes. The FDB has registered importers of cigarette products, and put in place a permit system to monitor and better regulate these importers. Almost all cigarette brands imported into Ghana have been duly registered (importers also have to register with Customs and Excise, see below). In 2010, the FDB introduced improved health-warning labels on all tobacco packaging. Finally, the FDB has a team of inspectors who could potentially play enforcement roles for a number of tobacco control areas.

The Research and Development Division (the RDD, formally known as the Health Research Unit) – a division within the GHS under the MoH – is the major stakeholder in tobacco control. The service is the secretariat of the National Tobacco Steering Committee, and coordinates all tobacco control activities in Ghana through the focal point for tobacco control. The RDD has been highly active in the development of legislation, pursuit of the implementation and enforcement of existing directives, education and awareness campaigns and research to support these activities.

Actors from other key national health institutions have also begun to play active roles in tobacco control. For example, staff members from both the Health Promotion Unit of the GHS (MoH) and the Accra Psychiatric Hospital have devoted their time as resource people to tobacco control efforts. Also, psychiatric nurses with counseling skills in drug abuse and HIV/AIDS were introduced to provide tobacco control cessation and counseling service to smokers in the capital.

Several other important agencies are playing important roles in tobacco control. The Customs, Excise and Prevention Service (CEPS) from the Ministry of Finance serves on the National Steering Committee on Tobacco Control and has been examining strategies to address smuggling. The attorney general's office in the Department of Justice and the Ghana Standards Board also serve actively on the National Steering Committee on Tobacco Control, and helped to facilitate the drafting of the National Tobacco Control Bill.

Civil society action is paramount to the success of tobacco control efforts in Ghana. Civil society groups aim to: influence policy change; sensitize communities to tobacco issues; create awareness about the dangers of second-hand smoke; and mobilize society for action to compel government to issue directives, as well speed up the passage of the tobacco control law. The Coalition of NGOs in Tobacco Control (CNTC), an organization made up of over 15 NGOs, is the key civil society group that leads the effort from the nongovernmental side. Specific NGOs include the Network for Community Planning and Development (NECPAD), Healthy Ghana, the Movement Against Tobacco and Substances of Abuse (MATOSA), the Communication for Development Centre (CfDC), Healthpage Ghana, Vision for Alternative Development (VALD), the Future Rescue Foundation, and the Integrated Social Development Centre (ISODEC). The coalition has so far sensitized stakeholders – including the media, the hospitality industry, the Ghana Actors Guild, etc. – on the need for a smoke-free ruling.

Healthy Ghana has played a pivotal role in recent years in tobacco control in Ghana. It is a health-based NGO created to establish a healthy population and a healthy environment, and to support comprehensively its identified social determinants of health. Since its founding in 2008, it has published extensively on healthy lifestyle issues and addressed many corporate bodies, schools and civil society organization. Healthy Ghana has also written extensively on exercise, environmental sanitation, air quality, dust inhalation, nutrition, economic and poverty issues in the Ghanaian print media. The executive director of Healthy Ghana, Professor Agyeman Badu Akosa, has been the pillar of tobacco control activities in Ghana. He is a past director general of the GHS, a position he held for five years, during which time he raised advocacy efforts on tobacco control. He is the past president of both the Ghana Medical Association and the Commonwealth Medical Association. He is also a recipient of the National Honor, the Companion of the Order of Volta, and a fellow of a number of prestigious scientific institutions. Currently, Professor Akosa is a professor of pathology at the University of Ghana Medical School.

Several major nongovernmental organizations – including particularly NECPAD, VALD and MATOSA – are playing major roles in promoting tobacco control in Ghana. NECPAD is a not-for-profit organization with a focus on sustainable community development, social justice, poverty alleviation, gender equality and related research and advocacy. It is committed to the use of participatory approaches (including poverty-sensitive, demand-responsive gender participatory approaches) and networking in the pursuit of its agenda. It has been involved in the fight against the use of tobacco in all its forms in Ghana by conducting awareness-raising programs and advocating for policy formulation on tobacco control. The organization is a key member of the Ghana Anti-Tobacco Use Alliance (GATUA). VALD was established to promote alternative initiatives and development at all levels of society. It engages in health promotion and information about tobacco control. The organization – particularly via Executive Director Issah Ali and General Secretary Labram Musah – has been very vocal recently about tobacco control generally, but also specifically about it being FCTC-compliant. MATOSA, headed by Oscar Bruce, has been a fervent advocate against anything related to tobacco. More generally, it has also been involved in public awareness creation and rehabilitation services of ex-addicts. Similarly, Frederick D. Aye, the executive director of the Consumers Association of Ghana, has focused mainly on advocating against anything that could be harmful or has negative health consequences on the ultimate consumer in the country. He has served on the National Steering Committee since 2002 and participated in almost all tobacco control activities in Ghana.

Finally, the tobacco control community has a great deal of academic support. In particular, the Department of Community Health of the School of Medical Sciences at Kwame Nkrumah University of Science and Technology and the School of Public Health at the University of Ghana have been heavily involved with conducting tobacco-focused research that will directly support advocates with evidence-based arguments.

Tobacco Industry

Production

The presence of the tobacco industry in Ghana dates back to the independence era when most companies sought to establish businesses in the newly independent state. For a number of years, three tobacco manufacturing companies operated in the country until British American Tobacco (BAT) became the sole local manufacturer in Ghana after its merger with Meridian Tobacco Company in 1999.[5] The core business of BAT was cigarette manufacturing and marketing. The company's current brand portfolio includes State Express 555, Embassy, Rothmans Kingsize, Diplomat, London Kingsize, Diplomat Menthol, London Menthol and Tusker. Their brands have both 10- and 20-stick packs. The company was formally listed on the Ghana Stock Exchange in July 1991. BAT held 55 percent of shares in the company with the remainder owned by Ghanaian and foreign investors.

In December of 2006, however, BAT–Ghana closed down its factory, indicating that the move was "part of its drive to optimize its business processes including its supply chain, which will enable the organization to take advantage of the emerging economic integration in Africa to benefit from a reduced cost base, in line with the strategy of the British American Tobacco Group." The firm has since delisted from the Ghana Stock Exchange.[6]

Employment

There is little information on tobacco industry employment in Ghana. In terms of cultivation of tobacco, BAT–Ghana sponsored its registered farmers to cultivate flue and air-cured types of tobacco. The farmers were assisted with loans and inputs like fertilizers, improved seeds and pesticides. They also benefited from extension services from the company's field staff that gave farmers close attention throughout the various stages of production, including seedbed and land preparation, field practices, harvesting, curing and grading. The company finally bought the farmers' produce at agreed prices and made prompt cash payment. BAT obtained over 80 percent of its leaf requirement from the domestic growing program and exported the surpluses to overseas customers. Ghana's BAT subsidiary reports that the provision of the necessary resources and extension service support resulted in high earnings for its farmers. In 2004, for example, farmers earned about 22.2 billion cedis from tobacco cultivation.

In 2005, BAT–Ghana employed 260 full time staff and 1,300 registered farmers who earned a living from growing tobacco leaf. There were 13 distributors with approximately 250 employees, 1,800 wholesalers and over 20,000 retailers.[7] Since BAT left Ghana, there have been no follow-up studies to determine how much these employment statistics have changed.

Interaction with government

Currently, there are no multinational tobacco manufacturing companies in Ghana, but there are importers who bring tobacco products into the country to market and sell. It is not known if foreign tobacco industries are actively involved in the political process related to tobacco control in the country. Thus, the tobacco industry's level of involvement in lobbying, political contributions, appointments to government committees or government commissions or former government officials holding posts within the tobacco industry are not known or visible.

However, the CEPS has signed a Memorandum of Understanding (MoU) with the tobacco industry. The MoU advocates equal roles and a common purpose for the two bodies to provide each other with information and training to eliminate smuggling and counterfeiting of BAT products on the Ghanaian market.[8] It is not known if these agreements will weaken the implementation of the FCTC in the country. Ghana has not passed any previous measures/policies with the tobacco industry, but there are no policies that regulate the MoH and other officials' meeting with the tobacco industry.

There are also no policies preventing joint ventures between the tobacco industry and the government. In previous years, the major tobacco industry lobbyists in Ghana were from BAT, and anecdotal evidence suggests that the tobacco industry influences policymakers. However, their direct or indirect influence in the drafting of tobacco control legislation remains unknown.

ATSA Review

The principal achievement of the ATSA team was the review of new draft comprehensive tobacco control legislation. As a logical companion to the review, the team continued and expanded efforts to sensitize MPs to the proposal. First, the team facilitated workshops with the health subcommittee on the draft bill, including a review of the Draft Plan of Action. In a broader effort, after the development of new information, education and communication (IEC) materials (e.g. leaflets, media briefs, "no smoking" promotional items, etc.), the team mounted a four-day exhibition at Parliament House (the first ever) by distributing folders with local and national information and data about the perils of tobacco and "no smoking" pins and T-shirts to 230 MPs. Finally, in related efforts, the team completed research on taxation, including a desk review of tobacco taxes and expenditure and empirical data to support tax increases on tobacco products. At the end of the program, the team was pleased that the government agreed to an increase on the ad valorem excise duty on cigarettes from 140 percent to 150 percent.

Notes

1 Sources: CIA World Factbook https://www.cia.gov/library/publications/the-world-factbook/; except Organization of Economic Cooperation and Development (OECD) for development assistance statistics, and Food and Agriculture Organization of the United Nations – Statistics (FAOSTAT) for tobacco production. See http://stats.oecd.org/index.aspx and http://faostat.fao.org/site/567/default.aspx#ancor respectively (accessed 20 July 2011).

2 E. Wellington, "Tobacco or Health in Ghana," unpublished report to the World Health Organization (1994).

3 J. Dennis-Antwi, S. Adjei, J. B. Asare and R. Twene, *Research Report – A National Survey On Prevalence and Social Consequences of Substance (Drug) Use among Second Cycle and Out of School Youth in Ghana* (Accra: Ghana Health Service and World Health Organization, 2003). Online at: http://www.who.int/countries/gha/publications/substance_abuse_report.pdf (accessed 10 July 2011).

4 E. Wellington, "Survey of the implementation of the FCTC in Ghana," report prepared for the International Development Research Centre (2005).

5 British American Tobacco, "Ghana Annual Report and Financial Statements" (2004).
6 British American Tobacco, "Ghana Annual Report and Financial Statements" (2007).
7 British American Tobacco, "Ghana Annual Report and Financial Statements" (2005).
8 Ghana News Agency, "CEPS/Philip Morris MoU Questioned," 26 November 2006/1 September 2010. Online at: http://www.ghanaweb.com/GhanaHomePage/business/artikel.php?ID=114520 (accessed 21 July 2011).

Chapter 11

KENYA

Kenya Tobacco Situational Analysis Consortium

Executive Summary

Kenya is at a very exciting – perhaps even crucial – stage for tobacco control. In 2007, the national legislature passed a comprehensive bill that has urgently required dynamic and systematic follow-up in terms of implementation and enforcement in all major areas (e.g. smoke-free policies, labeling, advertising, etc.). The highly active Kenyan tobacco control community is well aware of these challenges and has begun to take proactive steps to address them, including the training of inspectors to enforce both smoke-free policies and bans on advertising, promotion and sponsorship. Notably, the training is a combined effort of the Ministry of Health (MoH) and civil society organizations, with some funding from external donors. Graphic warning labels and tobacco taxation strategies are also on the list of activities for short-term pursuit by these actors.

Though the political situation in Kenya is fraught with violent unrest following the 2007 national election and a wholesale reorganization of government, the tobacco control community is actively navigating the new landscape and maintaining close working relationships with policymakers and permanent ministry officials (i.e. nonelected and nonappointed). There is some continuity in personnel at the ministry level, which allows for greater consistency in activities and efforts. But there is an essential need for the community to stay well connected to the government because the tobacco industry (both British American Tobacco (BAT) and Mastermind) uses Kenya as a subregional hub for its operations, and these firms are aggressive in both their subversive marketing and their efforts to affect the policy process.

Country Profile[1]

Population in 2009 (global and African ranking):	39,002,772 (34, 7)
Geographical size (global ranking):	580,367 sq. km (55)
GDP by purchasing power parity in 2008 (global ranking):	US$61.51 billion (84)
GDP real growth rate (2006–8):	5%[2]
GDP per capita (global ranking):	US$1,600 (193)
Main industries:	Small-scale consumer goods (plastics, furniture, batteries, textiles, clothing, soap, cigarettes, flour), agricultural products, horticulture, oil refining, aluminum, steel, lead, cement, commercial ship repair, tourism
Languages:	English (official), Kiswahili (official), 40+ indigenous languages including Bantu, Nilotic and Cushitic
Official development assistance (ODA) – total commitments/disbursements (2007):	US$2,388.7/1,131.5 million
ODA as a percentage of GDP:	4.2%
Largest donors (disbursements in millions of USD):	USA 325.3, EC 145.3, UK 137.5, Japan 111.8, France 67.4, Germany 65.8, Sweden 45.5, Spain 44.4, Demark 39, Global Fund 28.2
Tobacco production by volume (2007):	11,153 tons
Tobacco exports (2007):	Cigarettes: 7,641 tons at $12,350 per ton, #4 export; tobacco (unmanufactured): 24,970 tons at $1,323 per ton, #9 export
Tobacco imports (2007):	Tobacco (unmanufactured): 22,001 tons at $1,918 per ton, #4 import

Brief Description of Political System

Type: Kenya was a presidential republic until the 2007–8 political unrest, after which there was a brief hybrid regime (with both a president and prime minister) that brought together the major political parties. In August 2010, there was a referendum that authorized a new presidential system, but one with less executive authority.

Executive: As of 2010, Mwai Kibaki (National Rainbow Coalition (NARC))
              holds the presidency and Raila Odinga (from the Orange
              Democratic Movement (ODM), which is partly comprised of
              the old Kenyan African National Union (KANU) – Kenyatta
              and Arap Moi's party) holds the PM's job (newly created).
Cabinet: Appointed primarily by the president and headed by the PM. It
              is very large with many patronage positions that are needed to
              keep the fragile coalition together.
Legislature: The unicameral National Assembly (Bunge) has 224 seats –
              210 seats are elected by popular vote every five years, and
              12 members are selected by political parties in proportion
              to parliamentary votes and are appointed by the president.
              Since the 2007 election, the two largest parties, the ODM
              and the Party of National Unity (PNU), have 99 and 46 seats
              respectively. The new constitution provides for a bicameral
              legislative branch.
Judiciary: There is a high court and a court of appeal.

Scope of Tobacco Problem

There have been a number of tobacco prevalence surveys in the last decade,
and while the results vary somewhat, the main substantive finding is that the
prevalence of smoking is unquestionably increasing. In general population
terms, the 2003 Kenya Demographic and Health Survey (KDHS) estimated
smoking prevalence at 23 percent in adult men, but less than 1 percent in
adult women. When the Kenyan government implemented the Tobacco
Control Act in 2008, Dr James Nyikal from the Ministry of Public Health
(MoPH) said that 26 percent of Kenyans – 8.4 million people – were
addicted to tobacco, though it is not clear which research he cited for
this statistic.

Though prevalence rates for women are reported to be low, there are
widespread concerns about the empirical accuracy of these rates. Research-
wise, there is a knowledge gap on adult female smoking rates and accurate
prevalence data on this group need to be collected. Specifically, the KDHS
is administered to the head of the household, which in many instances is a
man, and because culturally it is inappropriate for women to smoke and they
are not open about this issue, many survey respondents may not be speaking
accurately about female smoking rates.

Some prevalence studies have targeted specific demographic groups, and
the data on youths are particularly rich. The Global Youth Tobacco Survey

(GYTS) in 2001 indicates that among school-going children (13–15-year-olds), 13 percent were smokers – 15.8 percent for boys and 10 percent for girls. Results from the 2003 Kenya Global School-based Student Health Survey (GSHS – with a total of 3,691 student participants) largely confirm these findings, indicating that 13.9 percent of the students admitted smoking cigarettes on one or more days in the 30 days prior to the survey. Notably, a subsequent GYTS conducted in March 2007 revealed very dramatic prevalence increases in young people: approximately 20 percent of all school-going children use tobacco according to the results.

The National Agency for the Campaign against Drug Abuse (NACADA) in 2001 and 2002 commissioned the first ever national baseline survey on youth abuse of alcohol and drugs in Kenya. This survey targeted young people aged between 10 and 24 years including both students and nonstudents. It provides data on the prevalence of those who have ever used tobacco, disaggregated according to the eight provinces of the country. It indicates that tobacco use was prevalent in all parts of the country with overall tobacco use of 31 percent and 58 percent among the students and nonstudents respectively. Targeting a related but slightly older demographic, a national situational analysis conducted between November 2002 and June 2003 by NACADA and the Kenya Institute for Public Policy Research and Analysis (KIPPRA) on Drug and Substance Abuse in Tertiary Institutions (i.e. post-secondary) in Kenya revealed that about 34 percent of students in Kenya are abusing tobacco, primarily through smoking cigarettes (~85 percent). If these prevalence rates are accurate, this reveals an alarming prevalence for young, educated adults.

Unfortunately, the generation of time-series prevalence data remains weak. For example, the NACADA and KIPPRA statistics are not easily comparable to other surveys, both because they used different methodologies and because there is no standardization of terms. For example, the term "ever used tobacco" may mean having smoked even once as opposed to the regular use of tobacco, which by all accounts within the tobacco control field is a more accurate indicator of prevalence. Thus, most advocates prefer to cite either the GYTS or the KDHS, which are widely considered to be more reliable by epidemiologists and statisticians. Future data collection efforts need to bear in mind the need to produce data that can provide accurate illustrations of change over time.

Though there is evidence that noncigarette tobacco use is a growing problem, data are limited. There are some data on the use of tobacco products beyond cigarettes, but only for youths. The GYTS 2001 notes that 8.5 percent of students between 13–15 years used tobacco products other than cigarettes (male 9.3 percent, female 7.7 percent). The GYTS 2007 notes an increase with 12.8 percent using other tobacco products (male 10.7 percent, female 14.5 percent). Finally, anecdotal evidence from advocates on the ground indicates growing use of chewed tobacco products among school children, especially an Indian product called Kuber, which as of early 2010 continued to have warning labels that do not comply with the requirements of Kenyan legislation.

The Politics of Tobacco Control

Existing laws and regulations

The Tobacco Control Act (TCA) of 2007 frames the existing laws and regulations. Many of the major policy areas are discussed in the policy-specific chapters, so this synopsis will focus on several other key aspects of the current regulations, including the establishment of the Tobacco Control Board (TCA Art. 5), the Tobacco Control Fund (TCA Art. 7) and enforcement (TCA Part VII).

The TCA 2007 establishes a fairly elaborate Tobacco Control Board that by statute has the power to advise the minister of health on tobacco control policy and regulations. Moreover, the minister cannot enact policies or regulations without consulting the board. However, abstractly, since the minister appoints the chair, there is potential for interference if the minister is pressured to appoint an ineffective chair. The legislation requires the participation of a number of key government bureaucrats (e.g. the director of medical services and the chief public health officer) and civil society representatives (e.g. members of religious and women's organizations) on the board. Though the inclusive membership might serve as a reasonable check on the health minister's influence, with 15 obligatory members, tobacco control proponents fear a very wide variety of opinions and the resulting strong possibility of a lack of action. While the board was inaugurated on 4 May 2009, it did not meet subsequently in 2009 due to a lack of resources.

Second, the establishment of a Tobacco Control Fund is another positive abstract idea because it would help to fund tobacco education programs. Unfortunately, however, the legislation does not identify a particular "earmark" for it – for example, money generated from tobacco taxes that goes directly into an account to fund tobacco control initiatives. Instead, it seems to generate its revenues from the goodwill of parliament and individuals, and also seizures from the actual TCA (from TCA s.52). In the 2009 budget, the minister of finance did not make any allocation to the fund.

Finally, another key component of the TCA 2007 generating concern in the tobacco control community is Section VII, which focuses on enforcement. This section is lengthy with 26 separate subsections; however, it is not clear that the actual wording of the legislation sets up the act for immediate success. The act is designed to be enforced by public health officers, police and local-level enforcement officers who already exist and enforce other public health laws. The power to appoint more officers lies with the director of medical services if he or she identifies a need for additional officers in besides those already on the ground. The challenge, however, is that the TCA 2007 is enforced alongside other laws such as those governing evidence and criminal procedure, and as a result, the enforcement of the TCA tends to receive a low priority. The allocation of resources – such as vehicles and personnel – particularly by local authorities, in addition to political interference, remain genuine potential obstacles to effective enforcement.

Overall political context

The African Tobacco Situation Analysis (ATSA) Kenyan baseline assessment, stakeholder consultation and in-country planning meetings all noted that there are good policy and institutional frameworks for tobacco control in Kenya and that the existing positive relationships between government and civil society present opportunities for substantial progress in tobacco control in Kenya. Importantly, the stakeholder meetings and the assessments involved a wide variety of actors with interest in tobacco control, including advocates from civil society organizations, academics, medical professionals and government officials. The eventual ATSA team consisted of representatives from civil society (e.g. the Consumer Information Network, the Institute for Legislative Affairs (ILA), the Kenya Tobacco Control Alliance (KETCA), Peace Pen Communications, the Social Needs Network, the Tobacco and Alcohol Free Initiative, and the Uzima Foundation), the government (e.g. the MoH and the Ministry of Education (MoE)) and research institutions (e.g. the Kenyan Medical Research Institute and the Institute for Natural Resources and Technology).

Stakeholders at the ATSA meetings also noted a number of important weaknesses in tobacco control efforts that the public health community must address. First, there is a lack of coordination of efforts among the actors seeking policy change. Second, there is weak capacity both within government and civil society for enforcement of the TCA 2007. Third, there is poor monitoring and evaluation of tobacco control legislation and regulation once they are passed. Fourth, there is still strong opposition from the tobacco industry to tobacco control, especially through the use of economic and trade arguments to influence policymakers. Fifth, there is low public awareness on the provisions of the law. Finally, there is a lack of formal cessation services.

As part of efforts to begin to address the shortcomings described above, one of the ongoing short-term goals of the Kenyan ATSA team and the tobacco control community more generally is to determine better the positions on tobacco control of the relevant (elected) ministers and the permanent (unelected) bureaucrats that are crucial to running the key ministries. These actors will almost certainly be part of the effort to reach these public health goals. Beginning at the highest levels, though they have not taken outspoken positions, the current president (Kibaki) and the PM (Odinga) have shown mixed support for tobacco control. For example, the president at one point interfered with debate on the tobacco bill by getting it pulled out from the order paper.[3] But, once the bill had passed through all the necessary stages, he signed it. When the PM was a member of parliament (i.e. yet to become PM), he supported the tobacco bill during debate; since becoming PM, his preferences have become less clear because he has not made any public declaration of his stance. The Kenyan ATSA team, however, argues that the PM's position might be changeable with education of his office on tobacco control issues. Similarly, though the two ministers that fall under the PM's jurisdiction (the president and PM share executive power in Kenya) – those of trade and local government – have expressed pro-industry positions, the team believes they are also educable. Since the minister of local government will be instrumental in implementing and enforcing smoke-free zones in the long term, support from this ministry will be undoubtedly important.

The Ministry of Public Health and Sanitation (or just the MoH) has been and will continue to be a pivotal actor in the pursuit of tobacco control goals. The current minister (as of early 2010) is known to be supportive of tobacco control. A report from the Kenyan Broadcasting Corporation quotes her declaring that text and pictorial warnings are "in effect" from the TCA 2007. The new chairman of the Tobacco Control Board, Professor Peter Odhiambo, echoed this declaration by stating that the deadline for compliance with the new law has run out.[4] New high-ranking permanent bureaucrats in the ministry will require sensitization and further education to the issues.

Three ministries that address issues concerning young people – Children and Gender; Education; and Youth – are also likely to be helpful and/ or influential in achieving tobacco control goals in the coming years. The permanent secretary in the Ministry of Children and Gender (as of 2010) is a known supporter of tobacco control and may be a useful conduit to other cabinet members if she decides to promote the issue. The positions of the minister of youth and the minister of education are not clear, but as natural allies, their support would be undoubtedly helpful in creating more of a critical mass for tobacco control in cabinet. The tobacco control community continues to pursue all of these avenues.

Over recent years, there has been mixed evidence of support for tobacco control from the Ministry of Finance. On a positive note, the ministry raised taxes on cigarette products by 10 percent each year in 2007–9. However, in the 2009–10 budget, there was no increase. For tax increases to work as a public health strategy, increases must keep up with changes in inflation and income. In a more positive recent development, the ministry sent a representative to the Intergovernmental Negotiating Body (INB) on illicit trade in 2009 in order to learn better techniques (other than simply lowering taxes) to address it. Finally, the Ministry of Health has been working with the Kenya Revenue Authority (KRA) to examine the possibility of further tobacco tax policy reform.

Returning to the aforementioned, recently inaugurated Tobacco Control Board, there is great hope among public health proponents that the board will be a force for improved tobacco control. The chair of this board, Professor Peter Odhiambo, is openly supportive of tobacco control and a former head of the National Tobacco Free Initiative Committee. He is well known amongst influential political figures, and the ATSA team hopes that he can reach out successfully to policymakers.

Moving to the legislative branch, the leadership (having changed considerably in the 2007 election) continues to require sensitization to tobacco control issues. Unfortunately, the majority of the champions and all of the vocal opponents of tobacco control were voted out in the 2007 election. However, since the major legislation has already been passed, support in the legislature will only become crucial if any actual legislative amendments are required (some existing loopholes – e.g. in labeling – can probably be closed by standard ministerial regulations). In any event, through a separate project, the umbrella organization of tobacco control NGOs, KETCA, has been conducting frequent one-on-one meetings with members of parliament (MPs) and has received expressions of support, especially from MPs coming from tobacco-growing areas and some female MPs concerned with issues that affect women and children adversely.

The Kenyan ATSA team believes that the attorney general's (AG) office lacks capacity and experience in tobacco control, but is open minded to support and input from tobacco control experts. In fact, the ILA has been offering the AG's office technical support through legal research in defending the constitutional cases that have been filed by the tobacco industry challenging the TCA 2007. The ILA is also working with the MoH and the AG's chambers to develop draft regulations under the TCA. The team also argues that it is important to work with the judges at the high court/chief justice level to ensure that sufficiently stiff penalties are handed out, especially to violations by the industry of the TCA 2007. These efforts to influence the office may be critical because there is evidence that it has experienced lobbying from the industry.[5]

Mastermind Tobacco and Bridgeways Logistics filed the two legal suits pending before the courts against the TCA 2007. The case filed by Mastermind has come up several times before the courts and each time, Mastermind has said it was not ready to proceed and sought more time to file additional documents. Mastermind has also changed lawyers and then sought time for the new lawyer to acquaint himself with the proceedings. As of 2011, the court had not yet heard the case.

The ATSA team has started to see prosecutions of violations. Court records demonstrate that in three municipalities (Nairobi, Kakamega and Eldoret), there have been arrests of people violating the ban on smoking in public. The fines, however, have been small. Though there have been violations by the tobacco industry on the ban on advertising, promotion and sponsorship, they have not yet been prosecuted, largely due to lack of cooperation from enforcement agencies.

Finally, the ATSA team argues that the tobacco control community must reach out to the military, whose members have access to cheap cigarettes through the military canteens (called the Armed Forces Canteen Organization (AFCO)). As of yet, no efforts have been made formally to reach out to this institution or its members, and there are no studies that have established the magnitude of the problem.

Politics of ATSA action – Smoke-free implementation and enforcement

On 8 July 2008, the Kenya TCA of 2007 came officially into effect, and the implementation of its many provisions slowly began, including an aggressive set of smoke-free regulations, a stiff ban on advertising and promotion and new restrictions and rules on tobacco package labeling. One of the key components of the TCA 2007 was a ban on smoking in all public places, which are defined as "all indoor, enclosed and partially enclosed places open to the public or any part of the public or to which members of the public ordinarily have access including workplaces and public conveyances generally."[6] The following places are named specifically in the act: offices, workplaces, restaurants, hotels, eating places, educational facilities, places where children are taken care of, places of worship, courts, jails, police stations, recreational facilities, hospitals and public transport (including trains, buses, ferries and airports).

However, the ATSA team members have noted anecdotally that in 2009, the ban was only being observed in government buildings and some workplaces, and that the ban was largely being flouted in entertainment spots including bars, hotels, restaurants, casinos and recreational facilities (e.g. local movie theaters within residential estates). There is also anecdotal evidence of smoking on public transport in terms of drivers and touts, but there is very little smoking by passengers, largely because a ban on smoking in public transport was put in place by ministerial decree several years before the national legislation was passed.

In order to enforce smoke-free policies, many of the key actors are at the subnational and/or local level, including mayors and other local authorities. Because they can help to implement the provision and provide resources to enforce it, provincial administration officials are important to engage. Therefore, the team proposes that a program to use the traditional chiefs for public education and enforcement would also be highly beneficial. Similarly, local mayors are not only able to pass bylaws but also play major roles in enforcement and public awareness. Without doubt, local enforcement agencies, which include not only the provincial administration but also the police and public health officers, must continue to be engaged and educated because they will do much of the actual enforcement. Quite simply, there must be "buy-in" from these groups for anything effective to happen in the area of smoke-free public places.

In the case of Nairobi, the city government is highly centralized with one mayor and a council, as well as a town clerk in charge of day-to-day administration. The position on the smoke-free policy of these local-level politicians is not yet known. The city council of Nairobi has designated smoking zones in three corners of the city and persons who smoke in public are arrested. However, attempts to enforce other aspects of the law by public health officers have been met with resistance by senior bureaucrats, and one public health officer in 2009 was reportedly facing trumped-up corruption charges intended to intimidate her into going slowly on enforcement. In addition, the city council has been slow to allocate sufficient resources for enforcement of the act in the form of vehicles for enforcement rounds. Public health officers have the power to inspect but not to arrest and need to be accompanied by city council police; sometimes, these officers are not allocated to the public health officers to assist with arrests.

Civil society will continue to play a major role in the success of smoke-free public places by continuing to put pressure on authorities to implement and enforce the policies. The Kenyan team identified a number of organizations that are not yet involved in the movement, but who, they argue, should be involved. The highly active and pivotal KETCA, which brings together a number of NGOs committed to tobacco control, would like to engage other NGOs involved in public education and awareness, including community-based organizations that address issues pertinent to women, children, youths, the environment, consumers and farmers. These organizations could be very helpful in the dissemination of information and to help conduct the public education and awareness campaigns for tobacco-related issues.

Professional organizations can provide support to civil society groups by lending both their legitimacy and the support base of their memberships. The KETCA has been actively engaging several professional organizations including the Kenya Medical Association and the Pharmaceutical Society of Kenya at stakeholder forums, and these organizations have indicated interest in further involvement in tobacco control. Tobacco control proponents also believe that other professional groups – e.g. teachers and nurses – could be potential and influential allies because they are on the frontlines of interacting with more potentially vulnerable groups, including young people and those using the healthcare system. Similarly, proponents recognize the important influence of community leaders – including those in religious communities – especially for public education. Religious leaders (Catholics, Protestants, Pentecostals and Hindus) are thought to be particularly influential with policymakers and should be actively engaged more in the broader tobacco control effort.

The tobacco control community recognizes that research organizations – e.g. the Kenya Institute for Public Policy Research and Analysis (KIPPRA), the Institute for Policy Analysis and Research (IPAR), universities, etc. – need to be engaged more, particularly considering the assistance that researchers could provide in terms of evidence-based research to present to policymakers. This goal returns to the issue of coordination (or lack thereof) across sectors because advocates, researchers and policymakers need to further discuss how they can help each other reach their tobacco control goals. There are ongoing efforts to overcome this obstacle.

The ATSA team argues that many other influential groups on the business side of civil society, while maybe not destined to be "allies," need to be sensitized to the smoke-free issue, with the explicit end goal of support for the campaign. For example, the constituents of workers unions (especially the Central Organization for Trade Unions (COTU), the Federation of Kenya Employers and the Kenya Association of Manufacturers) and the public transport sector (e.g. the Matatu Owners Association and the Matatu Welfare Association) need to be educated on the benefits of smoke-free places. In the case of public transport, benefits for both employees and customers should be emphasized. Finally, bar and hotel owners are particularly important to engage because these are the areas where stakeholders observe anecdotally that smoking in public is still continuing.

The Kenyan media outlets are not necessarily tobacco control allies or adversaries, but either way, advocates have experienced challenges reaching them. Participants at stakeholder meetings have noted that there are many journalists who smoke, and they argue that this group needs a targeted education campaign. There have been some recent related developments, notably a Bloomberg-funded project to build relationships with the media and secure more positive coverage for tobacco control. The campaign, which began in November 2009, bore fruit with increased coverage of Kenyan tobacco control by the media. There are also plans underway to set up a journalists' network specific to tobacco control.

The ATSA team identified a number of major opponents to smoke-free policies, many of which have perceived an economic stake in the changes. In terms of economic groups, the Kenya Association of Hawkers, the Hotel Owners Association and the Kenya Tobacco Growers Association have objected or expressed concern about the policies because they believe the regulations will generate negative economic impacts. Advocates will need to educate these groups about the impacts of these policies in other countries – i.e. these groups will not likely be affected by smoke-free policies. Some media and particularly editors of the business sections of newspapers have indicated opposition to the policies, and more education for these actors might help to change their views. Finally, the tobacco industry itself has strongly objected to smoke-free policies, but they are discussed in-depth elsewhere in this chapter. However, in a related development, there have been vocal objections from so-called "smokers' rights groups." These groups are a bit of a mystery because it is not clear who funds them. The ATSA team first interacted with them during hearings for the TCA 2007, and they only seem to surface when legislation is proposed. Tobacco control proponents will need to monitor these groups and better establish their connection to the tobacco industry.

On an important final note, there have been immediate challenges to the enforcement of smoke-free legislation, including allegations of corrupt enforcement officers. Notably, however, public health officers now have performance contracts and have been asked to give monthly reports on their enforcement efforts in order to encourage them to prosecute as opposed to extort bribes from offenders. A recent project funded in part by the Bloomberg Initiative to Reduce Tobacco Use to train enforcement officers has generated mixed success. Trainings have been carried out in ten towns, though only three have taken measurable enforcement action after the training in the form of declarations by town authorities that their town was going to enforce the smoke-free provisions of the law and arrests of ban violators. The officers have reported inadequate resourcing to carry out their duties and a lack of coordination between public health officers and the police in enforcement. Efforts are being made to convene roundtable discussions between all agencies and actors that are necessary for enforcement to occur.

Politics of ATSA action – Enforcement of the ban on advertising, promotion and sponsorship

Even though obvious advertising in print and electronic media no longer takes place, tobacco control proponents cite anecdotal evidence of widespread indirect advertising, sponsorship and promotion by the tobacco companies. For example, recent informal monitoring by the Kenyan Consortium has revealed sponsorship of events such as trade fairs, one-page advertisements in the newspapers listing products and prices and the use of corporate social responsibility (CSR) activities in the funding of economic development. However, tobacco control advocates have found it difficult to identify which specific interventions are required to address this issue. During the initial political mapping exercise, the team discovered that they need more information on the context for advertising, promotion and sponsorship in Kenya, including the improved identification of appropriate stakeholders. At present, the MoH is working to strengthen the legislation through the development of regulations for advertising, promotion and sponsorship that identify a formal monitoring system as a necessary component.

While it is not known definitively whether the industry provides campaign funding in order to influence policymakers, high-level policymakers are known at least to give private audience to the industry. Accordingly, the team expects that the following ministries will take an interest in any efforts at a more rigorous enforcement of the advertising, promotion and sponsorship ban: Information and Communication; Trade; Agriculture; Health; Finance; Youth and Sports; and Culture. Tobacco control proponents from KETCA are actively seeking to determine better the positions of ministers, deputy ministers and high-level ministry officials on this specific set of issues through face-to-face courtesy visits.

Beyond the actual principal ministries, there are several government agencies that play direct roles in this issue area. Both the Marketing Society of Kenya and the Advertising Board of Kenya have regulatory roles for marketing and advertising. Similarly, the Kenya Films and Censorship Board has a regulatory role over the content of films. Tobacco control advocates are continuing to assess the precise roles of these agencies.

The Kenyan ATSA team expects significant pushback on these efforts to enforce the ban from several key actors who do not want actual implementation or enforcement of these measures. They expect stiff resistance from the industry, especially British American Tobacco–Kenya (BATK). Similarly, team members anticipate that tobacco retailers and distributors will fight these measures vigorously. There is reasonable concern about resistance to enforcement from agricultural groups. In terms of farmers' associations, stakeholders at ATSA meetings noted that the industry had front groups who were agitating for the industry to be allowed to conduct promotional campaigns for farmers. In a related concern, tobacco control proponents have noted that the Agricultural Society of Kenya has received significant funding for its agricultural shows from the industry.

A critical part of enforcement continues to be a monitoring system to identify violations and have the violators properly prosecuted. There are continuing efforts to monitor all radio, television and newspapers to see where tobacco is mentioned and how it is presented. The training of enforcement officers is also helping with this effort. The officers being trained in the ongoing program are a mix of public health officers employed by the MoH and the police and enforcement officers employed by local authorities and councils. The training takes one day and covers four major aspects: the rationale for tobacco control, the provisions of the TCA 2007, how to monitor implementation of the act and how to prosecute offenses effectively. Over one thousand officers in provincial capitals have been trained in the program since 2009.

Tobacco Industry

The tobacco industry and legislation

The tobacco industry is economically powerful and politically well connected. Notably, until recently, the Kenyan government was a shareholder of BATK through its national pension program, the National Social Security Fund (NSSF). There has reportedly been a complete divestment, but scholars argue (through the citation of tobacco industry documents) that the company

> enjoys high political connections with some of its chairmen (former and current) and non-executive directors enjoying good relations with powerful individuals in successive political regimes, while some are strategically positioned in key sectors such as the education sector and the private sector. It is therefore not surprising that efforts to develop and implement legislation consistent with the FCTC treaty have been unsuccessful amid persistent reports of BAT influence. [7]

Of course, after more than a decade of trying, the tobacco control community *was* successful in passing the legislation. Nonetheless, this success does not deny the importance of BAT in Kenya. The industry has been particularly successful in shifting the terms of the debate from public health interest to the perceived damage that the tobacco control policies would have on tobacco growers, their communities, the national economy and even cigarette consumers.

The tobacco industry has proven creative in its opposition to tobacco control legislation. When the TCA 2007 finally progressed to the second reading in the Kenyan parliament after years of failure due in large part to industry influence, BATK and Mastermind Tobacco spent KSh7 million to lavish MPs with a beach holiday and retreat at an exclusive coastal resort in a final effort to influence the bill. Scholars have demonstrated that industry representatives sought to convince the legislators to do away with the act or at least to dilute it. One of the proposals included giving the industry a role in the Tobacco Control Board.[8]

The industry has also challenged legislation in court. First, when the MoH issued ministry-level directives for smoke-free legislation and health warnings consistent with the FCTC (LN 44 of 2006), BATK and Mastermind challenged the government in a court of law on the basis that they were not consulted and that they stood to incur massive losses if the rules were to be applied. They were successful at that time in getting the measures suspended. Subsequently, when city and town councils in Kenya invoked powers given to them by the Local Government Act to outlaw public smoking and designating smoking zones, the industry threatened that they would sponsor dozens of litigants to sue the councils for infringing on their constitutional right to smoke, though they did not follow through on the threat.[9]

The industry has also complained publicly about the unfair nature of the legislation. With the introduction of the TCA in July 2008, the tobacco industry has publicly complained that the compliance time is too short. During its annual general meeting in May 2008, BATK postponed the issuance of bonus shares to its shareholders, even after announcing a 17 percent growth in pre-tax profit to KSh2.1 billion and domestic sales growth of 12 percent, because they claimed that they wanted to determine the short-term effect of the act. Publicly, BATK has complained vociferously about the cost of implementation of the act, while Mastermind Tobacco is claiming that the law criminalizes smoking and should be restricted to protecting only nonsmokers.[10]

Interactions between tobacco companies and farmers

Despite the tobacco industry's public narrative that it is vital to the Kenyan agricultural sector (and the economy more generally), its relationship with farmers appears complex and strained. In tobacco-growing areas, farmers have complained of exploitation by the tobacco companies. Typically in Kenya, tobacco companies sign contracts with farmers, although reportedly, the vast majority of the farmers – who are frequently limited in their level of literacy – do not understand them. In particular, the contracts set the buying price of the tobacco and the points of sale. Inputs such as seeds, fertilizers and pesticides are loaned to farmers by the tobacco companies. The costs, often priced high above the normal shop price, are deducted by the company when the farmers sell their leaf back to them. In Bungoma, for example, Christian Aid analyzed BATK's figures for the region and found that farmers were being paid the price of seven cents per kilo. They actually received less than half this price once the cost of the agrochemicals and other inputs sold to them by the company had been deducted. [11] At best, farmers are essentially contract workers who must assume all financial risks; at worst, this is a system of near indentured labor. Stakeholders from the agricultural sector at ATSA meetings have also noted other major complaints from farmers including: a lack of provision of protective gear; a poor grading system; poor quality inputs; harassment when a crop fails (because of drought or hailstorms) and the farmer cannot repay a loan in full; and a lack of insurance for the curing barns, which often catch fire during the curing process.

Finally, labor organizers have reported anecdotally that BATK has been fighting any meaningful union representation that would give tobacco farmers collective bargaining powers. While there is no incontrovertible proof, many tobacco workers believe that previous attempts at forming a union collapsed due to behind-the-scenes tobacco company interference.

The tobacco industry and the media, advertising and promotion

Because the media is driven by advertising and marketing, the tobacco industry, as a multibillion dollar industry, has previously been able to utilize this outlet to a large extent. Tobacco control advocates note that they cannot realistically rival the industry's level of exposure with their limited resources. Despite the ban on advertising, promotion and sponsorship, the industry continues to find loopholes and has been taking out full-page advertisements of the prices of their various brands. They claim that they are only reporting prices and are not "advertising." This type of activity ensures that marketing by and for the industry is still achieved. Furthermore, tobacco control advocates have faced challenges in recent years as news stories that do appear about tobacco control have often been presented from a negative angle, or have often been brief and superficial. However, recent efforts by advocates in 2008–9 to sensitize the media have resulted in improved coverage of tobacco control in the media.

While the industry states that its only purpose in advertising is to promote brand loyalty, there has been evidence that it still utilizes tactics to attract new smokers by associating smoking with prestige, power, freedom and luxury. Targeting specific groups in advertising has become an issue of focus. While BATK denies targeting youths in its advertising and calls its market a "mature market," internal industry documents reveal that in the past there has been an attempt to target youths aged between 18–24 years as a response to declining market share due to increased competition resulting from market liberalization. [12] Similarly, women have also recently become a target of interest for the industry. Because low levels of female smokers in developing countries can be attributed more to cultural tradition than to actual awareness of the health hazards of tobacco use, the industry has been able to promote cigarettes successfully to women by using seductive but false images of vitality, slimness, modernity, emancipation, sophistication and sex allure.[13]

ATSA Review

In a final review of the ATSA-related activities, the program helped to facilitate a number of significant improvements in tobacco control in Kenya. These improvements include: a strengthening of the capacity of enforcement officers; the actual enforcement of smoke-free regulations; improved monitoring of tobacco advertising, promotion and sponsorship; a major effort to increase relevant research in tobacco control and to link research to action; and emphasis on the improved coordination of efforts among stakeholders.

The team participated in major efforts to build capacity for enforcement and education in tobacco control. In the area of enforcement, there were a total of 26 trainings in 20 Kenyan towns wherein a total of 1,115 enforcement officers (police, local authorities' officers, administration police, public health officers and chiefs) participated. More broadly, members of the team, more than 100 civil society representatives, 150 media individuals and other volunteers received training about key parts of the TCA 2007, including how to help with its implementation and enforcement. Among other tangible results of the trainings, there were a large number of successful smoke-free campaigns in schools (e.g. 1,793 entries in Nairobi province).

The team had a very active role in the development and dissemination of at least five major tobacco control publications. Firstly, early in the project, members of the team produced the "Situational Analysis of Tobacco Control in Kenya: Report of the Baseline Assessment," which was completed by the Kenya Tobacco Control Situational Analysis Consortium. Secondly, the team, building on the first document, completed the "Situational Analysis of Tobacco Control in Kenya: Report of the Full Analysis" nearer to the end of the program (much of this chapter is drawn from information in this report). In terms of tackling the misinformation regarding economic issues and tobacco specifically, the team helped to produce a report entitled "Golden Leaf? Debunking the Myths about the Economic Effects of Tobacco in Kenya." Similarly, in an effort to research efforts to address advertising and related issues more systematically, the team helped to develop "Turning off the 'TAPS': Strategies to control Tobacco Advertising, Promotion and Sponsorship in Kenya." Finally, the team was central to the development of "The National Tobacco Control Action Plan: 2010–2015."

Throughout the project, the ATSA team has continued to seek better coordination and information sharing, and these efforts are helping to generate many tobacco control victories. More than ten organizations involved in tobacco control, from both government and civil society, continue to actively coordinate efforts; this improved coordination continues to be critical in responding to the challenges of developing, implementing and enforcing better tobacco control regulations. Though there are many challenges ahead in tobacco control, the continuing widespread and profound efforts are engendering demonstrable public health gains for the country.

Notes

1 Sources: CIA World Factbook https://www.cia.gov/library/publications/the-world-factbook/; except Organization of Economic Cooperation and Development (OECD) for development assistance statistics, and Food and Agriculture Organization of the United Nations – Statistics (FAOSTAT) for tobacco production. See http://stats.oecd.org/index.aspx and http://faostat.fao.org/site/567/default.aspx#ancor respectively (accessed 20 July 2011).

2 Growth was 1.7 percent in 2008, which was largely due to the political instability following the 2007 national election.

3 For a longer discussion of high-level ties to the tobacco industry, see Preeti Patel, Jeff Collin and Anna Gilmore, "'The law was actually drafted by us but the Government is to be congratulated on its wise actions': British American Tobacco and public policy in Kenya," *Tobacco Control* 16.1 (2007): e1.

4 Zipporah Njeri, "Cigarette Manufacturers Put on Notice," Kenyan Broadcasting Corporation, 29 May 2009.

5 For example, see Patel et al., "'The law was actually drafted by us but the Government is to be congratulated on its wise actions'."

6 Government of the Republic of Kenya, Tobacco Control Act (2007), Article 33.2.

7 Patel et al., "'The law was actually drafted by us but the Government is to be congratulated on its wise actions'."

8 Ibid.

9 F. Machio, "Efforts to Write Tobacco Control Laws Meet Resistance in Kenya," Disease Control Priorities Project, 21 May 2007. Online at: http://www.dcp2.org/features/40 (accessed 1 September 2010).

10 Maina Waruru, "Kenyan firms challenge new smoking laws," AfricaNews, 30 July 2008.

11 For a discussion of this dynamic, see J. Asila, "No Cash in this Crop," *New Internationalist* 369, 1 July 2004.

12 *East African*, "Regional News," 3 December 2001.

13 For discussions of these issues, see J. M. Samet and S. Yoon (eds), *Women and the Tobacco Epidemic: Challenges for the 21st Century* (Geneva: World Health Organization, 2001).

Chapter 12

MALAWI

Donald Makoka, Kondwani Munthali and Jeffrey Drope

Executive Summary

Malawi demonstrates one the lowest levels of tobacco control in Sub-Saharan Africa, having enacted almost no tobacco control legislation or regulations. It is also one of the largest producers of tobacco leaf on the continent and in the world. Not surprisingly, it has not signed the Framework Convention on Tobacco Control (FCTC). However, prospects for policy change may be brighter than one might expect under these circumstances because there is a very active civil society–based tobacco control movement and the presence of the tobacco manufacturing industry is limited compared to most countries in Sub-Saharan Africa.

The tobacco industry, in the form of the usual players such as British American Tobacco (BAT), does not appear to be a major economic and/or political player. Malawians are generally very poor and prevalence rates are relatively low, so revenues from manufactured tobacco products are limited and the large firms have mostly stayed away from this country. Instead, it is the leaf-purchasing companies that wield significant political and economic power. To date, these companies have not had to face substantial tobacco control measures. It is difficult to anticipate how much resistance any new measures might face from these groups and others (particularly agricultural organizations). There is, however, already general resistance to tobacco control measures from some key parts of the government because of the economic significance of tobacco leaf; the product generates greater than 60–70 percent of export exchange depending on the year. For example, the finance and industry ministries have been promoting domestic tobacco manufacturing in their strategic planning, and the first cigarette factory opened in 2009. Similarly, many legislators and cabinet members are directly or indirectly involved in tobacco leaf cultivation.

In the African Tobacco Situation Analysis (ATSA) program, the tobacco control community proceeded with a study that examines the state of advertising, promotion and sponsorship in Malawi. Furthermore, the community has been networking to bring together likeminded organizations and to promote tobacco control through the media. The ATSA team and other stakeholders believe that there is presently a window of opportunity to lobby for tobacco control policies, but that window is likely to close significantly over the next five years as influential people promote pro-tobacco economic strategies. With the importance of the tobacco leaf industry firmly established, the Malawian tobacco control community argues unequivocally that all emphases concerning tobacco control must be placed on health concerns, at least for the foreseeable future, and not on production.

Country Profile[1]

Population in 2009 (global and African ranking):	14,268,711 (67, 17)
Geographical size (global ranking):	118,484 sq. km (106)
GDP by purchasing power parity in 2008 (global ranking):	US$11.81 billion (143)
GDP real growth rate (2006–8):	8.3%
GDP per capita (global ranking):	US$800 (208)
Main industries:	Tobacco, tea, sugar, sawmill products, cement, consumer goods
Languages:	Chichewa (official, 57.2%), Chinyanja (12.8%), Chiyao (10.1%), Chitumbuka (9.5%), Chisena (2.7%), Chilomwe (2.4%), Chitonga (1.7%), other (3.6%), English (official); data gained from the 1998 census
Official development assistance (ODA) – total commitments/disbursements (2007):	US$594.1/781 million
ODA as a percentage of GDP:	21.8%
Largest donors (disbursements in millions of USD):	Japan 221.8, UK 133.7, Global Fund 79.4, US 79, EC 77, Norway 54.8, Germany 24.4, Austria 22.9, Sweden 20.4
Tobacco production by volume in 2007 (global ranking):	118,000 tons (7)

Tobacco exports (2007):	Tobacco (unmanufactured): 130,183 tons at $3,247 per ton, #1 export
Tobacco imports (2007):	Tobacco (unmanufactured): 14,210 tons at $2,172 per ton, #1 import; cigarettes: 690 tons at $5,023 per ton, #10 import

Brief Description of Political System

Type: Malawi is a multiparty presidential democracy.

Executive: Since 2004, the presidential chief of staff and head of government has been Bingu wa Mutharika of the Democratic Progressive Party (DPP). He beat the 20-year incumbent president Hastings Banda with an anti-corruption and financial discipline campaign.

Cabinet: There is a 46-member cabinet appointed by the president.

Legislature: The unicameral National Assembly is comprised of 193 seats, elected every five years by popular vote. As of 2009, the DPP has 119 seats and the Malawi Congress Party (MCP) has 26 seats. There are also district assemblies.[2]

Judiciary: Supreme Court, high court, chief justice appointed by the president.

Scope of Tobacco Problem

The existing handful of prevalence surveys gives a reasonable snapshot of tobacco use suggesting that the problem is significant and growing. Though there are discrepancies between these surveys, this is likely the result of using differing methodologies, and the results are not dramatically different. First, a World Health Survey (World Health Organization (WHO)) from 2003 reports an age-standardized overall adult (18 and older) smoking prevalence rate of 12 percent (9.7 percent in urban areas and 14.8 percent in rural areas). A 2005 survey from the World Health Organization Statistical Information System (WHOSIS) reports that 15.0 percent of adults smoke (using a slightly different definition of adult: 15 years and above), of whom 6.2 percent are females and 23.7 percent are males. The same survey reports that 18.4 percent of adolescents (13–15 years of age) smoke tobacco, of whom 17.9 percent are females and 19.1 percent are males. The Global Youth Tobacco Survey (GYTS) from 2006 reports slightly different numbers for youths: a 17.9 percent total smoking prevalence, with 21.1 percent for males and 14.7 percent for females. Additionally, the GYTS 2006 cites youth usage of other tobacco products such as snuff and chewing tobacco at 16.5 percent.

Despite the discrepancies – these differences are actually not enormous compared to differences in prevalence surveys in many other countries – there are some notable patterns. First, female prevalence rates, though once much lower, appear to be catching up to their male counterparts. Second, tobacco prevalence rates in rural areas are much higher, which likely reflects, at least in part, the large amount of tobacco production. Both patterns should inform future strategies by the tobacco control community. Finally, some recent World Bank data suggest that since the 1970s, average individual cigarette consumption by volume among individuals older than 15 years has increased by around 15 percent, from 9.5 packs to 11 packs per year.[3]

The nongovernmental organization (NGO) Youth Alliance in Social and Economic Development (YASED) reports from its youth resource centers (in Dowa, Lilongwe and Salima) that many youths start smoking at drinking establishments, which are accessible even to those as young as 14. Moreover, most bars and pubs selling alcohol will directly sell cigarettes, even to minors. The alliance argues that future tobacco control programs will require partnerships between institutions dealing with substance abuse and youth outreach in an effort to incorporate anti-smoking messages holistically in their daily work.

Beyond the need to conduct more comprehensive studies of tobacco use in Malawi, there is also a need to examine the problems associated with the growing of tobacco leaf and the growth of the tobacco sector in general. Clearly, all of these issues are intrinsically related, particularly in Malawi. A more complete package of studies related to the broader health implications of both tobacco use and cultivation will help the tobacco control community to make a stronger case to the Malawian government to sign the FCTC and to move general public opinion in favor of more tobacco control. More specifically, in addition to using the existing well-documented effects of smoking on the human body, the Malawian tobacco control community would also like to be able to quantify the effects of smoke from the many processing plants, the effects of workers' long-term exposure to tobacco leaf and the long-term implications of environmental degradation due to tobacco cultivation (especially deforestation and its many problems, such as airborne dust and erosion).

Politics of Tobacco Control

Overall context

There is very little in the way of existing or pending tobacco control legislation in Malawi, and it is clear that tobacco leaf growing definitely frames the politics of tobacco control in the country. Only 5 percent of the tobacco crop is consumed nationally and much of that is by the farmers themselves or through informal marketing at the community level. Furthermore, large, multinational tobacco manufacturing companies have not traditionally marketed and distributed widely in Malawi. At the same time, however, incomes appear to be rising in the country and smoking prevalence is growing amongst the surging youth population (half of the population is under the age of 25). At the present time, the ATSA team and various stakeholders believe that there is some political space to push for tobacco control but that the "policy window" will likely close over the coming years (approximately five years) as manufacturing and consumption increase. With the importance of the tobacco leaf industry firmly established, the Malawian tobacco control community argues unequivocally that all emphases concerning tobacco control must be placed firmly on *health* concerns, at least for the foreseeable future, and not on production.

There is a concerted effort by the government to increase value-added processing capability domestically, which would naturally increase the availability of end-use tobacco products in the country. Most notably, the Malawi Growth and Development Strategy (MGDS) 2006–11, which is the country's overarching economic growth strategy, articulates that Malawi would maintain the position of market leader in burley tobacco and seek to increase the production of flue-cured and Northern Dark Fired tobaccos. It also emphatically endorses the promotion of manufacturing as one of the priority areas to achieve sustainable economic growth. It was not surprising, therefore, that the 2008–9 national budget emphasized the need to introduce a tobacco cigarette manufacturing company in Malawi. As a result of this emphasis, a new local cigarette manufacturing plant, Nyasa Manufacturing Company (NMC), opened its doors in November 2009. Furthermore, to protect it from dumped cigarettes (below cost products imported from other countries), the minister of trade has publicly promised protection to the industry.[1] This promise is a direct response to the 2008 National Budget Taxation Act Amendment in which the national government introduced incentives for companies wanting to manufacture tobacco in the country.

Beginning with the highest office, second-term president Bingu wa Mutharika has been mostly indifferent to tobacco control issues (though, somewhat encouragingly, no Malawian president has ever been a public smoker). Though the president can issue decrees and orders (that have to be based on certain existing laws), this has not been a realistic possibility in the case of tobacco control. Formal requests from civil society organizations for more tobacco control measures and ratification of the FCTC to the Office of the President have only generated formal responses that promise to take note of the suggestions, without any concrete movement on any measure.

In a related development in September 2009, the president expelled representatives of major international leaf-buying companies to protest their setting of prices below the floor set by the Malawian government. This was not in any way a tobacco control measure, but rather a strategy to pressure the leaf companies to pay more for the cultivated product. No rigorous examination has been completed in order to determine if this strategy is leading to price increases for growers.

At the cabinet level of the executive branch, there are some key, powerful ministries that play or will play pivotal roles in tobacco control, including those controlling health, education, finance and agriculture. From a policy perspective or regulation-making perspective more generally, some ministers can actually issue decrees. In addition to limited decree power, ministers can also develop policies and then submit them to the Ministry of Justice directly, which then converts the policies into draft laws to be considered by the National Assembly. However, it is also important to consider that ministers are political appointees – these are very fragile positions because they can be changed quickly. It is unusual for ministers to take a strong position clearly in opposition to the president. However, ministries are pretty stable in their permanent staffs from the chief bureaucrat – the permanent secretary – downwards. They are civil servants with minimal chances of transfers and/or dismissal, and these actors can be pivotal in policy change or other campaigns. It is therefore important to identify the knowledge, attitudes and practices of all of these actors, elected and nonelected.

The ATSA team investigated the preferences of major actors in the health and education ministries in early 2010 and concluded that there are key officials openly sympathetic to tobacco control. In the Ministry of Education, the deputy minister of basic and secondary, as of 2010, is a former teacher and is known to be very supportive of tobacco control, especially smoke-free schools policies, which might provide an opportunity for short-term education initiatives. Similarly, the long-serving permanent secretary is also openly supportive in face-to-face meetings with tobacco control advocates. It was not easy to identify strong positions in the Ministry of Health (MoH).

Like many economic and political elites in Malawi, many cabinet members are engaged in direct tobacco production on their own farms – 60 percent by preliminary estimates – and this is assumed to affect their position toward tobacco control negatively. In the late 2000s, the Tobacco Tenants and Allied Workers Union (TOTAWUM) and the Centre for Social Concern (CFSC) conducted field visits to tobacco estates with the media and reported that many farms are owned by politicians across the political divide. For example, the main opposition, MCP president John Tembo, who has enormous influence in parliament including assigning all parliamentary committee memberships in the National Assembly, is a well known tobacco farmer and for many years was board chairman for the Limbe Leaf Tobacco Company.

In terms of the legislative branch, it does not appear that any legislators are clear tobacco control advocates, and some are openly hostile to changes in tobacco control policies. The largest challenge is that politicians and the public often construe tobacco control as contradictory to production, and since tobacco leaf production comprises the largest share of the economy, this is a tremendously important issue. The National Assembly has 193 members, and is organized into area-specific committees for the sake of easier policymaking. The speaker of the National Assembly in 2004–9 was an influential political actor, and he owns a tobacco grading company. However, he is known publicly to be a devout Christian – an important, positive cultural attribute to most Malawians – and the ATSA team believes that he could be a particularly helpful advocate if he were supportive (at least of a smoke-free schools initiative for a start). Civil society organizations are seeking to open a dialogue with him about the perils of tobacco.

Chairpersons and members of key assembly committees (including those on health, education, commerce and industry, legal affairs and social welfare) are also powerful political actors in the legislature because they typically examine and approve proposed legislation before it goes before the complete legislature for discussion and a vote. In an encouraging sign, the former chair of the Health Committee participated in the initial ATSA stakeholder meeting. The ATSA team has been speaking to the new chair about tobacco control efforts. Team members suggest that it is important to concentrate on committee members from the three target districts of Mchinji, Kasungu and Lilongwe, which are the leading tobacco leaf–producing regions. It is also important to concentrate particularly on female members of the National Assembly because they tend to be more open about issues like tobacco that adversely and disproportionately affect women and children. From an institutional and pragmatic perspective, private members can sponsor bills on Thursdays; the ATSA team has suggested that advocating for a member of parliament to propose a tobacco control bill – for example, smoke-free schools – could be a realistic option in the short term.

Malawi recently formally adopted a more decentralized political system and this institutional change could provide new opportunities for tobacco control in the future. As a result of the structural changes, there are now district assemblies (DA), and though recently fraught with problems, they are an important institution and one that may grow in importance. The DAs now spearhead development projects, and the majority of national resources in all key sectors are directly transferred to them. In fact, the national budgeting process now starts at the district level. For stronger advocacy and positive opinion-building efforts, involvement of assemblies will be very critical as they are allowed to formulate bylaws that directly affect the general public. The issues relating to tobacco control require a multifaceted approach that not only challenges national policy and builds positive grassroots public opinion, but also carefully incorporates all appropriate levels of government.

The DAs, however, have been slow to obtain actual power. Though DA counselors are normally elected, elections have been suspended for a number of years (most recently in April 2011). National members of parliament (MPs) and chiefs are ex officio members of the DAs. Furthermore, in December of 2009, the Malawi parliament passed a constitutional amendment bill that empowers the country's president to decide the date when local government elections are conducted. In other words, for the foreseeable future, a great proportion of power continues to lie with the president, and to a lesser extent, the National Assembly. It is not clear when the DAs will be reformed – in fact, foreign donors have recently stopped sponsoring efforts to reform them. If and when the DAs becomes more viable, their official mandate suggests strongly that they could be involved in public health generally and tobacco control specifically.

Another fairly new legislative structure, the Law Commission, might also provide future opportunities for tobacco control. Since 2004, interest groups have been able to apply directly to the commission in order for it to consider draft legislation. Comments are sought from the public and the draft legislation is then forwarded to the National Assembly for consideration. The commission is a semiautonomous body under the Ministry of Justice. The members represent a broad range of interest groups and the current head of the commission is a child rights activist who is known to be supportive of issues relating to children and youths. More generally, the commission appears open to well-researched and evidence-backed arguments that can be represented by legal opinion. The approach of the tobacco control community is to ensure that any presentation to the Law Commission to formulate a special law on tobacco control must cover all legal, public opinion and national policy interests more than competently. This is one possible viable long-term strategy for tobacco control in Malawi.

The Chiefs' Council could potentially play a very important future role in tobacco control, but may also present some challenges. Traditionally, there were four levels of chief (headman, group headman, child and paramount chief), but now there are many levels and chiefs are paid, so the process has been politicized. For example, there are about 10 chiefs in Kasungu, 17 for Lilongwe and 10 for Mangochi. Chiefs wield tangible political power: they have some judicial powers; they are supposed to be on school committees; they can summon people to report; and they can issue fines and other penalties for violations of laws. Chiefs will require special training on tobacco control as well as systematic access to information. If convinced of the merits of tobacco control, they could play a vital role in shaping public opinion. Notably, since roughly the year 2000, they have been among the influential community leaders who are advocating reduction in growing tobacco leaf on the grounds of the negative environmental implications.

Active members of the tobacco control community widely believe that it is very important to build up a team to undertake effective advocacy, including strong representation from the health, education, media and traditional leaders sectors. Unfortunately, many organizations are currently more engrossed in advocacy in areas where there is greater funding, particularly from international donors, and engagement in tobacco control remains very limited. However, the YASED is continuing to host the "Smoke Free Malawi" campaign, which is comprised of the following organizations that have confirmed explicitly their interest in supporting tobacco control in Malawi: the Cancer Registry of Malawi; the CFSC; the Consumer Association of Malawi; Drug Fight Malawi; the Health Communications Department of the MofH; the Health Journalists Network; the Journalists Union of Malawi; the Link for Education Governance; the Medical Doctors Association of Malawi; the National Youth Council of Malawi; the Tobacco Workers and Allied Union of Malawi; and the WHO Communication Office.

Tobacco control advocates believe that it is imperative to have a sustained and broad education program that targets government officials, journalists, youths, children and women. Accordingly, in June 2009, Smoke Free Malawi held its inaugural commemoration of the World No Tobacco Day (a month late because of the national election) with a media briefing and a public presentation in Lilongwe. The two events were designed as a launch pad for a two-year public campaign to mobilize public opinion to ask the government to sign the FCTC and ban public smoking across the country. Presenters included representatives from government, civil society and the academy (e.g. the College of Medicine at the University of Malawi). In addition to the FCTC ratification and smoking ban, other main issues included the country's dependence on tobacco leaf cultivation and effective ways of reducing smoking. The speakers at the conference were recorded and aired on several radio stations. The media briefing was well attended (by 19 journalists). Subsequently, Star Radio (a Zodiak broadcasting station) and Joy Radio have offered up to 100 minutes worth of air time to the Smoke Free project to discuss issues on tobacco control, which is an opportunity that will extend the campaign's reach without any additional spending. Smoke Free Malawi, as well as institutions such as the CFSC and Drug Fight Malawi, are introducing a permanent weekly program on smoking and health as one of the outcomes in youth centers that are run by the three institutions. Dr Charles Dzamalala and other cancer registry medical personnel at the University of Malawi have offered to work with Smoke Free at no cost in an in-school public speaking tour on tobacco and health.

The organizers of the inaugural event pressed government hard, specifically on action. For example, they pointed out that local assemblies can institute bylaws to ban public smoking very quickly. But they also sought systemic change, pointing out that the Ministry of Justice, the Ministry of Health, the Ministry of Local Government and/or the Ministry of Youth and Sports could and should immediately introduce actual national legislation banning public smoking and the buying and selling of cigarettes to minors.

The tobacco control community is seeking to broaden the coalition of actors in active support of tobacco control. Organizers from Smoke Free Malawi have identified a number of major NGOs that could or should be engaged more in tobacco control efforts, including Linking Education and Governance (LEG, made up of education advocates), the Coalition for Basic Education, the Human Rights Consultative Committee, the Malawi Health Equity Network, the Council of NGOs in Malawi (CONGOMA) and the Medical Doctors Society of Malawi. The Malawi Economic Justice Network (MEJN) has been involved previously in tobacco control, and the network's vocal organization and effective advocacy would be helpful to the current effort. The National Organisation of Nurses and Midwives (NONM) could be willing to support tobacco control and might be particularly effective because they have a good network of nurses at every hospital. Incidentally, the health sector in general has received a tremendous amount of funding to support tuberculosis control, and there could be a useful link-in with tobacco-related diseases such as lung cancer. This avenue needs to be explored further in terms of cross-pollination of purposes and goals.

Stakeholders argue that tobacco control proponents should pursue opportunities that involve the media more directly and proactively in tobacco control. Kondwani Munthali from YASED highlighted great potential for integrating a media campaign into the work at the ATSA meeting in October 2008. For example, he suggested creating a regular column in a newspaper about the health risks of smoking; designing a small newsletter that can be inserted into national newspaper; and developing instalments that can be added to radio programs. The ATSA team identified most of the major media outlets that need to be incorporated into the awareness effort: TV Malawi, the Malawi Broadcasting Organisation, the *Nation* newspaper, the *Blantyre* newspaper, Zodiac Broadcasting, 101 Radio (a youth station), Capital FM, Star Radio, two community radios (Radio Maria in Mangochi and Dzimwe Radio), Abstract Beats and Transworld Radio. Notably, the team referenced a previous program that distributed free wind-up radios to schools (an EU-sponsored project), suggesting that radio may be one of the best media for reaching large numbers of people particularly in rural areas where tobacco use is highest. The team also noted the future possibility of engaging the Malawi Institute of Journalism (MIJ), which is a training institution in journalism and also owns a radio with a nationwide coverage.

The tobacco control community would like to engage more international support from organizations including the WHO, UNICEF, Plan Malawi, Care, World Vision, the International Labour Organization (child labor), the World Bank, the United Nations Population Fund (UNFPA), Action Aid and the Canadian International Development Agency. In fact, Plan Malawi recently released a report on child labor in the industry. Unfortunately, the organization also received a lot of criticism for the report because it had not substantiated its claims sufficiently about nicotine absorption. It is hoped that like Plan Malawi, some of these organizations could be engaged in tobacco control initiatives in Malawi in the near future. The legitimacy and expertise of these organizations should be helpful to domestic advocates.

The tobacco industry – in its various forms – is positioned to resist tobacco control efforts. In Malawi, the industry is arguably a little different than in many other Sub-Saharan African countries because the manufacturers of end products are not nearly as visible; the tobacco leaf companies, however, such as Limbe Leaf, are exceptionally prominent. It will be very important to monitor the industry throughout the current initiatives and over the coming years, particularly as tobacco processing and manufacturing increase in the country, as they appear poised to do. Other industry-related possible opponents include the government's Tobacco Control Commission (which monitors quality) and the Tobacco Association of Malawi (TAMA). It is important to note that TAMA is an association of tobacco growers in Malawi that would likely oppose tobacco control from the production standpoint, but might support it from the health front. In an encouraging development, the Tenancy Bill drafted recently with the support of these organizations makes it illegal to hire workers under the age of 18 (with a 5 million kwacha fine and/or two years of imprisonment). The Ministry of Labour has had a draft of the bill since late 2009, but as of early 2011, it had not yet been presented to cabinet for approval.[5]

A possible avenue for convincing elected officials that tobacco leaf growing is not a viable long-term economic growth strategy is to organize farmers in order to discuss openly and candidly the shocking economic and personal safety conditions of tobacco cultivation. According to advocates, there is considerable conversation among farmers about the lack of viability of the crop and their interest in alternatives (already, the

International Development Research Centre (IDRC) and the International Crops Research Institute for the Semi-arid Tropics (ICRIS) from India are sponsoring programs that encourage ground nut cultivation as an alternative).[6] There is a genuine political dimension to these discussions that needs to be pursued more by advocates – for example, the minister of agriculture has been publicly open to agricultural possibilities beyond tobacco leaf that she has now begun to pursue.[7]

ATSA action: Research to support an advertising ban

The ATSA team – comprised of researchers (e.g. the University of Malawi) and representatives from civil society organizations and the media – conducted a research study between July and December 2009 entitled "Tobacco advertising, promotion and sponsorship: A Malawi research agenda towards MPOWER No.5." The overall objective of the study was to provide research-based information and accurate data that can be used by policymakers to formulate legislation for an effective comprehensive ban on tobacco advertising, promotion and sponsorship in Malawi. The principal, more focused objectives of the study were: 1) to examine the extent to which newspapers, magazines, radio, television and billboards are used in tobacco advertising; 2) to analyze the attitude of smokers and nonsmokers towards tobacco advertising, promotion and sponsorship; 3) to analyze the extent to which tobacco promotional activities involve sports and entertainment industries; and 4) to determine the primary targets of these advertising, promotion and sponsorship activities.

An additional related objective of the study was to examine how different countries that are succeeding in promoting comprehensive bans in advertising, promotion and sponsorship in Africa are putting measures in place to ensure that the bans are effective. In other words, the study seeks to identify any best practices that Malawi can use in its formulation of legislation to ban tobacco advertising, promotion and sponsorship.

The study was conducted in the four major cities of Malawi (Blantyre, Lilongwe, Mzuzu and Zomba) where 258 respondents were interviewed. Among the interviewees, 46.6 percent were smokers and 53.4 percent were nonsmokers. It is important to note that only 16.7 percent of all the smokers were females, and since the data were representative of the population in the four cities, it can be seen that smoking is dominated by males in the urban areas of Malawi. There are several findings from the study that are important for tobacco control advocates in Malawi. First, while tobacco advertising persists in the print media in Malawi, there has been no radio and television tobacco advertising since 2005 following a directive from the MoH. Further, tobacco advertising in newspapers and other print media contains a health warning message.

Secondly, since 2005, there has been a total ban on tobacco sponsorship and promotional activities involving the sports and entertainment industries in Malawi. Furthermore, researchers have learned that the leadership of the Music Association of Malawi and the Football Association of Malawi, the governing bodies of musicians and football respectively, are in support of the ban and would favor a comprehensive ban on tobacco advertising, promotion and sponsorship in Malawi.

Unfortunately, in late 2009, much of the progress on advertising, sponsorship and promotion bans changed radically with the opening of the local cigarette manufacturing company, Nyasa Manufacturing. The company has waged an aggressive campaign in all forms of advertising including the use of misleading translations in local languages. In addition, they are reintroducing smoking parties and continue to use youthful celebrities (e.g. Joseph Nkasa and the Big Brother Africa Revolution reality show) in their campaigns.

Thirdly, the study suggests that health warnings are not very effective in Malawi. Concerning the health warnings that accompany tobacco advertisements in the print media, 44.4 percent of nonsmokers said the warnings are clear and educative enough, while 36.8 percent of nonsmokers indicated that the signs were clear but not legible enough. For the smokers, 40.8 percent said the warnings are clear and educative enough and 30.8 percent of the smokers indicated that the health warnings on tobacco advertisements were clear but not legible enough.

Further, public support for a ban, particularly among nonsmokers, is very high. When asked about the possibility of a comprehensive ban on tobacco advertising, promotion and sponsorship, 87.3 percent of nonsmokers indicated that they would support such a ban, while 10.7 percent of nonsmokers were indifferent. Less than 2 percent of nonsmokers would oppose the ban. For the smokers' category, it is encouraging to note that 55.4 percent would support the ban. Only 36.1 percent of smokers indicated that they would oppose the ban. This figure is significantly lower than anticipated. As such, a comprehensive ban on tobacco advertising, promotion and sponsorship would be supported by the majority of both urban smokers and nonsmokers in Malawi.

Finally, the study also sought the opinion of smokers on cessation support services. It was found that 77.5 percent of the smokers expressed willingness to get expert help on quitting smoking if such a service existed. On the other hand, only 8.3 percent indicated that they would not be willing to get such support, and the remaining 14.2 percent were indifferent. This result points to the need for support services in Malawi to help smokers to quit smoking.

If such a service existed, a significant proportion of smokers in Malawi would be getting the necessary support to help them quit smoking.

Tobacco Industry Monitoring

The powerful players in the industry do not come from the manufacturing side, but rather from the tobacco leaf industry, which generates more than 60 percent of Malawi's total export earnings. This is the largest business in the country, and there are not only tobacco auction floors in all of the three major cities (Blantyre, Lilongwe, Mzuzu), but new ones are being set up in the major growing districts of Malawi, such as Mchinji and Kasungu. The tobacco leaf companies have well-built infrastructure and employ over 3,000 people. It is thought that the most powerful forces behind Malawi's tobacco-dependent economy are US tobacco-growing subsidiaries, Limbe Leaf and Alliance One (Stancom and Dimon merged in late 2008 to form the largest member of the buyers' cartel), which together purchase over 95 percent of the tobacco crop and sell it to global tobacco firms like Philip Morris and BAT. The national government also gave license to the growers association, TAMA, who formed a company with United Kingdom–based Premium Tobacco called Premium TAMA. The Premium TAMA company has invested around MWK3 billion (US$22 million), and a plant to process tobacco was opened in October 2009, operating officially as Kanengo Tobacco Processors.[8]

Though the tobacco manufacturing industry does not appear to be currently involved in vigorous "pro-tobacco" activities in Malawi, a recent UN report suggests that BAT and other tobacco firms desire to keep a critical mass of tobacco-farming households in Malawi that have an interest in the status quo – i.e. continued tobacco leaf cultivation.[9] Furthermore, recent government measures to provide incentives to improve tobacco production and to encourage investment have already led to one local cigarette manufacturing operation. So while foreign manufacturing is not an issue now, manufacturing more generally is very clearly part of the government's long-term strategy, which has been endorsed publicly by the president and other members of the cabinet. It is not clear if the traditional large manufacturing players (BAT, Japan Tobacco International (JTI), Philip Morris, etc.) are interested in Malawi's strategy, but recent Chinese activity in the Zimbabwean industry might portend to interest from upstart Chinese manufacturers. Already, there is anecdotal evidence that the Chinese are becoming more active in terms of purchasing raw tobacco leaf.[10]

Returning to leaf production, and specifically the actual farming component, the market continues to be notably volatile, and the risks to farmers are large. A recent *Daily Times* article reports that production costs rose dramatically by

70 percent in 2008.[11] By the same token, the Bloomberg news service reported in June 2009 that Malawian tobacco prices had also increased dramatically by 64 percent.[12] Indicators suggest that the 2009 market season saw a downturn in prices of 23 percent, and a revenue decline of 9 percent (MWK66 billion to MWK61 billion, or US$473 million to US$423 million). It is not entirely clear what the longer-term effect of these changes will be – on one hand, if production costs get too high, farmers might opt for alternative crops, while on the other hand, if prices also rise, farmers could be motivated to stay in the leaf business. Tobacco control advocates hope that the recent downward trend will mean that more farmers will not be interested in growing the crop in coming farming seasons, which might also present an opportunity for more advocacy on leaf-growing reduction.

On a related note, whether price increases actually go to the farmer is an entirely different but important discussion. Recent scholarship suggests that farmers' incomes in Malawi have actually decreased in recent years, and the arrangement between tobacco estate owners and farmers is a fundamentally unequal one.[13] The secretary general for the central region of the TOTAWUM, Edson Gideon, said his organization was receiving many complaints from tobacco tenants about declining economic conditions. Similarly, the CFSC in Lilongwe said its research reveals that despite the fact that tobacco production is associated with economic development and employment provision and contributes over 60 percent of Malawi's foreign exchange, growers are clearly becoming poorer. Finally, tobacco-producing companies have come under criticism from their peers for using child labor.[14] Producers have recently begun to recognize that this practice could jeopardize their international trade in tobacco.

The industry continues to get a pro-tobacco message out to the population, particularly young people. For example, in terms of exposure to tobacco-related messages, the 2006 GYTS reports that 49 percent of youth nonsmokers and 60 percent of youth smokers had seen pro-smoking messages; 12 percent of male nonsmokers and 32 percent of male smokers had been offered free cigarettes by company representatives; and 38 percent of smokers owned an object with a tobacco brand logo.

Finally, in August 2009, Kondwani Munthali from YASED reported that BAT was engaged in a vigorous publicity campaign by advertising daily and donating 28 bicycles to the Ministry of Agriculture. In December 2009, it was reported in the local newspapers (*Malawi Nation* and *The Daily Times*) that a leading tobacco leaf company in Malawi, Limbe Leaf, had donated over MWK 2.4 million (the equivalent of US$17,142) to one of the leading Christian churches in Malawi, known as the Church of Central Africa Presbyterian (CCAP) for its reforestation program.[15] Commentators have since argued that the donation should not be seen as the company's CSR, but rather as repayment for the damage that the tobacco companies cause, since the tobacco leaf companies are responsible for the significant loss of forests in tobacco growing areas of Malawi.

ATSA Review

In part because of strong official resistance to tobacco control, achievements related to the ATSA program were limited mainly to the area of the monitoring of tobacco advertising, promotion and sponsorship. In addition to the major baseline assessment across different facets of tobacco control in Malawi, the team successfully completed a comprehensive, rigorous study of all radio and television stations, leading newspapers, the Football Association of Malawi, the Music Association of Malawi and a large, random sample of individuals. The ATSA team convened a widely attended and media-covered dissemination workshop to share the findings. Despite the challenges for tobacco control in this tobacco leaf–dominated economy, tobacco control proponents from civil society and research – led by Smoke Free Malawi – continue to pursue creative solutions to the major multiple public health threats posed by tobacco.

Notes

1 Sources: CIA World Factbook https://www.cia.gov/library/publications/the-world-factbook/; except Organization of Economic Cooperation and Development (OECD) for development assistance statistics, and Food and Agriculture Organization of the United Nations – Statistics (FAOSTAT) for tobacco production. See http://stats.oecd.org/index.aspx and http://faostat.fao.org/site/567/default.aspx#ancor respectively (accessed 20 July 2011).

2 District assemblies are part of the local government decentralization and devolution plan. There are 28 district assemblies, four city assemblies and eight town assemblies in three regions (North, Center and South). The central government appoints chief executives and district commissioners. The last local elections took place on 21 November 2000. The United Democratic Front (UDF) won 70 percent of the seats. More elections were scheduled for May 2005, but were canceled, officially due to famine; the president canceled local elections again in April 2011 after suspending the independent electoral commission.

3 M. A. Corrao, G. E. Guindon, N. Sharma and D. F. Shokoohi (eds), *The Economics of Tobacco in Malawi* (Washington DC: The World Bank, 2000). http://www.who.int/tobacco/statistics/country_profiles/en/TCCP2001.pdf (accessed 6 September 2011).

4 H. Mchazime, "Malawi's Own Cigarette Ready for Market," *Daily Times*, 14 December 2009.

5 F. Potani, "5,000 Malawian tobacco growers march against delayed law," AfricaNews, 15 April 2011.

6   M. Otañez, "Increasing Crop Diversification and Organizing for the End of Tobacco Farming in Malawi," paper presented at the 13th Conference on Tobacco OR Health, Washington DC, 2006.

7   Malawi Democrat, "Malawi cut 200,000 farmers from fertilizer subsidy," 11 May 2011.

8   F. Potani, "Growing Tobacco without Puffing Benefits," AfricaNews, 7 August 7 2009.

9   N. Okhoya and G. Mutume, "'Golden leaf' loses its luster: International tobacco controls spurring production shifts," *Africa Renewal* 18.3 (2004): 4. Online at: http://www.un.org/ecosocdev/geninfo/afrec/vol18no3/183tobacco.htm (accessed 21 July 2011).

10 S. Banda, "Malawi: Tobacco deal with China imminent," AfricaNews, 13 March 2008.

11 C. Kandeiro, "Tobacco Production Costs Up by 70%," *Daily Times*, 16 February 2009.

12 F. Jomo, "Malawi's Tobacco Price Rises 64% at Sale, Nation Says," Bloomberg, 16 June 2009.

13 S. Persaud and B. Meade, "Trade and Development when Exports Lack Diversification: A Case Study of Malawi," US Department of Agriculture, Economic Research Service Report #77 (2009).

14 S. Kaminjolo, "Child Labour Threatens Tobacco Market." AllAfrica, 11 February 2009.

15 J. Nankhonya, "Limbe Leaf Donates to Nkhoma Synod." *Sunday Times*, 29 November 2009.

Chapter 13

MAURITIUS

Premduth Burhoo, Deowan Mohee and Leelmanee Moussa

Executive Summary

Since 1999, Mauritius has made significant progress in tobacco control, and with new and improved legislation in 2008, Mauritius has emerged as one of the regional leaders in tobacco control. It has even emerged as a world leader in areas such as prohibiting corporate social responsibility (CSR) activities and compelling the inclusion of very large graphic warning labels on cigarette packages (65 percent of the package's largest sides). This progress has been important to address high prevalence rates which, though on the decrease generally, remain very high in some groups (the rate for adult male daily smokers as of 2009 remains greater than 32 percent).

There is clear support for tobacco control at the highest levels in the government. The Ministry of Health and the attorney general's office have been particular leaders. The tobacco control civil society movement, led by ViSa, is small but very active and a crucial watchdog of both the industry and the government's efforts to combat tobacco use. Currently, the tobacco control community is seeking to assess the successes and challenges of the recent legislative and regulatory changes, including the always demanding task of enforcement.

In general, the newest regulations are more than FCTC-compliant across most areas including advertising, sponsorship and promotion; labeling and packaging; and smoke-free places. Though not a part of the latest legislation, a tobacco-specific taxation strategy has a preliminary foothold and remains an area ripe for further development.

Country Profile¹

Population in 2009 (global and African ranking):	1,284,264 (154, 41)
Geographical size (global ranking):	2040 sq. km (187)
GDP by purchasing power parity in 2008 (global ranking):	US$15.27 billion (100)
GDP real growth rate (2006–8):	5%
GDP per capita (global ranking):	US$12,000 (91)
Main industries:	Food processing (largely sugar milling), textiles, clothing, mining, chemicals, metal products, transport equipment, nonelectrical machinery, tourism
Languages:	Creole 80.5%, Bhojpuri 12.1%, French 3.4%, English (official but spoken by less than 1% of population), other 3.7%; data gained from the 2000 census
Official development assistance (ODA) – total commitments/disbursements (2007):	US$171.2/94.2 million
ODA as a percentage of GDP:	1.38805%
Largest donors (disbursements in millions of USD):	France 57.6, EU 28.1, Japan 5.4, UNDP 1.3
Tobacco production by volume in 2007 (global ranking):	316 tons (107)
Tobacco exports (2007):	Cigarettes: 99 tons at $40,626 per ton, #5 export; tobacco (unmanufactured): 214 tons at $4,888 per ton, #15 country export
Tobacco imports (2007):	Cigarettes: 963 tons at $19,947 per ton, #6 import

Brief Description of Political System

Type:	Mauritius is a parliamentary democracy and has been one of the most stable democracies in Africa.
Executive:	As of 2010, Prime Minister Navinchandra Ramgoolam is the head of government. President Anerood Jugnauth is the chief of state.
Cabinet:	The Council of Ministers is appointed by the president on the recommendation of the PM.
Legislature:	The unicameral National Assembly is made up of 70 seats – 62 seats are elected and 8 seats are appointed to represent

minority groups. In 2010, the Alliance Sociale (a coalition that includes the Mauritian Militant Socialist Movement (MMSM), Mouvement Rodriguais (MR), Mauritian Social Democrats (MSD) and Parti Mauricien Xavier Duval (PMXD)) had 38 seats and the Mauritian Militant Movement (MMM) / Militant Socialist Movement (MSM) had 22 seats.

Judiciary: Supreme Court.

Scope of Tobacco Problem

Smoking prevalence rates in Mauritius are among the highest in Africa – approximately one out of every three male adults smokes regularly. However, the prevalence rate (particularly among males) has been decreasing since 1987 as a result of intensive noncommunicable disease (NCD) awareness campaigns and the new regulations under the initial Public Health Act of 1999. The principal prevalence statistics come from the Non-Communicable Disease Surveys (NCD Survey – conducted roughly every five years), the Global Youth Tobacco Survey (GYTS), the Global School-based Student Health Survey (GSHS) and the World Health Survey (WHS). The Ministry of Health and Quality of Life (MOH&QL) would like to integrate tobacco use data into the National Health Information System, but this remains to be implemented.

In terms of adult rates, according to the 2003 WHS, 32.1 percent of males are daily smokers with an additional 10.5 percent of males who are occasional smokers (N=3,888). Among females, the prevalence of daily smokers is 1 percent and 1.8 percent for occasional smokers.

The time-series data from the NCD surveys – presented in Table 13.1 – offer more information and demonstrate the decrease; the data also roughly corroborate the findings of the WHS. Prevalence has decreased from a high of 57.9 percent amongst males in 1987 to 35.9 percent in 2004. For women, the rate decreased from 7 percent in 1987 to a low of 3.3 percent in 1998, before rising to 5.1 percent in 2004 (this recent increase could perhaps be explained by the increasing prevalence among adolescent women who over time have become the adult population surveyed). The rate of prevalence among the total population decreased from a high of 30.7 percent in 1987 to 18 percent in 2004. The final results of the most recent NCD survey are awaited to confirm the decreasing trend.

In addition to overall rates, some of the existing survey data – particularly from the WHS – demonstrate how smoking prevalence and use are stratified based on urban/rural, age and income breakdowns. According to the WHS (2003), smoking prevalence is 17.5 percent in urban settings and 15.3 percent in rural settings. Table 13.2 presents prevalence by age.

Table 13.1. Mauritius prevalence rates – NCD surveys

Year	Total prevalence	Male prevalence	Female prevalence
1987	30.7%	57.9%	7.0%
1992	24.3%	47.3%	4.8%
1998	20.2%	42.0%	3.3%
2004	18.0%	35.9%	5.1%

Table 13.2. Mauritius prevalence rates by age groups

Age group	Prevalence
18–29 yrs	14.7%
30–44 yrs	18.2%
45–59 yrs	17.0%
60–69 yrs	17.1%
70–79 yrs	9.6%
≥ 80 yrs	6.2%

The breakdown from the WHS by socioeconomic status demonstrates a notable pattern: smoking prevalence clearly decreases with income. Prevalence rates by lowest to highest income quintile are: Q1, 21.6 percent; Q2, 18.9 percent; Q3, 17.2 percent; Q4, 12.9 percent; and Q5, 12.5 percent. In addition, it was noted by the ATSA team that

almost 20 percent of smokers spent more than MUR 300/week on tobacco products. The modal income for the survey sample was MUR 4,000–6,000/month (suggesting that some households could be spending as much as 30 percent of their income on tobacco).[2]

Clearly the economic impact of tobacco consumption is being felt by the citizens of Mauritius, and almost certainly the heaviest part of that burden is falling on the lower socioeconomic groups.

The WHS 2003 also gives information on average daily consumption of tobacco by adults. These statistics exist stratified by gender, residence, economic quintile and age, but one of the key points is that males across categories generally consume between eight and ten cigarettes per day, while females consume on average five and a half cigarettes per day. The only notable exception is males 60–69 years old, who consume on average 13.4 cigarettes per day.

In terms of youth smoking, according to the 2008 GYTS, smoking prevalence (i.e. having smoked on one or more days of the 30 before the survey) among 13–15-year-olds on the island of Mauritius was 20.3 percent for boys and 7.7 percent for girls (13.7 percent overall). This is a decline from the earlier 2003 GYTS, when rates were 21.6 percent for males and 8.5 percent of females (14.8 percent overall). Notably, the 2003 GYTS noted slightly higher rates on the island of Rodrigues (particularly among females): 26.6 percent of males, 13.6 percent of females (19.7 percent overall). An additional survey, the GSHS, was conducted in 2007 for students on the island of Mauritius and it revealed that 23.1 percent of males and 8.5 percent of females (15.4 percent overall) were current smokers.

However, the overall consumption level among students is much lower than the general population. In 2008, 36.6 percent of those who report being smokers smoke less than one cigarette per day, 32.8 percent smoke one cigarette per day, 22.9 percent smoke two to five cigarettes per day and 7.7 percent smoke six or more cigarettes per day.

The GYTS 2008 and 2003 and the GSHS 2007 also provide data on adolescent exposure to second-hand smoke. In 2008, 36.1 percent of students reported living in homes where others smoked in their presence. Though the measures are not identical, this statistic is comparable to 2003, when 33.9 percent of never-smokers and 69.6 percent of current smokers reported exposure to tobacco smoke in their homes. In 2008, 73.6 percent reported exposure to second-hand smoke in places outside their homes. In 2003, 60.4 percent of never smokers and 88.8 percent of current smokers reported exposure to tobacco smoke in public places. Males and females in Mauritius are nearly equally exposed to these dangers. In addition, the GSHS 2007 results corroborate the GYTS findings, reporting that 77 percent of students reported people smoking in their presence on one or more days during the previous week.

The GYTS also contains information on advertising, promotion and sponsorship. The GYTS 2003 reports that the main sources for pro-tobacco messages for school adolescents aged 13–15 years are the television, foreign magazines, newspapers and the internet. In 2008, over half of the respondents saw a pro-tobacco advertisement in a newspaper or magazine in the previous month. Fortunately, 84.9 percent of respondents reported seeing an anti-smoking media message in the same timeframe.

In terms of cigarette accessibility for youths, despite the prohibition of the sale of cigarettes to minors as per the Public Health (Restrictions on Tobacco Products) Regulations of 1999, the GYTS 2003 showed that over half of respondents buy their cigarettes directly from shops. Some factors reported by the survey that led to cigarettes being accessible to minors include: sale of loose cigarettes, proximity of points-of-sale to their place of residence, and offers of free cigarettes by tobacco representatives.

Some cessation and treatment data are also available from the GYTS. In 2003, approximately 11 percent of current smokers in Mauritius (aged 13–15) had developed a dependence on tobacco (signified by smoking a cigarette immediately upon waking up). In 2003, about two-thirds of current youth smokers had tried to stop in the last year but failed to quit; that proportion dropped to 58.5 percent in 2008. In 2003, 41.2 percent of smokers did receive advice to quit from a professional or program, while in 2008, 76.1 percent reported receiving help at some time to quit (though exact details of the professional or programmatic intervention are not elucidated). In December 2008, a pilot smoking cessation clinic became operational in the public health sector. The MOH&QL plans to open such clinics in multiple regions of the country in 2010. In addition, the Adventist Church sometimes offers group therapy for quitting smoking called the "Plan de Cinq Jours."

Finally, the health consequences of smoking have been tracked in the healthcare system. According to internal statistics from the MOH&QL, 7 percent of the burden of disease in Mauritius is attributable to tobacco-related diseases, principally vascular disease, cancers and chronic obstructive pulmonary diseases.

Politics of Tobacco

Inventory of existing laws and regulations

The 2008 tobacco control regulations have improved already strong legislation from 1999. The Public Health Act of 1999 provided some basic restrictions and a first major step to future restrictions, but the improvements in the Public Health Act of 2008 are vast and substantive and in almost complete conformity with the World Health Organization's (WHO) Framework Convention on Tobacco Control (FCTC). The regulations even exceed basic compliance in several cases. The FCTC was signed by Mauritius on 17 June 2003 and ratified on 17 May 2004; the new legislation demonstrates Mauritius' commitment to its treaty obligations.

On 28 November 2008, Mauritius passed new regulations on tobacco known as the Public Health (Restrictions on Tobacco Products) Regulations 2008. These regulations entered into force on 1 March 2009, except for the labeling requirements, which entered into force on 1 June 2009. In Mauritius, laws are adopted by the parliament, and regulations (like those on tobacco products) are adopted by administrative bodies (i.e. government ministries). The legislative and regulatory process in Mauritius was that the Public Health Act was adopted by the parliament in 1999, and then the new tobacco regulations in 2008 were adopted by the MOH&QL, which fall under the Public Health Act that the parliament adopted nine years earlier.

Until very recently, the Public Health (Restrictions on Tobacco Products) Regulations of 1999 governed the following aspects of tobacco in Mauritius: 1) advertising, promotion and sponsorship; 2) sale to minors; 3) smoking in enclosed public places; and 4) packaging and labeling. There have been marked improvements on the 1999 act in the 2008 regulations regarding these key aspects of tobacco control and they are highlighted in considerable detail in the policy-specific chapters. As far as the contents of tobacco products are concerned, the tobacco regulations of 2008 do not allow the display on cigarette packages of the tar or nicotine content of cigarettes or their carbon monoxide yield. These provisions did not exist in the 1999 tobacco regulations.

Also, wide-reaching education campaigns were run by the government (with support of various health NGOs) to inform the public, businesses and distributors about these new regulations in advance of them entering into force. The government also provides limited funding, roughly Rs 250,000, to ViSa, the principal tobacco control advocacy organization. However, there is no earmarked line item in the budget or a plan to dedicate any of the revenue generated by tobacco taxation to awareness-type programs, or a permanent tobacco control unit.

According to most stakeholders, compliance and enforcement have been an issue in the past in Mauritius. The fines for noncompliance range between Rs5,000 and Rs10,000 upon first conviction and up to 12 months in prison for a third or subsequent conviction. It is not clear how much of a deterrent these punishments are. The MOH&QL has set up an enforcement committee that has the responsibility to ensure that a proper enforcement plan is established. The enforcement committee is holding regular meetings to monitor enforcement, and the Health Inspectorate and the police are conducting compliance checks in public places and businesses. There is also an ongoing MOH&QL project sponsored by the Bloomberg Initiative to promote 100 percent smoke-free environments in Mauritius, including enforcement of the smoke-free regulations.

Overall political context

Politically, Mauritius is a somewhat exceptional African case in that the highest levels of the executive branch, including the prime minister, the MOH&QL and the attorney general, demonstrate active support for tobacco control. Furthermore, there appears to be momentum, particularly within the MOH&QL, to take action on tobacco control. The following quote from Prime Minister Dr the Hon. Navinchandra Ramgoolam, G. C. S. K., from

12 March 2009 – Mauritius Independence Day – demonstrates this commitment to tobacco control and to the newest legislation particularly:

The Public Health (Restrictions on Tobacco Products) Regulations have recently been promulgated. Contrary to what some may think, this is not a measure that restricts liberty. It is meant to free you from a scourge that was becoming far too widespread and wrecking innocent lives. Smoking, far from being a liberating act of defiance, is the first step to an addiction that enslaves you and destroys your health. Smoking is neither cool nor smart. Be resolute in resisting the pressure of your peers who would lead you astray.

In 2009, Mauritius began implementing the National Action Plan on Tobacco Control 2008–12 with the main objective of reducing tobacco-related mortality and morbidity by preventing the use of tobacco products, promoting cessation and protecting individuals from exposure to second-hand smoke. Since February 2009, the government – led by the MOH&QL – has started a national awareness campaign on the new regulations through mass media and other channels.

Also, a National Committee on Tobacco Control has been set up to advise the government, particularly the MOH&QL, on policy matters relating to tobacco control and to coordinate and monitor the implementation of the National Action Plan on Tobacco Control. The committee is comprised of representatives of government organizations (including the MOH&QL, the Ministry of Finance, the Ministry of Agro Industry and Food Security etc.), parastatal bodies and NGOs. The industry has sought – unsuccessfully – to have one of their representatives on the committee. The committee is chaired by the director of health services in charge of the prevention desk at the MOH&QL. The committee typically meets two or three times per year.

The Mauritian government is committed to strong tobacco control. In addition to the National Action Plan on Tobacco Control, new tobacco regulations were passed to be compliant with the FCTC and to implement the Action Plan. The main new tobacco control policies presently being implemented include:

1. Introduction of pictorial warning labels
2. Laws to limit environmental tobacco smoke
3. Complete ban on advertising, promotion and sponsorship
4. Elimination of product descriptors such as "light" or "mild" brands
5. Prohibition of sale of loose cigarette sticks; packages being sold must contain 20 cigarettes
6. Strengthening of regulations for sale of tobacco to minors
7. Control on illicit trade

The Cabinet of Ministers, which meets on a weekly basis under the chairmanship of the prime minister, is briefed by the minister of health and quality of life on all matters relating to tobacco control as necessary. The new regulations also went through the Cabinet of Ministers and not through the parliament because the Public Health (Restrictions on Tobacco Products) Regulations 2008 fall under the Public Health Act already approved by parliament (in 1999). Once the cabinet approved the regulations, the minister of health and quality of life used his statutory power and prerogative to promulgate them.

Civil society organizations, particularly ViSa, have so far made significant contributions to the gains that have been achieved in tobacco control. They contributed in the preparation of policy documents through valuable comments and strongly advocated for the implementation of the new policies. Some other nongovernmental organizations that lend support to the cause include Link to Life (Cancer Support Group) and the Heart Foundation, amongst others. Link to Life is a cancer patients' group that provides counseling, support and health information to its members and the public at large through cancer awareness talks and exhibitions at schools, youth clubs, municipal halls, public and private workplaces on request. The Heart Foundation organizes anti-tobacco awareness campaigns among the public through talks, walks and pamphlets.

The tobacco industry and its distributors, vendors and retailers remain problematic and antagonistic toward tobacco control (see discussion later in this section). Tobacco growers may also be problematic due to their alleged anticipated loss in revenue resulting from a decrease in tobacco sales, though the number of growers is rapidly declining for a number of reasons. Notably, growers are guaranteed both price and volume floors by the government (through the Tobacco Board) and BAT to sell their leaf crop, so these policy changes should not affect them.

The actual tobacco regulatory body is the Tobacco Board. The minister of agro industry is responsible for appointing the eight members of the board, which includes a representative from the tobacco growers, the Ministry of Finance, the prime minister's office and the tobacco industry (sometimes two from the industry). According to the board, its responsibilities include: 1) fixing the grades of leaf tobacco; 2) fixing the purchase and sale prices of those grades; 3) purchasing leaf tobacco produced in the country according to the approved grading system; 4) processing and selling leaf tobacco to the manufacturer; 5) managing the Statutory Funds established under the act; 6) licensing the import of leaf tobacco, manufactured tobacco and tobacco products; and 7) ensuring that every packet of imported cigarettes bears an approved Health Warning Clause. The board also offers the following incentives: 1) interest-free loans for the purchase of equipment and repairs of sheds and barns under the Mechanisation and Inputs Fund; 2) interest-free credit facilities for the purchase of inputs; 3) a Best Growers' Award Scheme to reward annually the three best performing growers for each type of tobacco; 4) purchase of leaf tobacco at a negotiated price; and 5) cash payment to tobacco growers on delivery of leaf. Considering this information provided by the board, balancing these responsibilities and incentives with public health concerns must be challenging.

ATSA action #1: To evaluate the impact of graphic health warnings on the population

It is important for tobacco control policies to be accompanied by rigorous evaluation because quality evaluation research provides not only concrete evidence for the effects of policies, but also has the potential to inform future policies. Accordingly, the ATSA team has been examining the patterns of smoking behavior and evaluating national-level tobacco control policies in Mauritius. The new regulations and action plan are innovative – for example, Mauritius is the first country in Africa to display pictorial warning labels on cigarette packages. In addition to being important to successful implementation of policy in Mauritius, the results of the policy evaluation can also be shared with other countries in the region to assist their own evidence-informed policy planning.

This study is a prospective cohort survey consisting of a minimum of two waves. Wave 1 was conducted between April and May 2009. The objectives were:

1. To measure the effectiveness of current text health warnings
2. To determine the prevalence of smoking in the population
3. To evaluate the level of support for cessation programs and smoke-free initiatives among smokers and nonsmokers

In December 2008, contact was established with the International Tobacco Control (ITC) Evaluation Project at the University of Waterloo (Canada) in view of collaboration and technical support for carrying out the study. Initial personal contact with the ITC team was made during the World Conference on Tobacco or Health, held in Mumbai in March 2009. After agreeing to collaborate, discussions centered on planning and implementation of different stages of the survey. Study proposal and survey instruments were finalized after regular conference calls and exchanges of emails.

At the request of the ITC team, the Mauritius ATSA team broadened the scope of the study by agreeing to the application of the complete (Wave 1) ITC questionnaire in Mauritius, with additional financial support from the

ITC Policy Evaluation Project. In other words, in addition to questions on health warnings, the whole set of questions that cover other FCTC domains (similar to ITC surveys conducted in other countries) were also included.

Widening the scope of the study will result in an opportunity to evaluate tobacco control policies in Mauritius more broadly and holistically. Thus, the next wave of the survey will not only evaluate the impact of the new graphic warnings and other measures with respect to packaging, but also support for and compliance with the new smoke-free legislation and support for proposed cessation clinics.

In order to gauge the efficacy of the new regulations – i.e. compare the new to the old – the ATSA team moved quickly to conduct Wave 1 interviews before 1 June 2009. Beginning in June, eight new rotating graphic pictorial warnings were supposed to be displayed on cigarette packages, though in reality the widespread introduction of the new labels was effective only in October of 2009 as existing stocks had to be cleared.

A total of 1,750 households were enumerated to establish an accurate sampling frame, from which a total of 600 smokers and 240 nonsmokers aged 18 years and older were drawn and surveyed using a face-to-face survey interviewing methodology. The IDRC sponsored the visit of two representatives from the ITC Evaluation Project Team from the University of Waterloo to provide training to the data collection team and supervise sample interviews in Mauritian households.

The next wave of the survey was executed between 30 August and 2 October 2010. Participants in Wave 1 of the survey were recontacted to respond to the Wave 2 questionnaire. This time-series, cohort design measure policy impacts in more fine-grained, individual-level ways, as compared to a repeat cross-sectional design (i.e. different samples of participants).[3] Among its many findings, the ITC results suggest that the pictorial warnings are more effective than the previous text-only versions and that smoke-free policies are having a marked and positive impact on multiple types of public and private (e.g. work-related) spaces.

Subject to the findings, additional waves may also be conducted to evaluate the impact of specific tobacco control policies that will be implemented in the subsequent five years. In fact, field work for Wave 3 is scheduled to begin in June 2011.

ATSA action #2: To support the joint MOH&QL/WHO smoking cessation initiative

For this action, the MOH&QL, partly in collaboration with the Mauritius Institute of Health (MIH) and the University of Mauritius, executed two studies. The first study is a survey of health professionals about tobacco use and smoking cessation called the Knowledge, Attitudes, Beliefs and Practices (KABP) survey. The objectives are:

1. To determine tobacco use among health professionals working in the public health sector of Mauritius
2. To explore their knowledge, attitudes, beliefs and practices with respect to tobacco use and smoking cessation
3. To assess their skills and training needs in smoking cessation techniques

The MOH&QL collaborated with the Mauritius Institute of Health (MIH) and the University of Mauritius in the implementation of this survey of health professionals. Since the MOH&QL is the ultimate user of this research, it is the key stakeholder for this action. The MIH played a central role in the implementation of the survey by providing logistics and other support. The stratified random sample was comprised of 350 registered doctors, specialists, dentists, nurses and midwives drawn from lists of healthcare staff working in the five health regions of Mauritius.

The second study is an assessment and strengthening of the existing Health Information System regarding tobacco use among NCD patients attending public health institutions. The objectives are:

1. To assess the present health information system regarding data collection, compilation and analysis on tobacco use by NCD patients of the public health system
2. To strengthen the existing health information system regarding tobacco use by NCD patients

The MOH&QL is the key government ministry in terms of this initiative. However, in addition, the Health Statistics Unit and the Medical Records Division are the two core elements of the Health Information System. The following three paragraphs outline the role of the specific agencies and departments in information collection, and neatly demonstrate how many actors are involved in the successful implementation of such a survey and/or any related future tobacco-related data gathering.

The Health Statistics Unit, headed by the chief health statistician, is responsible for the collection, compilation and analysis of data, and the presentation and dissemination of information relating to most aspects of health. The information generated in the Health Statistics Unit comes from the raw data that are collected from the various health institutions (hospitals, health centers, health offices, private clinics, etc.). The mode of transmission of the data is through pre-designed forms and electronic format. The data received in the unit are edited for completeness and accuracy, and then analyzed. The information generated is disseminated through weekly bulletins, monthly reviews and annual reports.

The Medical Records Division has the responsibility to collect, compile and present data pertaining to most types of services offered in hospitals. The Division is headed by the medical record organizer, and the staff of the Medical Records Cadre mainly compiles health service data from all hospitals and health centers (the records staff is responsible to record and maintain patients' medical files). Medical records staff posted in each hospital are generally the first point of contact with patients attending hospitals and provide an around-the-clock service. An accurate record-keeping process allows the collection of useful epidemiological and healthcare-related information.

Besides these two health-related entities for the survey, this ATSA action draws upon the assistance from all major health providers. In Mauritius, the public health delivery system comprises 13 hospitals (including five specialized hospitals), 26 area health centers, two medi-clinics and 127 community health centers. In the private sector, there are 13 private clinics. Finally, two other health entities that played roles in this action are the Non-Communicable Disease (NCD) Secretariat, which is based at each of the five regional hospitals and collects and compiles data on NCD patients in their respective health regions, and the National Cancer Registry, which collects data on cancer patients.

ATSA action #3: To support smoke-free initiatives in public and workplaces

Building on the recent national awareness campaign on the new tobacco control regulations, the Mauritius ATSA team called for a strengthened effort on all aspects of smoke-free regulations, particularly using strategic activities to target specific groups. Together with the implementation of the smoke-free regulations, there is a continuing need for rigorous monitoring of the smoke-free policy. Therefore, the team sought to monitor compliance by assessing the quality of indoor air through second-hand smoke (SHS) level measurements in public and workplaces. This assessment helps to provide evidence as to the extent that the new regulations are making indoor public places and workplaces (including cafes, bars, nightclubs and restaurants) smoke free.

The watchdog NGO, ViSa, has observed, for example, that some venues, particularly higher-end, mostly tourist-focused, establishments such as nightclubs and five-star hotels do not comply fully with the smoke-free regulations. Though authorities may be overlooking their noncompliance because of the economic importance of these businesses, this effort seeks to illuminate any such violations.

A smooth implementation of the smoke-free regulations requires a multisectoral approach politically, including particularly the Mauritius Institute of Health, the Ministry of Environment, the Ministry of Labour, Industrial Relations and Employment, the MOH&QL (including the following units: health, information, education and communication, occupational health and health inspectorate) and the private sector.

The Flying Squad of the Health Inspectorate Unit has been instrumental in smoke-free enforcement and plays a central role in all monitoring efforts. Furthermore, the regular police force and the environmental police also constitute an important ally for their role in an effective implementation and enforcement of the regulations.

It is also important to emphasize the involvement in advocacy effort of civil society organizations like ViSa, Link to Life (Cancer Support Group), and the Heart Foundation amongst others, which are playing key roles in the public awareness side of the smoke-free policies. In addition to civil society organizations, major employers and labor organizations need to be engaged more actively in terms of understanding smoke-free work places. At this point, it is not clear how supportive (or unsupportive) these groups are in the enforcement of the policy/regulations. Key groups include the trade unions, the Mauritius Employers' Federation, the manufacturing sector (particularly textile factories), and the owners of business premises. Efforts continue by the tobacco control community to reach out to these actors.

Notably, a small handful of businesses have been taking anti-tobacco initiatives on their own. For example, Moulins de la Concorde, a food production company employing more than 150 people, has implemented not only strict regulations on tobacco use for contamination and security (e.g. fire) reasons, but also provides direct health assistance to its employees. The company sets aside smoking areas away from other employees and the actual work environment, actively promotes a nonsmoking lifestyle and facilitates meetings for employees who are smokers and wishing to quit.

Although so far the tobacco industry has not shown open/explicit resistance regarding the implementation of smoke-free regulations, it is anticipated that it will act in less-than-obvious ways to undermine the policies out of concern for their ultimate impact on sales. In addition, tobacco control proponents continue to express concern about the reaction from the hospitality and entertainment industry, the vendors/retailers and owners of restaurants and night clubs.

For this study, written approval from the MOH&QL was sought to facilitate access to 60 hospitality venues, including cafés, bars, restaurants and nightclubs. A team of researchers from the Flying Squad of Health Inspectorate was trained by two experts from Public Health Agency (Barcelona, Spain) to assess second-hand smoke exposure by measuring particulate matter concentration (PM2.5) and nicotine concentration (using second-hand smoke passive samplers). The Global Smokefree Partnership helped to link these organizations.

Tobacco Industry

Tobacco manufacturing is on the decline in Mauritius. The number of cigarette sticks manufactured in Mauritius decreased dramatically between 2002 and 2007; the decrease is explained by BAT's decision to delocalize its factory to Kenya. All cigarettes and other tobacco products sold on the local market are now imported from countries like Kenya and South Africa. Notably, however, the sale of cigarettes on the local market increased slightly – in line with the population – from 998 million sticks in 2001 to 1,014 million sticks in 2006.

The Ministry of Agro Industry reports that the domestic production of leaf tobacco has declined from 556 tons in 2001–2 to 296 tons in 2005–6, and the acreage under cultivation has decreased from 395 hectares in 2000–1 to 291 hectares in 2005–6. There are 278 registered growers (growing both two-season Virginia Flue Cured and one-season Amarello Air Cured) with a labor force of 1400, of whom 75 percent are women. The main reasons for the decrease in leaf cultivation are most likely the following: inefficient/inactive growers; unwillingness to take over succession; climatic hindrances; lack of financial resources; and the high cost of production.

Recently, the industry's corporate social responsibility (CSR) programs have been deeply affected by the new legislation. BAT has noted in its annual report (2009) that the Public Health (Restrictions on Tobacco Products) Regulations of 2008 will restrict

> tobacco companies from engaging in any form of corporate social responsibility programs. Accordingly, all corporate social investments undertaken by BAT in Mauritius have been stopped. These included the undergraduate Scholarship Scheme which has seen 86 students enrolled in university since 2000 and the food baskets program that has been recognized for the support it provided to deserving households.[1]

In a negative development in early 2009, the tobacco industry took advantage of a loophole in the Public Health (Restrictions on Tobacco Products) Regulations 2008 by importing a very large stock of cigarettes (and presumably other tobacco products) prior to the entering into force of the labeling regulations on 1 June 2009. According to the new regulations (Regulation 9), labeling requirements do not apply to cigarettes or cigars imported before the regulations entered into force in November, 2008. It was estimated that this early imported supply lasted distributors and retailers in Mauritius until at least December 2009. Furthermore, though warnings appeared quickly on the least popular brand, "Dunhill Menthol," and the premium brand by Benson and Hedges, the most popular brand by Matinée still did not have compliant warnings after many months.

ATSA Review

Achievements of efforts related to the ATSA program included significant capacity building in tobacco control research at both individual and institutional levels and the further development of a broader and deeper tobacco control network. In terms of research, ATSA participants produced high quality and timely data that will help policymakers and advocates to produce better tobacco control policies. For example, one key part of the program was the rigorous measurement of the impact of the pictorial health warnings. Another aspect of the program was to generate data on the effectiveness of other new FCTC-compliant measures (smoke-free legislation, communication and education, pricing and taxation, and advertising and promotion bans). A third distinct part of the program generated baseline data for the establishment of smoking cessation clinics in the public health sector. Finally, the program helped to provide baseline information for more systematically incorporating the monitoring of tobacco use and treatment into the country's health information system.

The continued development of the network of tobacco control proponents was also central to the program. The ATSA team – comprised principally of permanent government officials (i.e. salaried, unelected and not appointed) – reports improved partnership among local stakeholders, particularly between government and civil society. The program also furthered opportunities for Mauritian tobacco control proponents to network with regional and global tobacco control agencies/partners.

Notes

1 Sources: CIA World Factbook https://www.cia.gov/library/publications/the-world-factbook/; except Organization of Economic Cooperation and Development (OECD) for development assistance statistics, and Food and Agriculture Organization of the United Nations – Statistics (FAOSTAT) for tobacco production. See http://stats.oecd.org/index.aspx and http://faostat.fao.org/site/567/default.aspx#ancor respectively (accessed 20 July 2011).

2 Quoted in an ATSA stakeholder meeting presentation held at the Mauritian National Institute of Health, Port Louis, 19 June 2008.

3 For the Wave 2 report, please see: http://www.itcproject.org/documents/keyfindings/itcmauritiusnationalreport_finalmay2011webpdf (accessed 21 July 2011).

4 British American Tobacco, "Mauritius Annual Report" (2009).

Chapter 14

NIGERIA

Nigeria Tobacco Situational Analysis
Coalition and Jeffrey Drope

Executive Summary

Nigeria is at a major crossroads in tobacco control, as comprehensive legislation was only passed by the National Senate in early 2011. The legislation is compliant with the Framework Convention on Tobacco Control (FCTC) and has been vetted by the domestic tobacco control community and its many international allies (e.g. Tobacco Free Kids (TFK), Framework Convention Alliance, International Development Research Centre (IDRC), etc.). With adult prevalence rates approaching at least 20 percent and increasing (and likely higher amongst youths), there is a clear need to address tobacco issues in the near term, especially in such a populous (> 150 million), varied (hundreds of distinct ethnic and/or linguistic groups) and poor country.

There appears to be considerable political support for the legislation at many high official levels, but Nigerian politics are very complex. Even before final presidential assent, the tobacco control community is shifting to consider the challenges of implementation and enforcement.

While seeking passage of national legislation, tobacco control proponents pursued other avenues. In November 2009, the tobacco control community team enjoyed a significant victory when Osun State passed a comprehensive smoke-free law (one of the African Tobacco Situation Analysis (ATSA) initiatives). The team had been sensitizing state legislators and the state-level executive branch (the governor and his staff) about tobacco control for months through education programs. The team has since shifted its efforts to enforcement. As a federal system, considerable power is decentralized to the states, so the "demonstration effect" of a successful smoke-free Osun State could have powerful positive demonstration effects.

As a veritable "practice run," the tobacco control community has been pursuing implementation and enforcement of the previously passed smoke-free Abuja law. After sensitizing the Abuja minister to tobacco issues, he officially incorporated a line item in the 2009–10 budget for tobacco implementation and enforcement activities. This action is an enormous victory for the tobacco control community because the laws are becoming more self-sustaining – i.e. not requiring as much external funding for awareness and enforcement. Abuja could also serve as an excellent model for implementation of the new legislation.

The challenges are large in Nigeria, including a very politically and economically powerful tobacco industry. In the mid-2000s, British American Tobacco (BAT) made Nigeria its West African manufacturing hub, and it has a large presence in the country. However, the tobacco control community is experienced, dogged and creative in its approaches. Currently, organizations working in tobacco control, particularly Environmental Rights Action (ERA)/ Friends of the Earth Nigeria (FoEN) and the Nigerian Heart Foundation, are seeking aggressively to expand their full-time tobacco control-focused staff, which is a necessity in a country this large and complex.

Nigeria Country Profile[1]

Population in 2009 (global and African ranking):	149,229,090 (9, 1)
Geographical size (global ranking):	923,768 sq. km (39)
GDP by purchasing power parity in 2008 (global ranking):	US$335.4 billion (36)
GDP real growth rate (2006–8):	6%
GDP per capita (global ranking):	US$2,300 (178)
Main industries:	Crude oil, coal, tin, columbite, palm oil, peanuts, cotton, rubber, wood, hides and skins, textiles, cement and other construction materials, food products, footwear, chemicals, fertilizer, printing, ceramics, steel, small commercial ship construction and repair
Languages:	English (official), Hausa, Yoruba, Igbo (Ibo), Fulani and Kanuri (country is comprised of more than 250 ethnic groups)
Official development assistance (ODA) – total commitments/disbursements (2007):	US$2,419.4/1,623 million
ODA as a percentage of GDP:	0.98%

Largest donors (disbursements in millions of USD):	UK 354.1, Netherlands 344, Austria 321.3, US 240.6, Denmark 94.4, EC 78.9, Global Fund 39.6, UNICEF 33.8
Tobacco production by volume (2007):	9,000 tons
Tobacco exports (2007):	Cigarettes: 760 tons at $13, 633 per ton, #7 export
Tobacco imports (2007):	Tobacco (unmanufactured): 12,278 tons at $2,921 per ton, #14 import

Brief Description of Political System

Type: Nigeria is a presidential federal republic with 36 states and one territory.

Executive: President Goodluck Jonathan was elected in 2011 and is the chief of state and head of government.

Cabinet: Federal Executive Council.

Legislature: The bicameral National Assembly consists of the National Senate and the House of Representatives. The National Senate is comprised of 109 seats with three seats from each state and one seat from Abuja that are elected every four years by popular vote. In late 2009, the main political parties in the National Senate were the People's Democratic Party (PDP) 53.7%, All Nigeria People's Party (ANPP) 27.9% and the Alliance for Democracy (AD) 9.7%. The House of Representatives is comprised of 360 seats that are elected every four years by popular vote. The main political parties in the House are the PDP (54.5%), the ANPP (27.4%) and the AD (8.8%).

Judiciary: Supreme Court (judges recommended by the National Judicial Council and appointed by the president).

Scope of the Tobacco Problem

National-level tobacco usage statistics differ widely among data sources in Nigeria, but evidence suggests that tobacco use is a significant and growing public health problem. The *Tobacco Atlas* (2010) cites tobacco prevalence rates of 9 percent for adult men, less than 1 percent for adult women, 9.7 percent for teenage boys and 5.7 percent for teenage girls.[2] Similarly, the Demographic Health Surveys (DHS) from 2003 cites a general rate of cigarette smoking of 8 percent for men and less than one percent for women, and less than two percent for noncigarette tobacco use.[3] In contrast, the 2008 Global Youth

Tobacco Survey (GYTS) data for Nigeria compiled by Dr Ima-Obong Ekanem, a member of the Nigeria Tobacco Control Alliance (NTCA), found that youth tobacco use (13–15-year-olds) has reached alarming rates: 17 percent to 27 percent of the adolescents surveyed were regular tobacco users (rates vary by region).[4]

Most data tend toward higher rather than lower rates. Two surveys by the Nigerian Ministry of Health (MoH) (1998 and 2001) found smoking prevalence rates of 17.1 percent among adults over 15 and 18.1 percent among youths aged 13 to 15. Also, the MoH has reported that total consumption of tobacco in Nigeria increased at an annual 4.7 percent rate between 2001 and 2006.

One notable statistic that remains low is consumption. Two-thirds of smokers report smoking one to five cigarettes per day, and only 16 percent report consumption of more than ten cigarettes. Of course, these patterns of low consumption are common across developing nations with serious poverty issues such as Nigeria, and the distinct challenges of low consumption should be considered in any tobacco control strategy.

A pessimistic appraisal of the data is also supported by recent mortality statistics cited by four Nigerian provinces in their separate lawsuits against BAT. The Lagos state government recorded more than 9,000 cases of tobacco-related illnesses in the state's 26 hospitals during 2006 alone; extrapolating to the whole country, more than 352,000 Nigerians suffer from tobacco-related illnesses annually.[5]

Politics of Tobacco

Inventory and a brief history of laws and regulations

In March of 2011 after approximately two years of consideration, the National Senate finally passed new FCTC-compliant comprehensive tobacco control legislation to replace an existing – and much weaker – statute from 1990. The legislation is entitled "A Bill for an Act to Repeal the Tobacco (Control) Act 1990 Cap T16 Laws of the Federation and to Enact the National Tobacco Control Bill 2009 to provide for the Regulation or Control of Production, Manufacture, Sale, Advertising, Promotion and Sponsorship of Tobacco or Tobacco Products in Nigerian and for other Related Matters." The short citation herein is the "National Tobacco Control Bill 2009." As of May 2011, as is legislative procedure in Nigeria, the bill was to undergo reconciliation with the House's version and then await final presidential assent. In brief, the bill seeks to ban smoking in public places, to forbid persons under the age of 18 to sell and buy tobacco products and to forbid communication between the manufacturers and consumers (i.e. advertising, sponsorship and promotion).

Previous attempts by the Nigerian government to regulate the activities of tobacco manufacturers date back to the early 1990s. The first significant policy was the Tobacco Smoking (Control) Decree 20, 1990. In 2001, the decree was converted to an act when Nigeria moved to democratic rule, and was titled "Tobacco (Control) Act 1990 CAP.T16." The act provided for a ban on smoking in specified public places, and it required warning messages on every tobacco advertisement and sponsorship. The highly ineffective warning message, "The Federal Ministry of Health warns that Smokers are Liable to Die Young," was enforced, but the ban on smoking was not enforced in all the specified places, such as schools and stadia. Since 1990, Nigeria has consistently marked the World No Tobacco Day (WNTD) with the tobacco control community creating awareness and disseminating information to members of the public on the adverse effects of tobacco on public health. These efforts were always driven by civil society, but in the late 2000s, the MoH also began to organize WNTD events.

After the 1990 legislation, there were a handful of hopeful signs of progress on tobacco control by the government. In 1999, in an effort to reinforce the government's position on tobacco control, a National Smoking Cessation Committee was inaugurated and a short-term plan of action was developed. These actions were shortly followed by a "total ban" on tobacco advertisement by the Advertising Practitioners Promotion Control (APCON) of Nigeria in 2002. In 2004, Nigeria signed the FCTC and subsequently ratified it on 20 October 2005. In 2007, an Abuja smoke-free policy was introduced by the minister of the Federal Capital Territory (FCT), banning smoking in public places. The federal government further demonstrated its political will to regulate the tobacco industry by paying its voluntary FCTC contribution to the World Health Organization (WHO) up to 2007 and halting the establishment of an N$80 billion tobacco factory by the Imperial Tobacco Group in Osun State. The successful mobilization against the proposed factory was the combined effort of MoH officials and tobacco control nongovernmental organizations (NGOs).

A national comprehensive tobacco control bill has been a central goal of the tobacco control community for many years. The path of the National Tobacco Control Bill 2009 was a long and often challenging one, particularly through the National Senate but a discussion of its journey serves as an excellent illustration of the power of persuasion and perseverance by its supporters, in and out of government. The National Senate version of the legislation was sponsored by Lagos East senator (and deputy minority leader) Dr Olorunnibe Mamora (MD), and received its official second reading in February 2009.[6] According to tobacco control advocates, British America Tobacco–Nigeria (BATN) actively sought to quash the bill after the reading, and it was only after vigorous efforts on the part of civil society organizations that the bill advanced to the committee stage. It was considered in a formal public hearing by the Senate Health Committee in July 2009.

During this time, the bill received a major boost from the minister of health, Professor Babatunde Osotimehin, who spoke out publicly in support of the proposed legislation. He stated, "I want to tell you that I am very passionate about anti-tobacco legislation. This British-American Tobacco people [sic] once came to talk to me on how we could work together but I said no! I cannot work with BAT people because the human cost of tobacco is enormous."[7]

Another influential national politician, Senator Jibrin Aminu (a former minister, former ambassador, two-time senator and chairman of the Senate Committee on Foreign Affairs), also spoke out publicly against tobacco. He urged stronger provisions than those in the actual bill, and he even suggested prohibition over regulation, saying, "I don't like that approach, we should discourage and prevent it completely. We should not be deceived by the sweet messages propagated by these tobacco companies."[8]

The bill also received vigorous support from many civil society groups inside and outside of Nigeria. For example, three major Nigerian NGOs – ERA/FoEN, the NTCA and the Coalition Against Tobacco – vigorously supported the legislation. The bill was also commended by international agencies and NGOs. The WHO country representative in Nigeria, who was represented at the National Senate public hearing by Dr Kayode Soyinka, said the hearing was a significant step by the legislative branch's upper chamber to rescue the lives of millions of Nigerians from tobacco addiction. In a memorandum to the National Senate, Matt Myers, the president of a leading tobacco control group based in the United States, Campaign for Tobacco-Free Kids, expressed support for the tobacco control bill "in its current form" and urged for it to be passed promptly.[9] The memorandum also stated that the bill is essential to bring Nigeria into compliance with its international obligations under the FCTC.

Expectedly, the issue was extremely controversial and faced enormous opposition, or at least skepticism. Initially, BATN attempted diplomatic opposition. While it agreed that tobacco had impacts on public health, it supported "appropriate" regulation of the industry that would help to reduce the impact of major policy change. According to then BATN director of regulatory affairs Tony Okwoju, "There are provisions in the bill, which we believe are either extreme and would have unintended consequences or will only make it difficult or impossible for the legal industry to operate, without necessarily achieving the desired objective of reducing the impact of tobacco on public health." He is also on public record stating that "we have seen cases where extreme regulation has resulted in an increase in the levels of illicit trade," and that "the effect of passing a law that is not adequately considered is that it will undermine its own intentions by placing tobacco outside of the control of the regulator, thereby leaving those who continue to smoke at the mercy of smugglers."[10]

In a related public statement, Saka Muniru, representing the Ibadan Progressive Union, told the Senate Committee on Health that the closure of the BATN factory located in Ibadan, Oyo State, alone would ultimately lead to loss of more than 500,000 jobs. This dramatic and preposterous unfounded claim was quickly and publicly refuted by ERA/FoEN.[11]

The committee hearing was spirited and the sides presented their arguments vigorously. Proponents of the bill worried about the outcome since the policy preferences of many of the senators were not clear. In opening the hearing on the bill, National Senate president David Mark, an influential leader in the legislature, remarked that "we are torn between economy and the health of Nigerians in passing this bill, but we'll not compromise because it's only those who are alive that can talk about economy." The Senate president, however, expressed some reservation about the bill saying, "I will remain neutral on this bill because the two key issues are health versus economy. How many jobs can we provide from the tobacco industry? How many people are going to lose their jobs now if the tobacco industries are not able to produce in this country? More importantly, if the tobacco industries here close down, will it stop Nigerians from smoking?"[12] Despite his somewhat mixed remarks, Senator Mark eventually supported the legislation.

Implicit accusations of graft also surrounded the hearing. Senator Mark commented on the bribery allegations concerning the bill, stating unequivocally that no senator had been bribed to influence the passage or otherwise of the National Tobacco Control Bill. Senator Mark said the issue of legislating cigarette smoking was contentious, as there are global lobbyists for a ban on tobacco smoking as well as organizations against the ban. He said, "I have heard all sorts of stories about lobbyists trying to see that the public hearing does not go on, or that lobbyists insist that the public hearing must go on."[13] Around the time of the hearing, tobacco control advocates gathered from highly reliable sources that BATN was offering to construct constituency projects for some parliamentarians.

In a somewhat surprising development on 21 July 2009, BATN changed its position, pledging to comply with the legislation. The director of regulatory affairs from BATN, Tony Okwoju, made the pledge before the committee hearing. Okwoju also took the opportunity to reinforce the positive effects of BATN for Nigeria, stating that in addition to paying N80 billion in taxes, the company in 2002 established the BATN Foundation, which had completed 77 community projects in 34 of the 36 states in Nigeria.[14] Notably, Okwoju was fired shortly thereafter from BATN.

Outside of the National Senate, support for the bill and/or tobacco from other government officials was also decidedly mixed. In a tidy and disturbing demonstration of opposition to tobacco control within the federal bureaucracy, as well as a sign of poor coordination across government agencies, a high-ranking government official publicly commended BATN in July 2009. Yet at the roughly same time, Dr B. E. Nwadialo, comptroller general of the Nigeria Customs Service, praised BATN for its commitment to the development of the Nigerian economy, especially through employment generation and prompt payment of taxes and duties to the government.

However, in a positive national-level tobacco control development in 2009, the federal cabinet banned fresh investments in the tobacco and allied industry.[15] Mustafa Bello, executive secretary and chief executive officer of the Nigerian Investment Promotion Commission (NIPC), made this disclosure at the second Nigeria–Japan Business and Investment Forum in Japan. Bello had said in response to an inquiry from a prospective Japanese investor that the federal government, in line with global efforts at stemming the use of tobacco products and isolating manufacturers of the product, may not be well disposed to fresh investments in that sector.

Litigation

Litigation has been one of the more recent tools employed by the tobacco control community in Nigeria. On behalf of the Lagos state government and ERA/FoEN, former attorney general and commissioner of Lagos State Professor Yemi Osibajo sued five tobacco companies (BATN, International Tobacco Limited, BAT, BAT (Investment) Limited, and Philip Morris International (PMI)) on 30 April 2007 in order to recoup the money – N2.5 trillion – spent on treating people who became sick from using tobacco products. He was the first government official to file a suit against tobacco companies when he was in office.

Before the end of 2007, three other states – Oyo, Kano and Gombe – and the Federal Government of Nigeria, taking a cue from the Lagos action, filed various cost-recovery suits against the tobacco industry. Oyo State is claiming, in punitive and anticipatory damages, N366 billion; Gombe, N600 billion; Kano, N3 billion; and the federal government, N5.3 trillion.

The cases in the various states have made little progress due to what government lawyers characterize as deliberate acts to frustrate the litigation. The defendants' counsel raised several preliminary objections, many of which were technical, in an attempt to delay or frustrate the cases from going to trial. However, there have been positive developments in states such as Kano and Oyo where judges have thrown out a series of objections and motions filed by defendants on the basis of lacking merit and acting in bad faith with a view to slow the judgment of the courts. Despite these early setbacks, four other states – Ekiti, Ogun, Ondo and Akwa Ibom – have subsequently joined the class-action suit.

The government legal team has actively fought back against the tobacco industry with legal means such as injunctions against the industry's efforts to stymie the suits. Also, ERA/FoEN has engaged in a series of workshops and campaigns to drum up high-profile support for the litigation in the newest states. The results of these efforts have been very positive, including favorable media coverage and an elevation of the general level of discussion on tobacco control and litigation in the states. As of mid-2011, these efforts are ongoing.

ATSA program

A major stakeholder meeting inaugurated the ATSA effort in June 2008, and several dozen stakeholders from around the country and multiple sectors attended the meeting. Participants came from universities (e.g. the University of Ibadan and the University of Nigeria), national government (e.g. the MoH, the National Assembly, etc.), local governments (e.g. the Lagos MoH), the media (e.g. *Guardian*, *This Day* and *Vanguard* newspapers), general NGOs (e.g. the Nigerian Medical Association) and civil society organizations with previous tobacco control experience (e.g. ERA/FoEN, the Nigerian Heart Foundation, the NTCA, etc.). The eventual ATSA team, anchored by the civil organizations with tobacco control experience, utilized many of these stakeholders and additional allies and resources to achieve their key goals of the enforcement of a smoke-free Abuja, smoke-free legislation in Osun and a review of tobacco taxation.

Implementation of a smoke-free Abuja
(Federal Capital Territory or FCT)

An Abuja smoke-free policy was promulgated by ministerial decree on 31 May 2008, but compliance has been mixed and enforcement efforts continue.[16] Abuja is well suited for a "demonstration" (i.e. for other states) of successful enforcement because the status of Abuja as the FCT makes the position of its minister (in this case, former FCT minister Aliyu Moddibo) equivalent to that of a governor of a state. According to the former minister, the rule was not intended to forcefully stop smokers from smoking but to create room for proper ventilation for residents of the FCT.

The ATSA team has achieved some notable success in terms of its goal to encourage the government to enforce the ban. One of the most important advances was the decision of the Abuja minister, Adamu Aliero, to earmark N1,870,000 for the purpose of enforcement in the 2009–10 FCT budgets. The money is designated for a mobile court to try violators and an awareness campaign. The ERA/FoEN considers this step an enormous victory for tobacco control because "success is when the government is putting in its own money."[17] The political mapping below helps to explain some of the processes that the team used and continue to use as they seek to enforce a smoke-free Abuja.

The political mapping conducted by the ATSA team for the Abuja smoke-free policy examines the potential influence and level of support of stakeholders to the successful enforcement of the policy. It demonstrates the many relevant actors in such an undertaking, how to conceptualize each of their roles and how to persuade them to pursue enforcement of tobacco control regulations. The analysis maps the stakeholders into four critical groups: advocates, low priority, problematic and antagonistic.

On 14 January 2008, the then minister of the FCT, Alhaji Aliyu Umar Modibo, made a public declaration that his administration would begin enforcement of the ban of smoking in public places beginning 1 June 2008. Prior to the commencement, the minister constituted an implementation committee that had two representatives from civil society, Akinbode Oluwafemi of ERA/FoEN and Toyosi Onaolapo of the Coalition Against Tobacco (CAT). Other committee members were drawn from the different departments of the FCT and law enforcement agencies. The committee mapped out a number of activities to support enforcement of the ban, including its official declaration on World No Tobacco Day 2008.

The ATSA team's mapping identified the president's office, the Abuja minister, the ministries of Health and Environment and the Abuja Smoke-Free Implementation Committee as key official institutions that generally supported the policy. Because Abuja as the FCT derives its policy directives from the presidency and the federal executive council, these high-level political actors are very important (typically in Nigeria, when a minister speaks in support of a policy, it is taken as the president's position). Unfortunately, the pro-tobacco control Abuja minister lost his seat in the December 2008 executive cabinet reshuffle announced by the then president Umaru Musa Yar'Adua. At the time of this development, the ATSA team suggested conducting advocacy meetings with remaining officials as well as new ones to consolidate what the former minister had initiated, as well as to ensure effective future enforcement of the policy.

The police were identified as a crucial stakeholder, particularly for the enforcement component. Moreover, the high level of support for enforcement from the executive arm of government guaranteed that the inspector general and the commissioner of police for Abuja would be compelled to comply with the policy directives. The police are the principal law enforcement organ in Nigeria and have the responsibility for enforcing every law passed by the government.

The ATSA team identified a number of key civil society organizations (CSO) that are or were actively engaging the government on these issues including the CAT, the Nigerian Heart Foundation (NHF), the Nigerian Cancer Society (NCS), ERA/FoEN, the All Nigeria Consumers Movement Union (ANCOMU), Educare Trust, Citizens Centre, People Against Drug Dependence and Ignorance (PADDI), Doctors Against Tobacco (DAT) and the Nigerian Tobacco Control Alliance (NTCA). The team's mapping also noted that these CSOs needed to be trained and incorporated into the planned advocacy effort to government on the enforcement of the policy, and a first major training occurred on 5 and 6 November 2009.

Though the "low priority" stakeholders are not directly involved in the enforcement of the policy, the ATSA team believes that they are capable of positively affecting ongoing efforts to enforce the policy. On the civil society side, the Nigeria Medical Association (NMA) is a potential ally in the campaign but has so far not taken any significant position on the issue. Tobacco control advocates continue to engage this powerful organization. On the government side, the ministries of Information, Justice, Women's Affairs, and Youth, as well as the Abuja secretary of tourism are all viable potential allies. Advocates would like to engage these actors with informational meetings but did not have a sufficient budget for such activities during the main campaign.

Beyond the federal ministries, several major national-level government agencies have been targeted as potential key actors and/or allies in the enforcement effort. The National Agency for Food Drug Administration and Control (NAFDAC) is a key tobacco regulatory institution that has sometimes supported tobacco control efforts. In a small glitch, the government replaced NAFDAC's leadership in late 2008, and advocates had to renew efforts to gain support of the agency. This agency remains a high priority in tobacco control more generally. Similarly, the Standards Organization of Nigeria (SON) is another regulatory body that must be sensitized to shore up its level of support for the policy priority. Under the former president (Yar'Adua), the Office of the First Lady of Nigeria was considered to be a strong advocacy agent to drive the enforcement of the smoke-free policy. At that time, the first lady's pet project was breast cancer awareness and prevention, which was a pursuit thought to offer an opportunity to involve her in the campaign for the enforcement of the smoke-free policy after adequate sensitization. First ladies – including the newest, Dame Patience Goodluck Jonathan – often take on health-oriented projects particularly involving women and/or children, so advocates will continue to pursue similar opportunities. The Consumer Protection Council (CPC) is another national body that has distinguished itself by its recent activities on tobacco control, and it has been duly informed about the efforts to enforce the Abuja smoke-free policy. The tobacco control CSOs continue to court these agencies, and notably, both NAFDAC and SON demonstrated public support for the tobacco control bill at the public National Senate hearing in July 2009.

A number of stakeholders likely oppose enforcement of the smoke-free policy, though explicit public pronouncements of this nature have been rare. Not surprisingly, the tobacco industry is a problematic and antagonistic stakeholder. While there is no clear evidence of intervention in the case of enforcement of the Abuja smoke-free policy specifically, the motivations outlined above to stop or change the national legislation suggest that they are not likely to support enforcement of the policy.

Depending on the specific actor, the media are potentially both supportive and problematic. The ban on tobacco advertising via the APCON directives has greatly stemmed the unwelcome and illegal practice by media of carrying subtle tobacco advertisements. The new national bill should improve the situation further as it makes the ban on advertising even stricter. But the media require engagement in order to educate them about the policy – tobacco control capacity-building for the media is an opportunity to promote effective enforcement of the Abuja smoke-free policy. Similarly, the entertainment industry continues to be problematic due to its influence on youths and uninformed consumers of its products. In the large and regionally influential Nigerian film industry, often called Nollywood, there has been consistent promotion of smoking in films; ERA/FOEN released a report on the smoking in films issue in 2005.[18]

Other independent actors can also try to influence the effort. For example, a private group believed to be both problematic and antagonistic is the Institute of Public Policy Analysis (IPPA). In recent years, IPPA embarked on campaigns in support of the tobacco companies through public dialogue and advertorials (an advertisement disguised poorly as an editorial). Unfortunately, not very much is known about this organization other than the fact that it did work directly funded by BAT.

Finally, tobacco control advocates concluded that it was quite necessary to conduct mass awareness campaigns on the policy to elicit the support of the general public in Abuja. This campaign should be in the form of rallies, dissemination of posters and stickers and engagement of role models in public pronouncement (which all comprised components of the eventual ATSA action plan). These awareness efforts and the overall enforcement of a smoke-free Abuja continue.

Smoke-free Osun State

As a key component of the ATSA project, the team pursued and achieved a smoke-free law for Osun State. The original ATSA team and its allies have since moved to the next phase of building support for the enforcement of the bill. Osun State is particularly pivotal in Nigeria for a number of very important reasons. Firstly, it is widely considered to be a culturally strong and important state in the southwest part of this large country. Secondly, Osun is located near much of the tobacco cultivation/production (there is a BAT factory in the bordering state of Oyo). Thirdly, Osun hosts an internationally known festival that is recognized by the United Nations Educational, Scientific and Cultural Organisation (UNESCO) as being culturally very important. This festival has been supported for the last five years by BATN. Fourthly, Imperial Tobacco sought to locate a factory in the state, but the plan was aborted after vehement objections by anti-tobacco activists, amongst others.

The preliminary mapping conducted for the Osun State smoke-free law – executed months before the law was passed – examined the magnitude of support/opposition of key actors including government institutions (especially the governor and state legislature), the private sector and community leaders. Like the Abuja mapping exercise, these potential stakeholders were mapped to the degree of their importance and levels of support.

Stakeholders placed a great deal of emphasis on the executive branch of government in Osun. Specifically, the governor was identified – correctly as it turned out – as an important actor whose support would significantly influence the outcome of the legislative process. The state commissioners of justice, health, and environment were also mapped as potential allies to the campaign. Accordingly, the ATSA team undertook extensive consultations and advocacy meetings with these officials. Undoubtedly, the support of these high-ranking officials was very helpful during the bill drafting, especially in determining the approach to adopt in tabling the bill either as an executive bill or private member bill (see below).

The state legislature in Osun was presumed to be equally as important as the executive. Prominent members of the legislature were identified as important advocates, and their individual positions and levels of support were investigated and reinforced (and countered if they were negative). For example, the ATSA team held a formal training for parliamentarians to sensitize them to the issues. The principal actors included: the chairman and members of the House Committee on Health; the House speaker; the majority leader; and both the secretary and clerk of the House. The mapping equally suggested further investigation of the House of Assembly to establish the most suitable approach to presenting the bill, either as a private member or an executive bill. Eventually, it was passed as a private member bill, sponsored by the chairman of the health committee, the Hon. Ayobami Salinsile. Furthermore, as the mapping anticipated, the explicit support of the speaker was critical to passing the bill.

A second major group of stakeholders was mapped as lower priority because of their indirect involvement in the legislative process and their potential capacity to influence and lobby the legislature and/or the eventual campaign for smokers to adhere to the new smoke-free law. This group included major religious leaders and the state commissioners for poverty alleviation, youth empowerment and women's affairs. Also, the ATSA team identified the head of sponsorship of the National Premiership (football) League, Mr Segun Odegbami, because of the overwhelming influence of the league on youths, who constitute a large proportion of the consumers of tobacco products. The league, more generally, presents opportunities to engage the football brand in the campaign against young people's initiation of smoking.

Advocates underscored the negative influence of the tobacco companies in Osun. As mentioned above, tourism is considered a vital source of income, particularly the annual Osun Oshogbo festival, which attracts an extensive international patronage and sponsorship from BATN. The mapping suggested adequate and continued sensitization of cultural leaders to limit the patronage of tobacco companies of their events. Similarly, the retailers and vendors of tobacco products were equally identified as antagonistic stakeholders for their current role in advertising and marketing tobacco product to end users. Their opposition to related tobacco control measures had emerged dramatically following the ban on all forms advertisement in the mass media through the APCON directives.

Due to their often close relationships with the tobacco industry or because members were heavy users of tobacco products, a handful of other groups were anticipated to be problematic stakeholders, including the media, the entertainment industries, patrons and operators of hospitality industries and the Road Transport Workers (particularly long-distance drivers). Advocates identified informational meetings with the leaders of these organizations and sectors as opportunities to reduce the influence of their activities on the legislative process and negative public opinion of the Osun State smoke-free law.

Taxation

The third ATSA priority on taxation was pursued based in large part on the impending review by the national government of current tax policies and the government's expressed intention of formulating future national budgets more on the income derived from tax earnings. Accordingly, the ATSA program was considered a timely opportunity to draw government attention to issues around tobacco taxes and how taxation can be used as an effective tobacco control mechanism. The tobacco control community is planning to pursue this issue with great energy in the near term.

Building on proposed research objectives of identifying the current government tax process, establishing optimal levels of a tobacco tax increase and considering smuggling implications, the mapping identified the following high-ranking officials and/or departments as potentially supportive advocates: the president, the minister of finance, the Ministry of Finance's chief executive officer and the Federal Inland Revenue Service. Tobacco control advocates believe that these actors will be supportive of tobacco tax policy reform because of the new policy thrust of the federal government to fund its future annual budgets more with the proceeds from taxes, thus necessitating an overhaul of the current tax policy regime. The general anecdotal impression of the ATSA team is that the current administration generally supports tobacco control and would like to increase revenues from new sources, which might include tobacco.

Several other governmental actors are thought to be critical to the success of future tobacco taxation efforts. The office of the customs comptroller general will be an important ally because of its role in monitoring the tobacco companies and the activities of the smugglers. The recent public statement, discussed above, in praise of BATN by the head of the customs division does indicate the sizeable need for future work to educate and to bring government agencies together. Nigeria's Economic Community of West African States (ECOWAS) secretariat is also considered to be an important stakeholder to engage, as the organization coordinates many of the economic policies of member states. Finally, the House committees on finance and appropriation are important because of their roles in coordinating the appropriation and budgetary processes of the House. Engaging the committee chairs and members will increase access to vital information.

The tobacco industry and its distribution vendors and retailers will likely be antagonistic stakeholders due to the anticipated loss in revenue resulting from any increase in tobacco taxes (and price potentially). In a related – and encouraging – taxation development, the government reviewed the Export Expansion Grant (EEG) policy, and BATN was removed from being a beneficiary of the program. Previously, in an effort to woo BAT (international) when it was consolidating its manufacturing in Africa, the federal government had granted favorable tax policies to the company.

It is worthy to note that the taxation mapping was largely based on anecdotal sources of information, which is insufficient to guide an evidence-based advocacy campaign for the review of tobacco taxation.

The NTSA coalition recommends further investigation of all identified stakeholders and others that might be of importance toward achieving the tax policy objectives.

Tobacco Industry Monitoring

Production

The status of Nigeria in the global tobacco trade has been changing in recent years – it is no longer a net importer of tobacco products, but rather has become a major producer and exporter. As recently as the late 1990s, Nigerian tobacco cultivation scarcely met two-thirds of domestic demand, and the country hardly exported. The tobacco production situation has changed dramatically since that time.

In recent years, BAT has implemented plans for Nigeria to become a regional hub for tobacco production that not only produces for the enormous domestic market, but also exports to Cameroon, Niger and other West African states. In 2001, BATN invested US$150 million in a state-of-the-art tobacco processing factory in Ibadan, Oyo State. With its construction and upgrades to an existing factory, located in northern Kaduna State, BATN offered inducements to farmers in western and southern provinces to take up tobacco cultivation.

It is not at all clear, however, that BATN needs or wants to boost domestic tobacco leaf cultivation in Nigeria. Because firms only pay 5 percent duty on imported leaves, it is likely that imported leaves are cheaper. However, there is still some leaf cultivation, and researchers note that Nigerians have not yet well understood that tobacco cultivation adversely affects food security by reducing the acreage available for cereals.[19] A principal concern is that the area where tobacco cultivation has been promoted by BATN is the "food basket" of the southwest of the country.

Employment

Though reliable statistics are lacking, every source concurs on the basic characteristics of tobacco industry employment: thousands of farmers fight an unequal battle of debt servitude to BATN and its agents (similar to most if not all other Sub-Saharan African countries). BATN purchases 80 percent of Nigerian tobacco produced; in many regions, it is the sole buyer. With a price-setting monopoly, BATN determines the value of tobacco leaves, and it often cheats the local farmers about the grade of leaves they pick.[20] Nigerian tobacco workers – primarily women and young children – are vulnerable to skin diseases because they handle raw tobacco leaves without access to proper protective clothing.

Advertising and promotions

BATN heavily advertises and promotes its products to large audiences in Nigeria using sophisticated methods. For example, the company has in recent years put advertisements on the sides of moving vehicles in order to circumvent Nigerian laws forbidding fixed advertisements. There is strong evidence that it uses BATN-promoted movies, concerts and fashion shows to gather crowds of youthful Nigerians and give them free cigarettes.[21] The new national law addresses these loopholes.

From the perspective of corporate social responsibility (CSR), BATN sponsors a wide array of community projects in Nigeria, including scholarships for tobacco farmers' children, potable water projects, tree planting and building a cassava processing facility. Its own Social Report,[22] recently updated through 2006–7, provides greater details of its myriad CSR activities.

Interactions with government

At all levels, BATN energetically works to subvert Nigerian government institutions. Infamously, it donated 21 jeeps to the Nigeria Consumers Protection Council (CPC) and still more to the Nigerian Customs Service. As mentioned above, a high-ranking official at the customs service has praised BATN publicly as recently as July of 2009. Also, BATN officials are known to hold periodic breakfast meetings with Nigerian media executives and to sponsor journalists' conferences and awards in order to foster pliant coverage of its activities. Local government officials often struggle to resist BATN's claims that its presence can generate much-needed investment.[23]

ATSA Review

The ATSA project bore direct fruit in the form of the revitalization of Abuja's existing smoke-free law, a new smoke-free law in Osun State and a review of tobacco taxation nationally. As described in detail above, the ATSA team aggressively sought to revitalize the existing Abuja smoke-free policy. One of the key achievements was to generate a provision for government funding of tobacco control, and specifically smoke-free enforcement, within the FCT budget. In Osun State, after months of educating and sensitizing the governor, the state legislature, the media and the general public, the team celebrated the passage and signing into law of the Osun smoke-free law. The Osun-focused part of the team has turned its efforts to enforcement. Both the Abuja and Osun efforts will be excellent practice for implementing and enforcing the comprehensive national legislation passed in 2011, a process in which the ATSA team members and their many allies played central and vital roles. Members of the ATSA team and their allies and colleagues will continue with these efforts related to the new legislation in addition to other proven strategies, including taxation and litigation.

Notes

1 Sources: CIA World Factbook https://www.cia.gov/library/publications/the-world-factbook/; except Organization of Economic Cooperation and Development (OECD) for development assistance statistics, and Food and Agriculture Organization of the United Nations – Statistics (FAOSTAT) for tobacco production. See http://stats.oecd.org/index.aspx and http://faostat.fao.org/site/567/default.aspx#ancor respectively (accessed 20 July 2011).

2 See http://www.tobaccoatlas.org/tobaccoatlas/about.html (last accessed 22 July 2011).

3 F. Pampel, "Tobacco Use in sub-Sahara Africa: Estimates from the demographic health surveys," *Social Science Medicine* 66.8 (2008): 1772–83.

4 The GYTS 2008 report for Nigeria is available from http://www.afro.who.int (last accessed 22 July 2011).

5 S. Salami, "Nigeria's war on tobacco," *Business Eye*, 10 January 2007.

6 The House version of the bill was sponsored by Bassey Etim and had its first reading on 11 December 2007 and second reading on 19 February 2008. It was then sent to the House Committee on Health and the House Committee on Justice on 14 May 2008, and finally had its third reading and passage on 14 June 2008.

7 I. Shaibu, "FG to stop tobacco smoking" *Vanguard*, 10 July 2009.

8 A. M. Jimoh, "Government committed to checking tobacco usage, says minister," *Nigeria Guardian News*, 10 July 2009.

9 Nigerian Best Forum News, "Groups Hail Senate Over Tobacco Bill," 26 July 2009. Online at: http://www.nigerianbestforum.com/blog/?p=18971 (accessed 13 July 2011).

10 Agence France-Presse (AFP), "Nigeria's tobacco lobby fumes over anti-tobacco bill," 21 July 2009.

11 B. Ezeamulu, "Group urges Senate to expedite action on Tobacco bill," *Next*, 23 October 2009.

12 Abdul-Rahman Abubakar and Turaki A. Hassan, "Senate denies bribery allegation on tobacco law," *Daily Trust/Weekly Trust*, 21 July 2009.

13 Ibid.

14 A. Folasade-Koyi, "BATN Backs Tobacco Control Bill," *Daily Independent*, 22 July 2009.

15 P. Ibe, "FG Bans Fresh Investment in Tobacco," *This Day*, 29 June 2009.

16 C. Onche, "More smokers defy FCT anti-smoking campaign," *Leadership*, 1 February 2009.

17 Personal quote from ERA/FoEN representative and tobacco control advocate, Akinbode Oluwafemi.

18 B. Ukwuoma and A. Ekechi Chukwu, "Global anti-smoking pact takes off," *Guardian*, 28 February 2005.

19 Salami, "Nigeria's war on tobacco."

20 Ibid.

21 Ibid.

22 BAT Social Reports can be accessed via http://www.bat.com/group/sites/uk__3mnfen.nsf/vwPagesWebLive/DO6RZGHL?opendocument&SKN=1 (last accessed 22 July 2011).

23 Salami, "Nigeria's war on tobacco."

Chapter 15

SENEGAL

Abdoulaye Diagne and Babacar Mboup

Executive Summary

While tobacco control had a very hopeful few years in the early 1980s when relatively comprehensive legislation (at least for the time and place) was introduced, advocates have struggled in recent years to make progress. In part due to an economically strong industry lobby and media support of the industry, most of the measures were rolled back in subsequent legislation (mainly in 1985). Consequently, there is very little in the way of current tobacco control measures in Senegal. Not surprisingly, perhaps, prevalence rates are high (though reportedly poorly and unsystematically measured), with adult smoking rates over 30 percent and perhaps greater than 40 percent. Youth rates appear to be lower at around 15 percent.

As of early 2011, a team of proponents of tobacco control is pursuing new comprehensive legislation within a Ministry of Health working group, though it is not entirely clear how much political will exists for a new law. Currently, tobacco control advocates have been focusing their efforts on an attempt to promote smoke-free policies in the influential religious center, the city of Touba. There is hope that this effort will lend moral authority to the tobacco control movement and put pressure on the national government to put tobacco control squarely back on the agenda.

Country Profile[1]

Population in 2009 (global and African ranking):	13,711,587 (68, 21)
Geographical size (global ranking):	196,722 sq. km (94)
GDP by purchasing power parity in 2008 (global ranking):	US$21.98 billion (100)

GDP real growth rate (2006–8):	5%
GDP per capita (global ranking):	US$1,600 (194)
Main industries:	Agricultural and fish processing, phosphate mining, fertilizer production, petroleum refining, iron ore, zircon, gold mining, construction materials, ship construction and repair, peanuts, millet, corn, sorghum, rice, cotton, tomatoes, green vegetables, cattle, poultry, pigs, fish
Languages:	French (official), Wolof, Pulaar, Serer, Diola, Jola, Mandinka, Soninke
Official development assistance (ODA) – total commitments/ disbursements (2007):	US$605.3/581.8 million
ODA as a percentage of GDP:	5.14906%
Largest donors (disbursements in millions of USD):	France 196.9, EC 97.9, Canada 39.8, Spain 39.4, US 39.2, Japan 31.9, Germany 27.1, 2007
Tobacco production/exports	N/A
Tobacco imports (2007):	Tobacco (unmanufactured): 3,276 tons at $8,694 per ton, #9 import; cigarettes: 1,190 tons at $19,883 per ton, #11 import

Brief Description of Political System

Type: Senegal is a democratic presidential republic.

Executive: As of early 2010, President Abdoulaye Wade was chief of state. Prime Minister Cheikh Hadjibou Soumare was the head of government.

Cabinet: The cabinet is appointed by the PM with the recommendation of the president.

Legislature: There is a bicameral parliament, comprising of the National Assembly and Senate. The National Assembly has 150 seats with 90 seats elected by direct popular vote. As of late 2009, the SOPI coalition had 131 seats. The Senate has 100 seats with 35 indirectly elected and 65 appointed by the president. The Senegalese Democratic Party (PDS) has 34 seats. Several opposition parties boycotted the 2007 elections.

Scope of Tobacco Problem

As a result of a lack of large-scale surveys in Senegal, little is known about the nationwide prevalence of smoking generally or its more specific demographic characteristics. The available data are also poor. Most of the existing information relates to small target groups and has been collected over very small geographic areas. Limited as these data are, however, they point to growing use of tobacco. According to the *Tobacco Atlas*, 32 percent of Senegalese adults smoke. Among young males, the prevalence is 7.9 percent, and among girls, it is 1.5 percent. According to the same data source, an estimated 5–10 percent of male deaths are due to tobacco-related illnesses; the figure is less than five percent for women. A survey undertaken between March and December of 1995 by the International Union Against Cancer (UICC) in five localities of the country found slightly higher rates: in a sample of 5,000 (95.3 percent of respondents were male) aged 15–67 years of age, 37 percent were smokers. In marked contrast, a 2003 World Health Survey (WHS) reports 19.3 percent male and 1 percent female prevalence rates. Tobacco control advocates hope to get tobacco-related questions onto the 2010 Ministry of Health (MoH) survey in order to begin to address the lack of good prevalence data.

One area in which prevalence statistics are good is in the health profession – tobacco consumption in this sector has been studied in significant detail over more than three decades. The *Tobacco Atlas* reports that 27.6 percent of health professionals are smokers. Researchers have also executed a number of studies covering a limited number of individuals. Baylet et al. executed two studies in 1974 that examined students in social education and medicine, but the samples were very small at 33 and 68 individuals.[2] In 1989, Ayad et al. examined smoking in medical students, and in 2003,[3] Ndiaye et al. executed a much larger study of a similar population with 1,547 individuals. The five other studies had samples ranging from 163 and 457 individuals. Ndiaye et al. also examined physicians in a related study (2002).[4]

Another demographic group for which there are good recent prevalence statistics is youth. The Global Youth Tobacco Survey (GYTS) from 2007, executed jointly by the World Health Organization (WHO) and the Senegalese Ministry of Health, reports that 15.3 percent of students (4eme, 5eme and 6eme) currently use tobacco products (males 20.1 percent; females 10.2 percent). For current cigarette smokers, the prevalence rate is 7.8 percent (male 12 percent; female 3.1 percent).

Politics

Inventory of existing laws and regulations

The 1981 tobacco control law was rather momentous for the time and place, particularly in terms of bans on advertising, but the Senegalese government backtracked significantly and rather quickly from it. This reversal was largely due to a strong tobacco lobby connected to the government and to the Senegalese media's vigorous support for tobacco advertising.[5] The domestic media complained vehemently that the laws did not apply to the foreign media and left them in a disadvantaged position. The law did in fact apply to all media, foreign or domestic, and the real issue was that it was simply never enforced. Law 85-1375 in 1985 essentially removed all of the strong components of the 1981 legislation, including bans on advertising, sponsorship and promotion, as well as on public smoking. The African Tobacco Situation Analysis (ATSA) team has been focused, in part, on advocating for legislation that more concretely enforces the Framework Convention on Tobacco Control (FCTC) requirements, which Senegal ratified in 2004.

The 1981 law addressed a number of major tobacco control issues – including smoke-free places, warning labels and advertising and promotion bans – most of which are outlined in the policy-specific chapters, and even included punitive fines that ranged from CFA 25,000 to 2,500,000. By all accounts, these fines were never applied, nor was much effort made even to identify who could apply them. For example, the 1981 legislation refers to "administrative authorities" in terms of the entities that could enforce the regulations, but does not identify them explicitly.[6]

Overall political context

The position of the country's powerful chief executive is not entirely clear. President Abdoulaye Wade demonstrated specific interest in the ATSA program by sending a letter to the director of the cabinet to instruct the MoH to support the program, but there are few other public indications of his support for tobacco control more generally. The president's explicit position on tobacco control has never been revealed in public statements. One indication that tobacco control has not been a recent priority, however, was the government's support of the building of a Philip Morris International (PMI) factory that came into operation in 2007. Furthermore, the government placed PMI's business in a very lenient environmental category, which holds the company to very low environmental standards. This decision was illustrative of the government's position, considering the problems associated with environmental smoke generated by PMI's products.

Support for tobacco control at the cabinet level does not appear to be strong. This may not be a particular issue, however, because power is highly centralized and ministers do not typically take on policy initiatives, or even public positions, that are not the president's. There is a MoH directive from 1998 that bans smoking on all ministry premises, which indicates at least some previous support for tobacco control from this ministry. More importantly, perhaps, the ministry has a working group on new tobacco control legislation and has appointed a focal person for tobacco, Dr Ndao, who has been a member of the ATSA team. However, even if the ministry is supportive of tobacco control, it is not clear that there is sufficient support from other members of the cabinet and their respective ministries or the president.

The Ministry of Finance is an important potential actor in tobacco control principally because of its role in taxation, but its policy preferences are not clear. It has actually instituted some reasonably aggressive tax policies that encompass tobacco, but these policies are aimed particularly at revenue generation, and the MoH has not played any role in the development of these policies.

The Ministry of Education (MoE) has taken a supportive position on tobacco control. For example, the ministry previously issued a decree banning smoking in schools and sent a representative to the initial ATSA stakeholders' meeting. However, effective enforcement of the decree will need to figure prominently on the agenda of tobacco control organizations because according to anecdotal accounts of stakeholders at ATSA meetings, violations of the ban continue to occur. Tobacco control advocates also report that tobacco control is not part of the school curriculum and suggest that there needs to be an aggressive campaign to make students aware of the dangers of tobacco use.

Through 2009 and early 2010, members of the ATSA team and others were part of a working group developing new comprehensive national tobacco control legislation. The group is reportedly diverse in experience. The new group's activities have included:

- Reexamining the draft bill proposed by the ATSA team
- Reviewing the wording of the bill for consistency with the various articles of the WHO Framework Convention on Tobacco Control (FCTC)
- Designating the FCTC articles to be transposed into domestic legislation
- Listing the FCTC articles to be covered by law
- Identifying the FCTC articles to be covered by regulation
- Making corrections to the text of the draft bill

As of early 2010, members of the group report that the wording of the draft bill has been revised, corrected, and finalized. This corrected draft bill is available and ready for submission to the competent authorities (the Ministry of Health and Prevention, once the bill is validated by the national tobacco control committee).

The ATSA team is also working with religious authorities and social movements in the city of Touba to implement smoke-free policies. The city of Touba is one of the main religious centers in a country that is predominantly Muslim. The Muslim leaders in Touba carry enormous moral weight and influence. Often, policies that start in Touba are then copied at the national level. Currently, there is a ban on the selling and using of tobacco products in the city. Though it is not binding by national law officially, it is widely observed and respected by citizens. There is even enforcement in the form of a youth association that monitors behaviors and report violators to the authorities, including the police. Tobacco control advocates hope not only that it will be an example for the rest of the country but that the leaders of Touba will champion the idea with national political leaders. In fact, with Touba at least partly in mind, the new proposed national legislation has a component that would permit municipalities to pass and enforce smoke-free policies.

But the politics of Touba are complex. While the leaders of the city have enormous influence, they do not usually press directly for policy change, but rather prefer to lead by example. They also do not like outsiders asking them to execute specific actions, nor do they accept money from foreign donors. In fact, they are well funded by a global network of members of the Mouride order who send regular and generous financial support. In any event, tobacco control advocates are seeking to give as much information about the public health benefits of tobacco control as possible to these leaders in case they decide that it is a cause they would like to support more openly.

Civil society continues to play a key role in pressing for better tobacco control policy. There are several important nongovernmental organizations (NGOs) promoting tobacco control, including the Association Sénégalaise pour la Paix, la Lutte contre l'Alcool et la Toxicomanie (ASPAT), the Association des Jeunes pour le Developpement (AJD-PASTEEF), and the Islamist NGO, Jamra, which for many years has fought what it calls "social evils," such as drugs and sexually transmitted diseases. There is also a National Network for Tobacco Control, though it is not a formal organization, but rather a loose collection of organizations that have an interest in tobacco control.

Finally, much of the media can be characterized as being either indifferent or even hostile toward tobacco control. Journalists are often motivated by the receipt of a per diem in order for them to cover an event, so it is necessary to have such resources to attract many of them. Not surprisingly, most tobacco-sponsored events have significantly more resources to attract media coverage than do tobacco control events. There is a network of journalists who cover health and though they have attended events organized by the tobacco control community, they are not active in it.

Tobacco Industry

The international tobacco industry maintains a strong presence, both in terms of manufacturing and aggressive marketing and sales. Previously, the Manufacture de Tabacs de l'Ouest Africain (MTOA), which was owned by the French tobacco company Coralma International, controlled 95 percent of the cigarette market in Senegal. However, in recent years, Imperial Tobacco (a subsidiary of British American Tobacco) bought the company, and Philip Morris, in particular, has greatly increased their market share and overall presence. British American Tobacco (BAT) used to license with MTOA to manufacture its brands, but since reorganizing to three regional hubs in Africa, BAT products are mostly imported from Nigeria. Philip Morris has been advertising heavily in Senegal and its share of the market appears to be increasing – one recent unsubstantiated report puts production at 5 million packs per year. Production has been increasing so dramatically such that, at least until recently, Senegal imports as little as 5 percent of its cigarettes.[7]

The former MTOA and now the industry more generally by most accounts are thought to have close relationships with the Senegalese government. The industry's lobby is effective and was able to help weaken Senegal's somewhat comprehensive 1981 tobacco legislation, one of the first of its kind in Africa. According to anecdotal reports, the industry and the media made a particular dent in the 1981 legislation's bans on tobacco advertising and sponsorship, which were essentially overturned by the 1985 legislation. The 1985 law has since become one of the primary obstacles to tobacco control in Senegal.

ATSA Review

In a very challenging environment, the ATSA team and its supporters have elected to lay the foundation for future tobacco control activities. In particular, the team sought to develop scholarly work to support tobacco control, generate opportunities to sensitize influential people about the issues, organize stakeholders more effectively and to develop draft local and national legislation.

In an effort to fill gaps in knowledge, scholars associated with the ATSA team produced a number of academic papers. Firstly, members of the team produced a political map of tobacco control in Senegal, including an emphasis on the organizations – official and nongovernmental – engaged in the fight against tobacco. In fact, the team produced a database of organizations and individuals who are involved in tobacco control and the activities that they have undertaken or are undertaking. Secondly, team members developed a working paper on taxation of tobacco products in Senegal. Thirdly, a group of interested journalists following a briefing workshop produced a book of articles pertaining to these issues. Finally, scholars with an interest in tobacco control completed a study on the influence of religion in Senegal, and particularly the case of the city of Touba.

Seeking to sensitize stakeholders and other interested parties to tobacco control issues, the team organized a series of communications, conferences, panels, public debates and lectures. There were also direct efforts to educate administrative and religious authorities, and the media, particularly by addressing community, legal, economic, institutional and health aspects of the fight against tobacco.

Finally, the team drafted two major legislative proposals. First, there is a new draft statutory instrument for the prohibition of smoking in the city of Touba. Second, after an exhaustive review, there is a new document that is a draft law on tobacco control. Tobacco control advocates are hopeful that authorities will consider these proposals in 2011–12.

Notes

1 Sources: CIA World Factbook https://www.cia.gov/library/publications/the-world-factbook/; except Organization of Economic Cooperation and Development (OECD) for development assistance statistics, and Food and Agriculture Organization of the United Nations – Statistics (FAOSTAT) for tobacco production. See http://stats.oecd.org/index.aspx and http://faostat.fao.org/site/567/default.aspx#ancor respectively (accessed 20 July 2011).

2 R. Baylet, S. Diop, N'D. Belinga and D. De Medeiros, "Enquête sur la consommation du tabac chez les élèves Assistants-Sociaux à Dakar," *Bulletin de la Société médicale de l'Afrique Noire de Langue française* 19 (1974): 80–7.

3 M. Ayad, M. Ndir, A. Hane, E. Chirazi, P. Kane, M. Badiane, I. Beye and A. Demazy, "Tobacco consumption among medical students," *Dakar Bull Int Union Tuberc Lung Dis* 64 (1989): 11–12.

4 E. Ndiaye, "Contribution à l'analyse des contextes environnementaux et des processus de socialisation des adolescents au tabagisme en milieu urbain: Le cas de Dakar," DEA sociology paper, Cheikh Anta Diop University, Dakar (2001); M. Ndiaye, M. Ndir, X. Quanttin, P. Demoly, P. Godard and J. Bousquet, "Smoking habits, attitudes and knowledges of medical students of Medicine, Pharmacy and Odonto-Stomatology's Faculty of Dakar, Senegal," *Rev Mal Respir* 20 (2003): 701–9; M. Ndiaye, M. Ndir, M. Ba, O. Diop-Dia, D. Kandji, S. Touré, N. Diatta, A. Niang, A. Wone and I. Sow, "Smoking habits among physicians in Dakar," *Rev Pneumology's Clinic* 57 (2002): 7–11.

5 San Francisco Department of Public Health (Tobacco Free Project), "Country Case Study: Senegal" (Washington DC: Campaign for Tobacco-Free Kids, 1998–9).

6 Government of the Republic of Senegal, Law n°81–58 (1991).

7 San Francisco Department of Public Health, "Country Case Study: Senegal."

Chapter 16

SOUTH AFRICA

Yussuf Saloojee, Peter Ucko and Jeffrey Drope

Executive Summary

The country's tobacco control success stands in sharp contrast to many other middle- and low-income countries where the tobacco epidemic is still growing. Large reductions in tobacco use have occurred in South Africa because of a combination of government commitment to comprehensive legislation and enforcement (four major pieces of legislation since 1992) and effective civil society–driven public health activism and community support. Moreover, research played an essential role by supporting both policy development and advocacy efforts. However, prevalence rates remain high (approximately 23 percent of adults are daily smokers; and noncigarette tobacco use, particularly in lower socioeconomic groups, is a continuing concern), the tobacco industry is powerful and the tobacco control community reports having to counter both public and government sentiment that tobacco control has "been done." By the tobacco control community's own admission, for every victory, the industry has tried to claw back part of the gain – they believe not only that there is more work to be done, but that it will require continued vigorous effort.

Most recently, the tobacco control community won a significant victory in ensuring that the 2010 FIFA World Cup would have smoke-free spectator venues. Currently, tobacco control advocates are examining the efficacy of existing tobacco taxation policies. While South Africa previously had excellent tobacco-oriented tax policies that directly decreased the affordability of cigarettes, recent falls in inflation and economic growth have made these policies less effective. Advocates are seeking to present new information to the Ministry of Finance to have these laws revised and to make decreasing affordability the centerpiece of the changes. The tobacco control community has also been working to provide the Ministry of Health (MoH) with sample regulations and materials for forthcoming graphic warning labels on tobacco packaging.

Country Profile[1]

Population in 2009 (global and African ranking):	49,052,489 (25, 4)
Geographical size (global ranking):	1,219,090 sq. km (32)
GDP by purchasing power parity in 2008 (global ranking):	US$491 billion (26)
GDP real growth rate (2006–8):	4.5%
GDP per capita (global ranking):	US$10,100 (105)
Main industries:	Mining (world's largest producer of platinum, gold and chromium), automobile assembly, metalworking, machinery, textiles, iron, steel, chemicals, fertilizer, foodstuffs, commercial ship repair
Languages:	IsiZulu (23.8%), IsiXhosa (17.6%), Afrikaans (13.3%), Sepedi (9.4%), English (8.2%), Setswana (8.2%), Sesotho (7.9%), Xitsonga (4.4%), other (7.2%); information gained from the 2001 census
Tobacco production by volume (2007):	20,000 tons
Tobacco exports (2007):	Tobacco products: 17,822 tons at $3,083 per ton, #17 export; cigarettes: 9,852 tons at $7,179 per ton, #12 export
Tobacco imports (2007):	Tobacco (unmanufactured): 30,499 tons at $2,667 per ton, #13 import

Description of Political System

Type: South Africa is a mixed republic.

Executive: Jacob Zuma is the current president and head of state. The president is appointed by the National Assembly every 5 years. Kgalema Motlanthe is the executive deputy president.

Cabinet: Appointed by the president

Legislature: Bicameral legislature. The National Assembly has 400 seats that are elected based on proportional representation. The National Council of Provinces (formerly the Senate) has ten members that are elected by each of the nine provincial legislatures, with special powers to protect regional interests. The legislature is dominated by the African National Congress party (roughly 65.9 percent of popular vote in the 2009 election); the opposition Democratic Alliance received 16.7 percent of the popular vote.

Scope of Tobacco Problem

According to some surveys, adult daily cigarette smoking prevalence rates demonstrated a steady downward trend between the early 1990s and the mid-2000s. Surveys by the South Africa Advertising and Research Foundation suggest that adult (15+ years) daily smoking rates fell by approximately a quarter, decreasing from 32.6 percent in 1993 to 23.4 percent in 2008. The major tobacco control nongovernmental organization, the National Council Against Smoking (NCAS), believes that rates have since bottomed out, partly as a result of inflationary trends overwhelming earlier tobacco taxation strategies (more discussion below). A South Africa Demographic and Health Survey from 2003 roughly corroborates the later findings with male daily smoking rates reported to be 35.1 percent and 10.2 percent for females.

Consumption (i.e. sales) patterns support the decreasing trend in the prevalence findings. In 2005, cigarette sales fell for the fourteenth consecutive year in South Africa. Annual cigarette consumption fell from 1.8 billion packs in 1993 to 1.2 billion packs in 2005 – a 33 percent decrease. Consumption fell despite an increase in population size, so the per capita decline in consumption was even larger – it fell by about 50 percent in the same time period.

Importantly to tobacco control, however, the positive overall trend masks the fact that smoking rates remain alarmingly high in certain demographic groups. Characteristics such as age, gender (reported above), "race," culture and socioeconomic status are all likely to have impacts on smoking prevalence rates.

In 1999, nationally representative data on tobacco use among adolescents in secondary school (grades 8 to 10) became available for the first time when South Africa participated in the Global Youth Tobacco Survey (GYTS). The survey was repeated in 2002. Among the key findings are statistically significant declines (at $p<0.05$) in cigarette smoking between the two surveys. The number of students who had never smoked a cigarette increased by 20 percent (from 53.3 percent in 1999 to 62.4 percent in 2002) and the number of frequent smokers (defined as those who had smoked on 20 or more days in the past month) declined from 10.1 percent to 5.8 percent between 1999 and 2002. It is noteworthy that in 2001 the government banned tobacco advertising, and the surveys provide data from before and after the ban. Although the declines in cigarette smoking cannot be definitively attributed to the ban, it is encouraging that the trend was in the expected direction.

Challenges remain, however, in the effort to address youth smoking. Despite the fact that the law prohibits the sale of tobacco to minors or its free distribution, 66 percent of the students in the GYTS reported that they bought cigarettes in a store. Furthermore, 22 percent of students in the same survey claimed that tobacco industry representatives had offered them free cigarettes.

Surveys show that large numbers of children are exposed to tobacco smoke pollution in South Africa. A 1990 study of 5-year-old children in the Johannesburg/Soweto metropole found that 64 percent of the children were exposed to second-hand tobacco smoke in the home. Colored children[2] were most frequently exposed, with 42 percent living in homes with two or more smokers. In Cape Town, 80 percent of 6–11-year-old school children were exposed to pollution from tobacco smoke. Using urinary cotinine concentrations to estimate exposure, the most important source of smoke pollution was maternal smoking, followed by smoking by the male parent and other household smokers.

In terms of income, survey data demonstrate that poorer smokers are more likely to quit than more affluent smokers. Between 1993 and 2000, there was an annual decrease in smoking of approximately −0.89 percent in households earning less than R1,400 a month, while smoking increased annually by approximately 0.33 percent in those earning more than R7,000 a month.

In terms of race, smoking prevalence is highest in the colored population (see Table 16.1). However, the white community smokes the most heavily (i.e. the highest actual consumption per smoker). In 1998, white smokers reported consuming an average of 18 cigarettes per day; the corresponding figure was 11 for Asians, 9 for coloreds and 7 for Africans. On average, women smoked about two cigarettes a day fewer than men. Income and race correlate highly and account partly, but not entirely, for these differences.

Tobacco products other than regular manufactured cigarettes continue to be popular in South Africa. Although manufactured cigarettes dominate, hand-rolled cigarettes account for about 21 percent of the market, and such use is particularly common amongst African and colored men. Similarly, while the overall rate of smokeless tobacco use in South Africa is relatively low at about

Table 16.1. Daily adult smoking prevalence rates by "race" and gender in South Africa, 2008

	% Male	% Female	% All
African	34.9	3.6	19.3
Asian	46.6	10.4	28.1
Colored	48.3	39.0	43.5
White	37.8	28.4	32.9
Total population	36.7	10.3	23.4

6 percent, black women are twice as likely to use snuff (12.6 percent) than to smoke cigarettes (5.3 percent). Of particular concern, the nicotine delivery from the commercial brands of snuff sold in South Africa is higher than from comparable brands in the United States. A typical commercial snuff user may be receiving nicotine concentrations equivalent to smoking 20 cigarettes a day. Homemade snuff (tobacco leaf ground with ash) seems to deliver lower levels of nicotine than commercial brands. Pipe tobacco consumption declined by approximately 4 percent in volume terms during 2007. Pipe tobacco is used both in the traditional manner and as roll-your-own.

Tobacco Control Policies

Existing laws and regulations

Since 1993, there have been four major pieces of legislation (and corresponding regulation-making to put these laws into practice), particularly by the MoH (and also the Ministry of Finance, in terms of taxation). The country's laws comply with most of the best recommendations of the Framework Convention on Tobacco Control (FCTC), in which the country was also a leading negotiator. Excluding snuff and snus, tobacco tax increases have been won and progressive legislation has been enacted, while smoking prevalence and the numbers of cigarettes smoked have declined. On the other hand, tobacco smuggling has increased; the tobacco industry remains influential; mass media educational campaigns are nonexistent; and law enforcement poses challenges. Tobacco control advocates believe not only that there is still work to be done, but also that tobacco control requires persistent monitoring of and rapid reactions to efforts by the industry and its allies. Because several ministries deal with potentially competing issues (discussed below), they demand well-executed and reliable scientific evidence before supporting tobacco control policies. Tobacco control advocates have been supplying this evidence on a regular basis for more than twenty years.

The original 1993 act empowered the minister of health to prescribe health warnings on advertisements and on tobacco packs. It allowed for the regulation of smoking in public places and also contained a prohibition on the sale of tobacco products to people under the age of 16, in addition to some restrictions on vending machines. It introduced a requirement that the tar and nicotine yields of cigarettes be printed on the pack. The first act led to the publication of the first set of regulations on 2 December 1994. These regulations contained details about the warnings on tobacco advertisements and packages, and also prescribed testing methods for determining tar and nicotine yields.

The second Tobacco Act (April 1999) is more extensive and introduced a ban on all tobacco advertising and sponsorships. It restricts smoking in enclosed public places, with certain exemptions. It restricts "point-of-sale" advertising to price and availability only, though the tobacco industry openly violated this restriction by advertising brands. The amendment, for the first time, gives the minister of health the power to prescribe maximum yields of tar and other constituents. It bans free distribution and rewards, and places further restrictions on the use of vending machines. The Tobacco Products Control Amendment Act, No. 12 of 1999 was published in the *Government Gazette* on 1 October 2000 and came into effect on 1 January 2001.

Four "Government Notices under the Act" were published in September 2000. The first notice deals with the maximum permissible yields of tar and nicotine and other constituents in tobacco products. The tar yield of cigarettes could not be greater than 15 mg per cigarette and the nicotine yield not greater than 1.5 mg by 1 December 2001. These maximum levels had to be lowered to a tar yield of 12 mg per cigarette and a nicotine yield of 1.2 mg nicotine per cigarette by 1 June 2006.

The second notice is an extensive piece of legislation regulating smoking in public places. A public place is defined as any indoor or enclosed area that is open to the public or any part of the public and includes a workplace and a public conveyance. The notice addresses the types of public places where smoking is permitted and the conditions under which smoking is permitted. In principle, a person in charge of a public place may designate a portion of the public place as a "smoking area" provided that the designated area does not exceed 25 percent of the total floor area, is separated by a solid partition with an entrance door and has a ventilation system that directly exhausts air to the outside. The notice also places special obligations on employers to protect their employees.

The third notice tackles the challenges of point-of-sale advertising of tobacco products. The signs may not exceed one square meter and must be placed within one meter of the point of sale. The tobacco products can be visible to customers, but merchandise cannot be handled prior to purchase.

The fourth notice codifies, with certain exemptions, the phasing out of existing contractual sponsorship and/or advertising obligations. All sponsorships taking place in terms of contracts that were in place as of 23 April 1999 were allowed to continue up to 23 April 2001.

The multifaceted tobacco control Amendment Act No. 23 was passed by parliament in September 2007. It was assented by the president in February 2008, published in the *Government Gazette* in February of 2009 and had a proclamation of commencement on 21 August 2009. The act provides anew for control over the smoking of tobacco products; makes provision for standards in respect to the manufacturing and export of tobacco products;

and extends the minister's power to make regulations and increase penalties. Provisions stipulated by the act include:

(1) No person may smoke any tobacco product in:
   (i) a public place;
   (ii) any area within a prescribed distance from a window of, ventilation inlet of, doorway to or entrance into a public place;
   (iii) any motor vehicle when a child under the age of 12 years is present in that vehicle; and
   (iv) in any prescribed outdoor public place where persons are likely to congregate within close proximity of one another or where smoking may pose a fire or other hazard.
(2) No person shall manufacture a tobacco product unless it complies with such standards as may be prescribed. The standards that a tobacco product must comply with include:
   (i) the amounts of substances that may be contained in the product or its emissions;
   (ii) substances that may or may not be added to the product;
   (iii) the ignition propensity of cigarettes; and
   (iv) product design and composition
(3) A manufacturer of a tobacco product must submit to the minister and to the public information in respect of:
   (i) research conducted into a tobacco product by a manufacturer or by a person who conducted research paid for in whole or in part by a tobacco manufacturer;
   (ii) the quantity of a tobacco product manufactured;
   (iii) marketing expenditure; and
   (iv) information on product composition, ingredients, hazardous properties and emissions
(4) The penalty for restaurants, pubs, bars and workplaces that allow smoking is increased from R200 to R50,000 (maximum). The fine for an individual who smokes in a public place will be a maximum of R500.

A third amendment act (Bill B24-2008) gives the government authority to regulate the promotion, packaging and the retailing of cigarettes. It came into force on 21 August 2009. Activities regulated in the bill include:

• direct or indirect advertising of a tobacco product, and the practice of paying film and television producers to show tobacco products on screen (so-called product placement) are prohibited;
• warning messages, with pictures showing the consequences of tobacco use, must appear on tobacco packages;

- "charitable" donations can be made by tobacco companies provided they are not used for purposes of advertising;
- "false" or "misleading" health claims on tobacco packages are barred – the use of labels like "light," "mild" or "low-tar" which falsely imply that such cigarettes are less harmful than regular cigarettes are banned;
- the free distribution of cigarettes and the use of coupons and gifts to promote tobacco sales and use is prohibited;
- self-service displays of tobacco products at retail are banned;
- the display of tobacco products at wholesale and retail is regulated;
- the sale of tobacco by and to those under the age of 18 is banned;
- mail order and internet sales are forbidden; and
- vending machines may only be located in places to which those under the age of 18 do not have access.

Overall political, economic and social context

The contemporary historical context (post-1980) of tobacco control has been addressed well in the academic literature and will therefore not be revisited extensively here.[3] Very briefly, however, after the collapse of apartheid in the early 1990s, the new African National Congress (ANC)–led government has been consistently supportive of many tobacco control policies. In particular, the first health minister in the Mandela administration, Dr Nkosazana Dlamini Zuma, followed by the late health minister in the Mbeki administration, Dr Manto Tshabalala-Msimang, were both very active and vociferous supporters of tobacco control domestically and internationally. Dr Zuma was instrumental in passing enabling legislation that banned tobacco advertising and smoking in indoor public places in 1999. Dr Tshabalala-Msimang was an important actor in moving forward the regulations for smoke-free policies and the advertising ban, and for negotiating the FCTC. Moreover, working in this relatively positive political climate, a professionalized tobacco control advocacy community has worked to develop and enforce progressive tobacco control policies.

   With major political changes in 2009 including a new president, changed ANC leadership, a new cabinet and many new legislators, there is some uncertainty as to the future status of tobacco control policies. That being said, there appears at least to be consistent support of tobacco control in South Africa from a number of key cabinet posts and major bureaucratic actors. Though the actual appointed post-holders in almost all ministries have changed recently, the actual policy positions of the ministries do not appear to have fluctuated markedly. President Jacob Zuma has expressed explicit support for tobacco control, though he has not initiated any policy directly. Accordingly, since the new Zuma administration took office, the advocacy community, led by the NCAS, is actively determining the positions of new ministers and deputy ministers in relevant departments. It is also continually mapping out the position of all legislators at the national level. With major positive changes to tobacco policy in 1993, 1999, 2007 and 2008, there is a clear track record of successfully affecting policy.

Taxation

South Africa has been successfully using tobacco taxation as a deterrent to tobacco use for well over a decade. However, because of inflation, economic growth and pricing tactics on the part of the industry, the tax strategy has lost some of its effectiveness. The African Tobacco Situation Analysis (ATSA) team is seeking to introduce a reconsidered taxation strategy to the Ministry of Finance and other key players – one that accounts effectively for inflation, cost of living and pricing – as a tool for tobacco control.

There is ample evidence to support the view that the price of cigarettes is the main short-term determinant of rates of tobacco consumption. As price increases, consumption falls and vice versa. Furthermore, many smokers have supported tax increases, as it provides them with an added incentive to quit. Poorer smokers – who are traditionally less responsive to health education – are more likely to quit when prices increase. Between 1990 and 1995, spending by poorer households on cigarettes has decreased, while spending by the richest households has increased fractionally.[1]

Since 1994, the government has adopted a progressive tobacco excise tax policy explicitly for health reasons (as opposed to other countries that have taxes on tobacco products mainly for revenue reasons). Between 1992 and 2008, the real (inflation-adjusted) price of cigarettes increased by 157 percent, real government revenues increased by 225 percent and cigarette consumption declined by 35 percent. Figure 16.1 plots part of this time period.

Despite the benefits, successive governments have been slow to tax tobacco more aggressively. Recent steep increases in the price of cigarettes were more a result of manufacturers driving up prices than of the government driving up taxation. Between 1990 and 2000, increases in taxes only accounted for 50 percent of the increase in real price; the other half of the change in price was due to industry-imposed increases in price. The industry has been profiteering, and its strategy seems to be to increase its profit margins at the cost of sales volumes.

The NCAS and its ATSA team partners elected to revisit taxation in order to obtain not only a new increase, but a better system that accounts for inflation and increases in income more effectively. The objective of this renewed policy initiative is to make cigarettes less affordable by lobbying for excise tax increases above the rate of inflation and above the rate of growth in

Figure 16.1. Cigarette price and consumption in South Africa, 1992–2001

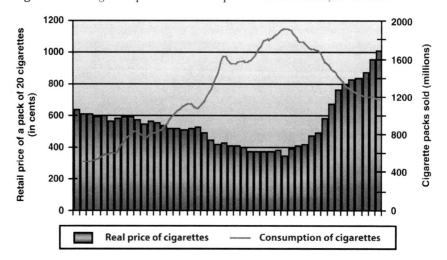

GDP. The NCAS argues that the first step is "information." Accordingly, the NCAS-led team hired an economist to develop a package of evidence-based tax research that will be submitted to the highest ministerial levels. It is crucial to be able to identify with sound economics the optimal tax rate from a health perspective and its revenue implications.

The ATSA team argues that it is important to make the effort to engage the pertinent political actors to press the case for increased tobacco taxation. In the case of taxation, the Ministry of Finance is a pivotal institution, with key actors at multiple levels.[5] The team argues that in addition to the minister and deputy minister, it is also vital to make direct contact with the ministry's director(s) general (or DG – the highest ranking bureaucrat in South African ministries), the deputy directors general (DDG) and others who have jurisdiction in this area. Since it is generally the DGs and the DDGs and their staffs who do much of the implementation and enforcement, it makes a great deal of sense to present the evidence-based tax research first to these actors, who will then – hopefully – take it up the chain of command. Often, it is easier to make contact with the bureaucrats than with the ministers.

That being said, the team recognizes the importance of "triangulating" by making direct contact, where possible, with the higher or highest levels of the ministry. As suggested above, the actual minister of finance and the deputy minister will be key players in executing such a tax increase. There are both a new minister and deputy minister in the Zuma administration, and the NCAS recognizes the importance of making a strong case to these high-level officials.

Not trivially, within the ministry, the support of specific key departments is crucial to any tax increase. In particular, the South African Revenue Services (SARS), including both the excise taxes and customs departments, is a pivotal institution for any taxation issue. The customs director is particularly important because s/he plays a major role in enforcement and smuggling.

Incidentally, tobacco control advocates are aware that the tobacco industry has lobbied Ministry of Finance officials in the past with its own set of "evidence-based" facts. In particular, the industry has obfuscated the benefits of increased taxation to both health and fiscal stability by claiming that increased taxation leads to an increase in the illicit trade of tobacco products. There is a multitude of international evidence that the tobacco industry has been involved in this illicit trade in many countries. In South Africa specifically, the chief executive officer of Mastermind Tobacco settled a suit for R57 million in June 2009, in which the company was charged with 25 counts of fraud specific to the nonpayment of excise duties, 25 counts of exporting goods illegally from the customs and excise warehouse and six counts of fraud related to nonpayments of the value added tax (VAT).[6] After attempting to pass off local cigarettes as exports, which are exempt from certain types of taxation, the company agreed to pay the penalties in exchange for not being convicted by a criminal court for a violation of the VAT Act, the Customs and Excise Act or fraud.

Other departments or ministries could also play secondary, but still important, roles. First, the Department of Trade and Industry (DTI) has a potential competing interest because of the possible implications for trade. Establishing the minister's views – ideally through a direct meeting – is important because his/her support could be very helpful, while a strong objection could be a major obstacle. Providing the evidence-based research to the minister that a tax increase would actually have positive, not negative, economic consequences for the country in the long run is a crucial piece of the argument that must be presented.

Second, again because of competing interests, the minister of agriculture is an important voice in cabinet. Because of agricultural tobacco production, in the past, the Tobacco Action Group (TAG)[7] has engaged the agriculture ministry in order to ensure that it did not oppose tobacco control legislation. With any new ministers, it will be important to meet them and present a set of evidence-based research to reassure them that taxation will not affect their constituencies. Incidentally, on a related note, the ATSA team argues that at some point in the near future, an analysis of tobacco farming in South Africa needs to be executed because tobacco production in the country has declined dramatically since 1988 and it could represent an affirmative case study on successful crop diversification.

Lastly, the MoH is generally supportive of tobacco tax initiatives and can act as a strong proponent of a proposed tax policy change with other ministries. It is therefore very important to get the support of the MoH by presenting it with an evidence-based set of arguments about the health merits of a tax increase and corresponding new and improved policy so that the ministry will convince cabinet colleagues that this is a worthwhile policy initiative. Again, with a new minister and DG in 2009–10, it is important to continue to make a persuasive case.

Warning labels

Though the new amendments from 2008 empower the health minister to promulgate regulations for the implementation of graphic warning labels, as of early 2011, the MoH had not yet decided definitively on the content of the new messages. For health warnings to be effective, it is important to ensure that the content and format of the warnings are appropriate for the target audience. The NCAS is pre-testing a range of messages to assess the comprehension, acceptability and potential effectiveness of health warnings. The aim is to identify warnings that are easily understood, informative, believable, relevant and most likely to lead to quitting. The NCAS believes that if the ministry were presented with appropriate professional materials as examples from which to work that it would move on the initiative relatively quickly.

The MoH is obviously the central political institution in this initiative. The minister of health has the final approval of relevant health regulations, so s/he must be engaged positively in the process. Importantly, within the ministry, it is the director of health promotion who has responsibility for tobacco control and who takes relevant proposed regulations up the ministry's chain of command to the DG and/or ministerial level. Meeting with the director and his/her staff to discuss potentially helpful activities related to packaging and labeling is vital.

Furthermore, the role of the ministry's legal department is crucial because it drafts both legislation and regulations. The recent legislative changes do not provide for the exact wording of the regulation for the labeling restrictions. The ministry has many pressures, so proposals based on model legislative and regulatory texts from other countries that highlight key components of the regulations within the South African context need to be developed and provided for their review and reference.

There will be private interests actively opposed to the implementation of warning labels. Undoubtedly, the tobacco industry will strongly oppose the initiative, attempt to delay and dilute it, appeal to the Department of Trade and Industry on the grounds of economic loss and argue for its intellectual property rights. Accordingly, the NCAS must have effective counterarguments for advocacy purposes, and will monitor and lobby relevant players as necessary.

There is a strong, free media in South Africa that is open to discussing tobacco control in an unbiased, thoughtful manner, and the ATSA team has been accessing the media in order to reach the public. For example, the team will hold media press conferences before new regulations are published for public comment, write media releases for wider dissemination, meet with journalists personally and do media interviews.

The initiative is being spearheaded by the NCAS. It also expects, when necessary, to call on its allies from the TAG for support, particularly to lobby, to disseminate information to the public and/or to rally its members and volunteers. The team expects that consumer rights groups, particularly the National Consumer Forum, will be similarly supportive, and is seeking to bring them – and other organizations – under the TAG umbrella.

A smoke-free 2010 FIFA World Cup

The 2010 FIFA World Cup was smoke-free in all spectator viewing areas. While South Korea (with the help of the World Health Organization (WHO)) hosted a smoke-free FIFA World Cup in 2002, the event was not smoke-free in Germany in 2006. The ATSA team believed, however, that it was possible to have a smoke-free World Cup in South Africa in 2010. With the World Cup being one of the largest sporting events in the world, this presented an unparalleled opportunity to showcase tobacco control policies both broadly and specific to South Africa. Furthermore, the residual positive effects for smoke-free public places in South Africa, particularly at sporting events and sporting venues, are very promising.

Importantly, the national cabinet under former president Thabo Mbeki passed a resolution in support of this goal on the recommendation of the then health minister, Dr Tshabala-Msimang. In early 2010, with two recent changes in presidential leadership and a change to Jacob Zuma leading the ruling African National Congress and several major cabinet shuffles, the status of this resolution was not entirely clear. Therefore, it was clearly a critical juncture in terms of holding the government to the original resolution.

The NCAS actively sought key stakeholders' positions, educated key cabinet members, lobbied supportive members to be torchbearers and lobbied less supportive members to change their positions. They wanted to be sure that the new cabinet stuck to the initial decision. Arguably, in this initiative, both the ministries of Health and Sport and Recreation were potentially important actors at the ministerial level, as their overt support would help the cause greatly.

In 2009, the NCAS sent a proposal for a smoke-free World Cup directly to the chief medical officer of FIFA, with an official copy also sent to the director of health promotion from the MoH. The MoH officially reiterated the cabinet decision regarding the smoke-free World Cup 2010. The Local Organizing Committee and FIFA agreed that World Cup venues would comply with the country's domestic tobacco laws and that all spectator viewing areas at the stadiums would be smoke free.

With the cup's major economic, social and reputational ramifications for South Africa, there were several other key organizations that were important. Firstly, the South African Football Association (SAFA) was a main component of the cup's organization, which included the facilities owners and managers and venue supervisors. The ATSA team had also developed a readymade strategy for management of stadia for the purpose of implementing the policy, which included a training program for stadia security, adequate signage including on the large electronic boards and prepared public address announcements. With considerable encouragement and support from the NCAS, stadia began to adopt and enforce such codes voluntarily to varying degrees.

Engaging the media and allies to publicize the initiative was an important component. Accordingly, the ATSA developed smoke-free advertisements for radio and television. It also engaged its TAG partners, including the Cancer Association of South Africa (CANSA), particularly for their lobbying capacity and membership.

The team expected resistance from several major areas. Of course, it anticipated that the the tobacco industry and the hospitality association would actively lobby against any such initiative. These counterefforts, however, did not change the positive outcome.

In a related legislative development, there has been a pending piece of legislation before parliament throughout 2009–10 entitled "Safety at Sport and Recreational Events," which now has a significant smoke-free section. In 2009, the NCAS addressed the parliament's Portfolio Committee on Sport and Recreation about a smoke-free component, and members of the committee were supportive of the idea.

Tobacco Industry

Tobacco manufacturers are a genuine economic and political force in South Africa. The industry had strong political connections with the apartheid government and still enjoys the support of some government officials. Perhaps most worrying and frustrating to advocates, the industry is continually finding new and creative ways to circumvent legislation. Fortunately, the advocacy community, led by the NCAS, monitors the industry closely and seeks to respond to its actions swiftly and firmly using both evidence-based research and publicity through the media.

The ATSA team has characterized the industry as powerful and cunning. It is comprised of both tobacco growers and manufacturers. However, tobacco growing is in serious decline (see Table 16.2), with the number of farmers, area planted and crop size all falling over the past two decades. In fact, the country has moved from being a net exporter of tobacco to a net importer, with substantial amounts of tobacco leaf imported duty-free from Zimbabwe and Malawi.

Tobacco manufacturing, in contrast, remains quite robust economically. Cigarettes, pipe tobacco and snuff are all manufactured in the country. About 35 billion sticks of cigarettes were manufactured in 2007, while 23 billion were consumed domestically. British American Tobacco (BAT) is the largest cigarette manufacturer with 90 percent of the market, while Japan Tobacco International (JTI)/Gallaher have 5.3 percent and Philip Morris International (PMI) has 1.8 percent of the cigarette market. Swedish Match (recently purchased by PMI) dominates the pipe and snuff markets and was the second largest tobacco manufacturer in the country.[8]

In 2003, 3,000 people were employed in manufacturing and 23,600 (including seasonal workers) were employed in farming, while R6 billion was paid in VAT and excise taxes resulting from the sale of tobacco products. To put these taxes into proper perspective, however, in 1993, the Medical Research Council estimated that tobacco use cost the South African economy R3 billion in medical costs of treatment and in lost productivity to business, which was twice as much as the industry paid in taxes that year.[9] Furthermore, the industry does not actually pay these taxes, but instead collects them for the government, and the actual cost of the taxes is borne by the consumer.

The tobacco industry has claimed that it supports reasonable and "enforceable" tobacco control legislation and suggests that it wants to work

Table 16.2. Tobacco farming in South Africa – 2000 versus 2007

	2000	2007
Farmers	615	150
Workers	31,000	12,000
Hectares planted	15,599	3,700
Total crop (million kg)	29	10

with government. Its position is that a balance should be found between health objectives and the economic and social contributions that the industry makes in South Africa. These industry "contributions" appear to include anything that impinges on their profits and their ability to market to any consumer.

To win support, the industry spends about R30 million annually on various corporate social responsibility (CSR) projects including HIV/AIDS awareness, black economic empowerment, crime prevention and bursaries for tertiary education.[10] The industry is permitted by law to make donations as long as it is not for the purpose of advertising. The NCAS has expressed grave objection to the vague wording of this component of the legislation, but parliament has not been sympathetic to its concern.

One of the most recent activities concerning the industry in South Africa was PMI's agreement to buy Swedish Match AB's South African operations for R1.75 billion (US$222 million). This announcement came after a previous agreement in February 2009, when PMI announced a 50–50 joint venture with Swedish Match to make and sell smokeless products like snus. PMI estimated that Swedish Match South Africa's pipe tobacco and snuff products represent about 31 percent of total tobacco consumption in South Africa, which makes the purchase a strategic gain for the company in South Africa. The country has proven to be an important international market dominated traditionally by BAT. As cigarette consumption declines and if smokeless tobacco products become more popular, this would put PMI in a particularly favorable market position.[11]

The ATSA team has expressed deep concern about a perception amongst sections of the public that the government pays too much attention to tobacco. In particular, there is a perception that the industry cultivates the support of politicians. The industry also portrays itself as a responsible corporate citizen – characterized by the tobacco control community as attempts to "buy" communities through CSR programs – claiming that it is a part of the solution and not part of the problem.

Longer-term challenges

In terms of challenges, advocates have complained about a lack of a formal government-sponsored system and database for logging complaints to municipalities and for monitoring prosecutions. In the meanwhile, civil society is bearing the cost of such monitoring, which may be less sustainable in the longer term. For example, when the NCAS identifies a violator, the council begins by writing a letter of cease and desist to the owner of the business. So for example, if a fast-food restaurant is permitting smoking, they will receive an official letter from the NCAS. If there is no response, the NCAS writes another letter, and where possible, sends a copy to the overarching organization (in the case of franchisees, the franchisor) and the real estate lessor, informing them that a criminal docket will be opened. If there is no response or a lack of compliance, the NCAS then opens an official criminal complaint.

Finally, advocates are also concerned about a gap in the education of health workers on cessation and the lack of dedicated government resources toward public awareness, prevention and cessation programs. In the case of professional health education, support from the government (including the bodies that regulate curriculum) and professional associations would be helpful. In terms of awareness, in the past, efforts have mostly come as a result of law promulgation. For example, the government published broad sheets in major newspapers about the new tobacco control regulations in 2001. But getting tobacco to stay on the agenda afterward has been a larger challenge, and it has not been the government that is paying for these efforts. Finally, while there is a government-supported quitline for smokers, cessation efforts also need to be devolved to local health clinics for which there will need to be proper training of staff. For this type of effort, there will need to be support from the national health ministry, and the provincial and city health departments that will do most of the implementation.

ATSA Review

The ATSA program has helped to generate important advances in tobacco control in South Africa, including in the areas of taxation, aid in developing new regulations for graphic warning labels on tobacco packaging and a smoke-free 2010 World Cup for spectators. First, partly as a result of ATSA-related activities, a strong case has been made to the government for reviewing and changing existing national tobacco excise tax policy. There is ongoing engagement with the Ministry of Finance and it is now established that the SARS plans to introduce a system for fighting the illicit trade in tobacco. Proponents of tobacco tax policy reform note some ongoing challenges, including continuing efforts by the tobacco industry to lobby SARS that excise taxes have been one of the root causes of the illicit trade in tobacco. These baseless claims are being countered with strong evidence-based research and the education of policymakers and the public on the industry's role in cigarette smuggling and how it benefits the industry. Despite the overwhelming evidence, however, it is a continuing challenge to change the status quo.

The program also helped to generate support for the development of important subsidiary regulation in the area of labeling. While enabling legislation is undoubtedly important, the follow-up regulations to implement new laws are just as crucial. Accordingly, the NCAS has been working to help find culturally appropriate graphic images for health messages on tobacco packaging. Critics and proponents alike have noted that images from other countries are not always relevant – in this case, images must be relevant to the South African context. For example, in early testing, some health messages that evoked fear were controversial and produced the most negative comment. However, the fact that they provoked strong reaction suggests not just that they will draw attention to the message, but also that people might be less likely to accept them.

In part due to efforts by ATSA team members, the 2010 FIFA World Cup was a smoke-free event in all spectator viewing areas. The tournament attracted 400,000 tourists from around the world and all spectators were able to watch the games free of the harm of tobacco smoke. Working with the South African government and FIFA, proponents of smoke-free policies were able to implement successfully the second-ever smoke-free World Cup.

In related recent advances, there are new regulations for standards in cigarette manufacturing and the tobacco industry has been dealt a huge blow with the court's dismissal of its challenge to the advertising and promotion ban. First, concerning reduced-ignition cigarettes, the NCAS helped to generate research on laws from other countries and made recommendations on best practices. In November of 2009, the Department of Health released draft "Regulations Relating to the Standards for Manufacturing of Reduced Ignition Propensity Cigarettes." The regulations were published in the *Government Gazette* in May 2011 and will come into effect in November 2012.

The industry's attempts to circumvent the ban on advertising and promotion by arguing that it violated their constitutional right to communicate one-to-one with customers was quashed in the North Gauteng High Court in May 2011. The plaintiff, BAT, or other tobacco firms will not be permitted to continue advertising in this manner and it is a monumental decision in light of the industry's clever tactics to undermine such bans.

The multiple and varied efforts of the South African tobacco control community demonstrate that the tasks related to promoting better public health policy are enormous and ongoing. Perhaps partly because the tobacco industry is so singular in its purpose of selling more dangerous products, these tasks require perseverance, creativity and doggedness from a public health community dedicated to serving and engendering the long-term vitality of its citizens.

Notes

1 Sources: CIA World Factbook https://www.cia.gov/library/publications/the-world-factbook/; except Food and Agriculture Organization of the United Nations – Statistics (FAOSTAT) for tobacco production. See http://faostat.fao.org/site/567/default.aspx#ancor (accessed 20 July 2011).

2 Racial classifications are still used by researchers in South Africa because they provide a measure of inequity.

3 B. E. Asare, "Tobacco regulation in South Africa: Interest groups and public policy," *African Journal of Political Science and International Relations* 3.3 (2009): 99–106; M. Malan and R. Weaver, "Political change in South Africa: New tobacco control and public health policies" in J. de Beyer and L. Waverley Brigden (eds), *Tobacco Control Policy: Strategies, Successes and Setbacks* (Washington DC: The World Bank, 2003), 121–51; C. P. van Walbeek, "Tobacco control in South Africa in the 1990s: A mix of advocacy, academic research and policy," *South African Journal Economic History* 19 (2004): 100–31.

4 See E. H. Blecher and C. P. van Walbeek, "An international analysis of cigarette affordability," *Tobacco Control* 13 (2004): 339–46; E. H. Blecher, "Targeting the affordability of cigarettes: A new benchmark for taxation policy in low-income and middle-income countries," *Tobacco Control* (Online First), 7 June 2010; E. H. Blecher and C. P. van Walbeek, "Cigarette Affordability Trends: An Update and Some Methodological Comments," *Tobacco Control* 19 (2009): 463–8.

5 The minister's actual boss, President (and leader of the ANC) Jacob Zuma, is supportive – he has actually called on all ANC officials to stop smoking – but he is not the key figure here as the Ministry of Finance will make the decision.

6 T. Jika, "Tobacco Company has to pay R57M," *Daily Dispatch*, 8 June 2009.

7 A coalition between the Cancer Association of South Africa, the Heart and Stroke Foundation of South Africa and the NCAS.

8 Euromonitor, "Tobacco in South Africa" (various years). See http://www.euromonitor.com/south-africa (last accessed 22 July 2011).

9 See Malan and Leaver, "Political change in South Africa."

10 BAT–SA, Annual Reports (various years). Available online from www.bat.com (last accessed 22 July 2011).

11 Associated Press, "Philip Morris to Buy Swedish Match South Africa," *Richmond Times-Dispatch*, 2 July 2009.

Chapter 17

TANZANIA

Tanzania Public Health Association

Executive Summary

In many ways, tobacco control in Tanzania is currently framed by the existing, problematic legal framework passed by the national legislature in 2003. By all accounts, the Tobacco (Products Regulation) Act (TPRA) requires serious reworking as many provisions are not compliant with the Framework Convention on Tobacco Control (FCTC), and furthermore, are too weak to be effective. Like many countries, implementation and enforcement were not well conceived, and not surprisingly, both remain very serious challenges.

Accordingly, the tobacco control community has elected to pursue FCTC-compliant legislation in the near term, and is considering the implementation and enforcement components of this new statute. It is apparent that they will face an uphill battle because as the Tanzanian economy struggles, the government has made tobacco cultivation one of the centerpieces of their new strategic economic plan. It is not clear how tobacco control and increased cultivation will comfortably coexist.

Country Profile[1]

Population in 2009 (global and African ranking):	41,048,532 (31, 5)
Geographical size (global ranking):	947,300 sq. km (38)
GDP by purchasing power parity in 2008 (global ranking):	US$54.25 billion (100)
GDP real growth rate (2006–8):	7%
GDP per capita:	US$1,300 (91)
Main industries:	Agricultural processing (sugar, beer, cigarettes, sisal twine), diamonds, gold, iron mining, soda ash, cement, oil refining, shoes, apparel, wood products, fertilizer

Languages:	Kiswahili (called Kiunguja in Zanzibar) or Swahili (official), English (official, primary language of commerce, administration, and higher education), Arabic (widely spoken in Zanzibar), many local languages
Official development assistance (ODA) – total commitments/disbursements (2007):	US$2,786.3/2,104.4 million
ODA as a percentage of GDP:	12.5%
Largest donors (disbursements in millions of USD):	Japan 721.7, UK 230.8, EC 193.9, US 166.9, Netherlands 128.1, Norway 114.3, Sweden 107.8, Denmark 77, Global Fund 74.9
Tobacco production by volume in 2007 (global ranking):	50,600 tons (14)
Tobacco exports (2007):	Tobacco (unmanufactured): 40,743 tons at $2,327 per ton, #2 export
Tobacco imports (2007):	Tobacco (unmanufactured): 1,224 tons at $4,079 per ton, #12 import

Brief Description of Political System

Type: Presidential republic.

Executive: The chief of state and head of government, as of mid-2011, is President Jakaya Kikwete (since 2005).

Cabinet: Appointed by the president from National Assembly members.

Legislature: The unicameral National Assembly (Bunge) is comprised of 274 seats (232 popularly elected, 37 allocated to women nominated by the president and 5 allocated to members of the Zanzibar House of Representatives, which has its own special regional powers). As of the 2009 election, the Chama Cha Mapinduzi party (CCM) has 206 seats and the Civic United Front (CUF) has 19.

Introduction

Between July and October of 2008, the Tanzania African Tobacco Situation Analysis (ATSA) team members carried out a baseline assessment and a stakeholder consultation meeting to identify policy gaps in Tanzania's tobacco control efforts. In partnership with International Development

Research Centre (IDRC) consultants, the team also did political mapping of the specific country context to identify priorities and create a work plan. This synthesis is an attempt to document the available information; the magnitude of tobacco as a public health problem in the country; to assess tobacco control efforts to date; and to identify challenges and opportunities for tobacco control in Tanzania.

Scope of Tobacco Problem

Available data on the incidence of smoking and associated health hazards make it difficult to assess the effects of tobacco use in Tanzania accurately. Data on the prevalence of smoking are fragmented, and mainly come from small, discrete studies done in segments of the population, thereby restricting generalization of the results. Nevertheless, the results of certain studies, including those done by Research on Poverty Alleviation (REPOA) and the Tanzania Global School-based Student Health Survey (GSHS 2008), are worth noting. There is also an ongoing study commissioned by the Ministry of Health and Social Welfare covering up to five districts that examines community-level knowledge, attitudes and perceptions of noncommunicable diseases and associated risk factors including levels of tobacco use and alcohol consumption.

There are no known countrywide surveys of smoking rates in Tanzania. However, discrete studies suggest a growing problem. For instance, in 2007, Mshiu and Siza interviewed 423 participants between the ages of 13 and 15 years in the Moshi Rural District of northern Tanzania, and they reported that the minimum age for experimenting with smoking is as low as 6 years.[2] A total of 26.4 percent (112 out of 423) of respondents reported that they had tried smoking. In another study, Mokiti and colleagues presented results of studies carried out in 2003 and 2008 on the prevalence of tobacco use among adolescents between 13 and 15 years of age in the three regions of Arusha, Dar es Salaam and Kilimanjaro.[3] Their study involved 6,343 participants from 75 schools. The authors reported an increase in the prevalence of girls who smoked in 2008 compared to the rate in 2003, whereas there was a slight decrease in the prevalence for boys. The study reported regional variations in prevalence and the age of onset. Respondents noted that aggressive advertisements that glamorize tobacco use were one of the main reasons for experimenting with smoking the first time. In these studies, the minimum age to start smoking was reported as 12 years.

A recent study based on the Adult Morbidity and Mortality Project (AMMP) in Dar es Salaam found that nearly a quarter (23.5 percent) of the (predominantly Muslim) male population smoked daily, and an additional

1.9 percent weekly. The average male smoker used 7.9 cigarettes a day. The AMMP (2000) also compared data for Dar es Salaam for 1992 and 1996, identifying a decrease in the smoking rate of 3.6 percent for men (from 18.1 percent to 14.5 percent) and of 0.9 percent for women (from 1.9 percent to 1.0 percent) over four years. There is a need to validate these reports through a more systematic study that seeks to document and account for ongoing changes in prevalence rates in the context of competing messages – on one hand, there has been sustained campaigning against cigarette smoking in Dar es Salaam, while on the other hand, aggressive tobacco advertising continues.

In a study from the early 1990s, Swai et al. found that 42.6 percent of adult males were smokers in rural Kilimanjaro, 28.2 percent in rural Morogoro and 8.6 percent in rural Mara.[4] Smoking rates increased substantially between the 15–24 and 25–34 age groups. Among women, 2.1 percent smoked in Kilimanjaro, 3.9 percent in Morogoro and 2.7 percent in Mara. The regional differences may be explained by sociocultural and/or economic differences as well as availability of tobacco products. In some regions, cultural restrictions may play a deterrent role, especially among females.

Jagoe et al. (2002) reported an "average age" of smoke initiation of 21.9 years for men and 22.6 for women.[5] However, it is reasonable to assume that these ages vary according to the population studied. For example, there have been anecdotal reports from rural areas where primary school students have been observed experimenting with smoking homegrown or locally made tobacco leaf rolled in some improvised paper or other locally available materials.

Awareness of the health hazards associated with smoking varies amongst youths, but appears to have increased significantly. In a 1995 study (Kiangi), less than one-third of students thought tobacco caused health problems.[6] Older respondents were more aware than younger ones, and boys more than girls. In significant contrast, a large majority (82 percent) of a 2003 sample of primary students (Nyinondi) thought smoking was "a bad thing," with the main reason given as "causing health problems" (by 77 percent of respondents).[7] Three-quarters of the participants said they would not like to see their younger sibling smoking.

Relatively little research has been done on smokeless tobacco such as snuff and chewing tobacco, both of which are common modes of consumption in Tanzania, particularly in some rural areas. According to Nyinondi et al. (2009) these products are the most affordable and accessible ways of getting sufficient nicotine for those already tobacco-dependent in rural areas. Anecdotally, the members of the Tanzania Public Health Association (TPHA) have reported that smokeless tobacco products are readily accessible in markets, shops and from street vendors.[8] These products, observed primarily in northern and north-central Tanzania, were mostly made from pure tobacco in rural areas, or blended with spices in urban areas.

More empirically, in 2006, Mnyika et al. reported a low prevalence of oral snuff (1.9 percent) and nasal snuff (0.6 percent) in the Rural Moshi District, northern Tanzania, in a sample of candidates ranging from 15–36 years of age.[9] The authors also reported a decline of cigarette smoking from 36 percent in 1991 to 23.1 percent in 1997 in males. They reported higher prevalence of oral snuff use in females (3 percent) than males (0.5 percent), whereas there was no significant gender difference in the prevalence of nasal snuff.

More innovative packaging of chewing tobacco is currently making its way into the urban communities. In a 2008 baseline study of adolescents carried out in Ilala Municipality, Dar es Salaam, Kaduri et al. report a prevalence of tobacco use of 5.9 percent (9 percent for males and 2.4 percent for females), while that of smokeless tobacco use was 3.6 percent, or "about half of all who have ever smoked."[10] The popular brands of smokeless tobacco reported in this study were Kuberi (44.8 percent) and Gutka (6.9 percent), which are nontraditional packaged commodities. It was further reported that 41 percent of the smokeless tobacco users were daily users. The study sample included 1,011 participants, 50.7 percent males and 49.3 percent females, with a mean age of 14.5 years for males and 13.6 years for girls. Although these observations do not provide reliable estimates for a countrywide generalization, they indicate the widespread use of smokeless tobacco among youths in Tanzania. The alarming concern was that these smokeless tobacco products used in the latter study area were branded as nutritional supplements, and blended to different tastes and with varying strengths, which are often tempting to adolescents.

Politics of Tobacco

Existing laws and regulations

Tanzania's parliament passed the TPRA in February 2003. Passage of this act was historic, as it marked the first time in Tanzania that tobacco was acknowledged as a public health issue requiring national regulation. Reportedly, the Ministry of Health (MoH) was a key player in the development of the TPRA. But there is general agreement in the tobacco control community regarding the need to make this law consistent with FCTC standards and/ or to enforce more effectively the spirit of what exists already. According to tobacco control advocates, awareness of the law is low and enforcement is weak as there are no designated enforcement officers. For example, tobacco advertising and sponsorship (particularly in the music industry) and smoking in public places are rampant. Improving awareness and enforcement of the law are seen as priorities. Of course, if the weaker version cannot be enforced, passing a stricter version will not necessarily facilitate better enforcement. Tanzania signed the FCTC in 2003 but did not ratify it until 2007.

The main objectives of the TPRA are to regulate the manufacture, labeling, distribution, sale, use and promotion of tobacco products and to prohibit smoking in specified areas. The specific objectives of the act are:

1. protecting persons under 18 and other nonsmokers from inducements to use tobacco products;
2. protecting nonsmokers from exposure to tobacco smoke;
3. ensuring the population is adequately informed about the risk of using tobacco products and exposure to second-hand tobacco smoke and about the benefits of quitting smoking;
4. ensuring that tobacco products are modified to reduce harm to such an extent as may be technologically and practically possible; and
5. promoting a climate that will lead to a smoking-free atmosphere in all walks of life.

Beyond the policy areas discussed in the earlier policy-specific chapters, the act prohibits the manufacture or import of tobacco products that do not conform to standards prescribed by the Tanzania Bureau of Standards. A manufacturer of tobacco products is required to provide the minister of health with information about the product, and its emissions must be written on the package. However, the current information required is inadequate and obscure, and there are no graphic illustrations to deter especially beginning smokers.

The act outlaws the selling of tobacco products in restricted places, including: a primary or secondary school; a heath care establishment or a social services institution; a child care center; and public places and other places specifically set aside for persons under 18. The act exempts membership clubs and clubs performing social functions or activities from the prohibition of selling tobacco products. In addition to the noted exceptions to the prohibition, the enforcement of the law is scarcely implemented, and the repercussions to the offender negligible.

The law empowers the government to formulate regulations to implement the law, though none have been made to date, hence the ambiguity of its implementation. The law also empowers the government to appoint inspectors to oversee implementation and to impose fines to offenders. On the whole, this law has only received limited follow-through in enforcement.

The majority of stakeholders at the ATSA meetings believe that although a considerable proportion of the political class are in favor of tobacco control, the actual interpretation of the TPRA 2003 has been at odds with the spirit of the law. This is not surprising as different segments of the political spectrum and society have conflicting interests on the matter. Additional advocacy and education directed toward law makers and the public in general, and farmers in particular, are needed.

Overall political context

The political context of tobacco at the highest political levels is not well understood. While the president and vice president are not known to support or oppose tobacco control overtly, tobacco is generally accepted by the national government as an important source of revenue, both on the domestic market as well as a foreign exchange earner. There is an urgent need to educate politicians on the health impact of tobacco use, particularly the financial impact of the direct and indirect costs of tobacco use.

The MoH is currently the driving force for the tobacco control effort and the current minister (2010–11) has been publicly supportive of tobacco control activities. After the ratification of the FCTC, the MoH commissioned a review of its anti-tobacco law to conform to FCTC best practices. This process is gradually continuing, but most of those involved expect the process to take some time before it is concluded. There is a special technical committee set up by the MoH to discuss issues relevant to all stakeholders, and the TPHA and partners have been among the active parties contributing input to the review process.

But the speed and commitment of the MoH to tobacco control has been called publicly into question by national legislators. According to a news report, the government was about to present a bill to amend the 2003 Tobacco Products Regulatory Act in order to align the country's anti-smoking law with the FCTC, but as of mid-2011, no bill had been introduced.[11] In late 2009, in response to questions asked by MPs during the health ministry's 2009–10 budget speech debate, the health and social welfare minister stated explicitly that the current law is not in line with the FCTC, hence the need to review it. Furthermore, in response to pointed questions from parliamentarians about activities by the tobacco companies that negate the principles of being a party to the FCTC, the minister of health stated: "The process of reviewing our law is at an advanced stage and the Bill to that effect may be tabled in Parliament during the next session."[12] Of course, the minister had also recently commented that tobacco advertising had no effect on prevalence, only on brand choice by the consumer. Specifically, a number of MPs openly questioned the minister on why these activities were taking so long and wondered why the ministry simply appears to be watching on the sidelines while cigarette manufacturers continue with indiscriminate advertising of their products despite the fact that the country has already ratified the FCTC. However, it is also well known in Tanzania that it is common for parliamentarians to change political parties, and their positions and line of questioning on many issues including tobacco control are not always consistent.

The technical committee set up by the MoH is comprised of key stakeholders, and proponents of a new bill hope that they will be more assertive in pushing the pertinent dialogue and arguments more generally. A team of tobacco control advocates, supported by the Bloomberg Initiative to Reduce Tobacco Use, is spearheading activities necessary for the new legislation. They have been at the forefront of the law review and the strategic plan preparation, in close association with the MoH. That said, the tobacco control community is still relatively small and is seeking to expand so that it can better reach the myriad political actors who require education on the issues.

In considerable contrast, in November 2009, a spokesperson from the Ministry of Agriculture presented the ministry's views on tobacco publicly, reassuring interested parties that there was no immediate danger of the government cutting down support for tobacco farming in the near future. In addition, some MPs were publicly encouraging their respective constituencies to increase the acreage under tobacco cultivation.[13] These public pronouncements were, of course, in preparation for the general elections in 2010. The contrast of the pro-tobacco leaf statements and actions, and the health-based concerns expressed by other members of the legislature, underscores the complexity of the health minister's position with respect to the tobacco control law. Many tobacco control advocates observe that this confusion is also reflected among the Tanzanian population and will only be dispelled with intense education efforts.

Similarly, advocates working on the new proposed national legislation have commented that more information and education are also needed in order to influence the attorney general's (AG) office. There are already people within this office who have indicated support for a favorable interpretation of the 2003 legislation, as well as for corresponding enforcement, but further education on the issues would likely buttress this effort.

In various stakeholder meetings, the ATSA team did preliminary mapping of the positions of some other key ministers and ministry officials. First, with the eventual intent of adding tobacco issues to the national education curriculum, the Ministry of Education and Vocational Training is one of the key entry points to influence change. Since implementation happens in large part at the nonelected bureaucratic level, there is also a need to educate additional ministry officials, including the deputy minister and the commissioners of primary and secondary education to support tobacco control in schools and institutions under their administration. Similarly, in light of their mandate to help women and children, the minister for community development, gender and children's affairs and the ministry's permanent secretary are thought to be amenable to supporting new tobacco control regulations in order to protect their constituencies.

From the civil society and advocacy side, the Tanzania Tobacco Control Forum (TTCF) is a key player in information dissemination and street campaigns, as well as advocacy for an anti-tobacco law review, a ban on advertisements and a smoke-free Dar es Salaam. The organization is working alongside the World Health Organization (WHO) office in Tanzania on revising the Tobacco (Products Regulation) Act of 2003 (TPRA), and is also playing a pivotal role in the development of the National Tobacco Control Strategic Plan draft document. The TTCF is a nongovernmental network of individuals and associations that works with other stakeholders to pressure the government to review the tobacco regulation law to conform to the FCTC.

The Tanzania WHO office has been working closely with the MoH, the TPHA and TTCF to revise the TPRA (2003) to conform to FCTC best practices. This relationship is ongoing, and when in need, other stakeholders are also invited to support the process. The ATSA team has worked closely with these entities.

In addition to the WHO and IDRC, other international partners have provided financial support for various tobacco control activities. The Canadian Public Health Association (CPHA) has financially supported community awareness activities, printing of Electoral Commission (IEC) materials and support for student studies on tobacco and attendance at conferences to present research. The International Union Against Cancer (UICC), the American Cancer Society and the Framework Convention Alliance (FCA) have provided financial resources for public awareness, advocacy to local policymakers and other tobacco project activities implemented at the TPHA. Lastly, the Bloomberg Initiative's Campaign for Tobacco-Free Kids has provided a grant that has allowed a more intense and sustained campaign by TTCF, particularly in terms of the current review process of the new proposed legislation.

There have also been domestic partners who have consistently collaborated with the TPHA and other tobacco control–oriented organizations in combating the tobacco problem. Sokoine University of Agriculture (SUA) has executed research on tobacco prevalence in small studies, provided student training on tobacco and facilitated information dissemination at scientific conferences through professional presentations. The Lawyers Environmental Action Team (LEAT) has provided legal advice about tobacco control. The Tanzania Association of Nurses has worked with the TPHA in their own professional area to support tobacco control activities. Lastly, Tobacco Farmers Tanzania has, in some locations, been helpful in encouraging the adoption of alternative crops.

Potential opponents of tobacco control efforts include, particularly, tobacco growers and tobacco product manufacturers. Tobacco growing organizations include the aforementioned Tobacco Farmers Tanzania and the Tanzania Tobacco Growers Association, whose members' livelihoods depend on farming and selling cultivated tobacco leaf. This opposition can be addressed, at least in part, with the provision of alternative crops to replace tobacco in their particular districts. Domestic manufacturers, such as the Tanzania Tobacco Company, Tanzania Cigarette Company (TCC) and Dimon Alliance One, that receive semiprocessed leaf tobacco and process it further by blending and packaging it, oppose new legislation. Individual politicians and other members of the public involved directly (growers or shareholders of TCC) or indirectly (have important constituents who benefit from the industry) may also oppose new efforts. Finally, advertisers and media houses receive revenue from tobacco advertisements and are likely opponents to tobacco control activities.

Tobacco Industry

According to 2008 tobacco production figures from the Food and Agriculture Organization of the United Nations – Statistics (FAOSTAT), Tanzania is Africa's fourth largest tobacco producer after Malawi, Zimbabwe and Mozambique. Estimates of the number of tobacco-growing households vary from 70,000 to 140,000. Trade liberalization in the early 1990s partly contributed to the steady increase in tobacco production from 22,000 tons of green tobacco in 1993 to 52,000 tons in 1997. Thereafter, there was a dramatic slump in production as farmers failed to pay back tobacco companies for loaned inputs and credit subsequently dried up. Farm gate prices decreased as traders tried to recoup their losses. Production began to recover in 2001, rising to 33,000 tons in 2003, when tobacco exports earned US$43 million, accounting for 20 percent of all agricultural exports. According to a recent public pronouncement of the deputy minister of agriculture, total industry production from 2003–8 was TSh340 billion (an average of US$51 million per year). According to the most recent FAO records (2008), the country produced 50,600 tons of tobacco from approximately 36,000 hectares under tobacco cultivation.

Tobacco is among the major export crops, ranking fourth after coffee, cotton and tea. Tanzania accounts for 0.3 percent of world tobacco production, a proportion that has been steadily increasing since 2001. According to some estimates, as many as 1.3 million people depend directly or indirectly on tobacco for their livelihood, though this figure is poorly substantiated and likely includes store owners and clerks that sell not only tobacco but many other products.

At present, tobacco is grown as a cash crop in approximately 11 of the 126 districts in Tanzania. Furthermore, tobacco farming is reported to be expanding in some of these districts. A news report from 2009 reports that "Over 1,500 farmers in Serengeti district are expected to get 1.6bn from tobacco this season."[14] In the late 2000s, the Morogoro-based Alliance One Tanzania Ltd company has been buying tobacco leaf from farmers in the district after the Ministry of Agriculture, Food Security and Cooperatives announced that farmers could grow the crop in compliance with national legislation on tobacco cultivation.

Producer prices in the tobacco industry are determined in a consultative process involving the key actors in the system. These include representatives of producers (such as cooperative unions and estate owners), buyers, processors and the Tanzania Tobacco Board (TTB). These stakeholders constitute the Tobacco Council of Tanzania (TCT). In the last six crop seasons, farmers have received 30–38 percent of free-on-board (FOB) prices.

The major tobacco buyers are Tanzania Leaf Tobacco Company (TOPSERVE/TLTC), and Dimon Morogoro Tobacco Processors (DMTP). These and other tobacco buyers make up the Association of Tanzania Tobacco Traders (ATTT), which deals with input supply and green tobacco procurement. The ATTT buys and distributes inputs to the primary cooperative societies. The societies in turn distribute them to farmers on credit. The credit is recovered at the time of selling green tobacco. As in many countries growing tobacco, there is the usual problem with high charges for inputs and low returns for farmers, thus individual farmers can seldom overcome poverty. In addition, the temporary labor demands of harvesting and other associated activities systematically deprive thousands of children of social and educational opportunities.

The Tanzania Cigarette Company (TCC) is the largest tobacco manufacturer in the country, and is a subsidiary of Japan Tobacco International (JTI). According to its own annual reports, the TCC has invested US$100 million in processing and marketing since 1995. The TCC's sales have been increasing steadily, from 2,500 million cigarettes in 1994 to 3,900 million in 2003. The TCC's regional and other international exports have been steadily increasing, also, and represented about 10 percent of sales volume in 2001. The company's total tax contribution to the treasury reached a record high of US$40 million in 2001. Anecdotally, supporters of TCC claim that 5 percent of Tanzania's tax revenue comes from the TCC, the TCC has been one of East Africa's "most respected companies" for a number of years, it is the best performer on the (very small) Dar es Salaam stock exchange and it has 7,000 local shareholders. The shareholders include prominent local businesspeople and many other public figures.

As mentioned above, a large number of children are involved in tobacco cultivation, many of them at minimal wages. Some of the International Labour Organization's child labor programs have attempted to remove young people from tobacco farms and reintegrate them into formal primary education. The "Anti-Tobacco Initiative: An Advocacy Approach," initiated in 2003 by the TPHA in collaboration with other partners, aimed to sensitize Tanzanians to the hazards caused by the cultivation and use of tobacco. Although tobacco farmers were open to the idea of producing alternative crops, they were concerned that alternatives needed to have a market.

Tobacco production has clear environmental costs in Tanzania. Soil depletion, desertification, bush fires and pollution from fertilizers and herbicides are the most serious negative environmental consequences of tobacco cultivation. After fuel-wood and house construction, tobacco curing is the largest cause of deforestation in Tanzania. The average amount of wood consumed for tobacco curing between 1991 and 1995 was an estimated 22,000 tons annually, which means that each year, about 40,000 hectares of forest are cut down to cure tobacco. A World Agroforestry Centre (ICRAF) study (1997) showed that one acre of tobacco consumed between $15m^3$ and $25m^3$ of firewood. For many years, observers have considered Tabora Region – the largest tobacco-producer in the country – to be at risk of desertification if steps are not taken to reverse the loss of natural forest resulting from tobacco cultivation. By the early 1990s, farmers had to travel up to 10 km to find wood for curing. The effects of desertification were already visible in terms of forest removal, drought, irregular rains and whirlwinds, which had been uncommon in the area previously. Though there have been no follow-up studies, the root causes have not been addressed, and the problem has in near certainty grown worse.

ATSA Review

The ATSA program in Tanzania focused on a thorough analysis of the political and economic landscape of tobacco control with the ultimate goal of passing new legislation that improves upon the problematic TPRA. The process, spearheaded by the TPHA, involved a wide range of actors in civil society, government and research institutions. In a related project, the IDRC also sponsored a study to determine the feasibility of a tobacco taxation reform as a tobacco control strategy. Advocates of tobacco policy change continue to engage vigorously with these challenging issues.

Notes

1 Sources: CIA World Factbook https://www.cia.gov/library/publications/the-world-factbook/; except Organization of Economic Cooperation and Development (OECD) for development assistance statistics, and Food and Agriculture Organization of the United Nations – Statistics (FAOSTAT) for tobacco production. See http://stats.oecd.org/index.aspx and http://faostat.fao.org/site/567/default.aspx#ancor respectively (accessed 20 July 2011).

2 E. M. Mshiu and J. Siza, "Adolescent risk behaviour initiation: Factors influencing cigarette smoking and alcohol intake among primary school adolescents in Moshi Rural District, Tanzania" (2007), unpublished report.

3 F. Mokiti, "Prevalence of tobacco use among adolescents in three districts" (2009), unpublished report.

4 A. Swai, Donald G. McLarty, Henry M. Kitange, P. M. Kilima, S. Tatalla, N. Keen, L. M. Chuwa and K. George M. M. Alberti, "Low prevalence of risk factors for coronary heart disease in rural Tanzania," *International Journal of Epidemiology* 22. 4 (1993): 651–9.

5 K. Jagoe, R. Edwards, F. Mugusi, D. Whiting, and N. Unwin, "Tobacco smoking in Tanzania, East Africa: Population based smoking prevalence using expired alveolar carbon monoxide as a validation tool," *Tobacco Control* 11.3 (2002): 210–14.

6 Geoffrey Kiangi, Aulikki Nissinen, Erkki Vartiainen, Daniel Mtango and Markku Myllykangas , "Access to health information on alcohol and tobacco among adolescents in Tanzania," *Health Promotion International* 10.3 (1995): 167–75.

7 S. Nyinondi, "Factors that Influence Smoking among Secondary School Students in Ilala Municipality" (2004), Master of Public Health dissertation, University of Dar es Salaam, Tanzania.

8 S. Nyinondi, "Determinants of smokeless tobacco use among selected populations in Tanzania," presentation at the 14th World Conference on Tobacco or Health, Mumbai, India, 8–12 March 2009.

9 K. Mnyika, E. Klouman and K. Klepp, "Cigarette smoking and use of smokeless tobacco in Moshi Rural District in Northern Tanzania," *East African Journal of Public Health* 3 (2006): 24–7.

10 P. Kaduri, H. Kitua, J. Mbatia, A. Y. Kitua, and J. Mbwambo, "Smokeless tobacco use among adolescents in Ilala Municipality, Tanzania," *Tanzania Journal of Health Research* 10.1 (2008): 28–33.

11 *Daily News*, "News report," 31 July 2009.

12 Ibid.

13 O. Kiishwe, "Government All Out to Increase Tobacco Production," *Daily News*, 26 November 2009.

14 J. Mungini, "Serengeti Tobacco Farmers to Get 1.6bn," *Serengeti Daily News*, 5 February 2009.

Chapter 18

ZAMBIA

Fastone Goma, Muyunda Ililonga and Jeffrey Drope

Executive Summary

Despite Zambia's sizeable tobacco cultivation and its significant resource constraints (it is rated 165 of 177 countries on the Human Development Index), it is emerging as a tobacco control story with promise. It has signed and ratified the Framework Convention on Tobacco Control (FCTC), and has existing, though decidedly problematic, laws and apparent will in several key sectors to take on new tobacco control challenges. Prevalence rates have been poorly measured for adults, but appear to be high relative to other Sub-Saharan African countries. By some accounts, 40 percent of male adults are smokers (though probably not daily smokers) while less than 10 percent of women are smokers. Youth smoking is lower at around 10 percent for daily smokers. Zambia also has a growing problem with noncigarette tobacco use.

By nearly all accounts, most of the existing legislation is vague and weak, and requires redevelopment. There is a movement in the advocacy community to seek these changes in the form of new legislation. This task, however, will require major efforts on the part of the advocacy community to educate (and seek to influence) policymakers using solid research. With a new government, there may be a genuine window of opportunity to pursue this avenue in the short term and many high-level policymakers have indicated overt support for tobacco control including the president, the vice president, the minister of agriculture and the mayor of Lusaka (the capital city). Moreover, there is an active tobacco control advocacy community, and several competent research professionals are engaged in tobacco control. Enforcement of the existing laws has been traditionally weak (even nonexistent in some areas). While waiting for new legislation, however, some new efforts to enforce the existing laws are in progress. There is a large (African Tobacco Situation Analysis (ATSA)–sponsored) movement to enforce the smoke-free laws in Lusaka, which has thus far received widespread public support including from high-level officials and the media.

The tobacco control community has also recently pursued the development of cessation programs and the incorporation of tobacco control into the healthcare curriculum. In 2009, four different clinics in Lusaka began to offer cessation services (which is very rare in most of Africa). Cessation and other aspects of tobacco control are being introduced into the curriculum of most healthcare professional programs including medicine, nursing and medical technology.

The tobacco industry is visibly present in the country and uses various marketing techniques and particularly corporate social responsibility (CSR) strategies to remain visible. Any new tobacco control legislation will need to address this challenge directly.

Country Profile[1]

Population in 2009 (global and African ranking):	11,862,740 (72, 19)
Geographical size (global ranking):	752,618 sq. km (46)
GDP by purchasing power parity in 2008 (global ranking):	US$17.5 billion (129)
GDP real growth rate (2006–8):	6.2%
GDP per capita (global ranking):	US$1,500 (199)
Main industries:	Copper mining and processing, construction, foodstuffs, beverages, chemicals, textiles, fertilizer, horticulture (including corn, sorghum, rice, peanuts, sunflower seed, vegetables, flowers, tobacco)
Languages:	English (official), Bemba, Kaonda, Lozi, Lunda, Luvale, Nyanja, Tonga, other (70+ indigenous languages)
Official development assistance (ODA) – total commitments/disbursements (2007):	US$1,028.2/830.2 million
ODA as a percentage of GDP:	7.3%
Largest donors (disbursements in millions of USD):	USA 165.3, Japan 94.6, EC 82.4, Norway 74.4, UK 74, Netherlands 71.5, Sweden 53.7, Global Fund 41.8, 2007
Tobacco production by volume in 2007 (global ranking):	48,000 tons (50)

| Tobacco exports (2007): | Tobacco (unmanufactured): 36,649 tons at $3,139 per ton, #1 export; cigarettes: 126 tons at $5,405 per ton, #18 export |
| Tobacco imports (2007): | Cigarettes: 965 metric tons at $8,824 per ton, #3 import |

Brief Description of Political System

Type:	Zambia is a presidential republic.
Executive:	President Rupiah Banda (since 19 August 2008); Vice President George Kunda (since 14 November 2008).[2]
Cabinet:	Appointed by the president from among members of the National Assembly.
Legislature:	The unicameral National Assembly is comprised of 158 seats. 150 members are elected by popular vote and eight members are appointed by the president to serve five-year terms. There is a movement for multiparty democracy. This movement holds 72 seats, whilst the Patriotic Front (PF) has 44 seats and the United Democratic Alliance (UDA) 27 seats.
Judiciary:	Justices are appointed by the president.

Scope of Tobacco Problem

The results from prevalence surveys in Zambia vary widely, as reported in Table 18.1, although consistently reports suggest that rates are comparatively high for Sub-Saharan Africa. Unfortunately, however, the surveys use different methodologies and are not easily comparable. One likely cause of the discrepancies in the surveys is the lack of distinction between "daily" smoker and "current" smoker – the latter category includes both those who smoke daily and those who smoke occasionally. For example, the Ministry of Health and Central Statistical Office estimated in 1998 that adult (>18 years) smoking prevalence rates were 35 percent for males and 10 percent for females.[3] The estimates for 2001 demonstrated a probable increase to 40 percent among adult males while there was a decline to 7 percent among females.[4] These surveys appear to be reporting current smokers.

In contrast, the Demographic and Health Survey (DHS) of 2007 showed a significantly lower smoking prevalence: 23.8 percent among men and 0.7 percent among women (15–49 years of age). Similarly, the World Health Organization's (WHO) most recent World Health Survey (WHS) in 2003 cites prevalence of daily smoking of tobacco (i.e. cigarettes and other products) to be 14.8 percent among men and 3.2 percent among women.

Table 18.1. Zambia – Most recent national prevalence rates

Year	Male	Female	Type of use and age	Source
2001	40	7	Current smokers > 18 years old	Ministry of Health report, 2001
2001	15	10	Smokeless tobacco > 18 years old	Ministry of Health report, 2001
2001	15	5	Current smoker > 25 years old	Ministry of Health report, 2001
2002	10.8	8.3	Current smoker, 13–15 years old	GYTS, 2002
2002	25.7	23.7	User of any tobacco product, 13–15 years old	GYTS, 2002
2003	14.8	3.2	Daily smokers > 18 years old	World Health Survey, 2003
2003	22.7	5.7	Current smokers	World Health Survey, 2003
2003	28.6	2.1	Daily smokers of any tobacco, 15–49 years old	DHS, 2003
2003	23.2	0.70	Daily cigarette smokers, 15–49 years old	DHS, 2003
2007	21.2	0.3	Daily cigarette smoking – urban, 15–49 years old	DHS, 2007
2007	24.7	1.1	Daily cigarette smoking – rural, 15–49 years old	DHS, 2007
2009	17.5	1.5	Daily cigarette smoking – > 25 years old (in Lusaka)	University of Zambia/WHO/ Ministry of Health

The much lower statistics from the DHS and WHO most likely reflect daily versus current users (daily and nondaily). However, in a country like Zambia, where many smokers cannot afford to smoke every day, it is important to consider both statistics.[5]

Research has also explored prevalence rates in important discrete groups. For example, researchers consistently find rural-urban differences in prevalence rates. While only 0.3 percent of women 15–49 years old were smoking in urban areas, more than three times as many (1.1 percent) were smoking in rural areas. The difference was smaller between urban and rural male smokers but still significant (21.3 percent urban versus 24.7 percent rural). The DHS 2007 also showed that smoking was more prevalent among the less educated, and those in the lower socioeconomic quintiles. The major tobacco types consumed in Zambia include manufactured cigarettes, hand rolled/refuse tobacco, piped tobacco, chewed tobacco and snuff. Furthermore, most of the adults reported that they started smoking when they were adolescents.

The Global Youth Tobacco Survey (GYTS), a school-based survey conducted among 13–15-year-olds, has been executed twice in Zambia. The GYTS 2002 demonstrated a prevalence of current smokers of 10.8 percent among boys and 8.3 percent among the girls, while in the GYTS 2007, researchers found that a slightly lower 8.2 percent of adolescents were currently smoking (10.4 percent for males and 6.2 percent for females). In Lusaka District, there were no significant gender differences observed in the current cigarette smoking rates between boys and girls in both 2002 and 2007 (9.4 percent males versus 8.7 percent females and 6.7 percent males versus 6.8 percent females, respectively).[6] However, the surveyors noted that there are significant rural-urban differences among youths as well, with rural youths having higher rates of tobacco use than urban youths.[7]

The GYTS surveys reveal other important findings beyond cigarette smoking. Notably – perhaps even dramatically – in the 2002 survey, researchers found that 25.7 percent of male and 23.7 percent of female adolescents in Zambia had been using *any* form of tobacco. Clearly, noncigarette tobacco consumption is a major issue. While there are few hard data on the subject, the consensus amongst stakeholders is that a sizeable proportion of the population – particularly in lower socioeconomic groups – uses smokeless tobacco products (such as chewed tobacco). It is also thought to be more prevalent amongst women (who do not want to be seen smoking cigarettes for cultural stigma reasons) and people in rural areas (perhaps most in the tobacco-growing areas). The GYTS 2002 reported a smokeless tobacco prevalence of 20 percent among males and 22.9 percent among females aged 13–15. But data on total consumption of forms of tobacco other than cigarettes are sparse, generating a concern that an overemphasis on cigarette smoking can obscure the pervasiveness of total tobacco use.

The latest prevalence data come from a survey of 1928 adults over the age of 25 that demonstrates an overall daily prevalence rate in Lusaka of 6.8 percent – 17.5 percent for men and 1.5 percent for women.[8] The study also focuses on body mass and makes a worrying connection between low body mass and smoking. It calls for more research on the association between tobacco use and poor nutrition.

More national-level prevalence surveys are needed to establish more accurately the tobacco challenges in Zambia. In 2010, Zambia was selected as one the countries in which the General Adult Tobacco Survey (GATS) will be executed.

Politics of Tobacco Control

Existing and pending tobacco control laws, executive orders and regulations

Zambia started its campaign against tobacco long before the FCTC. There has been active advocacy from civil society organizations for many years for better tobacco control policy. There has been sporadic support for these policies from the government, but with the signing of the FCTC and other positive indications, there is optimism in the public health field that this support is growing.

In 1992, the government passed a number of tobacco-related bills. Among other provisions, these bills banned the following: sales to minors under the age of 16 (Public Health (Tobacco) Regulation (PH(T)R) 1992), product giveaways (PH(T)R 1992 and Health Regulation-Statutory Instrument No. 163 of 1992, dated 7 December 1992), pro-tobacco advertising in the media and smoking in various public places (including, but not necessarily limited to, government buildings, private worksites, educational facilities, healthcare facilities and public transport). In addition, each tobacco product package had to read "WARNING: TOBACCO IS HARMFUL TO HEALTH." However, this forward-thinking legal framework was not effectively enforced, leading to a decade and a half of inertia in Zambian tobacco control.

On 28 May 2008, the Zambian government acceded to the FCTC. Later in the year, it enacted Local Government Statutory Instrument #39, which reiterated the ban on smoking in public places; moreover, it specified that the package warning be printed on the two largest sides of each packet in bold letters against a contrasting background. However, even this improved legislation has been said to be too vague and vulnerable to abuse. Tobacco control advocates widely believe that a single and more comprehensive law must now be enacted to reflect the demands of the FCTC.

The legal infrastructure to establish effective tobacco control in Zambia is already in place. Zambian elected officials, with the possible exception of certain MPs on the relevant tobacco control subcommittee, are not impeding tobacco control. Tobacco control advocates argue convincingly that there is a genuine opportunity for advancement in key tobacco control policies in the near term.

Overall political context

For a country that produces a large amount of tobacco leaf, there is encouraging evidence of support for tobacco control, even at the highest levels of government. There is also an active civil society that is engaged in the effort, and has proven to interact effectively with government on tobacco control issues. This civil society movement is also growing in size and scope.

It is worthwhile to note the important official and unofficial steps that advocates must understand and navigate in order to achieve policy change. The legislative process has six major steps in Zambia and requires support from a number of key actors and institutions. In particular, several key ministries will surely play pivotal roles in new tobacco control policies. All new legislation must be proposed by a ministry, and at any step in the process can be sent back to that ministry for redrafting. In reality, any draft tobacco control legislation is likely to go to the Ministry of Health (MoH) to begin the legal process.

Based on the typical legislative process in Zambia, comprehensive tobacco control policy will likely pass through the following steps:

1. The MoH adopts legislative text after consulting all "stakeholders" and forwards it on to the Ministry of Justice for review (each ministry has its own internal process for this step).
2. The Ministry of Justice reviews the legislation and proposes any changes to the initiating ministry. If the two ministries agree on the text, it is forwarded to the cabinet office for inclusion on the cabinet agenda.
3. The full cabinet reviews the legislation and if consensus is reached, it is scheduled for presentation to parliament.
4. A parliamentary select committee reviews the legislation and if approved, schedules a first and second reading in parliament.
5. If 50 percent of the 105-member parliament approves the legislation, it is forwarded to the president for final approval.
6. When the president signs the legislation, it becomes law.

At the highest level, there is some circumstantial evidence that the president (as of 2011), Rupiah Banda, supports tobacco control. The president took office when the previous president, Levy Mwanawasa, died in office in July 2008. Notably, Banda was the vice president when the FCTC was signed (Mwanawasa was reportedly openly pro-tobacco control). That role acknowledged, President Banda is also sympathetic to the cause of tobacco farmers and has pledged to help them get better prices for their products. In any event, tobacco control advocates identify the strong and continuing need to educate the president and his staff on the FCTC and to demonstrate that tobacco cultivation and tobacco control, at least at this point, need not be mutually exclusive. There is a presidential election in late 2011, and advocates will need to renew their efforts to communicate with this office after the election.

Similarly, the vice president for 2008–11, George Kunda, only took office after Mwanawasa's death, but he was the justice minister when the signing of the FCTC took place, and thus had some input into the broader tobacco control debate (including the accession to the FCTC). Importantly, the ATSA team believes that there is need for closer association with him in order to get his overt support. In a very encouraging sign in May of 2009, the vice president's office sent an official representative (the deputy health minister) to launch officially the smoke-free Lusaka initiative.

A number of key ministries will potentially have major effects on the success of any new tobacco control measures. Generally in Zambia, there is relatively high turnover among ministers. That said, the pool of applicants generally considered for this type of service is not too large, and pundits have observed that the same small number of individuals tend to hold these highest offices, though their actual positions change from time to time. For example, due to the recent change in presidential administrations in 2009, there are many ministers new to their particular ministry, though many are not new to cabinet. These dynamics could be viewed as both a challenge and an opportunity. On one hand, many of the ministers do not yet know very much about tobacco control, presenting a genuine chance to educate them. On the other hand, there is some stability to who holds the powerful positions, so education can be an effective tool. Clearly, establishing and maintaining relationships with multiple ministers is a very demanding task that requires enormous efforts and sufficient resources on the part of the tobacco control community. But, this task will be pivotal to the success of the community's efforts. The tobacco industry is no doubt making similar calculations.

The MoH is arguably the key ministry for tobacco control. In general, the minister, his/her deputy and the highest-ranking nonelected officials (especially the permanent secretary and the director for public health and research) tend to be pro-health, pro-tobacco control and keen to support initiatives that enhance the well-being of the general public. With high turnover at the ministerial level, there is need to give any new minister (and those under him/her) orientation on the matters contained in the FCTC and to enhance harmony with the other officers in tobacco control. There is a particular need to enlighten the highest-level ministry officials on the lack of implementation of the Public Health Act (1992) clauses on tobacco control in order to give them the necessary leverage for further policy development and implementation.

Moreover, the ATSA team argues that there is a serious need to lobby the ministry for the enactment of a comprehensive law on tobacco control. In a hopeful sign, after FCTC ratification, the ministry established a national tobacco control office and appointed a focal point person. This focal person has been active in tobacco control activities including the Lusaka smoke-free initiative in 2009 since his appointment.

The Ministry for Local Government is another important ministry for tobacco control generally, but perhaps particularly for smoke-free policies. The ministry played a key role in passing Instrument #39 – a regulatory instrument that reiterated the previous major tobacco-related public health legislation from 1992 (described in greater detail below). As of 2010, in addition to Instrument #39 that bans smoking in public places, the ministry is reportedly in the process of drafting more regulations to supplement this law. There is need to influence this ongoing process by meeting with ministry officials to ensure the drafting of competent regulations and/or guidelines.

The Ministry of Education (MoE) and the Ministry of Youth and Sport are also potentially important in tobacco control efforts. The MoE has not taken a strong stance on tobacco. For example, as of early 2011, completely smoke-free schools are not yet a reality in Zambia. Similarly, there is little inclusion of tobacco issues in school curricula. The Ministry of Youth and Sport has not taken a position on tobacco, but it is known that ministry representatives have been courted by British American Tobacco (BAT), which has sponsored sports events for youths. There is a serious need to educate these ministers and their staffs on tobacco issues and the tactics of the tobacco industry.

There are concerns in the tobacco control community that the Ministry of Agriculture may be opposed to the aims of tobacco control programs because of the economic importance of tobacco production. The first agriculture minister in the Banda administration, Hon. Brigadier General Dr Brian Chituwo, is a medical doctor and was the minister of health who signed the FCTC in the previous government. He is overtly pro-tobacco control, and was expected to be a strong advocate for alternative crops while rendering a strong voice for tobacco control. One of his early major policy decisions was to withdraw technical assistance to tobacco cultivation. Unfortunately, in late 2009, he was moved from the Ministry of Agriculture to the Ministry of Science and Technology. His replacement, the Hon. Peter Daka, did not have a known position on tobacco control but comes from the tobacco-growing region of the Eastern Province of Zambia. There is concern in the tobacco control community that he is likely to be one of the strongest adversaries in government.

The position of the Ministry of Commerce, Industry and Trade is more complex. In 2009, the minister, Felix Mutati, made some statements that could potentially be problematic for tobacco control. Specifically, he exhorted Zambians to do more tobacco processing in Zambia, rather than exporting leaf to other countries for processing.[9] He also said that he would be discussing the matter in greater detail with the minister of agriculture to see what the government could do to promote the effort. This economic program is an ongoing concern in a country where tobacco cultivation is on the dramatic increase.

One of the Ministry of Finance's primary foci is to maximize revenue collection for the government. A boost in tobacco production leading to increased tax revenue would be very appealing to the ministry. The financial burden imposed by heath care costs related to tobacco use is usually overlooked compared to the pressures of balancing the national budget. Persuading the ministry to be more attentive to issues of tobacco control will not succeed without a clear crop substitution – and therefore, revenue replacement – argument.

Legislatively, there has been evidence of solid support for tobacco control measures, as well as some focused opposition. First, the Parliamentary Committee on Health and Social Services has traditionally been enthusiastic to partner with research organizations who can feed into their information systems on any subject of public health importance. There is an immediate need to lobby this committee for the enforcement of the existing laws and for the enactment of a more comprehensive tobacco law. Similarly, the Parliamentary Committee on Local Government facilitated the signing of the Instrument #39, and is thus seen as a serious ally in the fight against tobacco use. However, longtime advocates expressed concern that committee members seem to be rather naïve towards the devious tactics of the tobacco industry, which has been seriously courting some of them. In terms of legislative opposition, the MPs from tobacco-growing areas and those courted by the tobacco industry may be opponents.

At the local level, tobacco control advocates recognize that mayors, city councilors, town clerks and local authorities will play very large roles in the success of some of these measures, particularly the enforcement of smoke-free policies. These local officials are important because they can sometimes pass even stiffer bylaws, but will definitely need to exert greater effort at publicizing and enforcing tobacco control bylaws in the municipality where they govern (see the discussion below on Lusaka).

Fortunately, Zambia has a vigorous civil society and academic community that have taken particular interest in these issues, and are actively involved in the tobacco control movement. The Zambia Consumer Association (ZACA) has been instrumental in spearheading the tobacco control campaign in Zambia. With support from international organizations such as the Bloomberg Initiative's Campaign for Tobacco-Free Kids (CTFK) and Corporate Accountability International, ZACA has worked closely with the MoH to foster the signing and accession of the FCTC and enhance the profile of the World No Tobacco Day (WNTD) commemoration. ZACA has also been a keen participant at the FCTC's Conference of the Parties (COP) meetings. It has held numerous events that sensitize important actors – journalists, senior civil servants, lawyers – to tobacco control issues. It has also begun to build a network of other NGOs – the Tobacco Control Network – with which it has worked on other consumer issues to help further the cause. These organizations include the Resident Doctors Association (RDA), the Young Women's Christian Association of Zambia (YWCA), the Female Lawyers Association of Zambia (FLAZ), the Young Men's Christian Association of Zambia (YMCA) and the University of Zambia Students Union.

The Tobacco Free Association of Zambia (TOFAZA) is a newer group with wide participation from the Mount Makulu Research Centre (an agricultural research organization), the Ministry of Agriculture and the general public. Membership in the association gives particular advantage when it comes to working with certain offices, particularly the Ministry of Agriculture. While it is strong when it comes to lobbying activities, TOFAZA also has capacity for research formulation, data analysis and scientific dissemination of information.

The Zambia Anti-Smoking Society (ZASS) has been a partner in all previous tobacco control lobby groups in Zambia. The society is strong at lobbying, especially at the MoH where it worked toward ensuring the signing of the FCTC.

The Mental Health Association of Zambia (MHAZ) is a professional organization that has identified tobacco as a substance of abuse and is keen to facilitate processes that would lead to its "cure." Thus, the MHAZ is keen to promote efforts towards preventing use/abuse of tobacco, and also in helping with cessation programs.

The University of Zambia (UNZA) is currently the leading institution in tobacco-related research, particularly through its School of Medicine (SoM) and the Institute for Economic and Social Research (INESOR). Several members of the Tobacco Control Consortium are from these institutions and will be instrumental in preparing the necessary evidence-based tobacco control research as the greater program matures and bears fruit. In particular, these professionals have been and will be instrumental in facilitating cessation programs in the various health centers. However, UNZA personnel have identified a need for some amount of orientation to build further capacity. In particular, scholars suggest that it would be desirable to set specific training for faculty (training of trainers), students and allied health workers in issues of tobacco use and tobacco control with emphasis on training for cessation of tobacco use. These actors will be pivotal in the dissemination of the tobacco control messages, especially from a health perspective. The current gap in knowledge is demonstrated by the results of the 2009 Global Health Professions Students Survey (GHPSS), which illustrate that tobacco is not incorporated effectively into the curricula of medical, pharmacy and nursing students (see below for further discussion).

Both print and electronic media have carried positive messages on smoke-free environments, but to a large extent there is need for training to have them as true strategic partners. Media organizations or personnel would not be opponents of tobacco control in the ordinary meaning of the word "opponent." However, they may be influenced by contractual relationships (especially advertising) and personal material benefits (for individual journalists or editors). Tobacco campaigns all over the world continue to use their abundant resources to peddle influence. The ATSA team argues that there is need to facilitate increased activity among the different media through capacity-building, and actively began such efforts in 2009.

Key potential opponents to tobacco control include the tobacco industry (discussed below) and the Tobacco Board of Zambia. The board is a parastatal organization that was established by the national government in the early 1970s to promote tobacco farming in Zambia, which was seen then as a potential foreign exchange earner outside of copper production. The board has offered technical advice and loans to small-scale farmers in order to increase their participation in tobacco farming in the past. Over time, the role of the board has changed to that of providing a trading platform (auction) for tobacco farmers and leaf buying companies. It has great influence in the tobacco trade in Zambia.

There are a number of other important agricultural organizations in Zambia that may be potential opponents. All of these organizations are comprised of members who benefit directly or indirectly from tobacco growing and trade. The organizations include: the Tobacco Association of Zambia (TAZ) – a grouping of commercial tobacco growers; the Agricultural Consultative Forum – a public/private organization that promotes dialogue and fosters partnerships in the agriculture sector; the Zambia Association of High Value Crops (ZAHVAC); Zambia Women in Agriculture (ZWIA); the National Farmers' Union (ZNFU); the National Peasants and Small-Scale Farmers Association; and the Zambia Export Growers Association (ZEGA).

ATSA Action – Enforcement of a Smoke-free Lusaka (Capital City)

Many of the most important political actors that will ensure the success of a smoke-free Lusaka are municipal-level officials including the mayor, the city council and high-level city and town clerks. Furthermore, relevant enforcement agencies – the police, the environmental health officers (EHOs) and members of the provincial/district administration – continue to be pivotal in implementing and enforcing smoke-free laws. Finally, health authorities are an integral part of the ongoing campaign. With a major initiative underway, there is an opportunity to examine closely the politics of this effort.

In terms of promoting a smoke-free Lusaka, UNZA, ZACA and the MoH have facilitated the formation of a consortium of NGOs, which was named the Zambia Tobacco Control Campaign (ZTCC). They have also identified and sought to engage other interest groups who should be involved in tobacco control, particularly those already involved in public education and awareness (including women, children, environment, religious, consumer, youth, farmers' and other community-based groups). Such groups can help to disseminate information and conduct the public education and awareness campaign for smoke-free places. The ATSA team proposed utilizing drama groups (see discussion below), local celebrities, other civic leaders, the National Arts Council and professional musicians in the public awareness campaigns (e.g. radio programs) and other targeted activities.

Similarly, a number of major professional organizations – the Zambia Medical Association (ZMA), the Zambia Nurses Association (ZNA), the RDA and other allied professional organizations – have been eager to contribute to tobacco control efforts. These groups – all comprised of health professionals – are important as potential allies in the campaign because people believe in health professionals to provide accurate information and frank advice in any health-related discourse. The ZMA is part of the tobacco control consortium and has proven to be an excellent ally in the information dissemination campaign, particularly providing information for the phone-in radio programs. Doctors presented tobacco-related topics in obstetrics and gynecology, pediatrics and surgical oncology, among other specific areas. The programs attracted widespread public attention because of the respect that health officers command in Zambian society, and because they were very lively with many hard-hitting questions and corresponding insightful answers. Though the ZNA did not join the consortium after being approached to participate, nurses are part of the cessation trainings in the ATSA-sponsored program, and a large number of nurses are being used to screen patients in the urban clinics. Finally, the RDA was approached but did not join the consortium. Notably, however, individual doctors, resident doctors and nurses are participating actively in the consortium.

At an early stakeholders' meeting in April 2009, the ZTCC leadership (spearheaded by UNZA and the MoH tobacco focal point official) brought together many of the key stakeholders. By the leaders' account, a major lesson learned was that there are many in the Zambian population who desire to participate in tobacco control, and a little stimulus (such as an inclusive meeting/workshop) goes a long way in engaging them. In fact, the city council was more than willing to take leadership in enforcement of the smoke-free law – they had simply lacked the means to get the whole process into motion.

After the April 2009 meeting, the ATSA team visited the following officials to discuss and solicit support for the ZTCC and the smoke-free Lusaka initiative: the permanent secretary for Lusaka Province; the town clerk of the Lusaka City Council; the director of public health and research at the Ministry of Health; Senior Chieftainess Nkomeshya Mukamambo II; the district commissioner for Lusaka; the permanent secretary at the Ministry of Local Government and Housing; the commissioner of the Zambia Police; the commissioner of the Drug Enforcement Commission (DEC); the permanent secretary of the Ministry of Justice; the administrator of the High Court; and the mayor of Lusaka. All of these officials would likely influence a successful campaign.

Beyond the overarching opponents to tobacco control described above, some key members of the business community, especially bar and tavern owners, may actively oppose smoke-free efforts as there is a perception that it will reduce their business clientele. Importantly, the team engaged the president of the Liquor Traders Association (from Lusaka), who has offered his support. There is a continuing need to educate these actors in order to comply with the tobacco-free environmental laws, including displaying appropriate "NO SMOKING" signs and not selling tobacco to minors.

Under the same initiative, TOFAZA led a workshop in May 2009 to build capacity in the area of disseminating information about smoke-free policies. In the workshop, a total of 20 TOFAZA members were trained. There was a particular focus on the utility of drama as an educational tool in city neighborhoods and other communities. A core team of 12 are being used as resource persons for training drama artists for creative dissemination to the general public, which addresses some central communication challenges including literacy issues. A drama group was subsequently identified from the Ng'ombe community, which had a number of educated, young men and women who understood English well but also performed well in their local language, which greatly facilitated the process since there was no need to translate the material for presentation. By the end of 2009, the actors were already trained and were actively utilizing drama groups for tobacco control dissemination activities.

The ZTCC project has received enormous support and a buy-in from the highest official levels. The campaign was successfully launched officially on 20 May 2009 at Lusaka's Mulungushi International Conference Center. In partnership with the Lusaka City Council's mayor, the town clerk and environmental health officers, ZACA organized the event. The event began with a 2 km march through city streets past a prominent shopping area to the conference center. The participants were led by the mayor, the deputy mayor, the town clerk, the ranking official from the district commissioner's office, and from the ZTCC, Dr Goma (UNZA) and Mr Musenga (ZACA). The permanent secretary for Lusaka Province and the commissioner of the DEC joined the team at the venue. Other important participants included ZACA officials, environmental health officers from the Lusaka City Council and the MoH, teachers, community members, TOFAZA members, media practitioners and consortium members. The vice president's office sent the deputy health minister, Mr Mwendoi Akakandelwa, to read the vice president's speech and cut the official opening ribbon. All of the speeches, including those of the mayor and the president of the Liquor Traders' Association, emphasized the need for enforcement of the smoke-free law. One of the highlights was a performance by the newly trained drama group from Ng'ombe about the perils of smoking, which was received with great enthusiasm by the attendees.

Building on their early success, the smoke-free Lusaka effort is ongoing. After the event, the ZTCC has followed up with vigorous public awareness efforts including leaflets, brochures, major distribution of "no smoking" signs, radio programs and television appearances by ZTCC members. A two-day training for EHOs within Lusaka District was conducted to prepare them for the implementation and enforcement of the smoke-free Lusaka campaign. Relevant materials were distributed by the EHOs to public outlets within the city.

After the event, local authorities expressed interest in following up on the enforcement of the law. Accordingly, ZACA and the town clerk met to discuss future actions. Shortly thereafter, the local authorities undertook to meet with various stakeholders in the city in order to sensitize them to the implementation of the smoke-free law in Lusaka. These stakeholders include: the Liquor Traders Association of Zambia, the Zambia Chamber of Commerce and Industry, the Zambia National Marketers Union, the Zambia Bus Drivers and Taxis Association, and the Zambia National Hotel Caterers Association. These groups are comprised of businesspeople who run bars and restaurants, marketers who sell cigarettes informally in street markets, and taxi and bus owners who must observe the law insofar as smoking in public transport is concerned. These meetings were held separately with each interest group in order to avoid conflicts due to vested interests.

Also, the local authorities undertook to carry smoke-free messages on their internally generated documents that go to the public, such as bills for house rent, bills for municipal water and sanitation services, bills for land rates, and other official correspondence. As of early 2011, these measures have not yet been implemented due to understaffing, the high expenses to alter existing documents, and technical limitations in the public relations unit. However, city authorities continue to assure the ZTCC and ZACA that they will follow through with the program. Finally, the city authorities expressed a desire for a study-tour of several cities that have successfully implemented smoke-free policies, and ZACA is endeavoring to facilitate such a tour.

ATSA Action – Tobacco Cessation

As described in the overall political context above, the Ministry of Health is generally supportive of initiatives that promote general health and well-being. While they will be keen to render support for cessation programs, there will be need for positive engagement so that for the sake of long-term sustainability, they will take ownership of the program and domesticate it within the selected institutions and existing health system. This is being done with the direct help of the ministry's tobacco focal point person who is a member of the consortium.

One of the first steps by the ATSA team was to inform and engage the provincial and district directors of health about the benefits of cessation programs, particularly in order to facilitate the processes for the implementation of the programs in the Zonal Health Centres. The implementing officers are health center personnel, the medical officers, medical licentiates, nurses and EHOs. These professionals need adequate competence training in various cessation techniques, and will need to interface with the community-based structures such as the Health Centre Committees (HCC), which will carry positive information into the communities.

The consortium sought to build capacity in the team by training trainers in cessation work. First, Dr Fastone Goma, a physician on the team attended the Training Enhancement in Applied Counseling and Health (TEACH Project) course offered by the Centre for Addiction and Mental Health (CAMH) at the University of Toronto, Canada. Second, to further the process of training, technical assistance was requested from the International Development Resarch Centre (IDRC), which sent Dr Lekan Ayo-Yusuf, an associate professor at the University of Pretoria with expertise in training motivational interviewing, to Lusaka to assist the team. The district medical officer allowed three to five healthcare professionals from each clinic to participate in this training. This first training had 19 participants who included clinical officers, dental therapists and nurses. It effectively covered two days, with the first day being dedicated mostly to theory and instructive lectures, whereas the second day was more about building skills. By all accounts of the participants, the training was very successful. Substantively, there is a deliberate inclination towards nonpharmacological approaches to the treatment of tobacco dependence in order to address poverty and the specific tobacco use practices in Zambia.

Following the training, each team from a selected clinic was given the task of formulating an action plan of how to implement the cessation program in their particular clinics. These action plans were discussed at a meeting held on 17 August 2009. These action plans were further harmonized at a consensus-building workshop. The participants of the meeting generated the following recommendations: 1) train all the health workers in the clinics so that cessation becomes a routine practice; 2) establish cessation "corners" for more in-depth counseling and follow-up visits; 3) train community agents such as community health workers and tuberculosis counselors in cessation of tobacco use; and 4) establish community-based tobacco use cessation support groups.

The processes to regularize cessation practice have commenced in the selected clinics. From inception, it is being made clear that this is an exercise that just enhances the traditional clinical practice and it is not a parallel program. Thus the brief motivational interviewing is to be routine practice for each frontline health worker. However, these workers have been supplied with additional records for the purposes of monitoring and evaluation. The cessation corners share facilities with other corners such as tuberculosis, reproductive health and anti-retroviral therapy, which have been running as routine counseling sites for the clinics. This structure should guarantee sustainability beyond the project's lifecycle.

An analysis of GHPSS 2009 data shows a deficiency of tobacco-related issues in the curricula of the health professional students – only 6.8 percent of respondents had received tobacco cessation training of any kind. There is need to lobby further for the inclusion of tobacco issues in the standard health training, so that it really becomes routine practice. The ATSA team is preparing for this eventuality. From the team of the previously tobacco-trained health workers it is proposed that a core of trainers can be readily identified who can then facilitate in-service training of their colleagues.

Tobacco Industry Monitoring

Production

Zambia is rapidly becoming one of the world's leading producers of tobacco leaf (as of 2008, according to the Food and Agriculture Organization of the United Nations – Statistics (FAOSTAT), it is seventeenth in the world and fifth in Africa). Production statistics from the Ministry of Agriculture demonstrate steady increases in the production of Burley and Virginia tobacco from 1989–90 to 2001–2, from about 5,000 to 13,000 metric tons (combined). In 2003–4, there was a large spike when production exceeded 20,000 tons for the first time. This increase is in large part a result of tobacco farmers fleeing the political and economic instability in Zimbabwe and immigrating to Zambia to grow tobacco (among other crops). There has also been a recent shift from cultivating Burley tobacco to Virginia tobacco, which is better suited for Zambian soil conditions. Tobacco is an important cash crop for government revenues, and the government has been giving subsidies to small farmers in order to encourage more tobacco growing. Zambia lacks tobacco-processing capabilities; instead, nearly 99 percent of Zambian tobacco is exported. The destinations of tobacco exports include neighboring countries like Zimbabwe, Malawi and South Africa, as well as the European Union.[10]

Employment

There is currently a gap in specific data on tobacco-related employment, both direct and indirect, in Zambia. There is anecdotal evidence that many Zambians are employed as growers, and BAT has argued publicly that robust tobacco control efforts would deprive many rural peasants of their incomes. Tobacco cultivators could, of course, explore alternative crops, and efforts to introduce such programs may need to be introduced in parts of the country with more tobacco growing.

Advertising and promotions (interactions with public)

BAT is very active in Zambia and targets most of its advertising to a younger audience. It sponsors the ambiguously named Youth Free Smoking Campaign, which underwrites community projects. Tobacco control advocates argue that the campaign's main purpose is to introduce children to tobacco since it seeks to attract the youth with attractive billboards, posters, and banners, and by giving away tobacco-themed T-shirts and baseball caps.

According to BAT's own annual reports, the range of community projects that it underwrites is enormous. Ironically, the projects are often related to community health, such as digging boreholes for drinking water, anti-malarial spraying and HIV/AIDS public awareness campaigns. BAT also interacts directly with schools through donations to individual schools and colleges and by sponsoring interscholastic trophies for athletic competitions. Many of these efforts resemble the "corporate good neighbor" behavior seen in post-industrial countries, suitably and effectively tailored to Zambian needs and cultural practices.

ZACA has closely monitored the activities of the tobacco industry (particularly BAT) in its attempt to influence health policy. BAT has unsuccessfully attempted to participate in workshops hosted by ZACA, but the association has stoutly refused to cooperate with BAT in any way. BAT had also presented to the Ministry of Local Government and Housing its own version of smoke-free regulations aimed at influencing the process: instead of 100 percent smoke-free environments, the BAT proposal allows for designated smoking zones. Further, at the time when the smoke-free law in Zambia was being hotly debated by the public, BAT invited the minister of local government and housing, the Hon. Sylvia Masebo, to officiate at the launch of its CSR program, the Youth Smoking Prevention Programme. At this time, the minister almost backtracked in her support for a 100 percent smoke-free law – ZACA had to hold a meeting with her to advise her of her responsibility as a public official under Article 5.3 of the FCTC.

BAT also donated a large quantity of T-shirts and caps to the Ministry of Local Government and Housing at the launch of the Youth Smoking Prevention Programme. The T-shirts were later donated to the Annual General Meeting (AGM) of the Local Government Association of Zambia (LGAZ), which is comprised of mayors and town clerks drawn from various cities and municipalities around Zambia. Rather cleverly on the part of BAT, the meeting's participants are the chief officers responsible for overseeing the implementation and enforcement of the prohibition of smoking in public places.

Interactions with government (at all levels)

Tobacco control activists believe that the national Zambian government generally favors effective tobacco control. Recent leadership from the executive branch, including from the key pro-tobacco control MoH, sets the tone. The government under the previous president Levy Mwanawasa was generally recognized internationally as more efficient and honest than previous Zambian governments, and generally aware of tobacco control issues, and the new administration overlaps considerably with the previous one. Certain ministers, according to the ATSA team, however, are not supportive of tobacco control; in particular, the minister of youth and sport has been open to sponsorship from the tobacco industry. Advocates believe that the current minister (as of 2011) and the ministry require more education about the health risks of tobacco.

Serious problems have arisen with the ability and willingness of local levels of government to enforce FCTC provisions. The Ministry of Local Government has been uneven in its performance. In 2008, the minister organized a public awareness campaign on the entry into force of Instrument #39, the law banning public smoking. Mixed results followed. Some local radio and print coverage supported the act, but a group of aggrieved smokers grumbled against it. The members of the Parliamentary Committee on Local Government have been mostly anti-tobacco by inclination – but BAT has

Table 18.2. Ranking of six public health programs in Zambia, 2008

Program	Government rank	Public rank
Vaccination	3	5
Portable water	4	2
HIV/AIDS	1	1
Tobacco control	6	6
Nutrition	5	4
Child health	2	3

Source: Stakeholders' Consultative Meeting – ATSA (2008).

been offering them unspecified incentives. Legislators are often a potential obstacle to the executive branch's wishes on these issues, especially on a low-priority issue such as tobacco control. At the first ATSA stakeholders' meeting in 2008, in a short survey presented in Table 18.2, the participants ranked tobacco control last among a list of six major public health programs. Keeping tobacco control on the agenda of both government and the public continues to be a challenge.

ATSA Review

Since the ATSA initiatives began, the Zambian tobacco control community has achieved several notable policy and/or programmatic successes. These achievements include: improved organization of stakeholders; the well-regarded launch of a new major tobacco campaign for a smoke-free Lusaka; several large media trainings; the first major trainings on cessation for healthcare professionals; the organization of existing research for use by advocates and policymakers; and a review of new draft comprehensive legislation.

While there have been a number of important tobacco control efforts in Zambia over the last two decades, during the ATSA initiatives, there was a new systematic and sustained effort to expand and organize stakeholders into the form of a new Tobacco Control Consortium. The new consortium brings together a number of different actors, including not only civil society organizations like ZACA and TOFAZA that were previously highly active in the effort, but also other organizations, government officials, academics and health workers committed to improving public health. The new consortium successfully sought political and social mobilization, in part by launching the ZTCC, which included public awareness efforts such as presentations on national and community radio and television shows, and the development and presentation of drama performances in high-density, low-income communities.

As a part of the broader mobilization, there were formal efforts to train and organize media in order to increase interest and knowledge in public health. In addition to a major workshop, there was also the official formation of a journalists' network against tobacco: the Zambia Media Network Against Tobacco (ZAMNAT). The trainings introduced media specialists who had prior experience in other parts of Sub-Saharan Africa.

As described in great detail above, the ATSA program provided for the first major efforts to organize training on cessation for healthcare providers. For the first time, frontline healthcare workers are being prepared systematically to deal with the challenges of tobacco addiction. In a related effort, there was the successful creation of a new quitline for the first time in Zambia.

Researchers with interests in tobacco control sought to set a research agenda that would be helpful to policymakers and advocates. According to all researchers, there is a paucity of documentation on tobacco use in Zambia. Thus to start, the ongoing research has been framed around the first ever overarching review of the existing tobacco control-relevant data, including a sustained and vigorous effort to collate existing epidemiological data for Zambia (e.g. from the Ministry of Health, the GYTS, DHS, WHO, etc.).

In addition to the documentation of the status of compliance to smoke-free laws in the city of Lusaka, the consortium worked vigorously on the formulation of the first draft of a new, comprehensive Zambian Tobacco Control Bill. The consortium continues to seek passage of this bill through sensitization, education and work with government officials. There is still a lack of coherent collaborative policies among the stakeholders in tobacco control. But the mood is very optimistic because there are a lot of parties interested in tobacco control in the country, and as the ATSA initiatives demonstrate, with only a little improvement in capacity, it is possible to generate enormous public health benefits. Though some individuals in key ministries are still naïve, there is obvious support from important community and government leaders. Public health proponents – armed with locally relevant, rigorous research – will continue the process of mapping out the preferences of these actors so that they can communicate effectively with them in an effort to generate more successes in this critical area of public health.

Notes

1 Sources: CIA World Factbook https://www.cia.gov/library/publications/the-world-factbook/; except Organization of Economic Cooperation and Development (OECD) for development assistance statistics, and Food and Agriculture Organization of the United Nations – Statistics (FAOSTAT) for tobacco production. See http://stats.oecd.

org/index.aspx and http://faostat.fao.org/site/567/default.aspx#ancor respectively (accessed 20 July 2011).

2 President Banda has been acting president since the illness and death of ex-president Levy Mwanawasa on 28 August 2008. He was elected president on 30 October 2008 to serve out the remainder of Mwanawasa's term. Elections are scheduled for late 2011.

3 Ministry of Health, Zambia, "Tobacco or Health Control in Zambia – A Situational Analysis 1993–1998" (1998). Cosponsored by WHO/AFRO.

4 Study executed by the WHO Regional Surveillance System for Tobacco Control in the publication "Regional Survey of Country-specific Data 2001" (2001). These same data are referenced in O. Shafey, S. Dolwick and G. E. Guindon (eds), *Tobacco Control Country Profiles* (Atlanta, GA: American Cancer Society, 2003). Tobacco control experts have expressed some concerns about the 2001 report because many data sources are unverified or not referenced. Moreover, the studies only provide "current smokers" and do not make any distinction between daily and occasional smokers.

5 World Health Organization. "World Health Survey," (2003). Online at: http://www.who.int/healthinfo/survey/whszmb-zambia.pdf (accessed 21 July 2011).

6 R. Zulu, S. Siziya and S. Nzala, "Tobacco smoking prevalence among in-school adolescents aged 13–15 years: Baseline for evaluation of the implementation of the FCTC in Lusaka District, Zambia," *Medical Journal of Zambia* 15.3 (2009): 100–4.

7 Authors' personal communication with S. Siziya.

8 S. Sisaya, O. Babaniyi, P. Songolo and M. Nsakashalo-Senkwe, "Prevalence and correlates for tobacco smoking among persons aged 25 years or older in Lusaka urban district, Zambia," *Journal of Public Health and Epidemiology* 3.2 (2011): 43–8.

9 *Times of Zambia*, "Mutati Warns Tobacco Farmers Over Exports," 2 November 2009. Online at: http://www.us-winston.com/mutati-warns-tobacco-farmers-over-exports/ (accessed 21 July 2011).

10 See FAOSTAT: http://faostat.fao.org/site/339/default.aspx (last accessed 22 July 2011).

Chapter 19

CONCLUSION: TOBACCO CONTROL IN AFRICA – PEOPLE, POLITICS AND POLICIES

Jeffrey Drope

Attempting to sum up the expansive work to change public health policy across 12 countries is a daunting but invigorating task. Arguably, the best avenue to a meaningful summary and final analysis is to reexamine and synthesize some of the themes that emerge from the preceding chapters, including several that might be less obvious to the casual reader. We, the authors and editor, have sought purposefully to be mindful of drawing too much inference from this research. This decision is a result of our dissatisfaction with earlier work that claims too much causality when the evidence is simply not strong enough or offers explanations that are too facile. While duly acknowledging these concerns, we believe that we have examined the roles of and relationships among key actors and institutions involved in tobacco control policy in Africa in ways that are both rigorous and generalizable, and moreover, useful to both practitioners and researchers in the health and social sciences.

As was cautioned in Chapters 1 and 2, there is no unified theory of public health policy generally or tobacco control policy specifically; improving tobacco control policy in such disparate political and economic contexts does not have a one-size-fits-all explanation or prescription. Fortunately, however, many useful patterns emerge from this collection that should help us to understand better these processes in developing countries both abstractly and systematically. It is important to note that many of the findings emphasize that developing countries are in many ways different from their developed world counterparts.

Thinking Systemically: Policy Change

It is very clear from these detailed narratives that policy change was or is at the heart of nearly every major recent tobacco control initiative in Africa. Most of the solutions that are being discussed and pursued tend to be systemic in one way or another – either specific policies (e.g. smoke-free initiatives) or comprehensive legislative and regulatory structures (usually Framework Convention on Tobacco Control (FCTC)-compliant), and/or the enforcement of these policies. But this research underscores that these tasks are inherently political, and almost without exception, very challenging. After making the determination that politics deeply shape the possibility of changing policy effectively, tobacco control advocates are taking the politics part of the challenge very seriously and are learning more effective ways to access and influence their own political systems. Politics is now a central part of the systems-thinking increasingly employed by public health policy reformers.

The first step to tackling major public health policy goals is to identify the specific political and economic contexts that shape both the opportunities for and the challenges to change. Some of the teams began their programs with very sweeping programs in mind, only to determine after more systematic and rigorous analysis that smaller steps needed to be taken first. But in any situation, knowing the structures of government and society better – including the roles and relative power of all of the relevant institutions and the various nongovernmental forces trying to affect policy – has been paramount to seeking substantive change successfully. Moreover, knowing how the official structures mediate the demands from competing groups for policy change helps proponents to move forward in their choice(s) of strategy.

The Underestimated Role of the Bureaucracy

While those seeking to reform public health policy in developing countries might naturally think to appeal first to the highest levels of governments – for example, the president – these narratives consistently illuminate the vital role that government ministries play in making policy. At a minimum, these agencies generate the companion regulations to new (or in some cases, existing) legislation, and then are largely responsible for implementing and enforcing them. Clearly, South Africa's tobacco control success has come in large part from the huge value that civil society organizations have placed on the role of the country's health ministry, and perhaps, too, the finance ministry. Advocates clearly cultivate strong, professional working relationships with these ministries predicated on evidence-based research, and the extensive regulations and amendments that reinforce the existing legislation speak to these relationships.

Notably, new public health regulation increasingly does not correspond directly to national legislation, but rather is generated using the inherent powers of the ministries or other government agencies. For example, in Ghana, the packaging and labeling regulations promulgated in 2009 originate directly from the country's Food and Drugs Board (FDB). These dynamics reemphasize that it is crucial for advocates of policy reform to establish and maintain strong working relationships with those in government who are charged with regulating the relevant policy area.

Finally, government agencies can serve a unique quasi-advocacy role for public health initiatives with other government actors. In many countries, pressure and/or high-quality counsel from government agencies to other institutions in government have been critical in changing tobacco control policies. For example, in Burkina Faso and Mauritius, government agencies have played key roles in developing and endorsing legislative initiatives to improve tobacco control. The within-government support dynamic can often provide added legitimacy to the broader efforts.

Thinking Smartly: Exploiting Opportunities

One of the exciting findings of this book is that advocates are taking advantage of opportunities for change as they present themselves, particularly by examining the structure of their political systems and the opportunities that result either from previously unexploited features of the institutional design or from recent structural changes. Moreover, while the desire for comprehensive national legislation is understandably strong, many advocates are recognizing that the struggle could be a long and arduous one, and in the interim are looking for new points of entry into the system. These "new" access points are sometimes merely the act of finally pursuing existing laws and/or regulations, or seeking policy change in a more limited substantive or geographical area. One of the most compelling parts of this strategy is that most of the micro-efforts do not preclude the macro-efforts, and in many cases may in fact promote them.

A relatively new point of access has come as the result of the recent reorganization of political structures across much of the continent: there is considerable potential to take advantage of many countries' recent efforts to decentralize power from national to subnational governments. For example, in Burkina Faso, advocates have predicated many of their most recent efforts on this structural change. While pursuing new national legislation, advocates also recognized the central role that local officials play in implementation and enforcement of many tobacco-related rules and have been concentrating their efforts on educating mayors and their staffs in order to encourage them to support tobacco control policies – particularly smoke-free places – in their districts.

Similarly, with significant progress on democratization in Nigeria, the country's federal structure presents outstanding opportunities to further tobacco control efforts. Where previously most authority rested with the national government, increasingly, states are finally getting the responsibilities that the formal institutional structure actually dictates. Direct results of these political changes include the successful smoke-free Osun State legislation and the enforcement of existing smoke-free laws in the capital, Abuja. Moreover, there is growing evidence that these changes and efforts are diffusing to other states. These subnational and local initiatives should effectively complement the new national legislation recently (2011) passed by the National Senate by providing a clear regulatory and pragmatic framework for implementation and enforcement.

The Next Frontier: Implementation and Enforcement

With creative and persistent proponents of tobacco control steadily generating policy victories around the continent, attention is now turning to implementation and enforcement of these policies. Both local and national governments will play enormous roles in the post-legislative environment. Furthermore, civil society's work will continue to be pivotal in putting pressure on governments to follow through on policy and offering solutions to these new challenges.

As the successes and struggles in a number of African countries demonstrate, decentralization offers important opportunities for effective implementation and enforcement of some types of policies. In Eritrea and Kenya, there is national-level comprehensive legislation, but in both cases, the enforcement activities at the subnational level will in great part determine the success of the new policies. In Eritrea, a country with a strongly centralized governmental structure, tobacco control advocates have identified that enforcement – particularly of smoke-free policies – is actually going to occur primarily at the regional level. Accordingly, advocates are engaging and sensitizing the *zoba* (regional) administrations to the tobacco problem and introducing tractable solutions.

More generally, Kenya is an excellent case study for imagining how implementation and enforcement might unfold in other countries. Because the process of ensuring that new laws are implemented and enforced effectively is complicated and resource-intensive, these efforts require significant support from a number of societal actors, including often those that previously had not been engaged in the process. Since enforcement of smoke-free policies – and to some extent, bans on advertising, promotion and sponsorship – is going to happen mostly at the municipal level, it has been necessary to engage local-level governments and enforcement authorities such as the police. But the effort is indeed complex because coordination and training at the local level have been spearheaded by both the national government – particularly the health ministry – and civil society organizations. In addition, much of the funding for the initiative has come from external donors. Success requires an enormous amount of cooperation among disparate agencies, multiple levels of government, private organizations and international donors.

As the Kenyan experience demonstrates, decentralization is no panacea to the coming challenges; national governments and civil society must remain highly engaged in implementation and enforcement efforts. In several of the countries with more advanced tobacco control regimes in place, including particularly Mauritius and South Africa, tobacco control communities that include national governments and civil society organizations are taking steps to improve implementation and enforcement. In Mauritius, the effort is led both by the government and civil society. On the government side, there is actually an official team in the Ministry of Health and Quality of Life (MOH&QL) – the Flying Squad – that is formally assigned to enforce the policies of the 1999 legislation and the new regulations of 2008. Of course, this is an enormous task for a small department, but it is an encouraging signal from the government that they are dedicating resources to the challenge, a rarity in the developing world. The civil society organization, ViSa, also plays a central role as watchdog and frequently reports violators of the regulations to authorities.

In South Africa, there is not a dedicated official enforcement mechanism, but the civil society organization, the National Council Against Smoking (NCAS), uses the available institutions of government to enforce existing regulations. For example, the NCAS successfully uses criminal dockets against violators of smoke-free laws to ensure compliance. In fact, some of the time, the simple act of reporting to a violator that a criminal docket will be opened is enough to obtain cooperation. This strategy is an indication not only of the creativity and will of civil society, but also of a government that must institutionalize enforcement more effectively.

Finally, the experiences of these countries suggest that it is more effective to incorporate implementation and enforcement into the development of new legislation and/or regulations. With a number of countries in the midst of legislative development (e.g. Cameroon, Ghana and Zambia), it is worth considering how to develop provisions – such as internal, sustainable funding mechanisms and clear designations of authority – that can engender better implementation and enforcement. The experiences with ineffective rules – e.g. Burkina Faso's Raabo and Tanzania's Tobacco (Products Regulation) Act (TPRA) – suggest that post-legislative changes can be very challenging to make.

The Legacy of Bad Rules

While some countries have been recently taking advantage of existing rules, Tanzania offers a cautionary tale as to the peril of passing poorly conceived legislation. By most accounts, Tanzania's TPRA (2003) does a poor job of most things, and advocates are trapped by a government that points out that there is existing legislation and instead is choosing to focus on promoting tobacco leaf cultivation as an economic growth strategy. Proponents of change sometimes wish that there were no legislation so that the starting point would be new to all stakeholders. Considering that just among the African Tobacco Situational Analysis (ATSA) countries, Ghana and Zambia (and possibly Cameroon) are actively pushing new comprehensive legislation, the importance of developing effective legislation at the outset that not only seriously considers future implementation and enforcement challenges, but also is legally sound, clear and binding, could not be more marked.

Another key take-home point from Tanzania's legislative experience is the need to minimize tobacco industry involvement in the development of new rules. The narratives demonstrate dramatically that the tobacco industry is highly active economically and politically across the region. In addition to Tanzania, there are problematic pieces of tobacco-related legislation around the continent that illustrate profoundly the past – successful – meddling of the industry. Part of Nigeria's recent fight to pass new tobacco legislation in the National Senate was to overturn the weak parameters of the Advertising Practitioners Promotion Control (APCON) directives that – at the strong encouragement of the industry – only loosely regulated tobacco. During 2010 in Burkina Faso, there were competing bills before the legislature, one authored by the tobacco control community and another deeply influenced by the country's powerful tobacco industry. Unfortunately, the tobacco industry-supported bill won. Not surprisingly, the bill had much weaker provisions than the one developed by public health professionals.

The Central Role for Civil Society

Fortunately, as omnipresent as the tobacco industry is in Africa, these countries demonstrate that a vibrant and active civil society can successfully offer an effective countervailing force. A central role for civil society organizations in the advocacy process is very close to a "necessary" – though not sufficient – component for policy reform. Across the continent, civil society is at the center of much policy change, in addition to subsequent implementation and enforcement. It is theoretically possible that policy reform can happen in the absence of effective civil society activity – i.e. government-initiated and directed – but would seem much less likely considering the broader patterns historically, particularly in developing countries. While the Cameroon chapter argues that the academic community – mostly in lieu of civil society – can partner with government to effect policy change, this scenario is problematic because while scholarly communities continue to be instrumental in providing the supporting research for tobacco control advocates and policymakers, the skill sets of most researchers are not naturally oriented toward effecting policy change.

Previous general policy and tobacco control-specific literature has noted and emphatically demonstrated the effectiveness of policy entrepreneurs or champions in changing policy, particularly in civil society, though also in government.[1] These country syntheses largely echo this important finding: people matter. But these narratives also greatly underscore the notion that getting more people involved in policy reform is now the critical challenge; the expansion of civil society generally and succession in existing organizations are paramount to continued success in public health policy reform.

Several countries – e.g. Mauritius, Nigeria and South Africa – have well-established organizations that advocate for tobacco control policy. Many of the key actors have been in the field for years, even decades. Fortunately, in all three cases, a concerted effort to introduce new, young professionals to the field is being pursued. In order to maintain the movement's effectiveness, this effort must be redoubled, and then redoubled again. Moreover, the types of actors involved must be widened as the challenges become more complex. There is a genuine need not only for public health professionals, but also for medical researchers, lawyers, policy experts, epidemiologists, economists, political scientists and media specialists, among other fields. Finally, these efforts to grow the tobacco control community in these countries will realistically require external technical and monetary resources in most cases.

Promoting Government Will

The other seemingly "necessary" component for policy reform is actual government motivation to make policy change. The level of will not only affects the success of policy change, but also then whether implementation and enforcement are pursued seriously. Thus, a major overarching puzzle is how do we engender more government will for change? These narratives offer some suggestions for engagement.

In South Africa, after nearly two decades of tobacco control policy reform and subsequent implementation (and some enforcement), the fairly sustained governmental commitment is evident. The late former health minister, Dr Manto Tshabalala-Msimang, was an open proponent of tobacco control policy and her involvement made a difference. But it is equally as important to underscore that the tobacco control community actively cultivated her interest. Advocates built relationships with the ministry and other important officials, and used evidence-based research to support their arguments for policy change and provide governments with the facts that they needed to make appropriate policy decisions. But as the enforcement discussion above illustrates, maintaining government will – even in South Africa – is an ongoing and challenging task.

In Zambia, government engagement is precisely the effort that the Zambia Tobacco Control Campaign (ZTCC) is currently making. In the smoke-free Lusaka initiative, there have been multiple efforts to engage every level of government and appropriate enforcement authorities. For example, there have been trainings, briefings and many invitations to government officials to be integral parts of new public health policy initiatives. The apparent initial success of the Lusaka effort and the "buy-in" from government officials suggest that you can promote official will. It is worth replicating these types of efforts elsewhere in the developing world.

In contrast, there appears to be little will for tobacco control policy in Senegal and a softer approach might not be the best strategy. Despite engagement from civil society, President Wade and other national-level officials have demonstrated almost no interest in tobacco control policy and have actually made tobacco manufacturing one of the centerpieces of the country's economic growth strategy. Faced with such a dire situation, advocates for change are pursuing a very creative alternative by engaging religious leaders in the important religious center of Touba. They hope that the moral pressure from this source will lead to change. It is difficult to say if this will be effective, but the options appear to be otherwise frustratingly limited.

With so little scholarly work in this area, an obvious and important conclusion of these syntheses is that the tobacco control community needs much more research on how to engender will amongst government officials. Some countries are having success engaging their governments on tobacco control issues, but it is reasonable to suggest that even faced with the hard facts of the harsh costs of tobacco most governments perceive that they have other larger issues to tackle first. Civil society must address these misperceptions quickly and effectively.

Early Interventions

Because some of the countries in this analysis are only beginning their tobacco control efforts, it is reasonable to observe some variation in terms of the initial interventions and activities. While the ATSA initiative – largely echoing FCTC emphases – vigorously promoted taxation, smoke-free policies, advertising bans and warning label provisions, a couple of the ATSA countries initiated other programs.

In Eritrea, the team initiated a schools-based initiative that incorporated both a prevalence baseline study and the promotion of existing smoke-free laws. While some tobacco control advocates might immediately question the ambition of such a program, the team argued that the government's acceptance of the president's 2004 tobacco control proclamation had been rather limited. They argued that they needed to demonstrate directly both the imminent threat of tobacco use and evidence of a quick and successful intervention. After determining through sound science that prevalence was far higher than initially thought, the schools initiative appeared to achieve its central goals as several of the key national ministries subsequently publicly embraced enforcement of the proclamation.

Another major area of tobacco control that is only briefly touched upon in this collection is cessation. The ATSA funders strongly discouraged cessation initiatives, mostly because of a strong preference for other types of more systemic policy interventions. While such a decision is reasonable from a resource-based perspective, the dearth of cessation services in Africa presents a genuine concern. But one large part of Zambia's ATSA effort involved cessation and actually serves to reinforce one of the broader program's overarching themes: strive for systemic change. In this case, the proponents sought specifically the incorporation of cessation training into higher education health curriculum and health clinics. Accordingly, the Zambian initiative sought to "train the trainers" – a clearly more sustainable approach. Moreover, the cessation effort in Zambia had the additional goal of reinforcing the importance of tobacco control within the biomedical community. A greater number of allies from this key sector will surely help the cause in the long term.

Tobacco Cultivation

The tensions between tobacco leaf cultivation and tobacco control are prominent in much of Africa and pose a genuine set of challenges. Leaf cultivation continues to be high on the economic agenda of many developing countries. Undoubtedly, because of its economic importance, it frames the entire tobacco control conversation in Malawi, and to a lesser extent, it is also important in Zambia, Kenya and a handful of other African countries. In a troubling development in Tanzania in late 2009, tobacco leaf has become a major focus of economic development strategists in the national government. It is evident from the Malawian case that concentrating on the public health rewards rather than the economic arguments is a superior strategy for proponents of tobacco control. Despite dramatic "comorbidity," advocates note that in the minds of most elected officials, poverty trumps public health in many circumstances. Thus, it is crucial to emphasize that country-specific tobacco control policies will not affect demand for tobacco leaf in the short term because demand stemming from global population growth continues to increase. In the meantime, governments with the help of international organizations and donors can help to develop and implement viable alternative crop programs so that farmers can make a better and healthier living growing other agricultural products.

The Continuing International Component

The very nature of the ATSA initiative with its international funders and its focus on the four major policy areas of the FCTC suggests that the international component continues to be crucial. Without doubt, the FCTC is deeply shaping the tobacco control agenda. For example, while stakeholders discussed many possibilities for different actions, teams gravitated back to their country's commitments to the FCTC. While the technical assistance and resources of international organizations are paramount to future success of tobacco control in developing countries, there should continue to be room to question the core assumptions of these actors. For example, the ATSA countries demonstrate that a huge emphasis has been placed on comprehensive legislation. But it should also be acknowledged that it took most countries quite a number of years to achieve that goal. In Kenya, for example, advocates fought for 11 years for the 2007 legislation. Similarly, the Zambian and Eritrean unorthodox approaches suggest that there is more than one approach to achieving tobacco control successes. International organizations and donors need to continue to be open-minded about alternative possibilities and paths.

There were some additional important lessons learned from ATSA in terms of international intellectual exchange, particularly the cultivation of south–south linkages. The program vigorously promoted intraregional cooperation. For example, a Nigerian-born South African expert in cessation and smokeless tobacco use assisted the Zambian team in training for and implementing its cessation clinics. Similarly, two activist-journalists – one from Malawi and one from Nigeria – helped to facilitate a workshop for the Zambian team to enhance its media efforts. More broadly, the ATSA program helped to support and grow the African Tobacco Control Regional Initiative (ATCRI) and the African Tobacco Control Alliance (ATCA), two organizations that have come to embody the coordinated African effort. Most recently, the African Tobacco Control Consortium (ATCC), "a coalition of public health organizations focused on preventing the tobacco epidemic in Africa" is seeking further to engender south–south cooperation.[2] These organizations in turn supported ATSA and helped greatly to improve the initiative.

Emphasizing the "Whole"

Earlier in the book, readers are implored to think about the "whole" – the broad context of how a country makes its rules and enforces them – because a meaningful conceptualization of the system of actors and institutions is essential to help advocates achieve their policy goals. The many separate initiatives that comprise the broader ATSA program underscore the fact that there is no single path to success, nor indeed, only one definition of success. Each county exists within a distinct political, economic and social environment at a particular moment in time. The programs, policies and processes that worked in the developed world, or even in an adjacent country, are not necessarily a guarantee for success in any other country. The ATSA team members learned to appreciate this fact and became skilled at analyzing their own environment, and then working toward goals suited specifically to it. International donors would do well to follow their example.

But at the same time, throughout the process, the ATSA teams also sought to share their experiences and to learn from others. At times this involved benefiting from the expertise found in developed countries but, increasingly, it involved learning from each other. The insight was gleaned from examining both the differences and similarities of their varying experiences. Though each situation is unique, participants found common ground that helped to inform their ideas and strategies. In many instances, participants found new and effective ways to bridge the occasional gap between research and advocacy. From these interactions, new relationships and coalitions have been formed which have greatly strengthened tobacco control in Africa and will doubtless support the efforts of these 12 countries and others as they move forward into the twenty-first century.

Notes

1 J. W. Kingdon, *Agendas, Alternatives, and Public Policies* (2nd ed.) (New York: HarperCollins College Publishers, 1995); J. de Beyer and L. Waverley Brigden (eds), *Tobacco Control Policy: Strategies, Successes and Setbacks* (Washington DC: The World Bank and IDRC, 2003).
2 See ATCRI's website at www.atcri.org (last accessed 4 June 2011).

NOTES ON CONTRIBUTORS

Editor – Dr Jeffrey Drope is an assistant professor of political science at Marquette University in the United States. He worked for more than two years with the African Tobacco Situational Analyses (ATSA) initiative, and was responsible particularly for spearheading the political context mapping program and coordinating overall data collection and analysis.

Foreword – Professor Oladipo O. Akinkugbe is a world-renowned expert on cardiovascular disease, particularly in developing countries. He is an emeritus professor of medicine at the University of Ibadan. He was the first chairman of the Non-Communicable Disease Programme in Nigeria in the early 1990s, and is a past president of the Nigerian Heart Foundation and the foundation president of the African Heart Network.

Preface – Jacqui Drope is the senior director of tobacco control for the African region at the American Cancer Society. In her former role as senior program officer at the International Development Research Centre (IDRC), she led and coordinated the ATSA initiative.

Policy Chapter Authors

Melanie Baier is a graduate of Marquette University's International Affairs Program and is currently an executive assistant to United States Representative Thomas Petri (WI-6th District) in Washington DC.

John Madigan, a former Peace Corps volunteer in Mongolia, is a graduate of the Masters in International Affairs Program at Marquette University. He is currently a program officer at ACDI/VOCA in Washington DC.

Joseph Struble, a former Peace Corps volunteer in Togo, is a graduate of the Masters in International Affairs Program at Marquette University. He is currently studying law at the University of Houston.

Country Chapter Authors

Burkina Faso – Mme Salimata Ki is the service coordinator for Health Research Services at the Direction for Research and Planning, Ministry of Health; Théodore Kangoyé is the former focal point for tobacco policy in the national government; Dr Laurent Ouedraogo is an associate professor of medicine at the University of Ouagadougou.

Cameroon – Dr Zakariaou Njoumemi and Dr Tetanye Ekoe are health economists in the Department of Public Health at the College of Medicine and Biomedical Sciences, University of Yaoundé; Daniel Sibetcheu is the focal point for tobacco control in the national government; Dr Eugène Gbedji was a program officer at the IDRC.

Eritrea – Zemenfes Tsighe is the director of the Bureau of Higher Education Administration and International Linkages at the National Board for Higher Education–Eritrea; Stifanos Hailemariam is an assistant professor of accounting and finance in the College of Business and Economics at the University of Asmara; Senai Woldeab is a lecturer in law at the College of Arts and Social Sciences at the University of Asmara; Goitom Mebrahtu is the director of Disease Prevention and Control at the Ministry of Health; Mussie Habte is the life skill–based health education expert at the Ministry of Education; Selamawi Sium is the youth empowerment team leader at the National Union of Eritrean Youth and Students; Ghidey Gberyohannes is the head of the Department of Nursing at the Asmara College of Health Sciences; Meseret Bokuretsion is a researcher at the National Union of Eritrean Women; Hagos Ahmed is the senior demographer and statistician at the National Statistics Office; Andemariam Gebremicael is the associate dean of the Orota School of Medicine and Dentistry; Giorgio Solomon is a pharmacist at Drugs and Narcotics Prevention and Control in the Ministry of Health.

Ghana – Edith Wellington is a research officer and the tobacco focal point in the Research and Development Division (RDD) of the Ghana Health Service (GHS); Dr John Gyapong is the director of the RDD-GHS; Sophia Twum-Barima was a country officer for the World Health Organization; Dr Moses Aikens is a professor of public health at the University of Ghana; and John Britton is a professor in the Division of Epidemiology and Public Health at the University of Nottingham (UK).

Kenya – Kenyan Tobacco Situational Analysis Consortium. The principal contact is Rachel Kitonyo at the African Tobacco Control Coalition (formerly at the Institute for Legislative Affairs).

Malawi – Dr Donald Makoka is a research fellow at the Centre for Agricultural Research and Development (CARD) at the University of Malawi and Kondwani Munthali is a media specialist at the Youth Alliance for Social and Economic Development.

Mauritius – Premduth Burhoo is a research officer at the Mauritius Institute of Health; Deowan Mohee is a health promotion officer for the World Health Organization in Mauritius; Leelmanee Moussa is a senior research officer at the Mauritius Institute of Health.

Nigeria – Nigeria Tobacco Situational Analysis Coalition. The principal contacts are Dr Kingsley Akinroye, the director of scientific affairs at the Nigerian Heart Foundation, and Akinbode Oluwafemi, the national coordinator for the Nigerian Tobacco Control Alliance and program manager at Environmental Rights Action/Friends of the Earth Nigeria.

Senegal – Professor Abdoulaye Diagne is the executive director and Babacar Mboup is a researcher at the Consortium pour la Recherche Economique et Social (CRES).

South Africa – Dr Yussuf Saloojee is the executive director and Peter Ucko is the director of the National Council Against Smoking.

Tanzania – Tanzania Public Health Association (TPHA). The principal contact is Dr Bertha Maegga, who is the TPHA executive secretary and chief research scientist at the National Institute for Medical Research.

Zambia – Dr Fastone Goma is the dean of the School of Medicine at the University of Zambia and Muyunda Ililonga is the executive director of the Zambian Consumer Association.

INDEX

Lightning Source UK Ltd.
Milton Keynes UK
UKOW051050131011

180249UK00001B/1/P